The Spiritual Quest

The Spiritual Quest

Transcendence in Myth, Religion, and Science

Robert M. Torrance

UNIVERSITY OF CALIFORNIA PRESS
Berkeley   Los Angeles   London

University of California Press
Berkeley and Los Angeles, California

University of California Press, Ltd.
London, England

Torrance, Robert M. (Robert Mitchell), 1939–
    The spiritual quest : transcendence in myth, religion, and
science / Robert M. Torrance.
        p.   cm.
    Includes bibliographical references and index.
    ISBN 0-520-08132-3 (alk. paper)
    ISBN 0-520-21159-6 (pbk: alk. paper)
    1. Spiritual life—Cross-cultural studies.   2. Vision quests—
Cross-cultural studies.   3. Indians—Religion and mythology.
    I. Title.
    GN470.2.T67   1994
    291.4′2—dc20   93-37644
                                                             CIP

Printed in the United States of America
9 8 7 6 5 4 3 2 1

"The Search" reprinted From *Where the Sidewalk Ends*, by Shel Silverstein, by permission
of HarperCollins Publishers. © 1974 by Evil Eye Music, Inc.

The paper used in this publication meets the minimum requirements of American
National Standard for Information Sciences—Permanence of Paper for Printed Library
Materials, ANSI Z39.48-1984. ⊗

For Donna
"All I had sought"

and my children

THE SEARCH

I went to find the pot of gold
That's waiting where the rainbow ends.
I searched and searched and searched and searched
And searched and searched, and then—
There it was, deep in the grass,
Under an old and twisty bough.
It's mine, it's mine, it's mine at last. . . .
What do I search for now?

SHEL SILVERSTEIN, FROM *WHERE THE SIDEWALK ENDS*

CONTENTS

PREFACE

I began my unfinished investigation two decades ago while preparing to teach a comparative literature course at Harvard University, "The Spiritual Quest: From Virgil to Kafka" (a course I subsequently taught, in different forms, at Brooklyn College and the University of California, Davis), and returned to it years later, after completing my book *The Comic Hero*. I originally intended to examine some of the major forms the quest has taken in Western literature and thought from ancient to modern times, but, like any true quest, this one took a direction that could not have been fully foreseen, and opened onto new and largely unexplored territory. My initial project, therefore, remains, in large part, for the future.

In this book I have undertaken, after extensive research in many fields as the dimensions of my subject became increasingly evident, to examine both the essential foundations or preconditions—social, biological, psychological, and linguistic—of the spiritual quest as a fundamental human activity and some of its principal variations, as manifested in religious practices of tribal peoples throughout much of the world. It is on the diversity of these practices, in the particularity of their widely differing cultural contexts, that ethnologists of our age, with deep respect for multicultural traditions and deep suspicion of facile universals, most often focus. Sharing this respect (and some of this suspicion), I have devoted the bulk of both my research and my book to examining variant forms the quest has taken among specific peoples of our richly polychromatic globe.

Yet skepticism concerning often dubious and sometimes ethnocentric affirmations of human uniformities (whether by Frazer or Freud, Jung, Lévi-Strauss, or their many popularizers and epigoni) need not eventuate in a relativism that rejects the very possibility of meaningful common human denominators. Ours is an age not only of "cultural diversity" but of "human rights," and true respect and understanding of our many differences requires recognition of the underlying commonalities that make us all—"by nature" or even "in essence"—equally human. We must grasp, with Tambiah (1990, 112), that "the doctrine of *the psychic unity of mankind* or *human universals* and the doctrine of *diversity of cultures/societies* are not contradictory dogmas," and with Geertz (1973, 51) that "there is no opposition between general theoretical understanding and circumstantial understanding, between synoptic vision and a fine eye for detail."

The quest, as I conceive it, is the culminating expression of a universal activity by which humanity is in large part defined as human: a formative activity, as opposed to a static category (like "religion," "marriage," or "property" in the "*consensus gentium*" whose emptiness Geertz and others rightly repudiate), which finds expression, however varied, in philosophical or scientific investigation no less than in the Native American pursuit of a guardian spirit or the Siberian shaman's perilous journey to worlds beyond yet embracing our own. The meaning and scope of my central terms will become apparent as the book progresses, but in brief by *spirit* I mean the dynamic potentiality latent but unrealized in the given (much as form, in Aristotle's terminology, is potential in matter), and by *quest* the deliberate effort to transcend, through self-transformation, the limits of the given and to realize some portion of this unbounded potentiality through pursuit of a future goal that can neither be fully foreknown nor finally attained. Because it *is* a formative process leading to varied and inherently unpredictable outcomes, the spiritual quest is a universal fully compatible with the diversity that is inevitably its product.

The originality of my enterprise lies in my contention that this activity is grounded in the structure of human nature (and ultimately of life and even of matter) and finds expression in every part of the world. The urgent quest to transcend the given limits of the human condition characterizes tribal peoples of Central Asia, West Africa, or the Amazon at least as much as ourselves. It is characteristic also, to be sure, of "advanced civilizations" both East and West, taking shape in the shamanistic processions of Japan chronicled by Carmen Blacker; in the restless search for the Taoist islands of immortality or for Eldorado or the Holy Grail, the philosopher's stone or the elixir of life; in pilgrimages to Benares, Jerusalem, Mecca, or Rome; or in the mystical aspirations of Muslim Sufi, Jewish kabbalist, Catholic saint, or Protestant Pentecostalist. Its complexly changing manifestations in the Western literary and philosophical tradition from the *Odyssey* (or indeed the *Epic of Gilgamesh*) and

Plato to our own time might well be the subject of another large book. But there could be no greater provinciality, no narrower ethnocentrism, than to think the questing spirit a monopoly of the Faustian West or an innovation of the Great World Religions. It is far more deeply rooted and more widely spread.

In Parts One and Six of my book, which explore the preconditions of the quest and venture some closing considerations toward a theory or "synoptic vision" of its nature and structure, I have drawn on a wide variety of thinkers who have in common, perhaps—in contrast to the deterministic behaviorisms, structuralisms, and post-structuralisms that have sometimes dominated the "human sciences" in our century—an emphasis on the dynamic and active dimensions of human experience oriented not toward an immutable past or inertial present but toward a future in the process of formation: thinkers as diverse as Bergson and Piaget, van Gennep and Turner, Peirce and Popper, to name but a few. Between these sections, the major portion of my book is an examination of forms that the quest has taken in different times and places, mainly but not exclusively in tribal societies. Part Two considers both collective rituals oriented toward a sacred past, in which openness to the new finds expression through irruption of the unpredictable wild, and myths in which mobility is inherent in the subject matter of the journey and in the variability of the word itself. Part Three explores incorporation of the unknowable beyond into human experience through the "two-way" communication of a seemingly passive spirit possession. In Part Four, the emphasis shifts from the communal to the individual quest as embodied in the shaman's daring journeys—in regions from Australia to the "shamanic heartland" of central and northern Eurasia—to other worlds on behalf of his people. Part Five, the longest of all, considers the intricate interplay of ritualism and shamanism in the cultures of Native America, from the Arctic to Tierra del Fuego and the Amazon jungles, culminating in the extraordinary vision quests of the northeastern woodlands and the Great Plains. Nowhere is the tension between closure and openness, stasis and change, collective ritual and individual aspiration that typifies the dialectic of the spiritual quest more striking than in the aboriginal cultures of the Americas, and nowhere does the drive for transcendence of the given attain more dramatic expression.

For several reasons, I have based my exploration primarily on ethnographic evidence rather than records from "advanced" civilizations: because detailed consideration of the latter would involve extended attention to long and complex historical traditions that lie outside the already vast scope of the present volume and because similar practices of apparently unrelated (or very distantly related) tribal peoples provide persuasive evidence for the frequency, if not universality, of the impulse to which these practices give shape. The self-transcendent questing impulse that finds expression in myths and rituals of hunter-gatherers, herders, and primitive agriculturalists from different parts of the world is a legacy common to peoples recently removed (as almost all are) from similar conditions, and therefore one from which we have much to learn about ourselves.

Not, of course, that the practices of tribal peoples are in any sense unproblematic or exempt from historical forces. Quite the contrary: ethnographers have become increasingly aware not only of the complexity and unresolved conflicts internal to "primitive" (as to all other) cultures, but of the tangled web of outside influences that each is continually assimilating, both from other tribal societies and from remote or intrusive imperial civilizations. But though the lives of tribal peoples, even the most seemingly isolated, far from being static, are inevitably embedded in history and change, emphasis on adherence to sacred ancestral patterns remains a striking characteristic of most. Change is typically resisted, if not denied, permitting us, too, to emphasize what is at least relatively constant within and among cultures devoted to the fiction of invariance. Nor is invariance solely a fiction; the shamanistic practices of the Scythians described by Herodotus are remarkably similar to those observed in Siberia and North America twenty-five hundred years later.

I have therefore generally used the traditional ethnographic present tense, with full knowledge that many of the cultures so depicted have since been transformed beyond recognition, have ceased to exist, or are even now being decimated in regions from the Sudan to the Amazon. And though the writing of ethnographers, far from being purely objective, necessarily reflects, as recent theorists stress, their own attitudes and presuppositions as much as those of the peoples they study, this obvious fact complicates but by no means invalidates their observations: every report is an interpretation, and no interpretation, whether by the ethnographer or the ethnographer's readers, can ever be value-free. Doing ethnography may indeed, as Geertz observes (1973, 10), be "like trying to read (in the sense of 'construct a reading of') a manuscript," and we who read the ethnographer must be cautiously aware that we are reading a reading: but how long has it been since we thought otherwise, or believed "facts" could speak for themselves? A wearisome self-absorption soon results when the ethnographer's predilections and rhetoric become the paramount focus of ethnography, when the situatedness of meaning and writing of culture, rather than more demanding questions of meaning and culture themselves, are stressed "to a point of exhibitionism" (Marcus and Fischer 42). I have therefore endeavored, after reading very widely, to choose my sources carefully and to cite them with appropriate caution, but not to exclude whatever cannot be certainly established, since this would be everything. It is one of my themes that truth, like the goal of every quest, is no less valuable for being ultimately indeterminate, or knowledge for being necessarily approximative. To recognize our inevitable limits is not to sink into the slough of aporia but to enter the always uncertain liminal realm in which the quest continually takes place.

ACKNOWLEDGMENTS

My research has been greatly facilitated by continued availability of a faculty study in Shields Library at the University of California, Davis. I am also grateful to the UC Davis Humanities Institute for supporting me for a quarter when I was beginning my revision of a much longer manuscript. Among those who encouraged me to persevere in arduous labors against the grain of an often shortsighted academic reward system, I especially thank Ruby Cohn and Roland Hoermann. I greatly appreciate the usefully critical suggestions of Mark Wheelis, who read part of the manuscript. Above all, I am grateful to Douglas Abrams Arava of the University of California Press for his enthusiastic responsiveness and consistent support, to the attentive readers for the Press who provided helpful commentary from the perspectives of their very different disciplines, and to Ellen Stein, whose scrupulous editing saved me from a number of inconsistencies and errors. Those that inevitably remain, in a book of this length and complexity, are of course nobody's but mine.

———

PART ONE

Animal Quaerens

The Quest as a Dimension of Human Experience

Chercher? pas seulement: créer.
PROUST

CHAPTER ONE

Religion and the Spiritual Quest

From Closure to Openness

We shall not look far in search of the quest; it will meet us at every turn of the way. For this business of seeking, of setting off in determined pursuit of what we are lacking and may never attain, is no incidental theme of our literature and thought, no bypath of history, but a fundamental activity that contributes in no small measure toward defining existence *as* human. All life is continually going beyond its given condition, and the primal origin of the quest may very well lie in the biochemical composition that links the proud members of our sapient species with everything else that grows before decomposing.

But the quest is pre-eminently a *conscious* transcendence, a deliberate reaching toward a posited—if by no means an unalterable—goal; and in this purposeful overreaching of our given status we are perhaps entitled to regard humankind, among the inhabitants of our planet, as being alone. We distinguish ourselves from lowlier beasts as kindlers of fire, makers of tools, users of language, but whatever innate dispositions may have evolved to render these activities possible, each of them was and remains, like everything specifically human, not an instinctive inheritance but a cultural acquisition, a capacity that must be attained. As the animal most imperfectly programmed by nature for the period between birth and death, the animal that must seek to acquire what it characteristically lacks to begin with, and to actualize by directed effort what is potential in its being but never knowable in advance, the human species may be designated *animal quaerens* with at least as much right as *animal rationale*.

What human beings lack in genetically programmed endowments they normally make good, to be sure, by an acculturation process so routine as to seem automatic: to speak one's native language, or to

3

manufacture a basic artifact, requires no one to go questing afar. Here culture is very nearly a second nature, and the most ordinary effort is all but certain not to miscarry. But awareness of this process may set human beings self-consciously apart from a no longer "natural" world which they strive to regain or surpass; the concerted effort to overcome this apartness is a cardinal condition of the quest. The very term *spiritual* is an index of this separation; for distinction from the body places the un-housed spirit in a state of incompletion and need. Whether or not the process of self-transcendence has its inarticulate origin in the protoplas-mic beginnings of life, so that evolution can be comprehended, as Berg-son somewhat fancifully thought (213), "only if we view it as seeking for something beyond its reach," it achieves awareness, and hence can be fully a quest, first in man; and not until man posits a mobile dimension at least partly independent of biological need does the quest become spiritual and specifically human. It lies in the nature of spirit, which owes its existence to the separation that it continually strives to overcome, rather to seek than to find.

TWO ASPECTS OF RELIGIOUS RITUAL

We naturally associate the spiritual quest with religions; we emphatically cannot identify them. Like technology and language, religion is a fre-quently cited differentia of humanity; insofar as it too is an institution of acculturation, it appears to be a self-contained system that leaves the spirit little to ask for. In this light, religion is less a manifestation of the individual quest than an alternative to it; it says not "Seek!" but "Seek no further!" This aspect of religion has been repeatedly emphasized by those who view religious beliefs as a reflection, and religious practices as a reaffirmation, of dominant social values.

For Marx it was axiomatic that the religious sentiment "is itself a *social product*" and that "the religious world is but the reflex of the real world" (Marx and Engels, 71, 135), "real" being equivalent to "socio-economic." Nor is this perspective exclusively Marxist: "In societies such as our own," Bergson remarked (13), "the first effect of religion is to sustain and reinforce the claims of society." For Peter L. Berger (1967, 33), "re-ligion legitimates social institutions by bestowing upon them an ulti-mately valid ontological status, that is, by *locating* them within a sacred and cosmic frame of reference." Within this frame religious and social institutions (which repeatedly overlap) are viewed as immutable, and re-ligion, by its claim to permanent status, acts as the hypostatized inertia (or "repository of sacred tradition") by which society collectively denies the potentially disruptive reality of change. It would be hard to imagine an institution more alien to the tentative in-betweenness and perpetual movement of the spiritual quest than this stolid objectification of willed social rigidity.   *Durkheim*

The study of "primitive" religion has found this model of particular value. In *The Elementary Forms of the Religious Life* of 1912 (115), Durkheim pronounced the totemism of aboriginal Australia, as recorded by Spencer and Gillen, Strehlow, and Howitt, "the most primitive and simple religion which it is possible to find," and therefore the one in which the essential features of all religions could best be studied. Many of Durkheim's assumptions now seem preposterous. Australian religions are neither single nor simple; and the hypothesis of universal religious evolution from a vague "totemism" unattested in much of the world was flimsy then and is untenable now. But by his single-minded insistence on the interdependence of the religious and social orders Durkheim exerted immense influence on the sociology of religion. His belief that society is "the highest reality in the intellectual and moral order that we can know by observation" (29) mounts to evangelical heights when he declares it "unquestionable" that to its members society "is what a god is to his worshippers" (236–37). And in this worship of society "the unanimous sentiment of the believers of all times cannot be illusory" (464): their adoration has the force of indefeasible truth.[1] Durkheim's collectivism is thus totalitarian in the strictest sense. Society as the Absolute, unlike lesser deities, allows no exceptions and tempers the necessity of its order with no merely personal mercy. Such a monolithic religion clearly leaves no place at all for the restless spirit to quest in.

Anthropologists have by no means unanimously acquiesced in Durkheim's fervid credo—"It was Durkheim and not the savage," Evans-Pritchard tartly observed (1956, 313), "who made society into a god"— but the social perspective on religion has been central to many. Thus for Malinowski (66–67), though society is neither the author nor the self-revealed subject of religious truth, religion "standardizes the right way of thinking and acting and society takes up the verdict and repeats it in unison." And for Radcliffe-Brown (1952, 157), the principal function of religious rites is to "regulate, maintain and transmit from one generation to another sentiments on which the constitution of the society depends." We need not subscribe to the unitary correlation between society and religion propounded by Marx or Durkheim to acknowledge their intimate connection. Religion is no luxuriant excrescence upon the trunk of

1. Bellah (1959, 458) must turn to early unpublished lectures for evidence that Durkheim "saw clearly that collective representations have a reciprocal influence on social structure." *The Elementary Forms,* Durkheim's last major work, whose very title has a Platonic resonance, offers little support. On the contrary, as Talcott Parsons writes (1937, 1:449), Durkheim was evidently "thinking of society as a system of eternal objects," timeless and unchanging.

society but a fundamental expression of underlying values that society can articulate in no more effective form. Insofar as such an articulation, unlike Durkheim's seamless weld, allows for variation and imperfection, however, and thus falls short of "unquestionable" authority in matters of ultimate truth, an otherwise inconceivable space for the quest may be imperceptibly but portentously opened.

Influential though orthodoxy, or "right opinion," has been in regulating social order, the orthopraxis, or "right practice," encoded in ritual has been more basic still; and ritual, which knits the social group together and validates its identity, is invariant almost by definition. The striking parallels between human and animal rituals have led to speculations concerning an instinctive disposition toward ritual behavior, even though ritual, like language, is culturally transmitted. Fundamental to its function of stabilizing social order is its repetitiousness. Every ritual must be performed over and over in essentially the same way, so that ritual has even been defined, by Kluckhohn (1942, 105), as "an obsessive repetitive activity." Since the rite re-presents a sacrosanct beginning, it must not be thought to change in any essential, however adaptable it may prove in practice (Firth 1967a, 41). Every performance is not only alike but *the same;* significant variation is excluded by the nature of ritual itself. What has worked before must not be altered lightly if it is reliably to work again, and again. . . .

In ritual the animal and the human indistinguishably meet and momentously diverge; ritual can no more be reduced to biology than restricted to spirit. Survival value appears fundamental to animal ritual (Lorenz 1966, 67). In addition to abating hostile tensions and cementing social bonds, human ritual often explicitly aims to assure the food supply on which survival depends; it is literally, in Hocart's phrase (37), "a co-operation for life." At the same time, while looking back toward primordial origins re-enacted ad infinitum and while sharing in the invariance of animal ceremonies, religious ritual decisively differentiates human from animal behavior by positing a goal no longer determined solely by chromosomal codes or physiological needs. By reaching *consciously* back toward consecrated prehuman beginnings whose distance from their ordinary condition they strive to overcome, the enactors of ritual thereby reach beyond them as well. They hypostatize ancestral animals not only as biological progenitors but as founders of the culture that distinguishes human from animal; their culturally acquired ritual effects, by its very existence, transcendence of the animal condition it celebrates. The very repetitiousness of ritual proclaims a distinctively human reality striving toward realization—a reality indeterminately in statu nascendi. Thus ritual is no mere inertial force but a potent agency of organic and social development. "Both instinctive and cultural rituals," according to Lorenz (1966, 77–78), "become independent motivations of behavior by creating new ends or goals toward which the organism strives for their own sake." Ritual "can have an adaptive and even creative function" (Firth 1967b, 23) in formation of the social order.

In this light, ritual seems an extension of the impulse to purposeful differentiation implicit in life; it is not stasis but regulated movement. Only after its adaptive rhythms have become mechanical does ritual assume the character of bureaucratic control assigned to it by Weber (1946, 267) and correspond only to religious "rules and regulations." Even so, the creative function recognized by Firth and others in no sense contradicts the maintenance of social equilibrium stressed by Malinowski and Radcliffe-Brown. The dynamic aspect of ritual may be no more perceptible to its participants than the evolution of life to a species in transition; ritual participants may be conscious only of perpetuating their group by scrupulous performance of practices prescribed since their foundation. Stability takes precedence of change (even though stability may be attainable only by nearly insensible change). "Ceremonies are the bond that holds the multitudes together," Radcliffe-Brown (1952, 159) quotes the Chinese *Book of Rites* as saying, "and if the bond be removed, those multitudes fall into confusion." A similar view underlies Kluckhohn's contention (1942, 101) that rituals (and associated myths) provide "the maximum of fixity" in a world where social order is continually threatened by spontaneity and change. In its coercive reduction of present and future to re-enactments of a domineering past, its insulation from time and denial of the change it may be unwittingly promoting, and its exclusion of all uncertainties arising from uncontrolled variation, ritual reinforces the equilibrium that every human society strives to maintain. In this it is the antithesis of the restlessly aspiring quest which is nevertheless, perhaps, latent within it.

The inseparable link between religion and social structure postulated by Marx and Durkheim thus appears to be abundantly established. Yet we should be wary, even apart from the dogmatisms of Marx and evangelical excesses of Durkheim, of assenting uncritically to the thesis of social priority and hence of seeing religion (by simple inversion, à la Feuerbach, of the religious viewpoint itself) as the reflection of a pre-existent social reality. "Durkheim's theory," Cassirer cogently observes (2 : 193), "amounts to a *hysteron proteron*," a placing of the cart before the horse. "For the form of society is not absolutely and immediately *given* any more than is the objective form of nature, the regularity of our world of perception. Just as nature comes into being through a theoretical interpretation and elaboration of sensory contents, so the structure of society is a mediated and ideally conditioned reality." To affirm the interdependence of the religious and social orders by no means justifies us in viewing either as the simple emanation of the other; and inasmuch as ritual is a creative force we might no less plausibly view society as the offshoot of religion than religion as the outgrowth of society. The antecedence of one or the other of these coordinate constructs of human culture is a moot, if not a meaningless, question.

Such considerations caution us against viewing ritual as a wholly static reflex of the society whose stability it asserts. (If ritual is an instrument of imperceptible adaptation, its very denial of change may be its supreme defensive stratagem: plus c'est la même chose, plus ça change. . . .) Nor can religion be confined to the collective and invariant aspects that permit it to be understood as a ratification of existing social order—the aspects in which it is farthest from any true quest of the mobile spirit. Bergson, who acknowledged the effectiveness of religion in sustaining society's claims, associated this dimension with a "relatively unchangeable" instinct directed toward "a closed society" (32). In contrast, the self-sufficient motion of "the open soul," far from being instinctual, "is acquired; it calls for, has always called for, an effort" (38–39). To these qualitatively distinct sources of morality and religion he respectively assigned the functions of "pressure and aspiration: the former the more perfect as it becomes more impersonal, closer to those natural forces which we call habit or even instinct, the latter the more powerful according as it is more obviously aroused in us by definite persons, and the more it apparently triumphs over nature" (50). In this second aspect individuals are no longer wholly identified with the collectivity, and no longer find their beliefs and practices adequately prescribed by social fiat in accord with biological predisposition, but must acquire them and make them their own. Here the human being, even in ritual movements which partake of both dimensions, parts company with the instinctually determined animal within as socially programmed religious behavior gives way to individually varied religious action purposefully directed toward an indeterminate outcome—religious action in which the spiritual quest has both matrix and paradigm.

THE INDIVIDUAL AND THE GROUP: RITES OF PASSAGE

Far from being, in Whitehead's phrase, "what the individual does with his solitariness" (1926, 47), religion in most societies is a quintessentially social activity. Even so, the Durkheimian equation of religious reality with "Society divinized" led Malinowski to ask (56) if primitive religion could be "so entirely devoid of the inspiration of solitude," leading him to the contrary conclusion (58) that "the *collective* and the *religious,* though impinging on each other, are by no means coextensive." In the solidarity of tribal society our accustomed antithesis of individual and group would no doubt be inconceivable. The very essence of the "participation" which Lévy-Bruhl associated with "primitive mentality" (and, he increasingly realized, with our own) is that "the subject is at the same time himself and the being in whom he participates" (1925, 345). Self-hood is achieved by identification with the group, not distinction from it. The religion of solitariness thought by Whitehead (1926, 35) to be the result of evolution toward more individualistic, less communal forms could have had no place (as he understood) in the unity of tribal society. Even so, the identity of individual and group has never perhaps been so complete as Lévy-Bruhl's much-disputed "mystical participation" suggests.

"Such facts as the seclusion of novices at initiation, their individual, personal struggles during the ordeal, the communion with spirits, divinities, and powers in lonely spots, all these," Malinowski reminds us (56), "show us primitive religion frequently lived through in solitude." And insofar as religion remains communal, the solidarity it ratifies is not an inheritance possessed ab initio as by the bees but a goal to be attained—often by strenuous effort—and periodically renewed. Far from affirming the undifferentiated cohesion of society, initiation ceremonies and other rites of passage suggest a relationship not of static invariance but of reciprocal transformation. Even in its tribal manifestations, then, religion presupposes (in Bergson's terms) not only instinctive "pressure" for the maintenance of a closed society but, at least in potential, the psychic "motion" of personal aspiration toward a community forever being achieved.

The importance of van Gennep's *The Rites of Passage,* published in 1908, four years before Durkheim's *Elementary Forms,* is evident from the title: ritual, the presumably immutable substratum of religious behavior, pertains not only to social stability but to transition, passage, and therefore change. The pattern underlying different rites of passage may indeed be remarkably stable—van Gennep (11) discriminated the three major phases of separation (*séparation*), transition (*marge*), and incorporation (*agrégation*), which he otherwise (21) called the preliminal, liminal (or threshold), and postliminal stages—but the rites affirm not structural fixity, in the first instance, but processual movement; not the apathetic self-sufficiency of a divine collectivity but the sometimes hazardous adaptation of its human components (whether individuals or groups) to a larger whole which, to that extent, is of their own making.

Van Gennep emphasizes (191–92) the importance of "transitional periods which sometimes acquire a certain autonomy" and of "*territorial passage,* such as the entrance into a village or house, the movement from one room to another, or the crossing of streets"; the passage defining these rites "is actually a territorial passage." It is therefore not the beginning or end points, the separation or incorporation, which these rites have in common—rites of birth, marriage, initiation, or death begin and end in wholly different biological and social conditions—but passage itself, the critical crossing of a threshold that is not a line but a region, a temporal and spatial in-between, "autonomous" because not governed by conventions prevailing before and after the crossing. Each passage, to be sure, presupposes a goal—it is a passage *to* something—but no goal entirely subsumes the passage to it (autonomy cannot be subsumed under law, or movement under fixity) or finally terminates the process of crossing, since every end-point is potentially a point of departure and "there are always new thresholds to cross" (189). What the rite of passage celebrates above all is passage itself.

Victor Turner, developing van Gennep's insights, repeatedly emphasizes that society cannot be understood in terms of fixed structure alone but is always a process, in which van Gennep's transitional stage is of crucial importance. Concerning this fluid, "antistructural" condition of "liminality," and the revitalized human relationship of *communitas* to which it typically gives rise, he writes (1969, 95–96):

> Liminal entities are neither here nor there; they are betwixt and between the positions assigned and arrayed by law, custom, convention, and ceremonial. . . . We are presented, in such rites, with a "moment in and out of time," and in and out of secular social structure. . . . It is as though there were here two major "models" for human interrelatedness, juxtaposed and alternating. The first is of society as a structured, differentiated, and often hierarchical system of politico-legal-economic positions . . . The second, which emerges recognizably in the liminal period, is of society as an unstructured or rudimentarily structured and relatively undifferentiated *comitatus,* community, or even communion of equal individuals who submit together to the general authority of the ritual elders.

The "communitas" emerging from liminality, in contrast to the hierarchies enclosing it on either side of the threshold, is for Turner the quintessentially religious aspect of human existence. The totality in which the individual transcends himself is not society as an immemorial static entity but an inherently transitional community perpetually in the process of realization.

Moreover, communitas, though originating in the liminal phase of rites of passage, need not terminate with it; jesters, saints, and other outsiders who "fall in the interstices of social structure, are on its margins, or occupy its lowest rungs" (1969, 125) provide society with a continuous (if not always welcome) reminder of communal values, and transition may even become a permanent condition when spontaneous communitas is normalized, as in the monastic orders of Christendom. Liminality is thus not simply a transient phase left behind once the ritual has accomplished its immediate object but a recurrent constituent of human culture, which it distinguishes (one might add) from the transitionless hierarchies of the ants and bees as an intrinsically unfinished process directed toward an incessantly redefined goal. The communitas fostered by this recurrent transitionality has an existential quality, as opposed to the cognitive, classificatory quality which Turner (with Lévi-Strauss) associates with structure; it has "an aspect of potentiality" and "is often in the subjunctive mood" (127).

Of the two complementary dimensions, communitas—the dynamic or potential—is therefore prior to the apparently stable configurations of the structural stasis which it is forever imperceptibly transforming. "Communitas . . . is not structure with its signs reversed, minuses instead of pluses, but rather the *fons et origo* of all structures and, at the same time, their critique. For its very existence puts all social structural rules in question and suggests new possibilities. Communitas strains toward universalism and openness" (1974, 202). This aspiration toward a more inclusive human community—all rites of passage, not excepting those of death, enlarge a corporate group—is one respect in which "communitas is to solidarity as Henri Bergson's 'open morality' is to his 'closed morality'" (1969, 132)—a force inherently expansive and incomplete. "Communitas is not merely instinctual," any more than Bergson's second source; rather, "it involves consciousness and volition" (188).

In major liminal situations a society *"takes cognizance of itself"* (1974, 239–40); for only in between obligatory fulfillment of structurally prescribed functions does the potential for purposeful change arise. The social order, for stability's sake, must therefore confine overt expressions of communitas to "interstitial" occasions and institutions. Clearly distinguished categories and relations are the essence of structure, and there is always danger in transitional states, as Douglas remarks (96), "simply because transition is neither one state nor the next, it is undefinable." The danger is one that the social order must strictly circumscribe, or it will soon be no order at all.

At the same time, anomaly which finds a recognized place in the social order—as in the Ndembu twinship ritual studied by Turner—may ratify that order by making it the guarantor of values seemingly antithetical to its immutable categories: by being assimilated, the anomaly is regularized and order is upheld. "Cognitively, nothing underlines regularity so well as absurdity or paradox. Emotionally, nothing satisfies as much as extravagant or temporarily permitted illicit behavior" (Turner 1969, 176). Rituals of status reversal, by making the low high and the high low, reaffirm the hierarchical principle without which high and low could not be distinguished even in reverse. But to reaffirm the principle is by no means to affirm any given hierarchy's perpetuity as actually constituted; on the contrary, continuous passage through a porous hierarchy whose only divisions are thresholds makes such an affirmation meaningless. Social life, as experienced by its participants, is "a process rather than a thing" (203)—not a fixed system but a dialectic "that involves successive experience of high and low, communitas and structure, homogeneity and differentiation, equality and inequality" (97). A society in stasis is a contradiction in terms, for ritual can truly affirm the social order only by continually reshaping and creating it anew.

Turner's argument is open to criticism for its excessively pliable terminology (*communitas,* like Lévy-Bruhl's *mystical participation,* is a catch-all of nearly undefinable limits) and its impressionistic use of evidence drawn from a grab-bag extending from African tribal rites to William Blake, Martin Buber, and the hippie counterculture of the 1960s. Granted that symbol and metaphor are fitter vehicles (as Turner suggests) than analysis for conveying the existential qualities of communitas, in these departments the anthropologist can hardly better the originals toward which he somewhat redundantly points us. Yet by his emphasis on ritual liminality as a formative component of a society in continual transition Turner, like van Gennep before him, fundamentally modifies the widespread view of religion (above all in its putative origins) as a passively reflective, obsessively repetitive ratification of a pre-existent social order which it thereby endeavors to immunize from the virus of change.

And by associating (even at the risk of prematurely equating) liminality and communitas, Turner discerns that far from merely dissolving the structural bonds among its members, leaving them isolated during their perilous crossing, the liminal phases essential to the rhythm of social life reconstitute those bonds by creating a deeper awareness of community as a shared human need than any static system of kinship roles alone can prescribe. It is in this sense, not by its coercive injunctions, that religion, to the extent that it is "liminal" and not wholly institutional, is most profoundly (as the etymology of our word suggests) a binding together. Through continually renewed assimilation of its members into a more comprehensive community in transitional rites that provide a fluidity integral to its existence if alien to its categories, a no longer static social structure achieves the capacity for self-renovation by which it becomes, in more than a manner of speaking, social life.

RELIGION AND SOCIAL CHANGE

This understanding of the dynamic role of ritual sharply contrasts with that of Durkheim or Radcliffe-Brown, for whom religion was essentially an epiphenomenon reinforcing the primary social order which it reflected. Other major thinkers of the early twentieth century also assigned to religion a formative function within a society seen less as a finished structure than a work forever under construction. Max Weber's primary interest, as Talcott Parsons discerned (1963, xxx), "is in religion as a source of the dynamics of social change, not religion as a reinforcement of the stability of societies." For Weber (1946, 245), the tendency of society to congeal in bureaucratic institutions is periodically subverted by the "entirely heterogeneous" force of personal charisma. Throughout early history, "charismatic authority, which rests upon a belief in the sanctity or the value of the extraordinary, and traditionalist (patriarchal) domination, which rests upon a belief in the sanctity of everyday routines, divided the most important authoritative relations between them" (297).

Both tendencies are therefore (like Bergson's two sources or Turner's structure and communitas) fundamental to religion; nor is the traditionalist solely an inertial or the charismatic a progressive force. Both (through "revelation and the sword") can be innovative, and both are subject to institutional routinization. Yet charisma, as a force essentially extraordinary, personal, and unstable, is for Weber, in the absence of external intrusion, the primary agency working against rigidification of social structures. The charismatic attitude "is revolutionary and trans-values everything; it makes a sovereign break with all traditional or rational norms: 'It is written, but I say unto you'" (250). By its highly personal disruption of the collective, its injection of the unpredictable into the routine, and its crystallization around the charismatic individual of an intensely motivated community within the larger society, religious charisma, as Weber portrays it, is inherently a force for change—a force equally destructive and creative in potential and always, from the observer's perspective, uncertain in outcome.

For George Herbert Mead, as for Bergson and Weber, the transformative agency in religion is not the liminal rite of van Gennep's or Turner's tribal societies but the dissident individual who gives new voice to his society's deepest, if nearly forgotten, aspirations. What gives unique importance to religious geniuses, such as Jesus, Buddha, and Socrates, is their "attitude of living with reference to a larger society," a society larger than their institutional communities; though each diverges from the prejudices of his age, "in another sense he expresses the principles of the community more completely than any other" (1934, 217). Only because society is a dialectical interchange between whole and part can any person achieve this unique importance by actuating the aspirations implicit in his social environment; he transforms his world by revealing to it, from his seemingly tangential perspective, the unsuspected novelty latent within it.

In Mead's social psychology, "the whole (society) is prior to the part (the individual), not the part to the whole" (7). The individual comes into being only through social differentiation and is a product of society, not its pre-existent component. Not until he can adopt toward himself the attitude of the "generalized other" constituted by his environment does the human being become a conscious individual. Ritual contributes significantly to this developing consciousness, since the self is a process in which the conversation with others has been internalized (178); the religious cult contributes toward evolution of the self by giving expression to an ongoing conversation with the world.

In contrast to the conventional "me"—the generalized other internalized in each individual—the response of the subjective "I" is always uncertain. "It is there that novelty arises and it is there that our most important values are located. It is the realization in some sense of this self that we are continually seeking" (204). And this "I," the individual's changing response to the institutionalized attitude of the community, in turn changes the latter by introducing something not previously present (196): the unpredictably responsive "I" is thus the dynamic agency of society's transformation. A reciprocal adaptation is always taking place, not only of the self to the social environment but of that environment to the self by which it is continually being reshaped. Thinking itself is "the carrying-on of a conversation between . . . the 'I' and the 'me'" (335), and because this conversation is forever introducing new situations, it is incompatible for long with any fixed form of society. The religious genius accelerates this often-imperceptible process by acting as "I" to society's "me," thereby actualizing what was potential. Not only primitive cult but religion in general is thus the open-ended conversation of man with his world.

For Peter L. Berger, too, social reality is a construct of human consciousness in turn structured by it through internalization of its own objectified projections: "the social world . . . is not passively absorbed by the individual, but actively appropriated by him" (18). By means of this "protracted conversation" society furnishes its constituent individuals with a *nomos,* or meaningful order, that shields them against the blankness of its unassimilable margins—with the result, however, that "the world begins to shake in the very instant that its sustaining conversation begins to falter" (22). Religion protects man against the terror of "anomy," or meaninglessness, by audaciously attempting to conceive of the entire cosmos as humanly significant. And although its projection of human meanings into an empty universe returns as a hauntingly alien reality, the religious enterprise "profoundly reveals the pressing urgency and intensity of man's quest for meaning" (100), which lies at the root of all his endeavors to impose order on what is beyond his control.

It follows that religion not only legitimates social institutions by bestowing ontological status on them, but relativizes these same institutions *sub specie aeternitatis* and hence may withdraw sanctity from them (97–98). Far from merely validating society's decrees, religion reveals the intrinsic incompleteness of all human attainments by holding out the possibility of an order transcending the approximative actual: the indispensable if unreachable goal of an all-encompassing nomos, an all-embracing communitas. For this reason, religion is a force not only, as Durkheim believed, of social inertia but no less intrinsically, as Weber understood, of radical change arising from the individual's aspiration toward a more meaningful order than the emptied legitimacies his given world can supply.

A similar conception of religion as continuous transcendence finds expression in Kierkegaard, who affirms through Johannes Climacus, the pseudonymous author of the *Concluding Unscientific Postscript*, "that it is not the truth but the way which is the truth, i.e. that the truth exists only in the process of becoming" (72). Existence "is precisely the opposite of finality" (107) and cannot be conceived without movement or reduced to any closed system, and reality is "an *inter-esse*" (273), "the dialectical moment in a trilogy, whose beginning and whose end cannot be for the existing individual" (279).

Since human life is by nature "steady striving and a continuous meanwhile" (469), then, the religious aspirant will renounce the mirage of absolute truth in this world for the road leading toward it and concur with Lessing's hard saying that "if God held all truth in his right hand, and in his left hand held the lifelong pursuit of it, he would choose the left hand" (97). The subjective thinker has no finite goal toward which he strives and which he could reach and be finished: "No, he strives infinitely, is constantly in process of becoming" (84). Religious aspiration requires a goal indeed, but requires that this goal be transcendent—attainable, if at all, only by a leap beyond the continuous meanwhile of human existence into another order of things whither neither Johannes Climacus nor we may follow. To the extent that religion pertains to the human it remains, for Kierkegaard's quixotically inward outsider no less than for the tribesmen of van Gennep or Turner, a never-completed transition.

Of the two conceptions of religion that we have examined, one is associated with passively habitual (if not "instinctive") affirmation of society as a closed structure immutably grounded in the past, the other with actively purposeful transformation of society as an open process perpetually in passage toward an unrealized future. In terms of the first, no quest is conceivable, since the answers are given in the fixed repetitions of ritual before the questions are asked. In terms of the second, the personal quest finds a collective paradigm in the liminal community's ritualized itinerary through society's margins toward an indeterminate outcome always leaving new thresholds to cross, and the individual's aspiration toward a more meaningful order may in turn become a potent instrument of social transformation.

Between the two, Bergson discerned (58), lies "the whole distance between repose and movement. The first is supposed to be immutable. . . . The shape it assumes at any given time claims to be the final shape. But the second is a forward thrust, a demand for movement; it is the very essence of mobility." The difference is not, however, as Bergson elsewhere implies,[2] a qualitative one that precludes interaction between them. On the contrary, the static and the kinetic, the closed and the open, the structured and the liminal dimensions of religion, neither of which can exist in isolation for long, are inseparable aspects of one another, through whose dialectical interplay the religious life of society comes into being and continues insensibly to evolve.

These aspects, though both essential, are nevertheless not equal; the primacy of the second derives, for Bergson, from the fact that "movement includes immobility" (58). Stasis is the temporary equilibrium that results from the variation in tempo intrinsic to motion; it is not an autonomous reality but a pulsation or pause in the movement that repeatedly creates and annuls it. The real is not only mobile but movement itself; and if we persist in regarding as real the momentary halts which are only the simultaneity of movements, and in fallaciously viewing rest as anterior to motion, this error reflects our deeply ingrained reluctance to accept the ineluctable mutability of a condition which suggests to our dissatisfied minds "a deficiency, a lack, a quest of the unchanging form" (244). To exist with irrepressible *consciousness* of impermanence, of the in-betweenness intrinsic to the transitional process of life, and to confront in perpetuity an openness offering no prospect of termination, is to be always aware of a lack—the lack of that very closure and fixity we so insistently affirm—fundamental to our existence.

Yet if the permanence we inherently lack and incessantly strive to

2. "But between the society in which we live and humanity in general there is, we repeat, the same contrast as between the closed and the open; the difference between the two objects is one of kind and not simply one of degree" (32). Bergson's "vitalism" rests, very shakily, on a similar dualism.

achieve should be a chimera incompatible with the mutability that defines and propels us as living and questing beings, it will be not only a will-o'-the-wisp forever beyond attainment but an object finally alien to our aspirations themselves—an ultimate goal of our quest, but a goal that can only provide fulfillment so long as we continue to lack and continue to seek it. For just as rest is a phase of the movement that includes it, finding can be no more than a momentary pause in the continuous process of seeking which has, by its nature, no end.

CHAPTER TWO

Biological and Psychological Foundations of the Quest

Religion as process is one source of the spiritual quest, suggesting that the individual's search, idiosyncratic though it may sometimes seem, gives intensified direction to an impetus shared in some measure with society as a whole. The outcast could not so frequently return as hero or savior if the needs to which she gives voice were not latent in those who initially cast her out. But if the human being is truly *animal quaerens,* a similar latency will be found in the biological, psychological, and linguistic conditions of human life and culture without which society and religion would themselves be inconceivable.

BIOLOGY AND PURPOSE: THE EVOLUTION OF OPENNESS

The quest, far from being an incidental activity, gives specifically human shape to processes basic to life. Distinctive of both is direction, or even, in some sense, purpose. Unlike modern physicists, who have rigorously rejected the notion of *telos,* many biologists find function or purpose a concept fundamental to understanding life. Thus for Simpson (86–87) "the purposeful aspect of organisms is incontrovertible"; for Bernštejn (in Jakobson 1973, 56) purposiveness is "a manifest, perhaps even decisive, difference of living systems"; and for Ayala (12) teleological explanations in biology are "indispensable."[1]

1. Ayala (8–9) distinguishes "three categories of biological phenomena where teleological explanations are appropriate," namely activity directed toward a consciously anticipated goal; "self-regulating or teleonomic systems"; and "structures anatomically and physiologically designed to perform a certain function" by the directive process of natural selection. See also the distinctions in E. Nagel, 275–316, and Mayr 1988, 38–66. Ayala

Yet the nature and origin of this biological purposiveness remain intensely problematic. The ancient Aristotelian teleology, "the doctrine of final cause, of the end's determining the means," which widely prevailed among biologists well into the nineteenth century, is one which Simpson (85) and all of modern science can easily dismiss as "anthropomorphic in a truly primitive way"; in its cruder forms this doctrine prodigally ascribed to everything in creation a purpose determined by its utility to man. So uncritical a teleology was demolished in principle by Kant's "Critique of the Teleological Judgment" of 1790, which both restricted the concept of natural purposiveness to the organism—in which "every part is reciprocally purpose and means" (222)—and argued that this concept is "not susceptible of proof through reason as regards its objective reality" (244). But Kant's scrupulous critique left open the very large loophole that *subjectively*, in his view (247), natural processes can only be understood by positing "a designing causality of a highest cause," since no human reason "can hope to understand the production of even a blade of grass by mere mechanical causes" (258).

This subjective conviction of a First Cause, which allowed Kant, after all his critiques of reason and judgment, to see in man "the final purpose of creation" (286), depended on the lack of any rationally convincing explanation of biological design—until Darwin dramatically supplied one in natural selection. Natural selection may not, as Darwin's horrified contemporaries too hastily concluded, wholly eliminate all question of purpose from the workings of nature expounded in *The Origin of Species*. Indeed, Darwin's language reveals the persistence of seemingly teleological and even anthropomorphic patterns in his thought. "Man selects only for his own good; Nature only for that of the being which she tends" (132), and Nature's productions "plainly bear the stamp of far higher workmanship. . . . It may be said," therefore, "that natural selection is . . . silently and insensibly working, whenever and wherever opportunity offers, at the improvement of each organic being" (133).

But the "purposes" we metaphorically or retrospectively ascribe to Darwin's selective Nature differ profoundly from those of Platonic demiurge, Stoic artificer, or Judaeo-Christian creator in accruing eventually, through reproductive selection of favored traits, not to the expendable individual but to the evolving species—and to man as a species like any other—and in unfolding in accord not with a predetermined plan or

---

further notes (14) that "Final Causes, for Aristotle, are principles of intelligibility; they are not in any sense active agents in their own realization." The "Aristotelian" teleology against which modern science reacted is a distortion of Aristotle's final cause, which he clearly discriminated from the efficient cause (the only cause normally signified by our word) with which a debased Aristotelian tradition confounded it.

"designing causality" but solely with the unforeseeable opportunities provided by random mutations or "sports." Nor of course does the process of evolution lead inevitably to greater adaptation, fitness, or survival: extinction, in the long run, is its normal outcome. Purpose survived *The Origin of Species*, if at all, in fundamentally altered form; behavior of individual organisms may no doubt be goal-directed, but evolutionary directionality seems purposive only when we deem it, in hindsight, successful.

To a great extent twentieth-century molecular biology has confirmed Darwin by explaining the mechanism of inheritance which he could only ascribe to a reproductive system of which he confessed to be "profoundly ignorant" (174). Insofar as this mechanism functions with nearly flawless efficiency, however, the directionality supposedly distinctive of life might seem inexplicable: for how do organisms mechanically reproducing their kind by invariable biochemical processes display more purposive direction than stars or planets whirled about by impersonal gravitational forces? To such questions Jacques Monod's *Chance and Necessity* of 1970 atempted to respond from the perspective of modern genetics in an "orthodox" neo-Darwinian form taken to a controversial extreme.

Monod reaffirms the characteristic "common to all living beings without exception . . . of being *objects endowed with a purpose or project*" (9). He calls this internal purposiveness *teleonomy*—a term drawn from cybernetics, which recognizes no essential difference between living and non-living systems—and considers it, along with autonomous morphogenesis and reproductive invariance, one of the three general properties distinctive of living beings. The very fact of teleonomy, however, constitutes an epistemological problem in that it seems to violate the ironclad postulate of the scientific method ("consubstantial" with modern science) that "objective" nature must be understood without reference to final causes. For Monod (21–22), "the central problem of biology lies with this very contradiction."[2]

The only solution he considers acceptable to modern science is "that invariance necessarily precedes teleonomy," preserving the effects of chance by submitting them "to the play of natural selection" (23–24). Invariance (encoded in the gene) is both precondition and end of teleonomy, whose project is "the transmission from generation to generation of the invariance content characteristic of the species" (14). Yet more complex forms of purposive behavior (which presuppose response to alternatives presented by variation) could surely never arise if invariance were absolute; rather, in the course of adaptation, *purpose itself*

---

2. On the term *teleonomy*, introduced by Pittendrigh in 1958, see Ayala (13–14) and Mayr (1988, 44–50). Ayala prefers "internal teleology" as a biologically appropriate term.

evolves—insofar as metaphorical extension of a term strictly applicable, as Kant already discerned, only to the individual organism can describe the blindly directional processes of evolution—as a cumulative consequence of the random perturbations that introduce variation into the resistantly invariant gene and gradually produce, through survival of the fittest mutations, developments of increasing complexity and refinement. Evolutionary directionality, without itself being purposive, is the indispensable condition for the genesis of truly purposeful goal-directed behavior, which is not the motor of evolution, as in Lamarck, but one of its products—an experiment whose end is not known. For the "goals" of Darwinian evolution are forever being determined by incremental preservation of advantageous mutations introduced through countless "choices" given by chance and winnowed by the "strictly . . . a posteriori process," in Mayr's words (1988, 43), of natural selection.

For Monod, to be sure, the organic system is "utterly impervious to any 'hints' from the outside world" (110–11) in a one-way relationship that is "thoroughly Cartesian: the cell is indeed a *machine*." This contention even leads him to the provocative assertion (116) that "*evolution is not a property of living beings,* since it stems from the very *imperfections* of the conservative mechanism"—as if imperfection were less a property of living beings than invariance. (For Darwin, in contrast, Gould remarks [1987a, 84], "The primary proofs of evolution are oddities and imperfections.") Others, however, have argued that the biological mechanism, even at the molecular or cellular level, is a system by no means closed to all influences from an outside world with which its relationships are not entirely one-way but reciprocal, even dialectical.

Thus for Piaget (1971, 81), investigating the biological basis of knowledge as an outgrowth of the process of life, "phylogenesis [is] dependent in part on ontogenesis" (evolution of the species on development of the individual), and not only the reverse, so that information supplied by genes "is not only transmitted but also transformed in the course of all this development." Since the genome contains a system of autoregulation, it is "a contradiction in terms to suppose that all connection with the soma or the environment can be cut off" (113) in a process excluding interaction between them,[3] for if *everything* were immutably programmed, there could be nothing to regulate.

---

3. The suggestion of interaction between genome and environment is the point at which Piaget's speculations most departed from orthodox genetics (for which the gene was a closed system and mutations random "mistakes" in conveying its messages) and became most hypothetical, for lack both of experimental verification and of any convincingly demonstrated mechanism of interaction. "For modern biology," Jacob writes (16), "there is no molecular mechanism enabling instructions from the environment to be imprinted into DNA directly, that is, without the roundabout route of natural selection. Not that such a

Given this hypothesized responsiveness of the genome to environmental stimuli, evolutionary selection becomes a reciprocal process at every level: organisms not only adapt to given environments but actively adapt environments to their own uses. Such dynamic activity continually produces new forms of equilibrium by interaction within a changing environment; it involves not only random mistakes in genetic transmission but endless readjustment through trial and error. For to Piaget—who rejects the "perpetual vicious circle" of attributing biological organization "to chances which are already partly organized and to selections which are themselves controlled" (276)—life inevitably entails purposeful modification of biological organization in response to a shaping environment which it in turn contributes toward shaping.

Piaget's speculations corroborate Bertalanffy's conception of the organism as an open system in continuous interchange with the environment. A permanent equilibrium would be contrary to life, which involves, for Bertalanffy as for Piaget, perpetual re-equilibration of the disequilibria continually introduced by the organism's interaction with the world; this progressive re-equilibration is one more formulation of biological purposiveness. The process is by no means one of aimless fluctuation, since organs or structures tend to become increasingly "mechanized" through progressive differentiation to suit the organism's overall purpose, thereby becoming decreasingly autonomous and adaptable in themselves. For Bertalanffy, as for Bergson, the open system or process is therefore prior to the closed system or structure, its temporarily equilibrated state: "Structures are slow processes of long duration, functions are quick processes of short duration" (1952, 134). The organism is accordingly "not a passive but a basically *active* system" (18), and its attributes necessarily include both individual and evolutionary *history* (109). Because life is process, and evolution (Monod notwithstanding) is its property par excellence, to study it as a structure abstracted from growth is to falsify it in essence.

Granted that the organism is an open autoregulatory system, the "purpose" inherent in the process of life will be not only self-preservation through genetically invariant reproduction but self-transcendence

---

mechanism is theoretically impossible. Simply it does not exist." Yet recent developments make such categorical assertions less sure. As Gould remarks (1987b, 157–59), the "central dogma" of Francis Crick, "that DNA makes RNA and RNA makes protein, in a one-way flow of information, a unidirectional process of mechanical construction," has been breached, in large part by the work of Barbara McClintock. In this new model, "the genome is fluid and mobile," and "a set of new themes—mobility, rearrangement, regulation, and interaction—has transformed our view of genomes from stable and linear arrays, altered piece by piece and shielded from any interaction with their products, to fluid systems with potential for rapid reorganization and extensive feedback."

in the direction of increasingly adequate adaptation to changing circumstances and, beyond this, to the incessant challenge of change itself. Biological purposiveness, in yet another formulation, is active resistance to the entropy that measures the degradation of energy, according to the second law of thermodynamics, in any closed system. In an open system responsively interacting with its environment, "the entropy balance," Bertalanffy asserts (1968, 48), "may well be negative, that is, the system may develop toward states of higher improbability, order and differentiation (although, of course, entropy increases in the larger system consisting of the organism and its environment)."[4] Only through the progressive differentiation characteristic, for Piaget, of all biological (and all cognitive) organizations can an open system of advanced complexity continue to live and to grow, thus achieving an always precarious negation of entropy and temporary postponement of extinction.

Monod speculates (167) that "the profound disquiet which goads us to search out the meaning of existence" through religious rites is an evolutionary inheritance of humanity. If so, it may be a quality selected not only for its advantage to tribal cohesion during our specifically human (and therefore recent) evolution, but still more fundamentally the highly intensified—because at least partly conscious—expression of the unstable organism's perpetual search for an equilibrium compatible with the always destabilizing process of transformation through growth. For if "both instinctive and cultural rituals," to quote Lorenz once again (1966, 77–78), "become independent motivations of behavior by creating new ends or goals toward which the organism strives for their own sakes," the profoundly unquiet search for stability expressed in the elaborate rituals of human religious behavior can be seen as a rudimentary property of living beings long antedating the upstart genus *homo*.

Which conception of evolution ultimately proves more nearly correct, the random mutationism of Darwin espoused by Monod, or Bertalanffy's and Piaget's dialectical interaction between an open system and its environment, will of course be decided by continuing observation and experimentation. For the present, few leading biologists would find the evidence for the latter sufficient to warrant serious questioning of orthodox Darwinism buttressed by modern genetics. The despotism of

4. Cf. Bertalanffy 1952, 127, and N. A. Bernštejn as quoted in Jakobson 1973, 56: "The organism . . . strives for the maximum of negentropy compatible with its vital stability." But increasing differentiation must not itself be seen as a purposeful evolutionary development, since, as Gould cautions (1993, 322–23), "life shows no trend to complexity in the usual sense—only an asymmetrical expansion of diversity around a starting point constrained to be simple. . . . Increasing complexity is not a purposeful trend of an unbroken lineage but only the upper limit of an expanding distribution as overall diversity increases."

chance deduced by Monod is far from being, however, a universally accepted consequence of his neo-Darwinian premises. For Dobzhansky (1974, 317–18), natural selection, as "the antichance factor in evolution," makes evolution directional by increasing the adaptedness of populations to their environments; Darwinian fitness is "not an intrinsic property of genetic mutation, but an emergent product of its interactions with the environment" (320). Evolution of an organism can therefore no more be attributed solely to chance than construction of the Parthenon can: evolution is essentially not a random but "a creative process, in precisely the same sense in which composing a poem or a symphony, carving a statue, or painting a picture are creative acts," and what it creates by bringing into being "living systems that would otherwise be infinitely improbable" is above all "order out of randomness" (1970, 430, 431).

There is of course in this impersonal creation no agent to which purpose in any usual sense can be ascribed; yet the undeniably purposeful activity evident in the search of advanced animal organisms for food, reproduction, and survival is itself the product of a blindly formative evolutionary process, "self-maintaining, self-transforming, and self-transcendent," in Julian Huxley's words (Hallpike 1988, 30), "directional in time and therefore irreversible, which in its course generates ever fresh novelty, greater variety, more complex organization, higher levels of awareness, and increasingly conscious mental activity." The a posteriori process of evolution through natural selection is not purposeful in itself (though hypothetical interaction between genome and environment leaves even this possibility open at a rudimentary level), but through its openness to the world, its responsiveness to change, its opportunistic creativity, and its continual formation of new if always provisional forms permitting survival in a constantly changing world, it enables the successfully adaptive organism to pursue the primary "purpose" or "meaning" of its existence. For the meaning in living creatures, Dobzhansky affirms (1974, 323), "is as simple as it is basic—it is life instead of death." In its restless pursuit of this forever variable goal (life being an order that can never be final), every organism created by the long random processes of evolution is inherently a quest in the making.

THE QUEST OF CONSCIOUSNESS

Biologists may speak metaphorically of a "search" even on the molecular level. But the quest is a search that is aware of itself and able to articulate its own goals; for its specifically human foundations, then, we must turn to psychology and linguistics. The fundamental distinction of psycho-analytical theory, as developed in Freud's last two decades, is not between unconscious and conscious but between id and ego. The id is the undifferentiated region of the psyche shut off (though never entirely) from consciousness and the outer world. Here "contradictions and antitheses persist side by side" (1959c, 20), the laws of logic are suspended, and time has no place. Though a source of vast psychic energy and potential conflict for the ego, to which it is "a chaos, a cauldron full of seething excitations" (1965, 73), the id impassively resists disruption of its self-contained equilibrium by any external disturbance. The only ordered movement evident in its inarticulate turbulence is an endless repetition manifested in the compulsive "ceremonial" of the neurotic which Freud compared to a religious rite, describing religion itself as "a universal obsessional neurosis" (1959a, 2:34)—a judgment to which he held firm throughout his long life.

The message cryptically communicated by the id in dreams and neuroses stems, as Freud especially emphasizes in his late writings, from "the *archaic heritage* which a child brings with him into the world, before any experience of his own"—a "phylogenetic" heritage (1949, 124; cf. 1939, 128) corresponding to instinct in animals. Instinct is not only conservative but regressive, *"an urge inherent in organic life to restore an earlier state of things"* embodying the inherent inertia of organic life (1928, 67–68), so that *"the aim of all life is death"* (70). In this turbid sediment of the mind ruled by the past and repetitively asserting its sameness while slipping backward toward primal nonentity the quest for an indeterminate future has clearly no possibility of coming into being.

The ego of Freud's late writings is "the organized portion of the id" (1959b, 23), somewhat as life is the organized portion of matter. It is quintessentially an open system, since it "owes its origin as well as the most important of its acquired characteristics to its relation to the real external world" (1949, 58). Freud stresses no quality of the ego more than this openness to the world, without which the id "could not escape destruction" (1965, 75). In contrast to the automatism of the id, blind to the impediments of reality, the ego must be flexibly responsive to contrary needs which it continually strives to balance. Despite its relative weakness, it is the truly active component of the mind which, by its "freely mobile function" (1959b, 79), counteracts the id's obsessive compulsion to repeat what has already been. It not only bridles and guides the powerful id, substituting the reality principle for the id's pleasure principle, but inventively mediates between the conflicting demands of those unreconciled principles and strives to pacify the unpredictable conflicts to which they recurrently give rise.

It follows that the ego's pathological states result from disruption of this openness to the external world (1949, 58) by which the ego maintains its precarious balance. Neurosis derives from conflict between ego and id, and psychosis from "a similar disturbance in the relation between the ego and its environment (outer world)" (1959a, 2:250–51). Neurosis tries to ignore reality whereas "psychosis denies it and tries to substitute something else for it": the healthy ego, in contrast, mediates between id and reality by seeking active achievement in the outer world. "It is no longer," Freud succinctly concludes (2:279–80), "*auto-plastic* but *allo-plastic.*" Because it shapes not itself alone but the other, the balanced ego escapes the repetitive monologue of the ritualized id and enters into conversation with an unpredictable interlocutor; it is not only open to the external world but actively engaged in transforming a reality of which, through its openness, it is inextricably part.

In sharp contrast to the id, the ego—to the extent that it can resist submitting to its overawing attendant—is capable of *development* in a purposeful direction "from obeying instincts to inhibiting them" in the "progressive conquest of the id" (1960, 45–46) to which psychoanalysis, by redirecting the ego toward reality, importantly contributes. Freud repeatedly returned in his later writings to the implications of his early hypothesis that progressive renunciation of instincts "appears to be one of the foundations of human civilization" (1959a, 2:34; cf. 1961b, 7; 1961a, 44); and even though the specter of an unappeasable guilt ominously rising from the depths of a repressive civilization lurked like a beast in the jungle (or an Unbehagen in der Kultur) in the darkening light of Freud's final decades, he remained convinced that civilization can only have arisen, and can only be sustained (if at all), by sublimation of the sexual instincts "through the mediation of the ego" (1960, 20).

To the development of the ego humanity owes the *history* of which that development is an integral part, for no more than biological life can the ego be understood apart from its history. In certain individuals this progressive ego-differentiation through the always imperfect repression of instinct becomes a restless drive toward an always unreachable future goal—a drive to which not only the individual psyche but human civilization owes its growth and its margin of freedom. "What appears in a minority of human individuals as an untiring impulsion towards further perfection can easily be understood as a result of the instinctual repression upon which is based all that is most precious in human civilization." In these few, Freud writes (1928, 76–77), the difference between satisfaction demanded and achieved "will permit of no halting at any position attained, but, in the poet's words, '*ungebändigt immer vorwärts dringt*'. . . . So there is no alternative but to advance in the direction in

which growth is still free—though with no prospect of bringing the process to conclusion or of being able to reach the goal."[5]

The mobile ego thus redirects the potent energy of repressed instinct
from regressive inertia to aspiration toward an unattainable future—an
aspiration that Freud associated not with the childish illusion of religion
but with science. The ego "represents what may be called reason and
common sense" (1960, 15), and Freud, an *Aufklärer in dürftiger Zeit*, held
fast despite his worst forebodings to the belief, reaffirmed at the very
time Hitler was seizing power, that "our best hope for the future is that
intellect—the scientific spirit, reason—may in process of time establish a
dictatorship in the mental life of man" (1965, 171). Only an Eros guided
by the rational ego can draw the mind progressively further from threatened subjection to the death-devoted id, and this supremely purposeful
work is the work of human culture itself, "not unlike the draining of the
Zuider Zee." For the id is the changeless past, the ego the indeterminate
future, the id what is reified and alien to us as evolving rational beings,
the ego our essential self, and *Wo es war*, this most pessimistic of realists
never ceased to hope, *soll ich sein:* "Where id was, there ego shall be"
(1965, 80).

For Freud, not only was the human id a phylogenetic inheritance but
its differentiation from the ego already existed in simpler organisms.
Only the extent of its development was unique to the human species,
and the task of psychoanalysis was to foster that development. Nor was
Freudian psychoanalysis alone in this emphasis; Jung, though far more
sympathetic to the archetypal and therefore inheritable unconscious
(which for him was not a menacing "it" but a beckoning mother), knew
that the human being could no more return to that universal matrix
than leave it wholly behind. He too stressed that it is "man's turning away
from instinct—his opposing himself to instinct—that creates consciousness" (1971, 4). Only active assimilation by the conscious mind can avert
disruption of the psyche by the chaotic *prima materia* from which it is
increasingly differentiated.

Man only discovers the world, Jung writes (1956, 2:417), "when he
sacrifices his containment in the primal mother, the original state of unconsciousness"; therefore the libido must not stick fast like Theseus and
Peirithous to the underworld but "tear itself loose from the maternal
embrace and return to the surface with new possibilities of life" (2:420).
In this emphasis on purposeful differentiation of consciousness from the
unconscious, Jung and Freud are fundamentally one—though for Jung,

5. The German words ("presses ever forward unsubdued") are spoken by Mephis-
topheles in Goethe's *Faust*, Part One, scene 4.

in total contrast to Freud, "the great psychotherapeutic systems which we know as the religions" (2:356) have consistently opposed the regressive tendency against which both repeatedly warned.

Despite the "discovery of the unconscious" widely regarded as the signal accomplishment of modern psychoanalysis, then—or rather in consequence of that discovery—for both Freud and Jung it is the organized activity of the *conscious* mind formed through interchange with external reality that most fully distinguishes the human species. The phylogenetic unconscious of psychoanalysis is all but impermeably self-enclosed, but consciousness is a process that continually opens toward a reality that transcends, includes, and reacts back upon it. The unconscious is inherited, but consciousness develops through interaction with others. By its purposeful differentiation from the repetitive unconscious, and its engagement with an unpredictable and changing world, consciousness is by nature incessantly in quest of the unknown.

No psychologist has contributed more to understanding the human mind's interactions with the world than Piaget. In early infancy the absorption of reality into the undifferentiated self, which Piaget designates "narcissism" or "absolute egocentricity," is nearly complete. The origins of this condition are biological, since the organism and its environment are at first a continuum. The child can engage in no true dialogue because she lacks "the art of seeking and finding in the other's mind some basis on which to build anew" (1932a, 133). No quest is possible so long as she fails to differentiate any object from herself or to conceive of any need born of its lack. "Objective" thought requires the subject to posit an object distinct from yet in continuing relation to itself: "the objectivity of thought is closely bound up with its communicability" (137). This process is eminently dynamic, and developing awareness of purposeful movement, "introducing a progressive differentiation within the primitive *continuum* of life and purpose" (1929, 236), is essential to its realization.

During the first phase of this process (250–51), self and things are confused in "participation between all and everything, and desire can exert a magical activity over reality." In the second phase, differentiation begins; in the third, thoughts and words are no longer "conceived as adherent in things" but are "situated in the head." The condition of separation in which the quest (like van Gennep's rites of passage) always begins is not, Piaget thus suggests, the sudden outcome of any one event such as the trauma of birth or weaning from the mother's breast but results from the gradual differentiation by which each individual becomes conscious of a world distinct from herself and of a self potentially deprived of its object. The same development of consciousness that gives rise to objective and thence to logical thought gives rise, by the separation it entails, to the possibility of unfulfilled desire and of a quest by the alienated self to overcome its lack of the global object from which it has been intrinsically but not incommunicably severed.

Two factors contributing to differentiation of consciousness as Piaget portrays it are especially important preconditions of the quest. One is emergence, at about a year and a half to two years, of "the capacity to represent something with something else, which is known as the symbolical function," manifested not only in speech but in play, postponed imitation through gestures, and mental pictures or interiorized imitations (1973, 16–17). Symbolism is a crucial step in development of consciousness because it entails relation between two initially differentiated "somethings," and because it exhibits intentionality independent of immediate need by evoking "the not actually perceived intended" (117). The development of increasingly adaptable symbolisms enables intention to be articulated and action to be oriented toward a goal represented in advance. As Bertalanffy affirms (1968, 20, 17), symbolism, the "*differentia specifica* of *Homo sapiens*," "makes true or Aristotelian purposiveness possible" by anticipating a future goal that may determine present action.

The second differentiating factor is the child's insistent asking of "why," reflecting a more advanced distinction of subject and object. The interrogative mood expresses heightened uncertainty about a world no longer at the subject's command, and the question "why?" evinces nascent awareness of the possibility that purposes in that unfathomable world might reveal "discord between desire and its realization" (Piaget 1932a, 235). Here in the obstinate questionings of the child is an embryonic quest both purposefully directed toward an indeterminate future goal (the answer sought but not known) and urgently concerned with purpose or meaning itself. To the extent that the mind chooses to undertake this effort, its development from egocentric self-absorption to objective and communicable knowledge is both precondition and prototype of the spiritual quest as a conscious human activity.

Piaget consistently emphasized the continuity of biology and cognition as assimilative open systems characterized by differentiation and growth. The most advanced instrument of this open-ended developmental process is the intelligence, characterized, in opposition to habituated training, by "a reversible mobility constantly widening in scope" (1971, 253). Intelligence not only reflects but constructs "objective" reality, since objectivity is "a process and not a state" (64), and intelligence, by its distinctive mobility, is the cognitive process par excellence. Only by organizing itself through evolution of its categories can intelligence organize the world it is perpetually constructing, and this progressive organization, which presupposes both initial differentiation and continual interaction of self and things, is the goal of the mobile equilibration that constitutes intelligence itself.[6] Otherwise put, the goal of the developing consciousness in Piaget's "genetic epistemology" is meaning and truth—not as subjective projections or hypostatized absolutes, but meaning (in Mead's words) as "something objectively there as a relation" (1934, 76) and truth (in Piaget's) as "an organization of the real world" (1971, 361–62). Without the discrimination of things from self in which the development of adult consciousness originates, no quest would come into being (for there would be no object to seek); but without the interaction between self and things by which intelligence organizes an objectively meaningful world, none could possibly be accomplished.

In contrast, then, to the inertial self-absorption of both Freud's id and Piaget's egocentric infantile consciousness, the adult consciousness, or ego, is for both an open-ended process continually organizing itself and its world in response to external reality and advancing toward provisional conquests of coherent meaning from inner and outer chaos alike. Such a restlessly forward-moving psyche has a precursor in the "Faustian" consciousness inherited from the Renaissance. "The human understanding is unquiet; it cannot stop or rest, and still presses onward," Bacon wrote (37; *Novum Organum* 48), "but in vain. Therefore it is that we cannot conceive of any end or limit of the world; but always of necessity it occurs to us that there is something beyond." But the consciousness of Freud or Piaget, as distinct from that of Bruno or Bacon, is rooted in the biological constitution of the human animal, which tempers the no longer limitless dynamism to which it gives rise and guides its choice of directions by genetically transmitted impulses and restraints.

Because the goal of so dynamic a consciousness is in the process of evolving (like consciousness and like the organism itself), it can never be predetermined or finally attained. Unlike the unconscious, which is "the principle of all regressions and all stagnations," consciousness, Ricoeur remarks (1974, 113), "is a movement which continually annihilates its starting point and can guarantee itself only at the end" toward which it incessantly advances but never fully arrives. And because it is reflexively

6. For Piaget (1967, 4), "the higher functions of intelligence and affectivity tend toward a 'mobile equilibrium.' The more mobile it is, the more stable it is." And equilibrium (151) is not passive but essentially active. The concept is central to his view of structure in biology, psychology, and linguistics.

aware of its own self-transcendent and self-creative activity, which thus becomes fully purposeful, "consciousness is not a given," Ricoeur affirms (108), "but a *task*." Through its awareness of forward movement toward a contingent goal in the unforeseeable future as the task it has purposefully taken upon itself and cannot abandon, human consciousness becomes, in its innermost nature, a perpetual quest.

CHAPTER THREE

Linguistic Foundations of the Quest

The self-transcendence inherent in life and intensified by consciousness can attain full expression only through the exclusively human medium of speech, which gives the inchoate questing impulse flexibly structured communicable form. Even though its object may be finally inexpressible (for how express what remains to be found?), the fully human quest presupposes the creative agency of the word—or sentence—that allows the always potential future to become the goal of present actions.

FROM COLLECTIVE INERTIA
TO RULE-GOVERNED CREATIVITY

That language might be essential to the search for an indeterminate future is barely conceivable in the structuralist linguistics of Saussure and his school dominant throughout much of the twentieth century. The fundamental distinction of Saussure's *Course in General Linguistics* (13–14) is between the collective system of conventions designated *langue* ("language") and the individual execution called *parole* ("speech"), grouped together as *langage*.[1] Only *langue,* as a homogeneous system capable of being isolated from the idiosyncrasies of human speech, can constitute the subject matter of a scientific linguistics. As a superpersonal "collective representation," *langue* (in contrast to *parole*) is "the product that the individual passively registers" (14), and it remains "external to the individual, who by himself can neither create nor modify it." It is

---

1. Saussure's English translator translates *parole* as "speaking" and confusingly reserves "speech" for Saussure's comprehensive *langage*. I shall employ the French terms in my citations, referring to the pagination of the English translation.

(73–74) of all social institutions "the least susceptible to initiatives," and like society as a whole, "being by nature inert, is pre-eminently a conservative force." Even more than religious ritual for Durkheim, *langue* is a "collective inertia" resisting all innovation.

Not that Saussure was unaware of the historical evolution of languages; he contributed, in the major work published in his lifetime, to the study of phonetic change, and one section of the posthumously assembled *Course* is devoted to "diachronic" linguistics. But the very dominance of historical concerns in the Indo-European philology of his time led Saussure to give firm priority to its "synchronic" aspect, to "static" rather than "evolutionary" linguistics. In his conception, "the opposition between these two points of view—synchronic and diachronic—is absolute and allows no compromise." The linguist who wishes to understand *langue* must ignore diachronic development, for if *langue* is a self-sufficient relational system it must be studied without reference to historical genesis. Whatever changes occur pertain to isolated components, not to the system of relations in which *langue* consists. Changes, like verbal signs themselves, are arbitrary, and *langue* as system remains unmodified by them: "In itself it is immutable; only certain elements are altered without regard to the solidarity that binds them to the whole" (84).

Above all—and from this both arbitrariness and immutability follow—*langue* is a self-contained and hence a *closed* system cut off from the external world. It is not a nomenclature, "a list of terms corresponding to the same number of things" (which would suppose fixed ideas pre-existing the words that named them); rather, the linguistic sign unites "not a thing and a name, but a concept and an acoustic image" (65–66). Both sound and concept are purely mental, sealed by their common closure from all connection with any reality beyond their reference to one another. The relation between the two components of the sign—"signifier" and "signified" as Saussure named them, reviving a terminology descending from St. Augustine and the Stoics (Jakobson 1971, 2:345)—is therefore wholly internal, and either or both may change (since in isolation both *must* be arbitrary) without in any way altering their permanently constitutive relation.

The inherently relational signs composing *langue* operate not by any intrinsic value (an arbitrary sign can have none) but by the differences among them that constitute the rules determining their function in the system. The components of *langue* are thus like chessmen, whose material form could be entirely altered without affecting their role in the system of rules which defines them. But in one crucial respect chess differs from *langue,* for "the chessplayer has the *intention* of making a move and exercising an action on the system, whereas *langue* premeditates nothing; its pieces are moved—or rather modified—spontaneously and by chance" (89). As a self-contained system of arbitrary components deriving significance solely from differences among themselves, *langue* is impervious to the intentions of its users.

In several key respects Chomsky's theories are akin to Saussure's, as Chomsky, who reacted against the American Structuralist school, has noted. For him, too, the object of linguistics cannot be the chaotic interplay of disparate factors in the *performance* of language—Saussure's *parole*—but the *competence* embodied in a speaker-hearer's implicit knowledge of grammar as a system of interrelated rules corresponding (in this regard) to Saussure's *langue*. Ever since *Syntactic Structures,* Chomsky has maintained that "grammar is autonomous and independent of meaning" (1957, 17)—a tightly organized system ideally isolable from other components of language. Great though his departures from structuralism may otherwise be, for Chomsky, "the classical Saussurian assumption of the logical priority of the study of *langue*. . .seems quite inescapable" (1964, 11).

Moreover, Saussure's assumption that *langue* is collective and immutable is reinforced by Chomsky's emphasis on linguistic universals as species-specific, indeed genetically programmed, properties of the human mind, so that "universal grammar" is the invariant "system of principles, conditions, and rules that are elements or properties of all human languages not merely by accident but by necessity—of course, I mean biological, not logical, necessity" (1975, 29). Such a system, being insusceptible to all but phylogenetic change, is impervious, like Saussure's, to individual variations, and Chomsky concludes (1965, 59) that the structure of particular languages, reflecting innate ideas and principles, "may very well be largely determined by factors over which the individual has no conscious control and concerning which society may have little choice or freedom." Thus Chomsky forcefully rejects the "commonsense" view that intentionality plays a central role in language. For if the genetically programmed language learner "does not choose to learn and cannot fail to learn under normal conditions, any more than he chooses (or can fail) to organize visual space in a certain way" (1975, 71), then purpose, at least in the sense of conscious intention, is strictly subsidiary if not wholly irrelevant. The question we must ask of language, Chomsky maintains (1972a, 70), is "what it is, not how or for what purposes it is used."

Yet the important affinities between Chomsky's thought and Saussure's should not conceal the still profounder differences between them. For Chomsky's structures, unlike the differentiated verbal signs of Saussurian semiology, are *syntactic,* and this distinction is of enormous consequence. Saussure limited the syntactic component of *langue* to linear combinations of signs, called syntagms. (With this syntagmatic relation he contrasted the associative—later called the paradigmatic—relation of possible substitutions for a given sign by others similar to it.) To *langue* belong only a few ready-made syntagms; others, including sentences, belong to *parole*, whose freedom of combination is not subject to rule. Thus syntax, in the dynamic sense of sentence formation, does not belong to *langue* and falls outside linguistics. For Chomsky this crucial distinction is the principal difference between his approach and that of structuralism in its various forms. Saussure, in Chomsky's view (1964, 23), "appears to regard sentence formation as a matter of *parole* rather than *langue*, of free and voluntary creation rather than systematic rule (or perhaps, in some obscure way, as on the border between *langue* and *parole*)." His view of syntax as a mere inventory is an "impoverished and thoroughly inadequate conception" which Chomsky (1965, 4) decisively repudiates.

In his own conception of linguistic competence, syntactic structures are not linear arrangements of signs but processes creating infinite possibilities through finite rules and constraints. A generative grammar, as Chomsky describes it in his once "standard theory"—later significantly modified—is the internalized system of rules comprising the speaker-hearer's "tacit knowledge" that generates both the set of sentences intuitively recognized as grammatical that constitute a language and—in a "stronger" sense—the structural descriptions of these (and no other) sentences that constitute an explicit theory of the language. The central syntactic component of this grammar "must specify, for each sentence, a *deep structure* that determines its semantic interpretation and a *surface structure* that determines its phonetic interpretation" (1965, 8–9). The syntactic component connects the deep structure of a sentence—approximating to its simple active declarative form—with the surface structure it finally assumes "by repeated application of certain formal operations called 'grammatical transformations'"; the semantic and phonological components determining the sense and the sound of the sentence are by contrast "purely interpretive" (16). In this "transformational generative grammar" the autonomous syntactic structures both generate and transform.

Chomsky's theories will stand or fall, as he has always affirmed, to the extent that empirical evidence sustains them. But his evolving conception differs from that of structural linguistics, despite their affinities, not in details but essentials. Above all, though Chomsky's competence like Saussure's *langue* may be a closed system—immunized from variation and change by being genetically programmed—it is also a generative *process*. What grammar—and specifically its syntactic component—generates is language itself, not as a sequence of self-enclosed signs but as an open-ended creative activity. Among Chomsky's central objections to

Saussure is that *langue* as "an inventory of elements" rather than a system of rules leaves no place for the "rule-governed creativity" of everyday language use (1964, 23). In contrast, the retrospectively defined tradition he calls Cartesian linguistics, stemming obliquely from Descartes and including the seventeenth-century Port-Royal grammarians and Wilhelm von Humboldt—who asserted (1972, 27) that "language is not work (*ergon*) but an activity (*energeia*)"—gave forceful expression to the essential creativity of language (Chomsky 1966, 19; cf. 1964, 17).[2]

In this conception, as developed by Chomsky, "the limitless possibilities of thought and imagination are reflected in the creative aspect of language use. The language provides finite means but infinite possibilities of expression constrained only by rules of concept formation and sentence formation" (1966, 29). Everyday language use is a creative and "mysterious ability" by which expressions new to experience are incessantly engendered (1972a, 100). The contradiction between this emphasis on open-ended creativity in language use and the seemingly deterministic insistence that linguistic structure is a biologically encoded system insusceptible to conscious choice is a contradiction in appearance only. For Chomsky's "rule-governed" creativity, if superficially paradoxical, places him firmly in an intellectual (and moral) tradition for which freedom itself, as opposed to license, is made possible by the laws defining it. Constrictions on attainable language *allow* a language to be attained; its innate schematism "*makes possible* the acquisition of a rich and highly specific system on the basis of limited data" (1972a, 174). A transformational generative grammar, by syntactically organizing the channels through which semantic categories find phonetic expression, *creates* the "infinite possibilities" constituting the nearly unrestricted freedom of linguistic performance—the creative use of language which remains, unlike the theoretically definable mechanism of competence, "a mystery that eludes our intellectual grasp" (1980, 222).

Unlike the unproductive Saussurian system, then, in which *langue* and *parole* are "absolutely distinct," and *langue* is imprinted on a passively receptive brain, the linguistic competence enabling creative performance reflects for Chomsky not "a 'passive' system of incremental data processing, habit formation, and induction" as in behaviorist learning theory, but an active potentiality like that of Leibniz in the rationalist tradition "for which external stimuli serve only as occasions for activating what is already dispositionally contained in the mind's own structure" (1975, 216). Indeed, despite Chomsky's reluctance to attribute purpose to language, performance is clearly the goal toward which the

2. For a critique of Chomsky's conception of a "Cartesian" tradition of linguistics, see Aarsleff, 100–119.

generative process of linguistic competence is directed. "There is, of course, no doubt," he asserts with uncharacteristically forthright acknowledgment of a broadened teleology, "that language is designed for use" (1972b, 199).

Among the most cogent objections to structural linguistics is that *langue* remains a closed system without essential connection either with speech through which it is realized or with the extralinguistic world. Under the "rule of the closure of the universe of signs," Ricoeur writes (1974, 83–84), "the act of speaking is excluded not only as . . . individual performance, but as free combination, as producing new utterances," though this "is the essential aspect of language—properly speaking, its goal." And language so understood "does not refer to anything outside of itself, it constitutes a world for itself" (1978, 90).

By his emphasis on open-ended creativity as essential to language Chomsky escapes the first of these objections. But his insistence, since his earliest work, that an autonomous grammar is "independent of meaning" (1957, 17) and that "semantic notions are of no use in grammar" (100) might make transformational generative grammar no less than Saussurian semiology seem "a world for itself" independent of all external reference. Some twenty years after *Syntactic Structures* Chomsky still "found nothing to challenge the absolute thesis of autonomy of syntax" (1977, 52), which remains a cardinal postulate of his theory of language.

Yet Chomsky does not identify this autonomous system with "language." On the contrary, he has tried to delimit as precisely as possible the role of syntax among the components of grammar and of grammar (including syntax) among the systems comprising language. Syntax, and grammatical competence in general, are the language system par excellence, since they alone are a structure-dependent, species-specific subsystem (or "organ") of the human mind whose only function is generation of language. But autonomy does not imply that no correspondences exist between grammar and meaning. On the contrary, the undeniable fact of such correspondences suggested to Chomsky in his earliest writings the need for a more general theory of language including a theory both of linguistic form and of language use (1957, 102), since the latter "obviously involves a complex interplay of many factors of the most disparate sort, of which the grammatical processes constitute only one" (1964, 10). Chomsky has always recognized the importance of such factors, even if he has sometimes described them as "extralinguistic" components of performance and considered them (like memory restrictions) "not, properly speaking, aspects of language" (1972a, 116). Increasingly, however, he acknowledges that the linguistic competence virtually identified in earlier writings with implicit knowledge of generative grammar comprehends also a "pragmatic competence" which (though not "language-specific" like grammatical competence) "underlies the ability to use such knowledge along with the conceptual system to achieve certain ends or purposes" (1980, 59; cf. 224–25).

Indeed, although Chomsky firmly rejects behaviorist learning theory and the doctrine that a vaguely defined general intelligence can account for language acquisition, he believes that several interacting components may be involved in knowing a language, including, besides the language-specific "computational" system of grammar, a more general "conceptual" system of object reference involving such relations as agent, goal, and instrument, so that knowledge of language "might consist of quite different cognitive systems that interweave in normal cognitive development" (54–55, 58). The fact that in Chomsky's view grammar alone and not language (of which it is only the central of several interacting systems) is autonomous, and that the less specialized "conceptual" system likewise integral to knowledge of language entails "object reference" and other potentially extralinguistic relations, sharply differentiates his conception from Saussure's self-enclosed system of internal values. "The idealization of 'grammar' will thus be entirely legitimate, but the theory of grammar will be in part 'open'" (1977, 37). The very fact of interaction with other components requires that grammatical competence be a less than hermetically closed system, and thus dictates that it can never constitute "a world for itself."

Reference to the external world, neglected if not precluded in Saussure's conception of *langue,* is one important function of the interdependent systems that comprise language for Chomsky. In this perspective, the autonomy of syntax (and its independence from determination by semantic categories) is what makes it possible for language to refer to extralinguistic reality and escape the *huis clos* of a solipsistic structuralism. For if semantic categories were themselves (as the short-lived theories of "generative semantics" supposed) intrinsic—thus "generative"— components of grammatical competence, "meaning" would be, as in structuralism, a predetermined, wholly intralinguistic affair.

Far from countenancing such tendencies, Chomsky, in developing his "extended standard theory" since the 1970s, has moved decisively away from any association of semantics with deep structure, suggesting "that perhaps all semantic information is determined by a somewhat enriched notion of surface structure" (1975, 82; cf. 1972b, 1977). "I doubt that one can separate semantic representation from beliefs and knowledge about the world," he writes (1979, 142–43). Such nonlinguistic systems of belief as expectations about three-dimensional space, human behavior, and so on, are crucial to an understanding of semantics, in which "there are many mental organs in interaction."[3] It follows that although semantic reference is an undeniable function of language, meaning is not a subject to be defined (much less prescribed) in terms of linguistic theory alone.

Far from being a "return to structuralism" (1979, 175–77), Chomsky's association of semantics with surface structure and extra-linguistic beliefs confirms his radical departure from Saussure's purely relational linguistics. For Saussure (1959, 114–17), both "signification" (the relation, within a sign, between signifier and signified) and "value" (the relation of signs to one another by which the signification of each is determined) are internal to *langue*. Meaning can only be an intralinguistic relation among signs or between their components, for in *langue* nothing else enters, and outside it all is freedom or chaos, not meaning. In Chomsky's theory, on the contrary, semantic representation incorporates beliefs about the real world which enter language through the openness of the lexicon and, in the strictly linguistic "logical form" mapped onto sentence structure by a generative grammar, constitute meaning.

This distinction between logical form and semantic representation recalls not Saussure's distinction between *valeur* and *signification* but that of Saussure's older contemporary Frege between *Sinn* and *Bedeutung*, "sense" and "meaning"; for Frege's *Bedeutung*, in contrast to Saussure's *signification*, designates an extralinguistic reference to a "thing meant," a truth-value established by correspondence with an objective state. Only the sense of a sentence, not its meaning (for which a knowledge of external conditions is necessary by definition) can be ascertained by exclusively linguistic analysis, and in grasping a sense, Frege observes, "one is not certainly assured of meaning anything" (61). Whereas Saussure's verbal sign relates only a sound-image and a mental concept so that external reference has no place, for Frege (61) "when we say 'the Moon,' we do not intend to speak of our idea of the Moon, nor are we satisfied with the sense alone, but presuppose a meaning" with reference to the external world.[4]

---

3. In affirming that our concepts "involve belief about the real world," Chomsky allies himself with Wittgenstein and Quine (and Frege). See Quine, 36: "It is obvious that truth in general depends on both language and extralinguistic fact." And cf. Austin's endorsement (108, 110) of Ayer's argument, against Carnap, that "there have to be some things we say the truth (or falsehood) of which is determined by non-verbal reality. . . . The idea that nothing at all comes in but the consistency of sentences with each other is, indeed, perfectly wild." As Cherry remarks (226), "Pilate did not jest about *syntactical* truth."

4. Cf. Dummett, 198: "The referent of an expression is its extra-linguistic correlate in the real world: it is precisely because the expressions we use have such extra-linguistic correlates that we succeed in talking about the real world, and in saying things about it

The linguistic sense—which Frege (60) associates not only with individual signs but with the "thought" imparted by their combination into sentences—thus mediates not between a signifier and a signified internal to the sign but between the ʳubjective idea and "the object itself"; and if we remain unsatisfied with the sense of a sentence alone and inquire also as to its meaning, this is because "the striving for truth . . . drives us always to advance from the sense to the thing meant" (63).[5] Toward the ascertainment of meaning as understood by Frege, then, sense (or in Chomskyan terms, logical form), though essential, can never be sufficient, since all sorts of considerations, Chomsky remarks (1979, 144), "determine the truth conditions of a statement, and these go well beyond the scope of grammar." Grammar (like the genome) may be a relatively closed system, but language (like life) is not; to the extent that it is open, through the multiplicity of its systems, to the larger reality which it makes accessible in the logical form imposed by its generative grammar, language may lead beyond internal sense to objective meaning.

Thus language is not a static system closed to the world beyond it but an activity constantly engaged in assimilating reality to consciousness. The apparent determinism of Chomsky's insistence on the innateness of universal grammar is deceptive, since only the constraints of grammar *enable* the creativity of language. Whether Chomsky proves to be right or wrong about the innateness of specific grammatical properties and the transformations posited by his evolving theory, the consequence of a generative grammar in which syntactic but not semantic categories are universal is not linguistic determination but freedom. For Chomsky (1973, 402; cf. Lenneberg, 377) as for Humboldt, "Language is a process of free creation; its laws and principles are fixed, but the manner in which the principles of generation are used is free and infinitely varied.

---

which are true or false in virtue of how things are in that world." In this position, Dummett remarks, Frege was "defying the whole idealist tradition" of contemporary German philosophy, to say nothing of the positivist and structuralist traditions that would later restrict truth or meaning to logical or linguistic relations alone. My quotations from Frege are from "On Sense and Meaning" (1892). Frege's "Bedeutung" is often translated "reference," as in earlier versions of Geach and Black's translations, and by Dummett. Dummett can even argue, as a result, that "reference is not an ingredient in meaning" (91)!

5. The "thing meant" can be a concept as well as an object, Dummett observes (203); therefore sentences as well as singular terms ("proper names") may have objective meaning as well as linguistically determined sense. On language as mediation between subject and object and thus as an opening of the self toward a world interpreted by language, see also Cassirer, 1:93 (language "effects a new mediation, a particular *reciprocal relation*" between subject and object); and Ricoeur 1974, 256 (language "is a mediation; it is the *medium*, the 'milieu,' in which and through which the subject posits himself and the world shows itself").

Even the interpretation and use of words involves a process of free creation."

This creativity never ceases to be rule-bound, however; and because semantic representation entails correspondences between the systems comprising language and extralinguistic reality, the freedom of language is limited—and given direction—not only by the internal constraints of grammar that determine its logical form but by the multiple conditions of reference that determine its meaning, or truth. To the extent that the former are given and the latter are not—the extent that syntax is closed and invariant but semantics open and indeterminate—language itself, as a biologically conditioned extension of consciousness into a limitless (and thus far meaningless) world which it seeks to appropriate to cognition through its infinitely varied combinations, is essentially, as Whorf (73) said of linguistics, "the quest of MEANING."

LANGUAGE ACQUISITION AND THE ENLARGEMENT OF FREEDOM

Intensive research in recent decades strongly suggests that Chomsky's conception of an innately programmed "language acquisition device" needing only to be "triggered" by external stimulus is a greatly simplified account of the process by which the child constructs a language. To say that "language grows in the child through mere exposure to an unorganized linguistic environment" (Chomsky 1980, 240) no more allows for an active role in language development than Saussure's conception of *langue* as a social product passively registered by the individual. Any adequately specified language acquisition device, Bruner writes (1978a, 202), must include not only syntactic structures but "some knowledge of the world, some dialogue routines, and some sense of 'what is to be accomplished' by communication." For Bruner, as for Piaget and others, linguistic knowledge (competence) cannot be divorced from action (performance), nor action from the interaction of which it is part. Language cannot be acquired solely by triggering an autonomous grammatical program in the brain but only through the overall development of child praxis.

"All speech rests on dialogue," Humboldt wrote in 1827 (137–38), ". . . and the possibility of speech is itself contingent on address and response"; recent research has corroborated the central role of active interchange in its earliest development. The interchange between infant and mother (or other caretaker) begins long before the child can speak as an "action dialogue" (Bruner, 1974–75, 284) of initially random but increasingly directed gestures on the child's part, such as grasping and pointing, verbally interpreted by the mother, which emerges as the foundation of a verbal language acquired not by passive absorption but by participation in the interaction of imitation and play.

For Bruner and others Chomsky's belief in the primacy of an innate syntactic component in language acquisition is "grossly wrong" (1978b, 245). Linguistic competence, far from being given, develops out of linguistic (indeed prelinguistic) performance; it is not an externally triggered genetic *program* nor (as in behaviorist learning theory) a *habit* inculcated by repeated imitation but a *construct* built up by activation of the child's innate cognitive abilities through continuous interaction with others. Primacy belongs not to the syntactic but to the pragmatic or semantic aspects of language, which are initially inseparable since meaning first arises through action. It is "inconceivable that syntax leads the way developmentally" (1978a, 211).

Yet to conclude from the temporal priority of pragmatic or semantic components of language development that syntax is a secondary and derivative system seems unwarranted. The prerequisite development of cognitive categories need not exclude the possibility, even necessity, of an autonomous grammatical component, such as Chomsky postulates, in the acquisition of language. Both deliberate sensorimotor gestures and patterned vocal utterances are common properties of widely varied animal species, and the young of many birds and mammals, as well as human children, learn structured behavior by imitation or play; "protosemantic" categories such as cause and effect have been experimentally verified in chimpanzees and are difficult to rule out altogether, given the vagueness of the concept, in any animal capable of learning from experience of the world. Yet no animal but man, as Chomsky stresses, acquires anything approximating to human language in complexity of structure or in creativity of use.

Granted the importance of prelinguistic sensorimotor categories in the child's acquisition of language, it "remains as great a mystery as ever," Bruner acknowledges (1978a, 211), "how he gets from this early semantic and pragmatic mastery . . . to an appreciation of syntax." For the moment, Chomsky's hypothesis of an autonomous generative grammar provides the most satisfactory explanation; in contrast, the "interactionist-constructivist model," embracing both linguistic performance and preverbal actions, is for Chomsky "difficult to assess, because it remains at the level of metaphor" (1980, 235–36).[6] Since Chomsky has never claimed that *language* is autonomous, but only the grammatical

---

6. Yet Chomsky acknowledges (1979, 85) that Piaget and his group have "opened up entirely new perspectives in the study of human knowledge." See the discussions in Piattelli-Palmarini.

component that permits its rule-governed creativity, his theory is compatible with the research of Piaget, Bruner, and others that has called its more rigid interpretations into question. Indeed, by allowing for multiple systems pertaining to language (including "conceptual" as well as "computational" components), and admitting "pragmatic" as well as "grammatical" competence into linguistic theory, Chomsky has conceded that language acquisition might be a more complex, active, and participatory process than he has often claimed—even conceivably that pragmatic activation of proto-semantic categories through interactive interpretation, and not mere passive exposure to random linguistic "input," might be prerequisite to the "triggering" of syntactic structures which would otherwise be a combinatory mechanism with nothing to combine.

In this conception, syntax, though developmentally secondary, retains its primacy, since without the potential for indefinite creativity which only a generative grammar allows, the language of the human being could never transcend the proto-semantic gestural and verbal signals of other mammals or of the human infant. Properly understood, then, recent research has not proved Chomsky's theory of linguistic competence "grossly wrong" but has placed it in the fuller context of cognitive development through interaction to which (for all its language-specific autonomy) it belongs, thereby enlarging the concept of linguistic creativity to embrace not only the uses of language but its acquisition through "an active search," as Cromer writes (in Bruner 1972, 50), ". . . for new forms." Syntactic structures may be genetically given in the structure of the brain, but within their constraints language must be discovered and rediscovered anew. It is "an *achievement* of cognition," Jason Brown writes (1977, 25), not a given but "something toward which the organism must strive." Because of the infinite productivity of grammar and the openness of the lexicon to a changing world, this quest, too, can never be completed; for there is no terminus short of death or aphasia to the continuously creative acquisition of language.

This broadened conception of language as a construct created through pragmatic dialogue, in accord with underlying cognitive categories and the transformations of generative grammar, emphasizes—in contrast to the conceptions of positivist philosophy, behaviorist psychology, and structural linguistics—its openness, adaptability, and freedom. The language generated by the combinatory creativity of this grammatical system in interaction with others cannot be sealed off from the extralinguistic reality to which it gives semantic representation consistent with logical form. Because language is learned not by habituated repetition or conditioned reflex (on the behaviorist model) but through creative imitation, play, and dialogue, it shares in the responsiveness of imitation to its models, the openness to the world characteristic of play, and the unpredictable give-and-take of conversation with others. The curiosity distinctive of the human being from infancy is nowhere more evident than in the inventive uses of language, especially in childhood; and inasmuch as the mind is characterized, as Goodman suggests (1971, 143), by "groping and grasping, . . . seeking and finding," language becomes its principal way of exploring a world subjected to its importunate scrutinies. Since languages, Humboldt long ago noted (in Cassirer 1955, 1:159), "are not really means of representing the truth that has already been ascertained, but far more, means of discovering a truth not previously known," the heuristic function of language evidenced in the child's insatiable questioning is among its prime characteristics. By its endless probings language is not only open to reality but is the principal means by which reality is opened to the inquisitive human mind. In Heidegger's terms (1971, 3), language "not only puts forth in words and statements what is overtly or covertly intended to be communicated; language alone brings what is, as something that is, into the Open for the first time."

In contrast again to Saussure's static view, an enlarged post-Chomskyan conception would concur with Humboldt (1972, 5) in seeing language as "continuously dynamic"—never an "accomplished fact," Ortega y Gasset writes (242), but always "in the process of being made, hence *in statu nascendi.*" Language does play a fundamental role, by its largely standardized lexicon and underlying grammatical structure, in reinforcing the stability of prelinguistically acquired concepts; without this regularity there could be no language but only a meaningless babble. Yet by his emphasis on linguistic stasis and his "absolute" distinction of synchronic from diachronic, Saussure falsified language (and even *langue*), ignoring, as Jakobson objected (1962, 220), the cardinal fact that "changes enter into synchrony," so that the static and dynamic dimensions of *langue* are inseparably linked. As Jakobson and Waugh (171) later wrote, stability and mutability necessarily interact in any linguistic code; hence "permanent variability . . . is the main universal of language" (234). Change—especially phonetic change—is not arbitrary but systematic, and a changeless linguistic system is a contradiction in terms.

The dynamic aspects of language are not confined to internal changes but pertain no less essentially to its acquisition and use. Not only the interaction through which words first acquire meanings but the meanings themselves "are dynamic rather than static formations," Vygotsky notes (1962, 124), which "change as the child develops"; they are never given but must be invented and found. In contrast to the fixed behavioral patterns of "lower" animals, moreover, play is a "special form of violating fixity" (Bruner 1972, 31), which promotes, in both its motor and verbal forms, inventiveness, variation, and flexibility; and so strong is the child's linguistic originality, Taine long ago remarked (257), "that if it learns our language from us, we learn its from the child." Because language learning is reciprocal between generations as well as individuals, the striking inventive variation of children never entirely ends,[7] and the dialectic of stability and change is at least potentially continuous in individual language development no less than in the linguistic system.

In consequence, normal use of language, Chomsky repeatedly stresses, is "innovative, free from control by external stimuli, and appropriate to new and ever changing situations" (1972a, 100). Being in essence activity, *energeia,* it is the most versatile human instrument for structuring an unpredictably changing world; through its inherently transformational processes it is a means, Bruner writes, "not only for representing experience, but also for transforming it" (1973, 330). The extension long past infancy of exploratory curiosity and playful inventiveness fostered by prolonged immaturity makes neurologically hypertrophied homo sapiens the opportunist (Bruner 1972, 47), the "great amateur" (Medawar and Medawar, 170), the "generalist par excellence" (Mayr 1976, 21), among more specialized animals; homo sapiens is programmed to learn from uncertainty and constrained to seek (and by seeking create) the adaptations to reality given in advance to less flexible, if possibly more contented, fellow creatures. Beyond all else it is language—as much the cause, perhaps, as the effect of his phylogenetic neurological development—which by its intrinsic responsiveness transforms naked and ill-adapted man into *animal quaerens,* the most astoundingly adaptive inhabitant of the earth.

Language is thus the furthest extension yet attained of the open biological program increasingly distinctive of higher animals, and in this openness lies the "creative freedom" ascribed to it by Humboldt and Chomsky. Its indeterminacy derives not only from absence of a rigidly pre-established program, like that of the genome, for its development, but from absence of any fixed goal marking a terminus for its uses. The structure of language embodies a progression from units compulsorily coded in accord with inviolable laws to a relatively unconstrained (though never unconditioned) freedom. In the hierarchy of linguistic units Jakobson (1971, 242–43) finds "an ascending scale of freedom" from combination of distinctive features into phonemes, where "the freedom of the individual speaker is zero," to the limited freedom of combining phonemes into words, the far less circumscribed formation of sentences, and finally the combination of sentences into utterances, where "the action of compulsory syntactical rules ceases, and the free-

7. No trace may seem to survive in the eight-year-old, Chukovsky laments (7), of the younger child's linguistic genius, but as Nelson and Nelson remark (272), "the periods of overlearning, repetition, and even rigidity that rightly are called 'closed' establish the best basis for new periods of flexibility."

dom of any individual speaker to create novel contexts increases sub-
stantially." At this level—the level of *parole* or performance which is an
activation of the properties inherent in competence or *langue*—conscious choice plays a potentially determinative role in language, which in
turn immeasurably enlarges its scope.

And since this structural hierarchy is also, to begin with, a developmental sequence (the child distinguishes phonemes before enunciating
words, and combines words into sentences before formulating complex
utterances), the process of language acquisition enlarges freedom and
choice. Evolution of language is characterized, Grace de Laguna writes,
"by a progressive freeing of speech from dependence on the perceived
conditions under which it is uttered and heard, and from the behavior
which accompanies it" (107). It is above all the "progressive release from
immediacy" (Bruner 1973, 349) achieved by this structured development of language from closure to openness, inflexibility to indeterminacy, that permits otherwise ill-programmed man to articulate and respond to the endless choices that confront us in our ineluctable search
for what no longer is (and can never again be) given.

LANGUAGE AND THE CREATION
OF A PURPOSEFUL FUTURE

Inasmuch as biological organization is goal-directed and language an
outgrowth of the open program emergent in consciousness, language is
the furthest extension of the purposiveness inherent in life. Its biological
determination is not a denial but a condition of its teleological orientation. An inchoate purposiveness is already evident in the child's early
sensorimotor praxis, defined by Piaget (1973, 63) as "a system of coor-
dinated movements functioning for a result or an intention"; in observ-
ing such behavior, Bruner (1973, 250) was struck by the extent to which
"intentionality precedes skill." In play, too, Vygotsky (1976, 55) discerned "a movement towards the conscious realization of its purpose,"[8]
which finds expression in progressive codification of rules and is nowhere more important than in the syntactically structured development
of language out of apparently aimless verbal interaction and play.

The inarticulate intentionality guiding skilled praxis takes on increasingly structured direction through play and gestural dialogue, but becomes fully conscious only in language. For purpose is not accidental but
essential to language, at once its indispensable condition and most mo-

8. Sylva et al. (250) found that "children given a prior chance to play are significantly
more goal-directed." See the classic account of the development of rules in the game of
marbles in the opening chapter of Piaget 1932b.

mentous result. Since language (even for Chomsky) "is designed for use," and performance is the goal of linguistic competence, speaking is an intrinsically purposeful action which cannot be understood without reference to its object. Language "cannot be analyzed," Jakobson insisted from the time of his earliest phonological writings (1962, 1; cf. 1978, 25), in opposition both to the neogrammarians of the age and to Saussure, "without taking into account the purpose which that system serves." Without this activating purpose language would remain a potentiality incapable of realization, a competence with nothing to do. Communicative intention brings language from latency into being by giving boundaries to its openness, stability to its adaptiveness, and direction to its freedom. Without it language would be (if not cataleptic silence or compulsive repetition) a random logorrhea, syntactically structured perhaps, but semantically a disconnected raving, a machinelike grammatical "creativity" running endlessly amok in a nightmarish world where colorless green ideas sleep furiously amid bloated sentences that drag recursively on forever.

If intentionality motivates the acquisition of language, fully conscious purpose results from it. Goal-directed behavior is an evolving characteristic of life from its beginnings, but only at the most advanced and specifically human "symbolic" level of brain development is there, according to Jason Brown (1977, 22), "a progression from purposive to volitional action," which "is bound up with language development." Even the single-word utterance (like the gesture) can indicate intention by designating a desired object; but only syntactic connection can express the progressively refined development of a hitherto largely latent purpose. Thus "it is not until predication is developed in the complete sentence," de Laguna observes (301; cf. 304), "that behavior becomes purposive in the full sense of the term. . . . The language of complete predication permits *both end and acts to be specifically denoted and hence distinguished.*"

This capacity of syntactically structured language to distinguish goals and acts is one that Piaget (1973, 73) finds at the origin of all symbols, which, when differentiated from their immediate significations, make it "possible to evoke objects and situations actually non-perceived, forming the beginnings of representation." Once the intended object can be evoked *in its absence* by precise and communicable linguistic designation, the possibility of fully conscious purpose arises for the first time and begins to orient human action away from preoccupation solely with the given and toward the premeditated quest of what, being absent and yet intended, remains to be found.

The most significant absence evoked by symbolism and in particular by language is the future—what will, or may be, but is not yet; for only then can the intended object now absent become present, and this possibility is the precondition of the purposeful quest. Symbolism, to quote Bertalanffy once again, "makes true or Aristotelian purposiveness possible. The future goal is anticipated in its symbolic image and so may determine present action" (1968, 17). Awareness of futurity as a time when what is will be other brings homo sapiens not only foreknowledge of death but the still more characteristically promethean opportunity of seeking in the indefinite interim what we now lack and of striving purposefully to become something other (or something more) than what we now are.

This future dimension, like the purposefulness that attends it, is again implicit in organic life from its beginnings, since one of the most general functions of living organisms, Jacob observes (66), "is to look ahead, to produce future as Paul Valéry put it. There is not a single movement, a single posture that does not imply a later on, a passage to the next moment. . . . An organism is living insofar as it is going to live, even if only for a short while." It is the nervous system which "ultimately became able to invent the future" as a conscious dimension (54). Indeed, according to Soviet neurological research cited by Jakobson (1980, 35), the left and right hemispheres of the distinctively bilateral human brain may demonstrate (like Freud's ego and id) "different temporal orientations," the left turned toward the future, the right toward the past; the left hemisphere is of course normally the locus of symbolic thought and speech. Futurity is implicit in life, emergent in consciousness, but fully apprehended as an essential determinant of action only through the specifically human symbolism of language.

For by its very nature the symbol, as distinguished by Peirce from both icon and index, is "a law, or regularity of the indefinite future" (2:166). Among Peirce's three classes of signs or "representamens," the icon is an immediate image evoking a direct analogy (as a portrait does) with its object; the index is connected with its object as a matter of fact or physical contiguity (as smoke signals fire). But the symbol, in contrast to both—and for Peirce all verbal utterances are symbols—is a purely conventional sign which refers to an object "by virtue of the idea of the symbolising mind, without which no such connection would exist" (2:168–69). Thus the symbol's "mode of being" is different from that of the icon and index. "An icon has such being as belongs to past experience. It exists only as an image in the mind. An index has the being of present experience" (4:447). Whatever is truly general, however, "refers to the indefinite future," and its mode of being is "*esse in futuro*" (2:79).[9]

---

9. Cf. 2:46–47 ("To say that the future does not influence the present is untenable doctrine"); 4:361 ("The value of a symbol is that it serves to make thought and conduct rational and enables us to predict the future"); and 8:19 (letter to William James: "The true idealism, the pragmatistic idealism, is that reality consists in the future").

The symbol intrinsically pertains to the future, which can be effective on human action only by its means.

If, as Peirce believed, "the future alone has primary reality" (8:152), only symbolic reference brings that reality into being, and this always provisional creation of futurity is the distinctive purpose of human activity. In syntactically ordered predication, moreover, language provides not only "anticipation of the end to be reached" but also, as de Laguna discerned (301), an organized though conditional series of intermediate acts leading purposefully toward that end, each stage of which "forms a new starting point for a fresh determination of the remaining stages" (302). This goal-oriented serial organization can be described, in Jason Brown's happy phrase (1972, 283), as a "continuous penultimacy, in that language development always incorporates into itself the meaning that is sought after in expectation of a coming stage," so that the development of speech out of thought is essentially "a pressure towards the future." Language not only frees man from the immediacy of the actual by its openness to diversity and adaptability to change, but gives direction to our freedom by evoking an indeterminate future goal for our actions and guiding us conditionally in quest of its forever penultimate realization.

CHAPTER FOUR

The Questing Animal

Without language social institutions would be as inconceivable as language without society; their interdependence is a primary condition of human existence. Our examination of language thus brings us back to consideration of society as the matrix both of communal religious experience and of the individual quest that can never leave this primal model and source far behind.

Saussure's conception of *langue* as a superpersonal, passively registered "collective inertia" immune to individual variation closely accords with Durkheim's exaltation of society as a transcendent entity to which its submissive constituents pay homage. No elementary religious form could work more pervasively toward the summum bonum of maintaining social stasis than the supremely autonomous language system postulated by Saussure, as absolute (and as arbitrary) in its dictates as any divinity. The more dynamic, open-ended, and purposefully creative conception of language that we have adopted more nearly corresponds, on the contrary, to society as conceived by van Gennep or Turner, Berger or Mead—not a given entity serenely pre-existing and impassively surviving its ephemeral members, who pay it the tribute of worship en route to personal extinction, but a perpetually transitional reality forever being formed and transformed by those who compose it. This is a dialogic and indeed a dialectic reality in passage (like the language with whose development its own is interdependent) toward self-created, always provisional goals that direct its continuous adaptation to a changing world and give it the flexible equilibrium that no closed system can long maintain.

Of Bergson's two sources of religion and morality, one was a closed and static structure upheld by habitual if not instinctive "pressure" to repeat an immutable past, the other an open and dynamic process impelled by the "forward movement" of purposeful aspiration toward an uncertain future; the second may be considered a cardinal source of the personal quest. The opposition between them—and the transformative potentiality their interaction fosters—is rooted in the biological, psychological, and linguistic preconditions of society and religion themselves and thus, we may safely surmise, in human nature.

This duality can be creative only because its apparently antithetical poles continuously interact in a dialectic embracing both. The instructions encoded in the closed genetic program of each organism, whose molecular structures obey the statistically invariable laws of physics, engender a system open to the environment to which it must adapt in order to survive, and the resultant interaction between organism and environment impels the contingent evolution of accidentally variant forms "selected" for reproductive success. Structure and process, closure and openness, are thus interdependent aspects of life, whose advanced forms are increasingly distinguished by an "open program" capable of acquiring information not only from genetically coded instructions but in response to the environment—capable, that is, of profiting from experience. "On the whole, and certainly among the higher vertebrates," Mayr writes (1976, 24), "there has been a tendency to replace rigidly closed programs by open ones," enlarging the organism's scope for purposive choice; expanded flexibility would thus appear to be an evolutionary product of the genetically "invariant" reproduction of life as an open system. (In the heterodox biology of Piaget, this interactive duality originates within the genome, so that even mutation involves an inchoate interplay of closure and openness.) Only if "system" and "program" are thought of as imperviously self-enclosed do the concepts "open system" and "open program," or the progressive expansion of genetically programmed openness, seem contradictions in terms rather than essential characteristics of life.

This dialectic of fixity and movement, structure and process, characterizes not only life in general but its extensions in human consciousness, language, and society. The structured psychological equilibrium achieved in normal development through assimilation of and accommodation to external reality is a "mobile equilibrium," Piaget emphasizes (1967, 151), which is "essentially active." In language, Chomsky's transformational generative grammar incorporates process in the very heart of a linguistic structure that must be activated, moreover (whatever its neurological foundations), by open-ended dialogue. And society, in Turner's words (1969, 203), is "a dialectical process with successive phases of structure and communitas" continually interacting to preserve stability while adapting to change. At every level structure and process are not antithetical but interdependent phases without whose perpetual interchange there could be no society, no language, no consciousness, and no life.

The question of primacy need not detain us; the structures of open systems are by nature processual and their processes inherently structured. What matters is the crucial role of *transition*. In organic structures process is continuous; there can be equilibrium, stability, rest in an open system, but no final stasis, for cessation is death. Such structures can incorporate regular change without disruption, but extreme or sudden change may upset their mobile equilibrium and result (if not in death or extinction) in intensified adaptation and re-equilibration eventually stabilized as a new structure evolved from the old.

Evolution, in Gould's words (1980, 213), "does not imply . . . that ceaseless flux is the irreducible state of nature and that structure is but a temporary incarnation of the moment. Change is more often a rapid transition between stable states than a continuous transformation at slow and steady rates. We live in a world of structure and legitimate distinction." Such transitions between stable states—not only biological but psychological, linguistic, and social as well—are of course restricted as to possible outcomes by the initial state: they are structured, not random changes. But because of the great internal complexity of these systems and their constituent openness to the most varied external influences, the outcome of any major transition between structures must be unpredictable: the emergent structure cannot be known in advance but will be essentially indeterminate.

Organic structures are thus repeatedly subject to transformation by their very adaptability to a mutable world, their constant need for an increasingly adequate if always provisional equilibrium. Thus "the idea of *structure* as a system of transformations becomes continuous," Piaget writes (1970, 34), "with that of *construction* as continual transformation." Every structure originates in another and is a beginning as much as an end; the passage between them is the phase of maximum openness and vulnerability when everything remains to be determined—the phase of recurrent *genesis* defined by Piaget (141) as a "formative" transition between a weaker and a stronger structure.

Transitions between no longer adequately adapted structures and others in the process of emergence are times of heightened responsiveness to the surrounding world. Conscious awareness of both the dangers and the transformative possibilities of such transitions—an awareness seemingly unique to our promethean species—impels the communal or individual quest for a future goal that can neither be fully known nor finally attained, but must (as in ritual) be repeatedly sought. Only by virtue of its provisional terminus, indeed, can purposefully pursued structural transition become truly a quest: a deliberate but uncertain passage no less intrinsically unending, and no less creative of its own perpetually transcended object, than the processes of life, thought, and speech from which it arose and continually arises.

In the spiritual quest the indeterminate self-transcendence of living things as open systems culminates in deliberate transformation of what Bergson called the "open soul" drawn beyond itself—hence beyond the previously given human condition—by the forward movement of aspiration toward an unforeseeable future. To persevere in this unending process with full awareness of its dangers—and full awareness, too, that the alternative to the movement of life is stagnation and death—distinguishes restless man among more fully adapted inhabitants of our earth as (at least in potential) the questing animal: *animal quaerens*. Our perpetual searching derives from the very extremity of conscious openness to an unpredictably changing world and is hence both the consequence and the cost of our precariously marginal freedom.

Rites of passage, which commemorate the hazardous crossing of an uncertain threshold, provide a communal paradigm for the individual quest. Insofar as they define a terminal (if temporary) condition attained by all celebrants alike, however, they differ from the true quest whose goal can never be prescribed in advance or by others but must be engendered through the process of searching itself. The quest thus characterizes the emergent individual no longer wholly defined by social role or wholly content with inherited structures. For him, or for her, the passage from one stage to another institutionalized in communal rites is often a solitary journey into unexplored terrain in search of what no other has found before and—possible failure being one hallmark of the quest—what none may find even now.

The quest resembles a pilgrimage in the high purpose that differentiates both from random wandering or haphazard exploration. But the pilgrimage is generally more communal and traditional (it may be repeated without essential change), and its terminus, whether Mecca or Jerusalem, Canterbury or Rome, is normally well established: only to the extent that it is unique and its goal (or the significance of attaining its goal) is in doubt will this rite of passage, like any other, become truly a quest.

Still more significant is the intrinsic connection of the quest and the question. Both derive from Latin *quaerere*, "to seek," and their meanings are closely linked. "Every asking," Heidegger writes (1953, 5), "is a seeking," and asking is indispensable to seeking because, in Gadamer's words (266), it "is the opening up, and keeping open, of possibilities" without which seeking would soon halt if it ever began. The child's earliest, un-answerable questionings are themselves an embryonic quest for resolu-tion of the newly discovered discord, in Piaget's words (1932a, 235), "be-tween desire and its realization" that lies at the origin of all questing. Only persistence into adulthood of our paedomorphic questioning, our childlike need to interrogate every provisional answer and rest satisfied with none, propels us to undertake the quest: for to search effectually, Claparède observes (Piaget 1932a, 230), "one must know what one is searching for, one must have asked oneself a question." And if a ques-tion incites the quest, another—or perhaps the same one transmuted past recognition—will be waiting at its end to lead us beyond what we thought was ourselves to further quests and questions potentially with-out end. Such is the promise of futurity, or the burden of incompletion, that the questing animal, man, receives as a birthright and cannot for-swear without abandoning what makes us most human.

Insofar as "spiritual" is more than a vague honorific it indicates the transcendent potentiality of the unknown: a true quest, Auden remarks (81), "means to look for something of which one has, as yet, no experi-ence." Spirit, far from being opposed to the biological (as in the Carte-sian dualism of body and mind), is the potentiality of human life—through conscious positing of future goals—for purposeful creation and growth. It is the possibility of structural self-transcendence made incipi-ently conscious in man, the capacity of neurologically advanced life "to invent the future"; it is not an existent reality but the aggregate of pos-sible realities open to unprogrammed human development. The spiri-tual quest is man's uncompletable endeavor to actualize, in some small part, the future which largely defines him, and thus to be fully himself by becoming continually more.

Spirit (like Aristotle's *form*) is distinct from matter not by difference of substance but as potential actualization from given condition, future from present, indeterminate from determined; the very term indicates man's separation from a condition in which he is no longer fully at home. Only when it is consciously represented does the futurity inherent in life become spirit; it therefore partakes of the differentiation of subject and object, self and world, in which consciousness is grounded. Spirit arises, like consciousness, out of a separation which it strives to overcome by purposeful orientation toward a future in which the contradictions that bring it into being and propel its forward movement would be re-solved—a resolution, were it to be attained, that would entail its extinc-tion. To the extent that this goal proves to be unattainable, the quest will, of course, be unending.

Its close connection with consciousness precludes exclusive linking of spirit with the irrational. French *esprit*, like German *Geist* and analogous terms in other languages, embraces "spirit" and "mind" in a single concept; hence the spiritual quest can include both the intellectual and scientific search for truth and the religious pursuit of salvation, which are fundamentally akin. Between the inductionist view of science as systematic progress by experimental verification toward establishment of manifest truth and the relativistic conception of shifting scientific paradigms not as "a process of evolution *toward* anything" (Kuhn 1970, 170–71) but as a "gestalt switch" (150) with "no coherent direction of ontological development" (206)—poles equally alien to the quest—is a science born of the recognition "that all we can do," in Popper's words (1965, 29–30), "is to grope for truth even though it be beyond our reach," since without the positing of a transcendent if never attainable truth "there can be no objective standards of inquiry; no criticism of our conjectures; no groping for the unknown; no quest for knowledge." The truth toward which science, in this conception, can provisionally lead, always subject to the refutations by which knowledge accrues, is uncertain and incomplete even in physics and mathematics (not to mention biology), as Heisenberg and Gödel amply demonstrated. Yet the ultimate indeterminacy of scientific truth need not entail a directionless relativism. On the contrary, an indeterminate goal engendered through purposive trial and error is a prime criterion for the spiritual quest (as for its biological and psychological antecedents), which thus attains in scientific inquiry one of its fullest expressions.

Intellectual pursuit of a finally undefinable truth is only one aspect, however, of the spiritual quest, since spirit comprehends but cannot be delimited by intellect. Our word derives from Latin *spiritus*, originally breath or breeze—one of many words, including Greek *psychê* and *pneuma*, Latin *animus* and *anima*, Sanskrit *atman*, and Hebrew *ruach*— associating breath or wind with the animating power of life. This association, which Tylor pointed out in his pioneering work in the anthropology of religion (16–17), is by no means limited to the Indo-European or Mediterranean cultural spheres but recurs among countless peoples as unrelated as the Nuer of the Sudan (Evans-Pritchard 1956, 1) and the Navajo of western North America (McNeley, 35). Spirit pertains most immediately, then, not to consciousness, by which it becomes self-aware, but to air as the force sustaining life.

The primitive association with breath and life is one hallmark of spirit; another, equally fundamental, is the wholeness by which it transcends or mediates divisions. For spirit, like the life-sustaining air, is both within and without, an embracing power connecting man with the world around him in the reciprocal bond of a truly open system. And because spirit connects with all living things, it counteracts the individual's potential isolation both from fellow-human beings and from other forms of life. By uniting inner with outer, self with others, present with future, spirit is a continuous mediation between the constricted actualities of our given individual existence and the transcendent though never limitless potentiality of our superpersonal being, the perpetual possibility of becoming more than we are. For the restless spirit, the Platonic *thymos* called by Ricoeur (1978, 32–33) "the mediating function par excellence," is an essence forever within and forever beyond us, reflecting "the fact that the self is never guaranteed," and that its search for itself "is in a certain sense without end."

The spiritual quest is thus a continuous questioning on the subject of life itself as an open system or structured process defined most fundamentally by the transcendent potentiality of its indeterminate future, which gives it direction and purpose. Insofar as human life is purposeful it will be an inchoate spiritual quest. For consciously goal-directed activity presupposes deliberate orientation toward a potentiality significantly different from the given: the quest is an effort to bring a fragment of that uncircumscribed future into being. Only man the forethinker, so far as we know from our hardly unprejudiced standpoint, can apprehend his incompleteness and look upon it as promise, consciously directing his self-transformation, and for this reason he remains uniquely *animal quaerens.*

There can be no certainty that the spiritual quest distinctive of the human species will continue; evolution most often eventuates in extinction, and the very foresight that enables man to pursue a transcendent goal also empowers him to engineer his destruction. Even short of that final quietus, the imperfectly anticipated goal of every quest will always be more elusive than the restrictive actualities that impel yet threaten to abort it through apathetic indifference or helpless perplexity, acedia or aporia. But though the former, the deadly sin of spiritual sloth, is potentially mortal, the latter condition, the "resourcelessness" of finding no way out of a seemingly hopeless dilemma, is not—as Plato, unlike the Sophists of his own day and later, well understood—a terminus but the possibility of a recurrent beginning; for only the soul that knows its own impasse searches, Ricoeur reminds us (1978, 22), to go beyond it and escape from the cave in which it is imprisoned: *aporei kai zêtei.*[1] The very remoteness of an intrinsically future, hence perpetually absent goal in

1. The phrase is from Plato's *Republic* 7, 524e. Aristotle, too, links searching with aporia in *Metaphysics* 1028b (cited by Heidegger 1962b, 255; cf. 1968, 212), where he calls the question *ti to on* ("what is being?") *to palai te kai nyn kai aei zêtoumenon kai aei aporoumenon* ("what was sought long ago and now and always, and always with no way out"). The aporia is an incentive, even a condition, of the quest, for if the quest is inherently without terminus, every unachievable goal is not an end but a provisional impasse that is always a potential new beginning, pointing beyond itself to another yet to be sought.

contrast to an actuality without prospect is the impetus without which no quest could begin; its elusively deferred attainment is at the same time its promise of incessant renewal.

In this way the spiritual quest is the *creative* process par excellence, the process by which human beings continually remake themselves in accord with goals forever beyond them: to search, Proust's narrator perceives at the outset of his immense exploration, *is* to create, and what searching creates is above all the self continually surpassed in another. In questing, therefore, is our essential humanity, our fidelity to our unfinished selves; and perhaps the wisdom by which we presumptuously distinguish our species in spite of all evidence of our folly is itself best conceived as a goal toward which we advance, if at all, only by continuing to hold it before us. We are at best *homo sapiens* not in the flesh but in spirit, that is, in unrealized potentiality; but inasmuch as our aspirations define us, the unachieved goal is itself the token of an incipient wisdom evinced in not wholly abandoning its pursuit. Sapience escapes us for now as a *differentia specifica* and will no doubt continue to escape us (as our highest goals always will); but in the "continuous meanwhile" of our contingent existence we are, if not *homo sapiens* in accomplishment, at least—or is it more, or even the same?—*homo quaerens sapientiam,* and in this more modest yet more promising title we may surely take justified and not inconsiderable pride.

PART TWO

The Spiritual Quest in Ritual and Myth

CHAPTER FIVE

Ritual as Affirmation and Transformation

If the spiritual quest is a fundamental human activity rooted in biology, psychology, and language, it will find expression throughout the world and throughout the ages in the supremely important acts and stories embodied in religious rituals and myths. But the rich diversity of human cultures suggests that the quest must be understood as much through the shifting forms it has taken in different times and places as through the common impulse to which these multifarious expressions bear witness. The widely variant cultural refractions of the quest are essential properties of a creatively self-transformative process irreducible to a single fixed paradigm, and this wealth of particular and ever-changing expressions must be fully taken into account.

ANCESTOR WORSHIP AND THE BACKWARD MOVEMENT OF TIME

Even in rigidly repetitive ritual celebrations of traditional order we have found a potential for variation and change. Such elaborate ceremonials nevertheless remain, like the "ancestor worship" with which they are often connected, oriented more toward perpetuation of an immutable past than toward the exploration of an indeterminate future essential to the spiritual quest.

In few areas has ritual been more elaborate than in southwestern North America. Among the Navajo, Kluckhohn and Leighton write (234), divinities themselves must "bow to the compulsion of ritual formulas" embodied in intricate "chantways" frequently lasting many days: Nightway and Mountainway, Windway and Waterway, Red Antway and Enemyway, to name but a few, and the Blessingway that underlies them all. By meticulous performance of hundreds of songs, daily drawing and erasure of sand paintings in strict accord with traditional designs, offering of food and prayer sticks, and repeated ritual purification, Navajo chanters labor to restore health and "good hope" to their tribe and to perpetuate the continually threatened harmony of their world.

The chanter undergoes a rigorous apprenticeship and seldom masters more than one or two chants; the eminent Hosteen Klah studied twenty-six years before acting, at age forty-nine, as principal chanter of his first Yeibichai or Nightway ceremony (Newcomb, 112–18). Great importance is given to detailed correctness—"if one word of the prayer . . . is missed, it is worthless and destroys its whole effect" (Haile, 123) [1]—and to outside observers the slow rhythmic dances sometimes seem monotonous or indistinguishable. The patterned invariance and formulaic control of these rites—the duly summoned divinity "is compelled to attend" (Reichard 1939, ix)—led Kluckhohn (1942, 101) to view ritual as "an obsessive repetitive activity" intended to attain "the maximum of fixity" (105) in an unpredictable world.

Navajo ceremonies are performed at no set times but whenever occasion (most commonly sickness) requires. Until recent centuries the sheepherding Navajo, like their Apache kin, were nomadic hunters; it is in the long-settled agricultural Pueblos that formalized ritual attained its fullest development in America north of Mexico. Among the Hopi, Zuñi, and others, a fixed annual cycle of ceremonies unrolls with the regularity of the seasons, aimed primarily at promoting not individual healing but fertility of the land. In ritual the submersion of individual in collective, ideally invariant existence characteristic of Pueblo life reaches its apex; in Zuñi, Bunzel writes (1932, 492), "The efficacy of a formula depends upon its absolutely correct repetition," and any departure from established practice causes "great perturbation." Nothing is left to chance or is subject to change.

Such rituals, affirming the rightness of what has been and sustaining the continuity of an immutable social and natural order, seem the perfect expression of Bergson's first source of religion, the inertial pull toward repose. To this extent Benedict would appear to have been justified in characterizing the Pueblo tribes (1934, 78–80) as "Apollonian" in their commitment to tradition. Their characteristic eschewal of excess, as Benedict portrayed it (with major omissions), is evident not only in the stately regularity of their ceremonies but in their supposed aversion to intoxication and their temperate offerings of feathered prayer sticks

---

1. Cf. Matthews, 24: "an error made in singing a song may be fatal to the efficacy of a ceremony. In no case is an important mistake tolerated, and in some cases the error of a single syllable works an irreparable injury."

and maize (rather than slaughtered beasts and human captives) to the gods who periodically dwell among them and fuse with them in the sacred dance of the kachinas.

Another contributor to communal conservatism in Pueblo society, as in many others, is the "worship of the dead," which Bunzel (1932, 483) calls "the foundation of all Zuñi ritual." There is "no ancestor worship in the restricted sense" in Zuñi, since "a man prays to *the* ancestors, not to his own ancestors" (510); but the influence of these deified predecessors (whom one is destined to join) in upholding ancient customs is everywhere. Present authority is rooted in what lies behind, not before it, so that significant human action perpetuates the past rather than striving to go beyond it in quest of an imperfectly envisaged future.

Ancestor worship, for Radcliffe-Brown, most fully realized the social function of a religious cult, namely (1952, 157) "to regulate, maintain, and transmit from one generation to another sentiments on which the constitution of a society depends." In sub-Saharan Africa, above all, British structural anthropologists who followed Radcliffe-Brown's lead have emphasized the function of ritual as an affirmation of social values.[2] Generally speaking, Fortes suggests (1976, 2), where ancestors are worshiped, not merely commemorated, "the medium of relationship with them takes the form of ritual"; conversely, among African peoples like the Nilotic Nuer or the Congo Pygmies where ritual is less developed, ancestor worship is frequently absent or marginal. In much of West Africa ancestral rituals have been central in promoting tribal cohesion. Among the Tallensi of Ghana, for example, ancestor worship, Fortes writes (1959, 19), "is the religious counterpart of their social order, hallowing it, investing it with a value that transcends mundane interests and providing for them the categories of thought and belief by means of which they direct and interpret their lives and actions."

Thus although ancestor worship "does not comprise the whole of any people's religious system" (Fortes 1976, 3), it is frequently—in tribal West Africa as in traditional China and Japan or ancient Rome—of central importance. The African villager may simultaneously worship spirits of forest and stream, of the earth and its crops, of animals wild and domestic, and pay homage to a High God such as Allah or Christ; but these divinities may be disturbingly distant or menacingly inaccessible even when well disposed (as who can know?). The ancestors, on the contrary, as continuing members of a lineage, are more familiar even when angered, as any family member can be; they may therefore reassuringly

2. See Fortes 1970, 260–78. As long ago as 1871 Tylor (201) noted that "on the continent of Africa, manes-worship [ancestor worship] appears with extremest definiteness and strength."

mediate between human and extrahuman. As the living-dead, they "oc-cupy the ontological position between spirits and men," Mbiti writes (90), and speak the language of both.

Nor is ancestor worship simply a generalized cult of the dead, since the religious status of an ancestor is normally achieved by a select few, mainly men of high social standing. Among the Yoruba of Nigeria, to become a benevolent ancestor, "a man has to live well, die well, and leave behind good children who will accord him proper funeral rites and con-tinue to keep in touch with him by means of offerings and prayer" (Awolalu, 55). Full membership in this powerful community is some-times postponed until successive obsequies have been performed and years, even generations, have passed; it is the culmination of a long and selective *cursus honorum* commencing with death. Two categories of an-cestral spirits are often distinguished, as among the Nsukka Igbo of Ni-geria (Shelton, 92), one of nameless generalized ancestors, another of those remembered by name; as a rule these groups are stages in a se-quence leading eventually, as the individual ancestor is forgotten, to an increasingly impersonal and authoritative spiritual status (cf. Mbiti, 32–34). The extent to which such a process is thought to culminate in a condition comparable to that of divinities, and deserving of equal wor-ship, varies greatly; it leads in any case to the highest spiritual condition a human being born in these times can achieve.[3]

In contrast to tribes, such as the Apache and many others, in which fear of the dead man prompts destruction of his possessions and avoid-ance of his name, the mortuary rites of many West African peoples not only separate the potentially dangerous spirit of the dead from the corpse but reintegrate it into the family, in which it becomes, en route to ancestorhood, an ever more honored if less personal presence. In some societies periodic ceremonies for the ancestors culminate in great annual or biannual festivals (often coinciding with agricultural rites), accompa-nied by sacrifices, songs and dances, and sometimes—as among the Yo-ruba—by masked impersonations of eminent ancestral spirits. Where ritual is most elaborately developed, as among the Dogon of Upper Volta (Burkina Faso) and Mali, or in Dahomey (Benin), homage is paid not only to forebears of individual lineages but to mythical progenitors of the tribe as a whole. And where hierarchical social classes and royalty prevail, as among the Ashanti of Ghana, only deceased lineage heads

3. The continuity between living elders and ancestors and subordination of the latter to extrahuman spirits have led some writers, such as Idowu (192), to reject the term "an-cestor worship"; others, such as Awolalu (63–65), find it appropriate. The very inconsis-tency of African beliefs would seem (as Messenger suggests, 67) to justify use of the term, with the caveat that different forms and degrees of veneration are suited to different kinds of spirits. See also Kopytoff; Brain; and Barber, 742–43, n. 15.

receive offerings and prayers from their successors (Fortes 1969, 189). Here ancestor worship ipso facto affirms the eternal legitimacy of existing institutions.

Among the Tallensi, as described by Fortes, the ancestors demand conformity to established moral values and fulfillment of social obligations, above all to one's parents; "the critical fact is that the individual has no choice" (1959, 40). All religion binds together those who share its practices, but ancestor worship most specifically binds the living to the dead and unborn in a generational solidarity that appears to preclude all change. "The ancestors, like public opinion," Gluckman remarks (1963, 74), "are always on the side of 'corporateness,'" and since in tribal life, as Mbiti observes (141), the individual "cannot exist alone except corporately," the ancestors become the guarantors not of a particular form of existence, a culture or way of life only, but of existence itself. Whatever particular form it may take, ancestor worship presupposes obligation of living descendants to the dead and deference to their supernaturally sanctioned authority—the *pietas,* as Fortes calls it, that continues the filial duty owed by children to living parents. Only by being first son and then father, and faithfully playing both roles as tradition prescribes, can a man of piety eventually hope to attain the culminating goal of spiritual union with the hierarchy of ancestors who begot him. So great is the prestige of the past, indeed, that it alone can be thought of as future.

Ancestor worship thus presupposes a conception of time fundamentally different from our accustomed notion of a linear forward movement. According to Mbiti (21–23), traditional African time has a long past and virtually no future; it "moves 'backward' rather than 'forward'; and people set their minds not on future things, but on what has taken place" (23). The Swahili *Sasa,* or "Micro-Time," the immediate present and its experiential extensions into the near future and recent past, is surrounded by the overlapping "Macro-Time" of *Zamani,* the "ocean of time" that is neither after nor before (28). Sasa is "the period of conscious living. . . . Zamani is the period of the myth" (29). Like history itself in these traditional societies, the individual moves slowly "backward" toward those who begot him, and death is "a process which removes a person gradually from the Sasa period to the Zamani" (32) in which the living-dead finally achieve the collective immortality of mythical ancestral spirits.

In such societies, Field writes of the Gã of Ghana (1937, 196–97), "The dead are always watching to see that the living preserve what their forefathers established." The ancestral Zamani provides an unchanging archetype of human behavior always valid for every member of the tribe. The order given from the beginning, often by a mythical founder, and embodied in the ancestors is the only conceivable order. Saint Augustine's restless search for spiritual repose in God "is something unknown in African traditional religious life" (Mbiti, 87), since the tribal African feels no need to seek what he already has: the transcendent validation of his existence which continuity with the ancestors, and through them with the gods, unstintingly gives.

Melanesia, along with Micronesia and Polynesia, is another region where forms of ancestor worship, comparable to those of Africa, have arisen. Where everything depends on supernatural ancestral forces, "the religious quest is essentially," as Read remarks of the Gahuku of highland New Guinea (115), "a search for this power, an effort to tap it and control it, to discover its source, and to enlist its aid" through mastery of ritual. Again the present moves toward absorption by the encompassing atemporal past; among the Kanakas of New Caledonia some old men are called ancestral spirits while still living, since their wisdom participates, Leenhardt writes (34), in the wisdom of ancestors and gods, whom they will soon definitively join. Here there can be no forward progression in time, for the past is continually being revived in the present. Even in tribes where short-lived ghosts never attain the prestige of true ancestors, and lack the good fortune of the Trobriand *baloma* spirits who slough off their outworn skin to be reincarnated in living wombs (Malinowski, 216), the future can only be envisaged as the past, since everyone living will become what his forebears have been. The open future of the spiritual quest would seem all but unknown in societies so strictly determined by eternal recurrence of the past.

The locus classicus of Melanesian ancestor worship is the Solomon Islands, for here, Codrington remarked in 1891 (125), spirits of nonhuman origin, prominent elsewhere in Melanesia, have almost no place, and supernatural power, *mana*, passes after death from powerful living men to their ghosts. Recent studies have largely confirmed Codrington's observations. The highest achievement of the living is to make themselves, through ritual appropriation of *mana,* as like as possible to the ancestral dead who are its source and whom some among them will soon rejoin. Among the Kwaio of Malaita, most populous of the Solomons, where all adult men and women become ancestral spirits, "the system . . . 'originated from the ancestors' and it is the duty of humans to follow ancient rules, not modify them" (Keesing 1982b, 210). Similarly among the Polynesian Maori of New Zealand, "to do the right thing is to follow the ancestors" (Johansen, 172). Significant innovation can only be a lapse from ancestral ways.

Pre-eminent among the right things bequeathed by the ancestors is ritual, to which correct performance is normally essential. Among the Tikopia, whose elaborate "Work of the Gods" Firth meticulously chronicled, ancestral ritual sanctioned a divinely instituted status quo, and ancestor worship, as in other highly stratified aristocratic societies of traditional Polynesia, was basically—like its counterparts in Ashanti or Dahomey—a cult of office-holders amounting, Firth remarks (1967a, 76), to "bureaucratic ancestralism." In Oceania as in Africa, or indeed ancient China, Rome, or Japan, ancestor worship is generally characteristic rather of settled agricultural than of nomadic hunting societies, and rituals to honor the ancestors often merge (as in Tikopia) with those intended to increase fertility of the crops. Among hunters and gatherers, the ancestors commonly honored are not the dead of recent generations and their anonymous forebears but the mythological founders and progenitors of the tribe at the beginning of time. Thus all legends in the Andaman Islands, Radcliffe-Brown writes (1922, 190–91), deal with the doings of the primal ancestors, mostly named after animal species.

Nowhere was the bond between the present and a mythological past stronger than in aboriginal Australia, where age-old sacred traditions tied tribes of hunters as closely to their local habitat as agricultural settlement tied people elsewhere. In many tribes the founding ancestors are continually present in the unchanging landscape through which the tribe repeatedly moves, embodied in the totem species whose name they share and in the sacred ceremonial articles (called *tjurunga* by the Aranda) which they have bequeathed from the distant past to the present. Everything of value to human society issued, like human society itself, from their hands, and since that time there has truly been nothing new under the sun.

Between that ancestral "Dream Time" (the Aranda *altjiringa*) and the present there is no unbroken connection such as that provided by the receding genealogies of some African and Melanesian peoples, no fading line of progenitors bridging the gap between then and now, but rather, as Maddock suggests (109), "a metaphysical discontinuity, a duality between men and powers." Since the Dream Time, human existence has been a pale shadow of the legendary past, "a dependent life which is conceived," Stanner writes of the northern Murinbata (n.d., 39–40), "as having taken a wrongful turning at the beginning, a turn such that the good of life is now inseparably connected with suffering," suggesting "some kind of 'immemorial misdirection' in human affairs," with no chance that living men can ever recover, much less surpass, the condition they have irretrievably lost.

Irretrievably, but not completely; for the Dream Time is not really past but lingers on in countless forms for the people of a lesser day. The ancestors never die but continue to inhabit the tribal landscape and the sacred objects. Among many Australian tribes the living are believed to reincarnate, and hence perpetually recycle, components at least of the ever-present ancestors; thus the Aranda child is assigned the totem not of his mother or father but of the ancestor thought to inhabit the spot where his mother first became aware of her pregnancy. It is the ancestor's "spirit child" that grows within her, engendered when she crossed his ancient tracks or passed near a sacred hill or spring or lay down by some long lost and buried *tjurunga.* Through his initiation at the time of puberty, Eliade remarks (1971, 58), "the novice discovers that he *has already been here,* in the beginning," and that the present itself is a shadowy reincarnation of a past that is always with him. Similar initiations into the mysteries of ancestral tradition were virtually universal in aboriginal Australia, even where belief in reincarnation was absent; and those few who passed through further initiations to become "medicine men" approached still more nearly to the potent ancestral status which none could now fully achieve.

Just as Australian initiation ceremonies identify each new generation with the ancestors of long ago, rites for the increase of plant and animal species associated with them are an attempt "to maintain the regular" (Elkin 1954, 205), to banish novelty from the predictable round of existence. Through ritual, Berndt observes (1974, 1 : 15), postulants seek to ensure that the ancestors' "vital life-giving power . . . is brought to bear on the affairs of men." But when this power is attainable only by repeating what others have always done, and men think of themselves as "passive recipients" of traditions eternally re-enacted in ritual, there will be no counterweight to the sacred past, no incentive to innovation, no human possibility other than following footsteps immemorially misdirected since the fabled ancestors vanished in propria persona from the tribal lands. Among the Aranda, even one who knew and admired them as intimately as Strehlow remarks (1947, 6, 35), "tradition and the tyranny of the old men in the religious and cultural sphere have effectually stifled all creative impulse. . . . The chants, the legends, and the ceremonies which we record today mark the consummation of the creative efforts of a distant, long-past age. . . . Nothing that the ancestors have done can ever be bettered by later craftsmen. In this respect, too, as in all others, it is unfortunately true that central Australia sleeps heavily under the all-oppressive night-shadow of tradition."

THE RITUALIZATION OF CHANGE AND CONFLICT

To the extent that religious ritual is an invariant commemoration of ancestrally hallowed tradition, there can be no future that is not an imperfect repetition of a timeless past lying ahead no less than behind; no individual departure from collective paradigms of behavior; no creativity that does not re-enact what has already been. There can be nothing to seek because everything of value has once and for all been long ago found.

Such a conception of ritual, however, overlooks the crucial role of conflict and change. A one-sided emphasis on affirmation of communal stability in tribal societies marks the views of Durkheim (deeply influenced by Spencer and Gillen's accounts of Aranda religion) and of Radcliffe-Brown and the British structuralists, or functionalists, who followed him. (In its neglect or denial of change French structuralist anthropology outdoes its empirically restrained British counterpart.) Hallpike, drawing on his studies of such dissimilar peoples as the Konso of Ethiopia and the Tauade of Papua New Guinea, is among those who have vigorously contested blanket claims that ritual serves to increase social solidarity, which he considers "the product of day-to-day relations, not of occasional ceremonies" (1972, 331). In his view, the functionalist model of human society, like that of behaviorist psychology, systematically ignores "the creative and the imaginative" and regards man and society "as essentially robot mechanisms, bundles of stimulus-response reflexes" (1977, 252). Functionalist arguments are reductive, circular, and devoid of significant content, "yet without such concepts, that of 'function' itself becomes meaningless" (281; cf. 1979, 41–65).

Whatever their sins of misplaced emphasis may have been in the eyes of a subsequent generation, however, the distinguished line of British social anthropologists from Radcliffe-Brown through Firth and Evans-Pritchard, Gluckman and Fortes, to the early Turner was by no means blind to the problematic aspects of "structure" and "function," or to the ubiquity of conflict and change. The Durkheimian exaltation of social solidarity was never uncritically accepted—"The Nuer conception of God," Evans-Pritchard wrote (1956, 320), "cannot be reduced to, or explained by, the social order"[4]—and van Gennep's emphasis on transformative rites of passage was a continuous influence on functionalist thought, cautiously commended by such orthodox representatives as Gluckman and Fortes, until it became dominant in the "liminality" of Turner (cf. Gluckman 1962; Turner 1969, 166).

Thus although they focus on rituals thought to perpetuate an ancestrally sanctioned order, these anthropologists recognized that change is essential to that order even when overtly denied. The Tikopia Work of the Gods, whose "adaptive and even creative function" Firth stressed (1967b, 23), ceased to exist when it ceased to adapt and create, for no living ritual can affirm an order belonging *solely* to the past. And despite

4. Over a quarter century earlier, he had asserted (1929, 22) that "it is one of the aims of social anthropology to interpret all differences in the form of a typical social institution," such as magic, "by reference to difference in social structure."

their belief "that the structure of the world and life was fixed once-for-all at a remote time in the past" (Stanner n.d., 151), the Australian Murinbata "welcomed change insofar as it would fit the forms of permanence" and thereby "attained stability but avoided inertia" (168). The distinction is crucial: the stability promoted by ritual is not an inertial inheritance but a continually renewed endeavor. Indeed, the stake the dead are thought to have in the future persistence of society, Fortes writes (1976, 6), paradoxically "gives ancestor worship a future orientation, rather than . . . a fixation on the past." Even this apparently backward-looking practice thus requires a ceaseless labor, in which living and dead are both implicated, to achieve a transcendent condition no longer given, as in the mythic age, but only attainable in a future potentially one with the supertemporal past. The transcendent Zamani of the long dead and the not yet born must be sustained by continuous effort in the Sasa which is here and now.

Such rituals affirm not simply the stability of society but the incessant activity necessary to achieve it. But to focus on the formalized rites of such traditional tribes as the Zuñi, Tallensi, Tikopia, and Aranda—as the tradition stemming from Durkheim and Radcliffe-Brown has done—grants a falsely privileged status to the fixed, repetitive, and invariant aspects of ritual compatible with a conservative social system which the ritual is thought to uphold. A fuller picture must take into account more disruptive dimensions, indicative of irrationality and conflict as well as of social cohesion.

The stately calendrical rituals of the Zuñi appear to support Benedict's claim (1934, 87) that these sober Apollonians "do not seek or value excess," but other rites greatly alter this picture. Frank Cushing, the first outsider to give an extended account of Zuñi life, describes (73–74) a Knife Dance at which he was threatened as a sacrificial "Navajo" by two Zuñi dancers who then accepted a yellow dog in his place, bludgeoned it to death and disemboweled it in a scene "too disgusting for description"—a scene he likens to Aztec war ceremonies or the animal sacrifices of "the savages of the far North-west," the very "Dionysian" peoples whom Benedict later categorically contrasted to the Zuñi. No less discordant with the Apollonian image is Matilda Stevenson's description (437) of the ritual eating of human excrement, in an "acme of depravity," by the Zuñi Galaxy Fraternity, after which "they bite off the heads of living mice, and chew them, tear dogs limb from limb, eat the intestines and fight over the liver like hungry wolves."[5] In these rituals, and others

---

5. Cf. Bourke's account (1920) of the "vile ceremonial" he saw in 1881 as Cushing's guest: "The dancers swallowed great draughts [of human urine], smacked their lips, and, amid the roaring merriment of the spectators remarked that it was very, very good."

where initiates thrust glowing brands down their throats, scourged themselves with cactus thorns, and swallowed swords, there is more than a pinch of Dionysus in the Apollonian stew—and a healthy reminder that highly coherent patterns of culture are as much imposed as extrapolated by the observer.

Far from merely ministering to prurient curiosity about the strange ways of "savages," awareness of such seemingly aberrant practices reintroduces into an excessively schematized picture the element of contradiction lacking so long as ritual was viewed as a fail-safe mechanism for the maintenance of dominant social values. Nor are ritualized outbursts of violence so alien as they might seem to the putative orderliness of primitive agricultural society. We conventionally think of "man the hunter" as aggressively savage, the brute Neanderthal of popular fantasy, and associate the pastoral or rural life (having more recently lost it) with serenity and peace, the Apollonian virtues of Benedict's homogenized Zuñi. But the opposite view is at least as likely, and in recent ethnographical literature (as in ancient myth) hunter-gatherers like the Congo Pygmies, Kalahari Bushmen, Australian aborigines, and California acorn-gatherers who live "naturally" off the land and celebrate in religious festivities their oneness with fellow-creatures of forest or bush whom they hunt yet revere, have been wistfully viewed as saving remnants or reproachful reminders of a harmonious and even "affluent" primordial way of life long endangered and now on the verge of extinction.

According to Turnbull, who elsewhere (1962, 92) extols the "molimo" ceremony in which the BaMbuti pygmies celebrate their "intimate communion" with their god the forest, not hunters but agriculturalists have been most aggressive toward a hostile "natural" world against which strenuous efforts to mold their environment have pitted them. The submissively adaptive hunter "accepts the world as he finds it and does not attempt to control or dominate it," Turnbull contends (1976, 14–15), substituting, perhaps, one stereotype for another. In contrast, African cultivating societies, in Turnbull's schematic view, are "much more dominating, aggressive, and at times even hostile," for now "the very earth is attacked with a hoe, reshaped and reformed and forced to produce crops determined by man."

From this viewpoint, the momentous worldwide change from a hunting way of life in harmony with nature to an agricultural one in conflict with the always encroaching wild has been seen as promoting not only social stratification and its attendant tensions but a more violent rela-

---

Though legerdemain, Curtis suggests (17: 147), may have substituted more palatable nutrients for "excrement" and "urine," the exaltation of excess nevertheless remained.

tion between human and superhuman, reflected in animal and human sacrifices that often represent—as Frazer's *Golden Bough* lavishly attests—the slaying of a deity. Killing is especially glorified, Adolf Jensen asserts (163), not by hunters but by root-crop cultivators, the chief practitioners of head-hunting and cannibalism; and among these tropical cultivators the central myth (91–93) is of a primal time brought to an end when its dominant beings, in plant or animal form, kill the deities who created the existing order. With the end of primal time mortal life replaces immortality, and crop plants arise from the deity's body, "so that the eating of the plants is, in fact, an eating of the deity." The ceremonial eating of fruit or sacrificial animals representing the deity, and their "drastic replacement" by cannibalism, actualize the primal event (in which ancestor worship has its origin) through dramatic cult reenactment.

Hypothetical though his speculations remain, Jensen's discussion highlights dimensions of ritual slighted (no doubt in revulsion from the lax generalizations of Frazer) by functionalist anthropologists. Ritual is not solely a homeostatic mechanism for bringing society into equilibrium through affirmation of its underlying values, a mass yea-saying to things as they are, but also a cathartic outlet for irrational fears and desires reflecting primordial realities of life and death from which all our carefully structured institutions offer imperfect shelter. And ancestor worship, as its frequent association with sacrifice makes clear, pertains not only to kinship systems but to blood and fertility and denial of ubiquitous death. In a society like the Zuñi, where collective ritual is systematized to "Apollonian" extremes, the flagrant excesses of the secret fraternities challenge communal coercion and introduce a margin of freedom into a culturally patterned existence that might otherwise seem more nearly automatism than life, or the life of bees rather than of men.

In this "society of strong repressions," Bunzel notes (1932, 521n) with a shrewdness lacking in Benedict's later account, delight in the antics of clowns springs from a "sense of release in vicarious participations in the forbidden." Nor is the "Dionysian" blood-lust found by Jensen among root-crop cultivators of New Guinea and Indonesia entirely foreign to these stately worshipers of the maize and the rain. In the masked impersonation of Zuñi dancers, "with its atmosphere of the sinister and dangerous," Bunzel finds hints (846–47) of human sacrifice just below the surface of impersonations symbolically representing "the extirpated fact." Be that as it may, the stability of this (as of any) society is not simply a datum to which its constituents passively subscribe on ceremonial occasions but a perpetually endangered creation of their incessant endeavors.

In Africa, too, ancestral ritual affirms not only a fixed social order but the uncertainty and change that attend it. The fact that blood sacrifices—including, in recent times, human sacrifices—are often made to ancestors concerned with the fertility of the earth suggests that the orderly continuity of living and dead, far from being automatic, has sometimes exacted a price beyond the normal expectations of filial piety. In the nineteenth-century West African kingdom of Dahomey, not only were human victims sacrificed to the royal ancestors at the annual "customs," and many more, including scores of wives, at a king's funeral, but a male and female slave of the king's are said to have been sacrificed each morning "to thank his ancestors for having permitted him to awaken to a new day on earth" (Herskovits 1938, 2:53). In this hierarchy of interlinked obligations buttressed by ancestral tradition, the coercive will of the gods known as Fá, or Fate, is offset by the contrary force of Da, "the mobile, sentient quality in all things that have life" (2:201), a divinity who incarnates "movement, flexibility, sinuousness, fortune" (2:255). And a way out is offered, as in many mythologies of the world, from the rigid mandates of divine and human authority by a celestial trickster, Legbá, whose capricious favor can overturn the dictates of Fate (2:295).

Like the religiously sanctioned clown of the Pueblos, whose reversal of norms offers release from conventional conduct, the African trickster affirms that control by gods and ancestors over human conduct extends only so far; unpredictable disruptions of order remain beyond their reach. Thus Ture, the trickster of the Central African Azande, "is a monster of depravity," liar, cheat, lecher, murderer, and braggart, an "utterly selfish person," Evans-Pritchard writes (1967, 28–29), who is still a hero because he "does what he pleases, what in their hearts they would like to do themselves . . . What Ture does is the opposite of all that is moral; and it is all of us who are Ture." In this lawless realm of saturnalian wish-fulfillment, whatever gods or ancestors may be looking on, in indignation or amusement, have no recourse but silence; for they will not be attended.

Saturnalian reversal of social norms characterizes not only legends but ritualized conduct in many regions of the world. Even apart from everyday "joking relationships," in which individuals insult others (mainly their in-laws) in socially acceptable ways (Radcliffe-Brown 1952, 90–116), ceremonial occasions may permit exchange of abuse and even blows between opposing groups (usually men and women) or, like the Roman Saturnalia, sanction temporary suspension of customary moral prohibitions. The verbal taunts, or flyting matches, are sometimes made in good spirit, as in the *Wubwang'u* twinship ritual of the Ndembu (Turner 1969, 78–79), where men and women belittle each other's sexual prowess and extol their own in a "buoyant and aggressively jovial" atmosphere. But sometimes hostilities run deeper: among the Gahuku of New Guinea, furious assault of male oppressors by women armed with "stones and lethal pieces of wood, an occasional axe, and even a few bows and arrows . . . convinced me," a bruised male observer reports (Read, 136), "that the ritual expression of hostility and separation teetered on the edge of virtual disaster."

WITCHCRAFT, THE WILD, AND INITIATORY TRANSFORMATION

Such open flouting of traditional norms is limited to specially designated occasions. So too are the rituals of protest or rebellion discussed by Gluckman, such as the Zulu agricultural rite in which young girls formerly donned men's clothing and shields, then went naked and sang lewd songs while men and boys hid inside their huts (1963, 110–36), or the Swazi *incwala* ceremony in which the king's subjects openly proclaimed their hatred of his rule (1966, 109–36). A far more menacing reversal of values is embodied by the witch, widely believed in tribal Africa as elsewhere in the world to pose a continuous threat to individual well-being from a realm in which moral and social norms have no sway. African witchcraft (in contrast to sorcery, which works through magic and medicines) is a psychic substance that transcends social control and ancestral authority (see Evans-Pritchard 1937, 21; M. Wilson, 92; Middleton 1960, 245–48). Witches are "innately wicked people who work harm against others . . . by virtue of the possession of mysterious powers unknown and unavailable to ordinary people; it is this," Middleton and Winter comment (8), "which sets them apart" and makes them so feared.

Once their congenital power has been activated by initiation or ill will, witches may inflict infertility, drought, injury, or illness, and they are widely thought to be the sole cause of death. Suspicions of witchcraft fasten on social and moral deviants (Nadel 1954, 171), whether solitary malcontents or the moderately rich and powerful envied for inexplicable success; the latter are also frequently victims of witches or sorcerers who strive to bring them low. But witches are not merely deviant members of society but the outright negation of natural and social order itself, eating human flesh and preferring night to day, practicing sexual perversions and "defecating on prepared fields . . . or urinating in drinking or milking receptacles," as among the Mandari of the Sudan (Buxton 1963, 103), or "flying through the air or walking upside down on their hands and smeared white with ashes," as among the Kaguru of Tanzania (Beidelman, 65). Witches among the Amba of Uganda (Winter 1963, 292–93) not only go about naked at night, transform themselves into leopards, and feed on people, but "sometimes stand on their heads or rest hanging upside down from the limbs of trees," eat salt when thirsty, and victimize members of their own village; such behavior not only differs from that of ordinary people, like the practices of sorcerers, "it is the exact reverse, an inversion of the moral code" (and indeed of human nature) in every particular (cf. Middleton 1960, 248).

Witches are thus a continual threat to an ancestral order dependent, in paradoxical symbiosis, on witchcraft to swell the ancestors' numbers through death, which would not occur in its absence, and to activate their protective intervention through malice toward the living. Witchcraft is the indispensable counterpart by which ancestral order, or social order in general, is defined, the chaos (or rather the anti-cosmos, for witchcraft too has its order) against which the socially sanctioned cosmos is measured and without which its sanctions would have no force.

Up to a point, the seeming irrationality of witchcraft can be reconciled with a functionalist model of society. Kluckhohn's study of Navajo witchcraft (1944, 106–112) contends that witchcraft beliefs are both psychologically adjustive in providing a channel for expression of tribal tensions and sociologically adaptive in affirming the tribe's solidarity against disruptions. Yet though belief in witches no doubt serves important social functions, such explanations seem wholly inadequate to account for its disturbing power. For witches are not, like ancestors, easily subsumed under social categories; they embody something other, a fundamentally extra-social threat to the fragile order that can sometimes channel but never fully contain it. They are associated not with culturally engendered ills but with the most uncontrollable powers of nature, the sharks that devour shipwrecked sailors in the Trobriands, the blight that ravages crops, the disease that mysteriously weakens and kills.

If this power were directed by or against strangers it might indeed be an instrument of social cohesion, but the widespread belief that witches choose their victims exclusively from their own village and even from their nearest kin, Winter comments (1963, 283), is tremendously disruptive of group integration. Witchcraft is "the enemy within"; it blames incomprehensible disease and destruction on those closest at hand, and thus works both against social adaptation by increasing internecine conflicts and against individual adjustment by arousing fear, as in Cochiti Pueblo, that one may be unconsciously guilty of witchcraft through "bad thoughts" responsible for another's illness or death (Fox, 266). And because it confounds all carefully constructed categories of kinship and community it detracts far more from stability than it could ever contribute. Witchcraft, Winter remarks of the Amba (n.d., 152), in contrast to the ancestor cult which increases the solidarity of the group, enhances "negative feelings of hatred which tend to pull it apart and destroy it." For this reason, the sociological determinism of Radcliffe-Brown and his school, Winter concludes (1963, 297–99), presents a very one-sided view of social phenomena by ignoring the disintegrative effects of witchcraft. The "formal congruence between the set of ideas and the social structure" in the Durkheimian tradition may even, when one term inverts instead of reflecting the other, produce disruption instead of cohesion—or rather a perpetual tension between them, a precariously dynamic rather than a statically harmonious equilibrium.

The running conflict between integrative ancestors and disintegrative witches is one prominent manifestation in tribal religion of a larger opposition between society or culture itself, the realm of humanly perpetuated if divinely founded order, and everything that lies threateningly (or invitingly) outside its control. The two are sometimes understood as opposing aspects of a single divinity. Thus among the Lugbara (Middleton 1960, 250–57), God, or *adro*, in his transcendent celestial aspect is creator of men, women, and cattle (and hence of society), but in his evil or immanent aspect this same adro stands menacingly opposed to the social order: "He is an 'inversion' of both God in the sky and of man. He lives in rivers and the bush, the waste places between the compounds, which are feared as 'outside' and uninhabited places," and is associated, as the "bad God," with witches and sorcerers, rain groves, and inexplicable manifestations of miraculous power, known also as adro.

More commonly, the uncontrollable "outside" forces are embodied as demonic spirits of the wild who may unpredictably intrude on the social domain at any time and assault its members with spirit possession or disease. Their targets are typically chosen (in contrast to persons chastised by offended ancestors) at random. Such spirits may be the familiars of witches, or opposed to them, for they are characteristically not malevolent but amoral, as much leprechaun as devil. Their outsideness is their essence, pitting them ipso facto against everything normal. Their very unpredictability is a continual danger to human beings who can never safeguard themselves against capricious attack.

Similar spirits, from impish poltergeists to menacing trolls, are of course common throughout the world. Not only these picturesque sprites, however, but any outsider not readily subsumed by established social categories is "inherently linked with the Wild," Hallpike suggests (1972, 325), thereby becoming a source simultaneously (in Douglas's terms) of purity and danger. Many peoples of the world, like the Lugbara, and like the Dinka of the Sudan, make a "clear distinction between the wilds (*roor*) and the homestead (*bai*), 'the desert and the sown'," a distinction reflected, Lienhardt writes of the Dinka (63), "in a division of Powers into the non-rational and rational, the purposeless and the purposeful, those which share men's social life and those which . . . are merely menacing to human beings."

Nor is the menacing realm of the wild invariably negative; it can embody a potentiality for transformation. Among the Ehanzu of central Tanzania, to undo the effects of sorcery, Douglas relates (94–95), a "simpleton" is sent wandering into the bush, symbolizing a venture both "into the disordered regions of the mind" and "beyond the confines of society. The man who comes back from these inaccessible regions brings with him a power not available to those who have stayed in the control of themselves and of society." Through this hazardous journey into the wilderness the seemingly closed structure of tribal society opens momentarily onto an uncharted space in which a spiritual quest for the transcendent and unknown becomes a possibility at last.

An essential tension thus exists in many tribal religions between ordered social structure and the uncontrollable wild; moreover, the social structure itself is not a unitary construct but one that incorporates continuous conflict and change within its overall solidarity. As Gluckman has repeatedly emphasized, "Conflicts are a part of social life and custom appears to exacerbate these conflicts: but in doing so custom also restrains the conflicts from destroying the wider social order" (1966, 2). Conflict and resolution of conflict is the "pervasive theme" of Turner's early study of the Ndembu of Zambia, *Schism and Continuity in an African Society*—a theme (1957, xxii) reflecting the views of those, like Gluckman, who "regard a social system as 'a field of tension, full of ambivalence, of co-operation and contrasting struggle.'" Here a dynamic view of society (and of the ritual which expresses its dominant values) emerges from adaptation of the Durkheimian model inherited through Radcliffe-Brown.

The strength of Turner's analysis stems from apprehension not merely of social conflict in general but of the particularly labile form of Ndembu society, in contrast with Fortes's more stable Tallensi. Ndembu society is matrilineal and virilocal; that is, inheritance is traced through women, yet a woman moves when married to the village of her husband and *his* matrilineal kin (to whom she and her children will be unrelated), thus repeatedly breaking up the residential unity of the kinship group. No sharp opposition between ancestral integration and the disintegrative forces of the wild can thus obtain in this society, since unlike that of the Tallensi, which "is related to the land, to agriculture, and to permanent residence on the land of well-defined corporate lineages," the Ndembu ancestor cult "is associated with the bush, its dangers and blessings, with the transience of settlement, with the hazards of life, and with the mobile human group itself rather than its specific habitation" (173).

Such a fissile society can hardly give rise through divinization of its unifying values to the transcendent solidarity thought by Durkheim to be the object of ritual; on the contrary, "norms and their supporting values can only *appear* to be consistent, since they must cover the pres-

ence of contradictions within the structure itself" (124). Instead of affirming established social structures, Ndembu ritual "compensates for
the deficiencies in a labile society" (303) and repeatedly restates "a group
unity which transcends, but to some extent rests on and proceeds out of,
the mobility and conflicts of its component elements" (316). Thus not
only invariance and immutability but conflict and change may be integral dimensions of ritual itself.

It is surely no accident that Turner's recognition of mobility and conflict in Ndembu society eventuated in rediscovery of van Gennep and
formulation of the concepts of liminality and communitas. The exem-
plary *rite de passage,* in which van Gennep's stages of separation, transition, and incorporation are clearly demarcated, is the initiation rite signaling a change from one social status to another—notably from
childhood to adulthood, as in the *Mukanda* rite of male circumcision
studied by Turner among the Ndembu. In this ritual, involving (like
many others from Africa to Australia) the segregation, after painful circumcision, of a group of boys from their family surroundings, instruction during the period of healing, and reintegration into society as
adults, Turner found social divisions giving way, during the transitional
period, to a transcendent sense of community. Through "the mystical
efficacy of ritual," he writes (1967, 265–66), "*Mukanda* strengthens the
wider and reduces the narrower loyalties," emphasizing the unity of
males irrespective of matrilineal connections. It effects not only a transformation of jural status but an expansion of human outlook, a heightened awareness of commonality that might never have come into being
without it.

Mukanda marks not only a biosocial transition, then, but "a complete
change in the novice's ontological status," as Eliade says of initiations in
general (1959, 187), through death to one condition and rebirth to another. Both by intense instruction and by confrontation during seclusion
with a world radically dissimilar to the one they had known the initiates
are profoundly transformed. Rites of passage thus both acknowledge
and redress the divisions inherent in all societies; they affirm the processual nature of society itself by continual reaggregation of the individuals
and groups that compose it and effect a fundamental reordering of previous allegiances.

Transference of a boy's attachment from the maternally dominated
childhood family to the world of men is central to initiation in New
Guinea. Here rituals organized (as among the Ilahita Arapesh or the
Baktaman) in elaborate sequences in which all males participate at different ages frequently involve—along with revelation of cult objects—
bleeding of the nose and penis and lashing of the genitals; treatment of
young novices as "wives" subjected to homosexual intercourse; enact-

ment of rebirth by crawling between men's legs; and public exhibition of new initiates in the ostentatious regalia of manhood, eliciting assault upon them by the excluded and infuriated women.[6]

One principal objective of these initiations, Tuzin remarks (103–04) of one rite of the Tambaran cult to which all Ilahita Arapesh males belong, is "to transform the novices into whole men by severing once and for all the ties of substance and affection which bind them to women, especially their mothers." The very extremity of these continual New Guinean initiations suggests the extent to which separation from childhood dependency and attachment to women in such fiercely warlike masculine societies is difficult if not impossible to achieve; here ritual at its most fanatically transformative affirms not the overall solidarity but the unresolvable internal conflicts of a society bent on transmuting or extirpating, regardless of cost, all affiliations not subordinated to its paramount object.

Initiatory rites effect a transformation of attachment and outlook not merely by mandating passage from one social dimension to another but by bringing the social order itself, in the person of initiants fully attached to neither dimension, into contact with the unsocialized "wild" that encompasses it; only thus can space for passage between the opposed conditions be opened. Van Gennep, who placed such stress (192) on territorial passage between stages, emphasized the "neutral zones"—"ordinarily deserts, marshes, and most frequently virgin forests" (18)—that formerly separated one territory from another and at the same time linked them together; it is in these pathless *marges* over which no social order can claim dominion that the crucial liminal phase of the rite of passage takes place.

Most initiatory rites marking the transition from boy to man involve collective isolation (in contrast to the individual seclusion of girls at first menstruation) in a hut beyond the edge of the village, and ritualized encounter with the wild is a frequent condition for the candidate's transformation. A Baktaman youth's first initiation begins when the men of the village, adorned with feather headdresses and pigs' tusks, suddenly sweep down at night, "tear the boy loose from the protesting and beseeching mother, and drag him off into the dark, frightening forest where till then he has not been allowed to go at night for fear of spirits and ambushes" (Barth, 51). Confrontation with supernatural monsters like the "hippopotamus" of the Kenyan Akamba or the "crocodiles" of the New Guinean Busama is often a central experience; among the key

6. See Tuzin on the Ilahita Arapesh and Barth on the Baktaman. On novices as wives, see Bateson, 131; on homosexuality, Keesing 1982a, 10–11, and Herdt 1981. Both Barth (65, 67) and Tuzin (236) refer to rebirth by crawling through men's legs.

mysteries revealed in many societies is the identity of those behind the masks and of the flutes or bullroarers that supply their voices. The very segregation of men from women that begins in the boys' initiation hut reinforces the belief, held by the Busama and many others of New Guinea, that men are akin to spirits whereas women can never attain sacredness (Hogbin 1947–48, 54).

Not by exclusion of the wild but by encounter with it are individuals transformed and the dynamic equilibrium of a mobile society maintained. Man belongs both to desert and sown, whose perimeters he must discover since neither is given; only by seeking out and assimilating the alien wilderness, society's defining antithesis, can he cultivate a place in a world that he will thereafter experience as fully his own.

Because they bring expansion of knowledge through absorption of extra-social powers, initiatory rites are a paradigm—however repugnant the New Guinean instance may be to civilized man, to say nothing of civilized woman—of the questing hero's encounter with the beyond. Awareness of their interdependence with vital forces outside their control is the essential knowledge, embracing all lesser mysteries, which the initiates gain through their encounter. And since every revelation of ritual secrets reveals a deception, this knowledge is both of transcendent truths and of the illusions by which such truths are apprehended or invented—an epistemological paradox not irrelevant to the quest (see Barth, 81–82; Tuzin, esp. 261–68). Assimilation of this transcendent dimension results in the "ontological" self-transformation these rites bring about, as when Liberian novices, having been "killed" by the Forest Spirit and then resuscitated, seem to have entirely forgotten their past experience (Eliade 1958, 31, citing Frobenius) and can no longer perform the most basic acts which society had painstakingly taught them before their transformative confrontation with its self-projected opposite.

Liminality can be at once a negation of preliminal social structure and an affirmation of another order of things (Turner 1974, 196) because it incorporates an alien perspective indispensable to society as interactive process. Ritual, the vehicle for cultural assimilation of the wild, cannot be understood as merely affirming a pre-existent social reality, even the complexly fissile reality of Ndembu society analyzed by Turner; for in contradistinction to ceremony, to which Turner assigns the confirmatory function, ritual is transformative in essence (1967, 95). It is the "realm of pure possibility whence novel configurations of ideas and relations may arise" (97), the channel through which the unpredictable and indeterminate periodically subvert and renew the categories through which reality is perceived. Like the *Chihamba* rite of affliction studied by Turner (1975, 185), ritual in general aims "to break through the habitual patterns formed by secular custom, rational thinking, and common sense, to a condition where the pure act-of-being is directly apprehended," the supremely liminal condition of man face-to-face with a radically unfamiliar world over which—until he can enlarge his newly inadequate categories of understanding by assimilating its influence—he has no control. Here on the threshold of the spiritual quest Durkheim and Radcliffe-Brown's intellectually provocative reduction of ritual to repetitive affirmation of social order must, as in the rites of passage themselves, be left firmly behind; for society, so conceived, cannot alone be the source of what transforms and creates it.

CHAPTER SIX

Myth and the Journey
beyond the Self

Ritual is by no means, then, merely a mechanism for denial of change. On the contrary, by incorporating forces potentially disruptive of social order it can be a potent instrument of communal transformation. When we turn from ritual act to mythic word the movement toward openness—the realm of the quest—is still more pronounced.

THE MYTHIC WORD AND THE SACRED JOURNEY

Ritual changes only gradually, except in times of crisis, since it finds validation in a timeless past viewed as a pattern for subsequent ages. Variation does in fact continually occur (see Firth 1967a, 233–60), but invariance is commonly held to be indispensable to its effect. The spell or invocation, as the verbal aspect of ritual action, is also ideally fixed; formulaic prayer, like every magic spell, achieves "compulsion by exactness of word" (Reichard 1944, 10), from which the slightest departure suffices to render it void. But degrees of fixity differ greatly from culture to culture; thus Evans-Pritchard (1929, 631–32) notes in Zande ritual performance a laxity which would "horrify a Melanesian" and invalidate the magic act. Language, as a creative faculty distinguishing man from more rigidly programmed animals, is especially susceptible to variation; unlike the fixed "compulsive word" of the Navajo, Nuer prayers, for example, have "no set form and order," Evans-Pritchard reports (1956, 22; cf. 212), and each may be used "anywhere and at any time."

Nor is this flexibility peculiar to the relatively unritualistic Nuer; among the Tallensi, with their rigid ancestral obligations, the body of a prayer, Fortes writes (1975, 135), "is apt to be a free and *ad hoc* construction reflecting the particular features of the occasion, though stock phrases will be used and stock sentiments and attitudes exhibited." The variability latent (even when strenuously denied) in culturally transmitted ritual becomes potentially limitless when the ritual word begins to free itself from subordination to fixed ritual action, and thus begins to open, however tentatively, from coercive exactness toward indeterminate exploration of the unknown.

Together with patterned actions and utterances, the sacred objects of ritual form an apparently closed symbolic system susceptible, however, to changing verbal interpretations. To the extent that multivocality, or diversity of potential signification, is its essence, the symbol is dependent on a continuing hermeneutic process for its existence. Its creativity lies not in sacral immutability but in the multiplicity of meanings to which it gives rise within this interpretive framework. The dynamic interdependence of fixed symbol and provisional word, not the symbol in isolation (for there can be no symbol in isolation), "actually 'creates' society," Turner writes (1974, 56), as a dialectic of structure and communitas, stasis and change. This relational meaning must in the end be verbally apprehended, for *logos* is relationship, and the word itself is a symbol oriented not toward an unchanging past but toward an indefinite future.

Verbal interpretation of ritual symbolism finds its most significant expression, among many tribal peoples, in myth. Not that myth is reducible to mere commentary on ritual. W. Robertson Smith (18) contended over a century ago that myths, insofar as they were explanations of rituals, were in almost every case secondary derivations from them. The hypothesis had a fertile impact on Frazer, the "Cambridge anthropologists" such as Jane Harrison, and the British and Swedish "Myth and Ritual" school, which interpreted myths as scenarios of rites demonstrating a pattern of divine kingship throughout the ancient Near East. But this view was easily reduced, by neglect of Robertson Smith's qualification, to Lord Raglan's claim (41) that "all traditional narratives originate in ritual"—an extreme position thoroughly rebutted over the last half century, at the risk of authenticating the no less untenable antithesis that association of myth with ritual "is nearly always trivial and casual" (Kirk, 18).[1] The frequently close connection between them suggests, on the contrary, that inasmuch as myths can be seen (as by no means all can) as explanations or interpretations of associated rituals, they are not mere "secondary" reflections but verbal counterparts dynamically interacting with them. Such being the case, as Lévi-Strauss suggests (1963, 230), "we shall have to give up mechanical causality as an explanation and, instead, conceive of the relationship between myth and ritual as dialectical."

---

1. For criticism of the "Myth and Ritual" hypothesis and Frazer's school, see respectively Brandon and Fontenrose.

This dialectic of repetitive act oriented (insofar as it is fixed) toward the immutable past and of variable word oriented (insofar as it frees itself from rote incantation) toward the potential future is another expression of the interaction of closure and openness, stasis and change, fundamental to life, consciousness, and language itself: here Bergson's two sources of morality and religion as inertial habit and forward thrust find one of their most fundamental expressions. Myth too, through close association with ritual, may fulfill the conservative function of validating the past by providing a "pedigree" for magic, according to Malinowski (141), and establishing a "sociological charter, or a retrospective moral pattern of behavior" (144). But like the blithely inconsistent explanations of ritual symbolism which native informants often bestow on baffled ethnographers, preliterate myths continually vary; they are pedigrees and charters, if at all, under constant revision. The same informant, Radcliffe-Brown long ago observed (1922, 188), "may give, on different occasions, two entirely different versions of such a thing as the origin of fire, or the beginning of the human race," and a similar variation characterizes the legends of many tribal peoples. Greater standardization no doubt occurred in more settled societies, but the flexible innovativeness of myth by no means came to an end, as the divergent renditions of Greek drama or the alternative versions of creation in the Hebrew bible abundantly demonstrate.

The characteristic variability of myth gives play to the indeterminacy latent in the ritual process (above all in its liminal phase), despite its adhesion to unchanging tradition. Far from being a structureless flux, however, mythic variability expresses the creative capacity of human consciousness and speech to assimilate unforeseeable experience in logically apprehensible form not by habituated repetition but by innovative recombination; myth, as the mobile complement of ritual, is thus an instrument not principally for control of a menacing outside world but for its exploration and transformation. It extends the reach of ritual, as word does of act, by transcending the immutability of a divinely given past—the sacral moment in which every time and place is the same—through projection, in the forward thrust of its narrative, of a potentially transformative future.

This dynamic conception sharply contrasts with Lévi-Strauss's structuralist tenet (which logically precludes dialectical interaction) that "mythology is static, we find the same elements combined over and over again, but they are in a closed system . . . in contradistinction to history, which is, of course, an open system" (1979, 40). Variability eludes the structuralist "quest for the invariant" (8), just as creative activity has no place in a human mind conceived as a "purely passive" crossroads where all that happens is a matter of chance (4).[2] In contrast to this assumption, the linguistically structured variability of myth permits the latent liminality of ritual to unfold through interaction with a perpetually changing world where the quest for an indeterminate goal becomes a possibility, if not a necessity.

Among the most common ritual symbols are the road or journey enacted by performance of the ritual itself. The image of a sacred road marking out the journey through life and beyond is widely diffused in native American religions, as in many others. Thus the White Path drawn on the floor of the Delaware (or Lenape) Big House leads to "the western door where all ends" and finds a celestial counterpart in the Milky Way along which souls of the dead travel to the spirit realm (Speck 1931, 2:23). In the Pueblos, where ritual has often seemed a monotonous denial of change, the symbol of the road embodies the mobility essential to even the most traditional religion. Among both Hopi and Zuñi, Elsie Clews Parsons observes (1939, 1:360−61), a line of meal sprinkled from the altar to the door of the sacred *kiva* is the road by which the spirits travel. Myths of mankind's emergence from beneath the earth to the "fourth world" of the present, and of the tribe's long wanderings before reaching the solstitial middle place ordained as their homeland, are further dynamic dimensions of Pueblo rituals, whose participants repeatedly re-enact the primordial tribal journey generation after generation.

Similar myths are explicit in such Navajo chantways as Upward Moving and Emergence Way, but every Navajo ritual is a journey along a road that eventuates, through purification and healing, in a *change* in status. Even the meticulously drawn but quickly obliterated "sand paintings" that are part of most rites are an indication, despite their seemingly static symmetry, of a transfiguring passage. "The corn with its four bars and four pollen footprints," Newcomb writes (155−56) of one painting, "was the ladder of life through its four stages, and above it was the blue bird indicating peace and happiness as a final goal," thus reminding the participant "that only by personal effort in mounting the ladder of life can spiritual strength be acquired." Movement is fundamental to any conception of ritual in which a purposeful journey plays so central a role. Indeed, in a broadened sense of van Gennep's term, not only initia-

---

2. Contrast Cassirer 1955, 2:69: "Nowhere in myth do we find a passive contemplation of things." Lévi-Strauss (1969, 10−12) rebuts "the illusion of liberty" by attempting to show "not how men think in myths but how myths operate in men's minds without their being aware of the fact." Of his analysis of mythologies and other taxonomies of "savage thought" in linguistic terms, Chomsky (1972a, 74) writes: "Nothing has been discovered that is even roughly comparable to language in these domains."

tions and other rituals marking formal alteration of the individual's bio-social status but virtually every rite, insofar as it maps out a path and invites to a voyage, is an incipient rite of passage or guided quest—for what seeker has not begun by following in the footsteps of an-other?—for renewal and transformation.

Even among sedentary peoples like the Pueblos, then, where cere-monies exalt recurrence and deny innovation, the suppressed dimension of the wild may reappear with a vengeance, and a vestigial quest survives in ritual imagery of the road. Among the Navajo, who are centuries closer to a hunting existence, undercurrents of mobility are perceptibly stronger. But an agricultural quest myth appears most prominently, among North American tribes, in conjunction with the rites of a more northern people, the Pawnee, who combined a planting and a migratory way of life, leaving solid earth lodges and carefully tended corn crops on the Great Plains of Nebraska several times a year (before their removal to Oklahoma) to encamp on the prairie and hunt the buffalo.

Affinities with the Pueblos and even possibly—in their sacrifice, as recently as 1838, of a captive maiden to the Evening Star—with the Az-tecs suggest, if not an origin "somewhere in Old Mexico" (Grinnell 1889, 227), at least a significant southwestern influence which sharply differ-entiated the Pawnee from other Plains tribes. Pawnee ceremonies, like those of many agricultural peoples, were considered, Weltfish writes (8), "as the means for keeping the cosmic order in its course." As in Zuñi and other Pueblos, seasonal ceremonies were in charge of a priesthood, but—as among nomadic hunters of the Plains—were performed in re-sponse to a visionary call (5–6). Sedentary life was thus infused, for these cultivators and warriors, with mobility and individualism.

The remarkable ritual sequence described almost a century ago by the Pawnee Ku'rahus, or priest, Tahirussawichi, in Fletcher's mono-graph, *The Hako*, may once have been widely diffused throughout north-eastern and midwestern America. In its Pawnee form the symbolism of the road is actuated as a communal quest for fertility. There was, Fletcher remarks, no stated time for performance of the Hako, which was not connected with any tribal festival, but was (26) "a prayer for children, in order that the tribe may increase and be strong." The cere-mony's central object, an ear of corn with its tip painted blue to represent the sky, with four blue lines descending from it, symbolized the vital power of earth, "mother breathing forth life" (44), as fertilized by the heavens, and the possibility of human reproductive and spiritual power. But the fertility of the sacral ear was not passively given to man, a boon descending like the rains from heaven, but had to be actively sought; and the long and difficult road leading to it was no sooner finished than undertaken anew.

The procession went forth singing, on "a way which has come down to us from our far-away ancestors like a winding path" (69), leading through otherwise uncharted margins between known territories. Alone in a land of strangers, the Ku'rahus remembers (70–71), "we call upon Mother Corn and we ask her: 'Is there a path through this long stretch of country before us where we can see nothing?' . . . Then our eyes are opened and we see the way we are to go." Their guide, Mother Corn, introduces into this unfamiliar realm the perennial life-sustaining rhythms that mark a path—the path of oneness with the rhythms of earth and sky—through the inhumanly pathless wild. At dawn, when the old is made new, Mother Earth unfailingly hears the questers call: "She moves, she awakes, she arises, she feels the breath of the new-born Dawn," and everywhere life is renewed. "This is very mysterious," the Ku'rahus remarks (125), ". . . although it happens every day." The renewal of earth is the pathway to renewal of humanity, for women beget children just as earth brings forth the corn (190).

The quest led by the corn mother through threatening wilds culminates in discovery of the child through whom the fertilizing powers of heaven descend to renew the people, and the final ritual is appropriately that of Blessing the Child. "As I sing this song here with you," the old Pawnee priest told Alice Fletcher (258), "I can not help shedding tears. . . . There is no little child here, but you are here writing all these things down that they may not be lost and that our children may know what their fathers believed and practiced in this ceremony." Here too the quest finds a fulfillment that must, like the blessing of children, be repeatedly renewed lest it wither and perish.

In the Hako ceremony, with its striking similarities to ancient Mysteries of the Mediterranean world (see Alexander, 126–30), the mythic quest was identified with the immediate experience of its celebrants; its territorial passage was not mapped in corn meal or pollen on the floor of hogan or kiva but trod by foot through open country in which even familiar sights appeared new. No object met on the journey seemed ordinary, Fletcher observes (302): "The trees, the streams, the mountains, the buffalo were each addressed in song," becoming like the people themselves part of a myth pertaining not to a paradigmatic past but to a forever unfolding present involving both human beings and the world around them in fervently sought renewal.

MYTHS OF THE HEAVENLY QUEST

In other myths the path leads to a qualitatively different world of the gods or the dead across distant seas, under the earth, or in the heavens. "At the beginning of the world men and God were in a direct relation, and men could move up and down from the sky" by rope, bamboo tower, or a tall tree, a Lugbara myth relates (Middleton 1960, 270). But when this bridge was broken, "men fell down, scattering into their present distinct groups each with its different language," so that separation from heaven entailed division from one another as well. In a similar myth of the Sudanese Dinka, sky and earth were originally connected by a rope, and "men could clamber at will to Divinity. At this time there was no death" (Lienhardt, 33–34). But when accidentally struck by the first woman's long-handled hoe, Divinity withdrew to his present great distance from the earth and sent a small blue bird to sever the rope which had given men access to the sky. Since then, "the country has been 'spoilt,' for men have to labour for the food they need, and are often hungry."[3]

Such African myths explain not only the origins of work, sin, or death, but man's remoteness from God on a continent where the vague sky deity of tribal religions is seldom worshiped (as by Nuer and Dinka) with the intense devotion accorded to spirits of the earth and the dead. The heavens are inaccessible in most of tribal Africa, even in myth (except for the trickster's occasional foray), since not even the greatest heroes could ascend to a world to which the passageway had forever been cut. "It is remarkable that out of these many myths concerning the primeval man and the loss of his original state," Mbiti remarks (127), "there is not a single myth, to my knowledge, which even attempts to suggest a solution or reversal of this great loss," nor any "evidence of man seeking after God for his own sake; or of the spirit of man 'thirsting' after God as the pure and absolute expression of being." There can be no quest for heavens from which the separation is so stark and the distance so forbiddingly great. Not that ascent to the skies and marriage between human and celestial beings are wholly absent from African folklore, but they are seldom deliberately sought and often suggest the baleful consequences of overcoming such a division.[4]

The tribal African was typically intimate with transcendent power in terrestrial, not heavenly form. In other mythologies the celestial journey, even when barred to the living, plays a more central part. Thus in a Micronesian myth from Ulithi Atoll (Lessa 1961, 15–19), once the half-divine trickster Iolofäth reaches the sky world, Lang, on the smoke of burning coconut shells, nothing impedes him from joining his father, the sky god, nor can death prevent him, when caught *in flagrante* with

3. Cf. the myths in Evans-Pritchard 1956, 10, and Buxton 1973, 22–23. For other African stories of man's separation from God, whether by accident or transgression, see Mbiti, 122–29.

4. Cf. Radin 1970a, 69–72; Werner, 50–80; sections F0–F199 ("Otherworld Journeys") of S. Thompson, vol. 3, and of Clarke.

an avian divinity's wife, from returning to human foible. In another myth he adopts a boy, Discoverer-of-the-Sun, who has climbed to heaven after his human mother left him to go up to her husband, the Sun. Here, in contrast to most African tales, "There is two-way traffic between Lang and earth," Lessa comments (1966a, 12), "and the passage is traversed by both deities and mortals."

In pagan Polynesia the human soul partook of a "psychic dynamism manifesting itself physically" throughout the universe (Handy, 26), and because so many of the *atua* (gods or spirits) had once been souls of persons charged with mana, there was no gulf but a continuity between "natural" and "supernatural" (6). The dynamism of a mana common to men and gods and the relative accessibility of the heavens in Polynesian myth made the quest for a world beyond a possibility, if not for living individuals in so hierarchical a society, at least for the gods and heroes of old, in whose exploits transcendent aspirations denied an outlet even in ritual act found fulfillment in word.

In Polynesian myth the division of heaven and earth resulted not from human folly but from the effort of their offspring, oppressed by the dark intimacy of their union, to open a breathing-space between parents henceforth parted but still in continuous contact. In the primordial night known by the Maori as Po, the sky father Rangi and earth mother Papa embraced in darkness, all but suffocating their children. But their first-born, Tane, in Best's Tuhoe Maori version (1972, 1: 749–51), "lay down upon the breast of the Earth Mother, with his head downwards he raised his legs and pressed his feet against Rangi and so thrust the sky upwards until the heat of Ra, the sun, was no longer unbearable." This forced separation, though no doubt the origin of strife, was a *felix culpa* creating light and motion from darkness and stasis, and opening a passageway through the mediating space between conditions no longer fused in androgynous oneness.

Among those who remained below in the space thus created were the newly spawned race of human beings who were at first only males. Hence the search for the mortal female "became the great quest of the gods": far and wide, Best writes (1924, 41), "they wandered throughout the universe, ever seeking the female element, and ever failing to find it," until Tane formed a human image from the body of the earth mother and instilled it with life from the "primal origin of all things," Io (35; cf. 1954, 23–26, and 1959). Human beings, like the gods their souls might become, were distinguished by *wananga*, or celestial knowledge, brought down by Tane (Handy, 55); they belonged not to earth alone but in aspiration, at least, to heaven as well, as the frequent celestial journeys of both gods and humans attest. Even the more terrestrial female may ascend to the skies, like Heipua, "Wreath of Flowers," in a

Society Islands tale (Handy, 82–83), who dies of heartbreak when her celestial lover leaves her, but seeks him above and overcomes every danger to bring him back to earth, where she reawakens on her flowery bier to find him again at her side.

But the outcome of the quest is not always happy, as several Maori legends make clear. Rupe climbs from heaven to heaven in search of his sister, who cast herself into the sea after Mani transformed her husband to a dog; he succeeds, but perishes from the effort (Grey, 62–68; Best 1972, 1:816–18). Tawhaki seeks his baby daughter by the goddess Tangotango, who took her up to the sky when he refused to wash her. By climbing a vine rooted in earth and not looking back, he finds her, but in Best's Tuhoe version, he insists on ascending higher to obtain the dogs of his ancestor Tama and falls from the uppermost heaven when Tama rebuffs him (Grey, 46–61; Best 1972, 1:910–17). The Polynesian unlike the African heavens are invitingly open, but to leave terrestrial roots behind in a vertiginous quest with no comprehensible object may not be given to human beings, who inhabit neither earth nor sky but the liminal margin that severs and joins them.

When the object of the quest is comprehensibly urgent, however—not the dogs of Tama, but the conquest of death—its pursuit against impossible odds ennobles the hero who attempts it. The exploits of Maui of a thousand tricks were famed throughout the Polynesian islands which he fished from the sea: how he lengthened the day by netting the sun and fetched down fire from the goddess Mahu-ika, barely escaping incineration. To this mortal divinity not even his mother's prophecy that "you shall climb the threshold of the house of your great ancestor Hine-nui-te-po, and death shall thenceforth have no power over man" (Grey, 22–45) seemed beyond him.

Between Maui and Hine a dispute arose "concerning the permanence of death. Maui argued," in Best's version (1972, 1:944–47), "that man should die as dies the moon, which wanes and dies, but comes to life again strong and vigorous. . . . But Hine would have none of this, and said: 'Let man die for all time, that he may be lamented and wept over.' So Hine persisted in slaying man," and Maui persisted in endeavoring to exempt himself and his fellow mortals from death. "I intend," he tells his parents in Grey's polished account (22–45), "to go on in the same way for ever." Here is a truly transcendent effort to breach the irrevocable condition of man, resourceless only in fleeing from death, and despite his father's warnings, Maui resolves to visit his great ancestress in her dwelling place at the horizon.

Not in the uppermost heavens scaled by Tawhaki, then, but at the meeting place of earth and sky, evanescent juncture of the eternally disjoined Papa and Rangi, will Maui encounter Hine-nui-te-po, queen, like

Greek Persephone or Babylonian Ereshkigal, of the lower world, yet continuously in touch, at the horizon, with the living: a goddess of the greatest threshold of all. She has tried before to slay Maui, who always returned to life; once she obtains a drop of his blood, however, and works black magic upon it, he must perish. But Maui resolves to confront her, and finds her lying asleep. Warning his companions not to laugh, he enters Hine through the passage by which man is born; but a bird laughs, and Hine's genitals crush him to death. His quest to return to a prenatal condition has failed, but this *culpa* too is *felix;* for only in between, not before or after, birth and death can life—and the quest—take place. Man as *animal quaerens* belongs neither to the earth from which he arises nor to the heavens to which he aspires, but to the horizon.

In such Polynesian myths of celestial transcendence, which seem never to have been closely connected with the ancestral and calendrical rites of these once rigidly stratified islanders, the forward thrust of the creative word prodigally compensates for the invariance of the repeated act; the myths are a "charter" not of things as they are but of their potentiality for becoming, like the questing heroes of myth, something other or more. Among southwestern American peoples, too, myth—though viewed by the Navajo as secondary to the fixed rite (Reichard 1939, 20)—articulates the quest for transcendence implicit in the pollen path and the sequential dry paintings of ritual. The great myth of these peoples, adapted by the Navajo and Apache from the Pueblos, tells of the people's Emergence from underground into the present fourth (or fifth) world where, in primordial times, they sought the Center of the Universe which became their tribal home. This myth of the people's collective quest for a place in the world resonates throughout Navajo ritual; not only the "Upward Moving and Emergence Way" but virtually every chantway celebrates the never-completed emergence that pertains as much to the open-ended future as to the determined past.

The Navajo chantway myths are stories whose hero undergoes a series of misfortunes and is restored by the supernaturals (Katherine Spencer, 19–28); from them he acquires sacred knowledge which he bestows as curing ceremonies. These heroes, at first rejected by their family, prove themselves by their ordeals as outcasts. Far from passively submitting to trials, they actively bring them about: "Why is it," the Chiricahua Windway hero exclaims, "that I suffer those hardships! It appears as though I were seeking the frightful things that are putting me to a test!" The heroes' trials thus take the form of deliberate quests, following exclusion from normal society, for knowledge transforming both hero and world. The pattern of these myths (and of the rituals they accompany) is that of van Gennep's rites of passage: separation, transition, incorporation.

The hero, having sought out the wild and made it part of himself, returns with superior powers: henceforth he will establish the norm for his world, until another hero comes to reject and renew it.

No Navajo myth more fully expresses the quest for transcendence than the search of Changing Woman's twin boys for their father, the Sun. This myth, linked to the Male Shootingway chant and, unlike the formulaic chants, subject to continued variation, finds closer analogues among the recently migratory Apache than the long sedentary Pueblos,[5] for the mobility of the journey is familiar to the hunter as it no longer is, except in nostalgic memory, to the planter. In the time of monsters after the People's emergence, the myth relates (King, 21–29), Talking God found a baby girl in a flower bed by a rainbow, born of darkness and the Dawn: a creature of the horizon. Because she changed with the seasons, she was called Changing Woman. One day she wandered from her hogan and fell asleep in the noonday sun; when she awoke, she felt someone had come in her sleep, and saw tracks in the east. Four days later she gave birth to a boy and in four more to a second (four is the sacred number of many American tribes); the two babies "grew every four days, like corn," and at age twelve disappeared. They had gone to find their father, the Sun.

Warned by Old Age that they would die before reaching their goal, but rejuvenated by him (for they are Changing Woman's sons), and protected by eagle feathers Spider Woman had stolen from the Sun, the twins after many adventures reach the house of the Sun. His daughter warns that her father will kill them when he returns; instead, the Sun subjects them to a series of trials to test whether they are Holy People worthy to be his children. Aided by Spider Woman's talismans and timely advice from the Sun's daughter and a helpful inchworm, they survive an overheated sweat bath, poisoned cornmeal, and slashing flint knives. The Sun names the elder his son and the younger his grandson, then lets them descend to earth from a hole in the sky after they have identified the fog-covered mountains that delimit the Navajo homeland below.

Donning heavenly armor and wielding spears of lightning, they slay the monsters infesting their land, then revisit their mother and the mountain from which their journey began and receive songs from Talking God to augment their new power. When they fall sick from their toils, the Holy People cure them by performing "Where the Two Came

5. I follow Navajo chanter Jeff King's version, recorded in 1942–43 by Maud Oakes. Others, all but the last recorded earlier, include Matthews, 104–34; Curtis, 1 : 98–106; Reichard 1939, 37–49; Klah, 73–99; and Link, 24–36. For Apache versions, see Opler 1938, 47–109 (esp. 47–55) and Goodwin 1939, 3–12, 16–26. A Pueblo analogue in E. Parsons 1926b, 99–102, does not involve a deliberate quest by heroes who simply "go where their father is."

to their Father"—that is, the healing chantway that re-enacts their heroic quest and conquest—four times. "Then . . . they talked of living in the future, and of the making of the future people." Thus ends this ancient legend of the celestially engendered seekers to whom warriors of old would pray, through the Male Shootingway chant, for a share in the sacred power won by their quest and brought back for the benefit of their people from the distant skies.

CHAPTER SEVEN

Mobility and Its Limits
in Communal Ritual and Myth

The collective bias of many twentieth-century views of society and religion was challenged, as we have seen, by such thinkers as Weber, Mead, Turner, and Berger. Karl Mannheim, too, asked (206), "From what should the new be expected to originate, if not from the novel and uniquely personal mind of the individual who breaks beyond the bounds of the existing order?" To break beyond the given toward exploration of the unknown is the essence of the spiritual quest, which is only conceivable when the individual no longer sees her existence as wholly defined by the collectivity.

For Firth, too (1964, 233–34), individual actions "tend to have structural effect"; thus the individual search may importantly influence the religious system, as it could never have done for Durkheim or his followers. Others may follow interpretations and actions learned from adventuresome seekers, who may impel social change. Hence examination of individual meanings, Firth writes (47), is indispensable to the study of religion, for without such investigation, "we cannot give satisfactory answers to the problems of religious transformation."

Structure has so often connoted fixity (in British as in French structuralist anthropology) that some writers, including Firth and Turner, have employed the more flexible terms *organization* or *process*. If structure implies order, Firth writes (61), "organization implies a working towards order—though not necessarily the same order." Turner likewise suggests (1967, 271) that without some discrepancy between its principles of organization, there could be no such thing as society, since society is "a process of adaptation that can never be completely consummated." This adaptation, like all others, is directed toward an evolving

94

end in a logical progression from mediate goals to final goal—insofar as any goal of an unending process can be "final."

Structure is necessarily adaptive, since in a changing world, as Rappaport notes (1979, 147), maintenance of homeostasis requires constant change of state and, in most cases, occasional structural changes whose outcome can never be predetermined. In such a purposively adaptive social organization, continually subject to indeterminate structural change through individual actions, above all on the part of its deviant seekers, ritual and myth play a crucial role. For together they run the gamut in tribal society between collective convention, immutably given and repetitively reaffirmed, and the "forward thrust" of more variant aspirations to transcendence. Rituals express conflict as well as conformity; and rites of passage, by confronting their celebrants with a socially uncontrollable Wild, provide a paradigm for the mythical explorations of questing heroes like Maui and the Navajo twins—a paradigm of radical separation from the known, perilous sojourn in an alien yet alluring liminal realm, and (in the Navajo if not in the Polynesian case) transformative re-incorporation into a world defamiliarized and reoriented by the heroes' triumphant return.

Such quests could not arise in a monolithic social order where ritual endlessly reaffirms what has always been and must be; but in a social organization unpredictably "working towards order" they are of central and formative importance. Just as the stake of the dead in continuity of their living descendants gives ancestor worship a "future orientation" (Fortes 1976, 6), so the seemingly static ceremonies of the ritualized Maori or Navajo actually open, through the creative variability of myth, toward a future initiated by the heroes of old but still—like the myths that tell of their exploits and even the slowly changing rites that enact them—in the process of formation.

Even so, the quest remains for the most part inchoate in ritual and myth, a latency awaiting realization. Rituals of rebellion and rites of passage accommodate dimensions of social conflict and mobility excluded from the static Durkheimian model, but their effect is not to challenge traditional society in the name of alternative values but to reinforce its essential rightness. Gluckman repeatedly affirms that "these rebellions, so far from destroying the established social order, work so that they even support this order" (1966, 28), since their controlled expression in ritual serves to resolve conflicts and thus to justify society as it is. Only a society fundamentally beyond question could permit such ritualized expression of open dissent and unbridled excess: "for the order itself," being immune from challenge, "keeps this rebellion within bounds" (1963, 127).

For Turner, Ndembu ritual affirms schism as an aspect of continuity, and tribal ritual in general acknowledges the individual only "by pre-scribing that he subordinates his individuality to his multiple social roles" (1968, 270). Rituals like the *Mukanda* thus function as a mechanism tem-porarily abolishing or minimizing deflections from normative behavior (1967, 269–70): such departures from the norm, by being safely con-tained in a circumscribed liminal arena, in the end reinforce normalcy. Therefore Turner's assertion (1968, 198) that in rites of passage the le-gitimacy of crucial Ndembu principles is endorsed does not contra-dict—though it importantly qualifies—his emphasis on liminal commu-nitas as a realm of pure possibility and a source of novel configurations, for this is a temporary and strictly limited liberty showing (1967, 106) "that ways of acting and thinking alternative to those laid down by the deities or ancestors are ultimately unworkable and may have disastrous consequences." In a similar way, anomalous events may be the occasion for reaffirming communal unity, and rites of status reversal may cor-roborate the hierarchical principle by demonstrating the absurdity of departure from it.

Thus the circumscribed mobility to which tribal rituals give expres-sion remains marginal to society. The urgent concerns most often ad-dressed by religion are not transcendental but worldly: food, drink, pro-creation. As Lawrence and Meggitt (18) write of New Guinea, "Religion is a technology rather than a spiritual force for human salvation." There is small place and smaller motive for deviant individuals to quest for some faraway goal; for in the immediacy of shared human need there is little to distinguish one individual from others nor much to seek—so long as the rains and the crops are dependable and no catastrophe su-pervenes—beyond what human labor and the revolving seasons regu-larly bring. The questing component of ritual therefore remains largely potential, even though this momentous potentiality belies reduction of ritual to mere repetition of the past or affirmation of the status quo. Individual variation remains essential, as Mannheim and Firth stressed, for change in tribal as in all societies, but the very slowness of such change (and the insistence with which it is denied) suggest how rare de-viation from ancestral ways is. The change institutionalized in rites of passage from one stage of life to another permits, in its carefully delim-ited transitional phase, only slight individual variation from socially es-tablished patterns: its goal, unlike that of the true quest, is fixed in ad-vance and all but infallibly obtained. Through ritual, change thus becomes a dependable constant in tribal religion, whose rites repeatedly celebrate not so much stasis as the regularity of a change without past or future.

This assimilation of cyclical change with no clearly distinguished futurity makes progressive changes inadmissible (Turner 1968, 277), since "norms must be maintained at the expense of novel ways of thinking and acting." In the end (which is very like the beginning), the fluidity and flexibility of primitive religion, Bellah writes (1970, 29), "is a barrier to radical innovation. Primitive religion gives little leverage from which to change the world"—and little stimulus to the individual quest which might give rise to change. For such a quest could only call society's values in question if it led beyond them toward others unknown, as the passage meticulously mapped out in tribal rites, for all its enlarging potential, can never do.

Thus the liminal phase of rites of passage is itself a transition between the relative closure of confirmatory ritual and the exploratory openness of the quest; its domain is the cyclical change which is simultaneously stasis and movement. "In the liminality of tribal societies," Victor and Edith Turner remark (3), "traditional authority nips radical deviation in the bud," eliminating "open-endedness" and any "possibility that the freedom of thought inherent in the very principle of liminality could lead to major reformulation of the social structure." Myth, through the variability of language and oral transmission, may entail greater open- ness than ritual toward the undetermined future. Yet the vast majority of myths from every part of the world are also concerned with more mundane needs than ascent of the skies or conquest of death. Here again, the quest is latent or marginal,[1] though even the earthiest trickster may sometimes incongruously remind us of his never quite severed ce- lestial connections.

The heavenly spirits of tribal peoples, who in some mythologies em- body at least a former possibility of transcending ordinary humanity, are generally subordinated as objects of worship—quite apart from futile questions of temporal priority—to those of the earth and ancestral dead, just as myth is often subordinated, in religious practice, to ritual, from which it may be entirely severed as it shrivels toward the practically in- consequential and readily predictable fantasies of the fairy tale. Even when myth is closely connected with ritual, as among the Navajo, it usu- ally remains secondary, again suggesting that the opening toward the quest articulated by myth is a potentiality awaiting fulfillment, a forward thrust restrained by the massive inertia of the ceremony to which it is

---

1. In Thompson's six-volume *Motif-Index*, only tales of sections F0–F199 ("Otherworld journeys") and H1200–H1399 ("Tests of prowess: quests") pertain directly to our theme, and in most the object of the hero's journey is fulfillment of a practical need giving little indication of a transcendent dimension. Such stories might be called metaphors of the spiritual quest, but what might not? Much of the perennial charm (and eventual mo- notony) of folktales lies in their firm adhesion to the touches of untranscended nature that dependably make the whole world kin.

adjunct. The mobility embodied, for example, by the symbolism of the road and the myth of emergence in so formalized a religion as the Pueblo is kept to a well-contained minimum, since the road is identical for everyone and always leads to the same middle place; the only choice—which is virtually none at all—is to begin the journey, for once that is done, there is no other road to follow.

The Hopi, Waters remarks (192), "is content to move slowly and in unison with all around him in this pattern into which he has been inducted at birth." Navajo ritual likewise leads infallibly toward a preestablished goal. And if myths like that of the Navajo twins give splendid expression to the quest, infusing the seemingly all but mechanical chantways with a measure of variability and openness, even these—because they are so clearly handed down from a sacred past and so closely associated with chants held to be eternally changeless—draw their listeners as much backward as forward. To the latter-day Navajo the celestial quest and the possible transformation it symbolizes is forever closed except insofar as he identifies himself with mythical heroes of the past memorialized in the monotonous repetitions of ritual. For within his traditional religion, the past, made potentially variable by myth, is the future, and adherence to it his only transcendence. The Navajo, treading his pollen path, thus partakes vicariously in the indeterminate quest of myth while scrupulously performing the rites whose efficacy the slightest deviation would instantly annul.

Ritual is praxis, undertaken to produce a concrete result. But it is also communication among its participants, and what its putative invariance communicates is that nothing is new. Ritual, A. Wallace writes (1966, 233), is "communication without information," since each ritual "allows no uncertainty, no choice, and hence . . . conveys no information from sender to receiver. It is, ideally, a system of perfect order and any deviation from this order is a mistake." Sanctity itself, Rappaport suggests (1979, 209), derives from the "*quality of unquestionableness*" imputed to unverifiable postulates. From this updated Durkheimian perspective, the opportunity for questing (which presupposes questioning, and possible novelty and choice) would again seem to be minimized or precluded. Yet far from simply reaffirming the certitude of stasis, the stereotyped communication of ritual serves a "mobilizing and coordinating function" (Wallace 1966, 235–36) by preparing the organism to act more quickly than less stereotyped and more informational communication could do, since this would require time and effort, because of the novelty of its message, to be absorbed. "The accomplishment of the ritual reorganization of experience is thus," Wallace writes (239), not mere indoctrination in society's pre-established values but "a kind of learning," or at least a propaedeutic to the intensified learning that action, once initiated, will inevitably bring.

It is even possible that the sanctity associated with the invariant repetitions of ritual may have been, as Rappaport speculates (1979, 231), the stable foundation without which language and social order could not have developed during man's long evolutionary prehistory. In this case an apparently rigid structure would again have given rise to a flexible process capable of self-transcendence through adaptation to novelty and change: a prototype of the conscious quest that would eventuate from it. Quite apart from such conjectures, however, the call to action communicated by ritual in Wallace's conception endows it with a dynamic function not in the distant mythical time of foundations but in the unfinished present. The very unquestionableness of ritual, which seems to preclude the quest, may paradoxically foster it by serving as the fixed springboard for otherwise impossibly bold initiatives whose intrinsic uncertainties, outside the protective closure of ritual, demand continual adaptiveness to change and repeated choice among unpredictable alternatives— qualities inherent in every living, thinking, speaking human being, but focused most intensely in the questing hero who deliberately sets out to realize the transformative aspirations that remain potential in others.

Inasmuch as priestly ritual is conceived in tribal society as the primary form of communication with the spiritual world, it becomes the indispensable intermediary between divine and human. The role of the priest as the conservative guardian of established ritual, Firth observes (1970, 32), is reaffirmation of the existing order and traditionally accepted meanings. Through this institutionalization of religious transcendence the dynamic potentiality of ritual is safely contained and its powers channeled toward maintenance of tested traditions rather than exposed to the hazards of untried innovation. A society continually in quest of self-transformation would risk centrifugal disintegration; priestly ritual, with its orientation toward an unchanging past, offers the stabilizing assurance (as Durkheim and his school rightly stressed) that what has been found need not continuously be sought anew. Its invariance is no doubt a fiction masking a latent impetus toward change, but the fiction is supremely valuable, insofar as universally shared, in upholding the continuity of communal tradition on which the very existence of social order largely depends.

PART THREE

Spirit Possession as a Form of the Spiritual Quest

CHAPTER EIGHT

The Varieties of Spirit Possession

Communal ritual and mythic tradition are thus great stabilizers of social order. Yet if this order, like every organic structure, is a dynamic equilibrium forever adapting to change, and if man is a questing animal open to transcendence of his given condition, the very tendency of priestly ritual and heroic myth to perpetuate an immutable past guarantees their insufficiency. Variation cannot be so nearly excluded nor communication confined to one-way transmission of formulaic chants and sacrificial offerings, nor can collective ceremonies wholly satisfy the need for personal contact with the indeterminate and the wild. This uncontrollable power, safely assimilated in the liminal phase of rites of passage but never banished far from the clearing or subdued for long, can suddenly intrude with the shattering transformative force of disease or madness against which cultural prophylaxis and priestly exorcism may be, in the end, unavailing.

SPIRIT POSSESSION AS DIALOGUE: OCEANIA AND ASIA

Just as the wild irresistibly encroaches on man's laboriously tilled crops, its untamed spirits perpetually menace the cultivators themselves, who view their onslaught with panic, fear, and trembling. For not only in ritually hedged liminality do these forces bring power or destruction; the individual who survives their seizure and submits to their sway may be endowed with a capacity for communication with the divine rivaling that of the institutional priest. Among the Lugbara of Uganda, God "in his evil or immanent aspect," who lives in waste places outside the compound and is an inversion of both sky God and man, "possesses adolescent girls and drives them into the bush," Middleton writes (1960, 256;

cf. 1969, 224), whence they emerge with powers of divination. Similar experiences are common in many tribal cultures, where unforeseen possession (of both men and women) and ensuing illness often initiate a diviner's or medium's vocation.

"A Tikopia priest talked to his gods and ancestors, but they did not talk back," Firth observes (1970, 261–62); "an ordinary Tikopia, through a spirit medium, could hold two-way converse with such a spirit." Here is a relationship with the superhuman inherently more variable and dynamic than communal ritual can provide, for by inaugurating a *dialogue* the medium opens a space, which ritual had carefully fenced off, in which the unexpected and undetermined have entry. Here too there will be pattern and structure, of course, but no fiction of invariance and little coercive control: the spirit who speaks through a medium can be questioned but not commanded, anticipated but never foreknown.

Communication with the divine through spirit possession is widespread in tribal (as in other) societies from almost every part of the globe. Sometimes, as among the highly centralized Ashanti of Ghana, the spirit speaks through his priest (Busia, 194). More commonly, in Africa and elsewhere, the office of medium or diviner is distinct from the priest's, although the same person may hold both. In some tribes the diviner is identical with the medium, whom some anthropologists call "shaman." Where the two are distinguished, it is through the medium that the spirit speaks directly, whereas the diviner, though he may at first be empowered by unpredictable possession, thereafter interprets signs such as the patterns of scattered stalks or winnowed grain in accord with strict rules and conventions.

The office of medium, though not restricted by family or class (as the priest's frequently is), may be inherited by those of a given lineage who show aptitude for trance; sometimes different mediums communicate with different classes of spirits, such as ancestors or tribal gods. After first being possessed, the medium may contract a lifelong association, even a formal marriage, with a particular spirit, or may become a receptacle open to various spirits as summoned. He or she may experience trance alone, delivering oracular words which another interprets, or may share the experience with others caught up, through rhythmic dance or rhapsodic speaking in tongues, in the contagious rapture of possession. Some prophesy only on formal occasions such as festivals, others whenever requested and paid; some convey advice or information about the dead, others diagnose and prescribe for disease, or combat it by assaulting the spirits that cause it. In nearly every case, however, possession of the disciplined medium, in contrast to the demonic fury of random seizure, is a communication with the beyond voluntarily solicited, in the interest of others, through the heightened condition of trance—ranging from ecstatic frenzy to cataleptic torpor—in which the medium's ordinary self is either entirely displaced by the spirit who speaks through her mouth or strictly subjected to the dominant will of the spirit who "rides" her.

A few accounts of spirit mediumship in tribal societies, and in the popular strata of "civilized" cultures, will suggest both the phenomenological diversity and the underlying unity of its forms. (The ethnographic material has been greatly enriched since Oesterreich's classic study, *Possession*.) In Polynesia, spirit possession was no less typical of the ancient religion than ancestor worship, agricultural rites, and human sacrifice, which it complemented by permitting direct contact with the gods outside the elaborate pyramid that reached its apex in the sacrosanct chief through whom all ritual was ultimately channeled. By his mastery of magic incantations and esoteric traditions, the aristocratic priest (and a fortiori the chief) of the New Zealand Maori was believed to resurrect the dead or slay the living; yet despite his lack of such miraculous capacities, not to mention social prestige, the humble medium, when possessed, spoke with no less authority, since the god himself spoke through his mouth.

Early travelers in Polynesia, like William Ellis in Tahiti, left vivid descriptions of seances.[1] Possessed by the god, the oracular *taura* medium "became violently agitated, and worked himself up to the highest pitch of apparent frenzy," muscles convulsed, features distorted, eyes wild and strained. "In this state he often rolled on the earth, foaming at the mouth, as if labouring under the influence of the divinity by whom he was possessed, and, in shrill cries, and violent and often indistinct sounds, revealed the will of the gods." Transcendence of the everyday human condition could scarcely be more emphatic.

Throughout Micronesia, too, spirit possession is widespread. In Ulithi the medium, who trembles and may fall into an epileptic fit during possession, is the channel through whom the ancestors provide information sought by the living (Lessa 1966b, 51). In Palau "the god may possess the medium at any time, without warning. He or she will shout loudly and then start speaking in the voice of the god" (Leonard, 157). In Melanesia and New Guinea manifestations of possession trance are as varied as attitudes toward the ghosts and ancestors who are its agents. In the Solomon island of Florida, sudden trance was a vehicle for prophetic utterance; a villager, "known to have his own *tindalo* ghost of prophecy, would

---

1. Ellis, *Polynesian Researches* (London, 1829), 2:235–36, in Oliver, 80. Cf. Oliver, 94: "The distinction between shaman [*taura*] and priest [*tahu'a pure*] is quite clear-cut; the former served as a medium through which a spirit addressed humans, while the latter addressed spirits as a representative of humans."

sneeze and begin to shake, a sign that the *tindalo* had entered into him; his eyes would glare, his limbs twist, his whole body be convulsed, foam would burst from his lips; then a voice, not his own, would be heard in his throat, allowing or disapproving of what was proposed" (Codrington, 209). Among the Manus of the Admiralty Islands, as among the eastern Kyaka of the New Guinea highlands, the medium communicates between ghosts and the living through whistles, which she then interprets (Fortune, 32; Bulmer, 145). Elsewhere in highland New Guinea, the Tsembaga "smoke woman" invoked by tobacco and ritual songs enters the medium's body through the nostrils, after which the medium "dances about the embers in a low crouch, sobbing, chanting, and screaming in tongues" (Rappaport 1968, 119–20).

From the sneezing and whistling, thumping and gibbering, of Melanesia to the stately dances of Bali two thousand miles west, the cultural distance could hardly be greater; yet spirit possession is here far more central than among the warlike pig-breeders of New Guinea or the rugged mariners of the western Pacific. The everyday behavior of the Balinese, Belo notes (1), "is measured, controlled, graceful, tranquil. Emotion is not easily expressed. Dignity and an adherence to the rules of decorum are customary." Yet these people, defying Benedict's bifurcation of cultures, show a striking susceptibility to states of trance, ranging from riotous to quiescent, in which the ordinary personality is transformed by a transcendent spirit; in some places "they claimed that *all the members* of this village group, down to the smallest children, could and had entered into trance" (53). Group trance might take violent forms, as when maskers impersonating Rangda the Witch or Barong the Dragon "would go wild, rush out of the accustomed performance place into the crowd, . . . then fall unconscious and have to be revived" (3). In Gianjar district, the temple court would at times be filled with wild figures brandishing krisses, leaping, and shouting, as they enacted the giant Pig, Lion, or Witch that possessed them (66–67), and the rapt followers of Barong, men and women alike, would stab themselves with their krisses and frenziedly "hurl themselves forward to suck the gushing blood" from a fellow trancer's wounds (164). But individual mediums also communicated with the gods in more controlled ways. Those known as *sadegs* dance, shout, ask questions of the gods or answer in their name, jump up, swivel their heads, or hurl themselves backwards into the arms of others.

In parts of Sumatra, as in the very different cultures across the Strait of Malacca, communication with spirits through a medium is frequently practiced despite the influence of Buddhist, Hindu, Muslim, Christian, and secular European civilizations. In Chinese Singapore a spirit of vast powers possesses the body of the *dang-ki* medium "and enables him to inflict injury upon himself without feeling pain, and to speak with divine wisdom, giving advice to worshippers and curing their illnesses" (Elliott, 15). During a seance (63–64) the possessing *shen* spirit is summoned by deafening drums, gongs, and monotonous chants amid burning incense while the medium sits with icy body and bowed head, until trance begins. Limbs quivering, body swaying, hair flying, he staggers up as if intoxicated, then slobbers and rolls his head as he prances and mutters. As frenzy mounts, he cuts his tongue with his sword, sticks spikes through his cheeks, or climbs a sword ladder. Consultations follow as an interpreter translates mutterings supposed to come from the *shen* into an intelligible dialect (67). Finally the medium leaps into the air and is caught by an assistant. "He will never admit that he has more than a few vague memories of what has happened since he went into trance" (65).

In the north Malaysian provinces of Perak and Kelantan, a dancer enters a state of *lupa*, forgetfulness, during which he becomes a spirit's medium (Endicott 1970, 20) and rises up, possessed by a tiger-spirit; he draws blood from his arm, fights an invisible foe, sits, claps, and lies down exhausted. In Buddhist Thailand and Burma, as in Hindu Bali and Muslim Malaya, this ancient form of contact with the divine by no means vanished with the advent of "higher" religions; its need is felt most intensely in times of crisis. In northeast Thailand, the *tiam* medium diagnoses disease by answering questions in the name of the possessing guardian spirit (Tambiah 1970, 278–79). Extreme maladies, such as malignant spirit possession, require the more potent services of a "medium *cum* exorcizer" (313) who learns an incomprehensible foreign language during trance and speaks in the voice of the Buddhist angels within him as he kicks and whips the patient, or stabs him with a tiger's tooth, so that the afflicting spirit will cry out and reveal its identity (322–29).

The "*nat* wife" of village Burma becomes a medium because a nat falls in love and wishes to marry her (Spiro, 208), even against her will. As curer, she either identifies the nat responsible for an illness or learns in trance from her spirit husband the remedy of the disease. Severe mental illness may require the services of an exorcist, the "Master of the Upper Path," not a medium but a master of esoteric lore who induces possession of the patient by the offending nat whom he attempts to command (230–36). This quasi-Buddhist Master seems (241) to have taken over the original function of the female medium, leaving her role far more marginal than in many societies.

Among the Kachins of highland Burma, where mediumship may coexist with Catholic or Baptist Christianity, "the medium in a trance state is able to transport himself to the world of the nats and consult the nats in person" (Leach, 193)—a form of spirit journey reminiscent of northern shamanism. On the Indian side of the mountainous Burmese border, too, the medicine man of the Ao Nagas, on recovering from trance, speaks of having seen the patient's soul in the heavens and visited friends among the spirit-doubles dwelling there (Mills, 245). And among the Konyak Nagas, shamans were believed to visit the land of the dead in trance, and to be able to bring back a soul kidnaped from a sleeping body (Fürer-Haimendorf, 93).

Soul flight is exceptional on the Indian subcontinent, even among many Naga tribes; but spirit possession pervades the countless "Little Traditions" of village India. In many regions, from the Himalayas south, communication through mediums in trance complements the less flexible institutions of the dominant priestly religions. The frenzied Kachári medium of Assam "seems for the time to be lifted above the world of time and sense" as she decapitates a sacrificial goat in search of knowledge concerning the cause and cure of disease (Endle, 40–41). Among the Buddhist Lepchas of Sikkim in the Himalayas, everything in the lamaistic religion is theoretically fixed, like the horoscopes of the hereditary priesthood. By contrast, in the indigenous Mun religion, possession of mediums by a "private god" is not astrally predestined but inaugurated by unpredictable sickness (Gorer, 215–19). In the mountainous borderland between India and Nepal, the Brahmin priest of the Indo-Aryan Paharis performs or directs the "carefully prescribed, stereotyped, highly ritualized religious activity" of the learned or great tradition, above all through annual ceremonies and life-cycle rites (Berreman, 55–56). His actions are determined by well-known precedents and his prestige derives from inherited class status and from elaborate religious education (60–61). Complementing these priestly functions, a variety of non-Brahmanical religious practitioners concern themselves with the worldly welfare of their clients, which they promote through personal contact with the supernatural world (56).

During ceremonies of the wild Baiga tribe of tropical central India, who have been little affected by Hinduism, mediums fall into frenzy, Elwin writes (1939, 381), and "throw themselves on the ground, their limbs twitch spasmodically, they wag their heads desperately to and fro" as the god rides upon them. Among the neighboring Kol, many of whom consider themselves Hindus, acts of the Brahmin priest have more a social than a religious validity (Griffiths, 147), and worship of the local goddesses is conducted by a village medium, the *panda*, who in trance "begins to tremble, then shout, beat himself upon the ground, and become in appearance a totally different person" (159). The Hindu priest of the savage Bondo of the Orissa highlands is likewise consulted for routine matters, the medium for anything out of the ordinary. He diagnoses the trouble, Elwin writes (1950, 161), "by means familiar throughout aboriginal India; he falls into trance and prophesies; he commands the winnowing fan and the gourd; he gets drunk and his ravings are interpreted as the voice of the god."

Another Orissa tribe studied by Elwin, the Hill Saora, are noted for the complexity of their indigenous religious practices. The male medium's knowledge derives from spiritual marriage to a wife from the Under World (1955, 130–31), and the female medium is similarly wedded, despite initial refusal, to "a suitor from the Under World who proposes marriage with all its ecstatic and numinous consequences," including birth of a spirit child (147). Both male and female mediums "torment themselves with clonic convulsions; they roll on the ground, tear at their hair, sway to and fro in complete abandon, dance on their knees" (215) when possessed by the supernatural consorts who endow them with knowledge of a condition transcending their own. In all these instances from tribal cultures (as in many others, to be sure, from Hindu devotional cults of Shiva or the Goddess), the contrast with the ascetic self-denial of the learned brahmanical tradition of India could hardly be more pronounced.

TRIBAL AND INTERTRIBAL CULTS: AFRICA AND AMERICA

So widespread is spirit possession in tropical Africa, and so fully documented in anthropological literature (see Beattie and Middleton, and Zaretsky and Shambaugh), that a few examples will stand for many. Among the Dinka of the Nilotic Sudan, the "Powers" (*jok*) may possess an unsuspecting tribesman, who has little or no control over trance; a medium, on the other hand, translates the twittering sounds spoken by the divinity through him and thus channels for the public good an experience intermittently shared by others (Lienhardt 1961, 57–72). Among the neighboring Nuer, not the leopard-skin chief or priest but the prophetic medium, who alone is the "owner or possessor of Spirit" (Evans-Pritchard 1956, 44), wields greatest influence through charismatic inspiration. The priest's virtue resides in his office, the prophet's in himself, and "whereas in the priest man speaks to God, in the prophet God, in one or other of his hypostases, speaks to man" (304). Thus the medium of these nomadic and nearly anarchic cattle-breeders, far from being secondary to the priest, takes on the authoritative dignity of prophet.

Among the Mandari of the southern Sudan, possession ranges from mental disorders caused when "Spirit-of-the-Above" falls upon them to several clearly differentiated kinds of mediumship employed in healing others. The medium's call "is typified by mental crisis involving withdrawal to the bush, wandering there aimlessly, and refusal to eat, speak, or take part in social life" (Buxton 1973, 45); it is thus an individual

counterpart to the tribal initiant's liminal separation during ritual exposure to the wild. At a seance for a patient the afflicting Power (*jok*) might
either speak directly through the possessed doctor or engage in a dialogue after possession—during which the doctor's body might be uncon-
trollably convulsed and hurled against a wall, or the hut might begin to
tremble—had run its course.

In parts of Africa where ancestor worship is more prominent, spirit
possession is often closely associated with it. Among the Tallensi of
Ghana, to be sure, domination of tribal thought by the ancestors leaves
little room for other supernatural forces (Fortes and Mayer, 11), and
divination, through which ancestral demands are revealed, is "a matter-
of-fact business," making possession by a departed ancestor or any other
supernatural agency inconceivable. Elsewhere in West Africa, ancestors
are often among the spirits thought to possess their devotees, especially
at festivals in their honor. Thus among the Fon of Dahomey (Benin), the
spirits of impersonated ancestors descend into the heads of dancers possessed by them (Herskovits 1938, 1:212–18). The wild behavior characteristic of possession among other peoples is largely absent, however,
in their ceremonies both for the ancestors and for the *vodun,* or gods:
"Even during the strongest frenzy it is evident that a dancer is most
rarely, if ever, completely in a trance" (2:199). In this well-ordered former kingdom, where divine dispensation was traditionally revealed not
through ecstatic trance but through meticulous divination in the cult of
Fá, or destiny, spirit possession has been thoroughly assimilated to ritual,
in which only the most marginal variation can be granted entry. Among
the Nago-Yoruba and other Yoruba tribes of Nigeria, too (Verger, 50),
possession trances are the culmination of elaborate festivals for the *orisha,* gods widely held to be of human origin, hence not fundamentally
different from ancestors. The future is revealed through divinatory
practices such as the famous Ifá, in which the multiplicity of poems and
stories associated with each figure makes it possible for the diviner's client to choose among them (Finnegan, 154), but spirit possession permits
a more personal communication with the divine than even the inspired
interpretation of palm nuts or cowrie shells can provide.

In Ashanti, and elsewhere in southern Ghana, less relentlessly regulated forms of spirit possession find place, although the normal identification of medium with priest restrains their never-unbridled excess. An
Ashanti seized by an *obosom* spirit in the excitement of a festival may
suddenly run forth into the wilderness, whence he or she may emerge,
if at all, as an *obosomfo* priest, and even after becoming a trained mouthpiece of the spirits may unexpectedly vanish into the bush for hours or
days at a time, as if to renew inspiriting contact with the wild. Here ancestor worship is largely a prerogative of the consecrated chief; among

the neighboring Gã, where a more typically West African form of ancestor worship prevails, the agent possessing a medium at either an annual
festival or a private seance may be not only a spirit or god but one of the
dead. When possessed, rarely more than once a year at her god's big
dance, the medium "speaks with a voice not her own and greater than
that of any human being" (Field 1937, 100). Several weeks of emotional
disturbance verging on madness normally follow, and several years'
training may be required before she can recognize the spirit possessing
her and speak in its name. At a dance she trembles and struggles while
attendants dress her; then a whole string of gods come rapidly upon her:
"She may be a lame man or a hunchback, she may assume the gait and
posture of a pregnant woman or a most amusingly coquettish young
damsel," or may bark or go on all fours when seized by an animal god,
or speak a language she does not know, until she collapses in her attendants' arms (105–07).

African spirit possession remains for the most part tribal, yet a medium will often have a following nearby (the most authoritative spirits
frequently speak a foreign tongue), and the cult of one influential tribe
will sometimes be adopted, and adapted, by another, as the *jok* possession of the Dinka was by the Mandari. Even when such a complex crosses
tribal borders, however, and is acknowledged as foreign in origin, it is
usually (as diverse Nilotic usages of *jok* suggest) transformed, far more
quickly than an international religion "of the Book" such as Christianity
or Islam can normally be, in accord with existing tribal beliefs and practices, which it transforms in turn.

A notable instance is the *Cwezi* complex of the Bantu-speaking
peoples bounded by lakes Tanganyika, Victoria, and Albert. Among the
Banyoro of western Uganda, traditional religion centers on Cwezi spirits
"associated with a wonderful race of people supposed to have come to
Bunyoro many centuries ago, to have ruled the country for a couple of
generations and performed many wonderful things, and then to have
vanished as mysteriously as they came" (Beattie 1964, 143), leaving behind them the *mbandwa* mediumship "through which the Nyoro people
still retain access to the magical power and wisdom which they represented" (1969, 160). Among the Zinza of northeastern Tanzania, on the
other hand, the Cwezi spirits (*bacwezi*) are considered recent, foreign,
and malevolent, in contrast to the old and beneficent *mbandwa* (Bjerke,
42–43): "They are the spirits appropriate to a changing and anomic
world" (53). Unlike the traditional (usually female) *mbandwa* medium,
the "shaman" who protects the social order against the "*bacwezi* of the
outside" can control the spirits who possess him (140), combining the
powers of medium and medicine man, diviner and exorcist. At a seance
he shakes his rattle, sings, and calls upon the *bacwezi* to fall upon him,

but in his "lucid" possession he conveys their words in indirect discourse rather than passively surrendering himself to them.

So fundamentally do spirits bearing the same name differ that Cwezi possession is no more a truly intertribal cult among Bantu peoples of this region than is *jok* possession among Nilotic peoples further north. Only the *zar* cult—diffused through much of Ethiopia and the African horn, North Africa, and the Arabian peninsula, where Christianity and Islam had long since breached the barriers of tribal religion—deserves, for all its local variations, to be called international. (The somewhat similar *bori* cult of Nigeria and northwest Africa also crosses national borders, but is mainly concentrated among the Muslim Hausa.)

Thus in Ethiopia, patients (usually married women) afflicted by such symptoms as sterility, convulsive seizures, or extreme apathy, and thought to be possessed by amoral *zar* (or *wuqabi*) spirits, are treated by a healer who has mastered their power. Through his offices, "the zar's identity is revealed by the patient's 'individual' zar dance ('gurri'), which the spirit obliges his human 'horse' to perform publicly while the doctor watches and directs," without himself entering trance (Messing, 286; cf. Leiris, 15–18). The procedure is essentially identical in Egypt, where the practitioner attempts to convert the zar from evil to protective spirits (Fakhouri, 52). Zar possession thus resembles exorcism in that the specialist induces trance in the victim of malignant possession, with the crucial difference that here the spirit is not expelled but conciliated, so that the patient, by induction into the cult, becomes in effect a medium capable of communicating in trance with a spirit both within and beyond her, and thus of bringing under her own control dimensions of her existence previously alien to her.

Only with the near disintegration of tribal ties in the cataclysm of overseas slavery, however, did black African spirit mediumship find new forms of expression, above all in the Caribbean and Brazil, that necessarily transcended old tribal barriers. In Haiti, the complex amalgamation known in English as voodoo (from *vodun*) incorporated components of African religions, especially the Dahomean, along with others from Native Americans and French Catholic colonizers, into a new religion in which possession trance is central. Here the spirit possession frugally meted out at the annual festivals of Dahomey is dispersed, in very different degrees, among the "servitors" at large; as they dance and sing to the beating of drums in the peristyle of an *hounfor* temple after sacrifice has been made, each may become the "horse" of a *loa*—a divinity usually thought of as human in origin—who temporarily displaces the servitor's soul (*gros-bon-ange*) and animates his or her body during possession. Various degrees of initiation separate the lowest grade of *hounsi*—"spirit wife," though few are ritually wedded to a loa (Courlander, 71; cf. Métraux 1959, 212–19)—from the female *mambo* or male *houngan* medium at the top of the hierarchy. But each is repeatedly ridden, pre-eminently by the loa lodged in the servitor's head (whether by birth or ceremonial initiation) and known as *maît' tête,* who normally takes possession of the body when solemnly invoked in the ancestral *langage* of the *prière Guinée.* Any devotee can be possessed, but for important matters a trained houngan or mambo should be consulted.

Possession varies widely, not only with the individual's capacity and stage of initiation but with the nature of the loa, for these comprise a colorful pantheon of divinities from different "nations," who manifest their characteristics in those they ride. Thus a mambo possessed, as Métraux describes her (1959, 125), by the battle god Ogoun, jams a saber into her stomach, duels wildly with the temple's master of ceremonies (*laplace*), hacks at the center post of the peristyle and chases the terrified *hounsi:* possessed by another loa on another occasion she will act in a wholly different way. The American artist Maya Deren, who found herself drawn into the voodoo dances she attended in 1947, gives an extraordinary personal account (260) of the first occasion when the goddess of love, Erzulie, mounted her head:

> There is no way out. The white darkness moves up the veins of my leg like a swift tide rising, rising; it is a great force which I cannot sustain or contain, which, surely, will burst my skin. It is too much, too white, too bright; this is its darkness. "Mercy!" I scream within me. I hear it echoed by the voices, shrill and unearthly: "*Erzulie!*" The bright darkness floods up through my body, reaches my head, engulfs me. I am sucked down and exploded upward at once. That is all.

In Spanish-speaking America, the cult of *Santería,* centered in the Caribbean but with offshoots as far north as New York, has also assimilated, along with a medley of magical practices, gods worshiped in the African homeland—mainly Yoruba *orishas* identified with Catholic saints—who are capable of possessing their devotees when summoned, at a fiesta or *tambor,* by the sacred drums. But it is in Brazil that possession cults of African origin have had the widest influence, outside Haiti, on the religious life of the western hemisphere. As in *Santería,* the Dahomean *vodun* and above all the Yoruba *orishas* generally prevailed over other tribal gods and of course over local ancestral spirits (Bastide 1978, 128), and were syncretized with Catholic saints, becoming known interchangeably as *orixas* or *santos.*

In the *candomblés* of Bahia State and its capital city, Salvador, "the deities have African names and are thought to have permanent residences in Africa, and all of the songs the faithful sing are in what are supposedly African languages" (Leacock and Leacock, 284–85). As in

Dahomey and Nigerian Yorubaland, the trance states of participants in the public candomblé ceremonies "are rarely if ever spontaneous; rather, mediums always go into trance on cue, they dance together as the deities, then they come out of trance together," so that with rare exceptions the ceremonies always follow the expected pattern (286).[2] They give expression not to a Durkheimian "collective ecstasy" but to "an ordered set of individual trances," each of which, Bastide argues (1978, 237–38), has its own distinctive character.

The influence of African spirit possession on Brazilian religion permeates other cults to which various non-African peoples have more richly contributed. No sharp distinction is possible between groups known in different regions as Macumba, Umbanda, Batuque, and so forth, but in each the African nucleus has been enriched—or corrupted—by elements drawn from Catholic liturgy, Indian folklore, and European spiritism, especially in the mid-nineteenth century form given it by Hippolyte Rivail, who wrote under the name of Allan Kardec (McGregor, 86–119).

Macumba is the amorphous term most widely applied to Afro-Brazilian cults, especially in their more popular forms. (In Rio de Janeiro, where macumba originated, the word is often used in deprecation, like English "mumbo-jumbo," being replaced by Umbanda when a more respectable synonym is needed.) The medium in charge of a *terreiro*, the cult center where sacrifice is made and initiates are possessed to the beat of drums, is known as the *mãe* (or more rarely *pai*) *de santo*, the mother (or father) of the "saint" or god, translating the Nago-Yoruba terms employed also in the Candomblé. In the words of one *mãe de santo*, Maria-José, as reported by an enthusiastic French pupil, "The terreiro represents Africa, the source" (Bramly, 44), the land of life and origins, force and power (199). When possessed, "The medium has no will, no memory, no personality," and once the god has left can remember nothing that happened during trance (37). But possession is not random, for the initiate—usually female in macumba as in the candomblés—makes "a kind of pact with a god" (53) who becomes the master of her head, until, through progressive initiation, she becomes his "bride" and experiences her first controlled trance (55), which she will henceforth enter at will.

In Belém (or Salvador), the largest city of the Amazon Basin in northern Brazil, the central feature of the "Batuque"—a name also used for the cults of Rio Grande do Sul half a continent to the south—is a kind

2. Yet spirit possession is much more widely experienced even in this most conservative Afro-Brazilian cult than in the tribal festivals of West Africa, where "a small number of privileged persons" fall into trance (Rodrigues, 101).

of contract by whose terms, Seth and Ruth Leacock write (52), "the human receives the spirit and allows it to participate in ceremonies, and in return the spirit looks out for the welfare of the human being." Possession takes place, as in other Afro-American religions, to the beating of drums, the shaking of gourds, and the singing of songs and invocations at a public ceremony (*batuque*) in the open pavilion of the terreiro, and its forms again vary widely in accord both with the possessing spirit and the person possessed. Younger and less experienced initiates are especially prone to frenetic seizures. When the demonic spirits called *Exus*—after the divine intermediary of Yoruba mythology who sometimes, like Dahomean Legbá, displays unpredictable malice—are invoked at midnight (23–24), young people seized by them dance contortedly, roll on the ground, and bark like dogs to rapid clapping, drumming, and singing. But what is most admired in the accomplished medium, the Leacocks affirm (171–72), "is very often the behavior that appears the least frenzied and the most normal to the outside observer."

Finally, the merger of African spirit possession with the megalopolitan world finds expression in Umbanda, a term plastic enough to be expropriated by other sects, but referring more specifically to the syncretistic cult widely practiced in the great urban centers of Rio and São Paulo. The various Umbanda sects, whose devotees in this vast multiracial country include educated members of the predominantly white middle class, draw their core components from other Afro-Brazilian cults like the despised Macumba, segregating the sacrificial ritual and black magic of the latter from itself as Quimbanda (its dark twin and secret sharer), systematizing the spirits of its polyglot inheritance into an elaborately ordered hierarchy, and overlaying the whole with the spiritism of Kardec and the spirituality of Jesus. Of the five major types of spirits distinguished in one account from São Paulo, the Yoruba *orishas*—syncretized not only with Christian saints but, in some versions, with the Olympian gods (Pressel, 335–37; McGregor, 185–86)—are considered "so powerful that a medium would explode if possession were to occur"; they therefore send spirits of the dead from the other four categories in their place (Pressel, 338). Possession, despite occasional frenzies, is thus generally less shattering than in other Afro-Brazilian cults, tamed to the point of becoming nearly routine.

In a modern Umbanda consultation, as Bastide sums it up (1978, 332), "each client has a number, handed out to him at the entrance. . . . The medium is in paroxysm, but the initial violence has worn off. . . . The clients, also seated on low benches, recount their sad stories— unemployment, a missing husband, a rebellious child, a persistent illness. . . . The séance ends with a moral homily or a prayer." At a session in São Paulo described by Pressel (341–45), the directors collect dues and signatures in a guest book. "Somewhere near the entrance there may be a bulletin board on which various items have been posted: a notice of a fund-raising picnic; a reminder that women are not permitted to wear slacks in the center; and perhaps a few photographs of members possessed by their spirits, taken at a religious *festa*." After a brief sermon on Christian charity, some mediums spin round while spirits descend into their "horses." When the drumming stops, clients wishing to consult a spirit wait in line, sometimes taking a number at the door; the consultation may cover any subject from aches and pains to family difficulties, love problems, or even poor grades. After receiving advice the client "is rid of his bad fluids"—a Kardecist heritage—in a ritual known as *passes*. "A spirit may occasionally," despite the general decorum, "possess a member of the audience, causing the individual to shriek and shake violently," but the cult leader or an assistant, who is not himself possessed, restores calm.

Manifold though its variations may be, spirit mediumship is everywhere a potentially transformative experience of communication with a transcendent force that displaces the everyday self. But here in Umbanda a sanitized and prepackaged, almost parodic possession trance tailored for the metropolitan masses no longer threatens to shatter those whom it routinely seizes or to communicate anything of the unknown that could not have been easily conveyed by a competent guidance counselor. Despite its exotic trappings and nostalgic yearning for a mysterious Africa that is in fact all around it, this synthesis of Christ and Kardec with a spirit mediumship smacking of the palmist's salon if not of the dentist's office seems as distant from the ancestral Africa of voduns and orishas, bacwezi and jok, as it does from the age-old tribal and popular religions of India, Thailand, Malaya, Bali, or Tahiti. What is missing from spirit possession in Umbanda, for all its spinning mediums and batteries of gods, for all its elaborate spiritism and ostentatious spirituality, is precisely its spirit: the continual possibility of a never wholly predictable alteration of the given human condition through the overpowering intrusion of the divine.

CHAPTER NINE

Possession and Transformation

In Delphic priestess, Hebrew prophet, Muslim Sufi, Christian Pentecostalist, and many others outside tribal religions, communication through spirit possession is complexly intermeshed with divergent ideologies of spiritual ascent; of salvation through adherence to law, submission to God, or infusion of grace; of emancipation or extinction of the self. By contrast, the core belief of tribal spirit-possession cults—that it is not man who raises himself to the heavens in these postmythical times but the gods who descend, with individually variant and never fully predictable results, upon man—remains consistent in most instances from the tropical or subtropical regions we have been examining.

THE ARDORS OF PASSIVITY

What connection does spirit possession have with the questing dimension of religious experience? At first blush, very little, for the quester actively seeks what the medium—repeatedly described as an instrument, a vessel, a vehicle, a horse ridden by a power she cannot resist—passively awaits. During mediumship a person loses his own being, Mbiti writes (226), "and becomes simply an instrument of the spirit in him," like a radio transmitting messages between divine and human (230).

The initial call is typically conceived as an onslaught of madness or disease against which the patient struggles in vain before submitting to a destiny, a *tremendum,* too great to withstand. Even if the call is initially rejected, Buxton writes of the Mandari (1973, 277), "it is believed that the chosen individual must eventually acquiesce." The medium is helpless before a vastly superior force and can only submit to its dictates; she does not seek but is sought and, being sought, cannot refuse. Choice is

117

thus reduced to a minimum or annulled: in the Batuque, the Leacocks observe (59)—and the same might be said far beyond Brazil—"it is the encantado who initiates the relationship and not the human being. . . . No matter how much an individual may feel drawn to a particular encantado, or how much he may want to be possessed by it, there is no way in which this may come about except through the volition of the supernatural." The medium's coerced (though possibly desired) union with a familiar spirit is often a bond until death, and where change from one dominant spirit to another is possible, as in the Haitian ceremony of *lavé tête* or "washing of the head," mental derangement is a frequent consequence of so dangerous a severance (Courlander, 21–22).

Nor is the medium's self-effacing submission limited to the initial call; on the contrary, every experience of possession entails temporary annihilation of the self. Action, like choice, is indispensable to the quest, but what the possessing power requires of his vessel is not activity—only the invading spirit can act—but passivity: not actions but, Lienhardt suggests (151), their etymological opposite, *passiones,* "sufferances" (we might translate the term) which give carte blanche to the spirit's overriding superpersonal will. In this dissociated condition, as we have repeatedly seen, the medium becomes another, or a series of others, who speak and act through him; having "ceased to exist as a person," the entranced individual "is in no way responsible for his deeds or words" (Métraux 1959, 132).

Stripped of initiative, action, will, choice, and hence responsibility, the medium is less a questing voyager than the road traveled by another—a not-uncommon metaphor to express her receptive function. The journey is for the spirit to make, from his otherworldly home to the world of men, and whatever exertion it involves is the spirit's alone. "When a spirit comes into a person he may have to struggle through because," Firth writes (1967a, 301), "in Tikopia terms the person does not present a clear path or, as we should say, is not a good medium." But although the path may be blocked, the will of the medium, as always, has no effect on the outcome: "The spirit just comes all the same," and no merely human power can conceivably prevent him.

Yet the practiced medium's passivity is not the bewildered neophyte's; it is an *achieved* passivity in which the medium's exertions, though attributed to another, find fulfillment. The very word passivity, insofar as it connotes inertness rather than passionate sufferance, is misleading. Neither vehicle nor horse is static, and a vessel—the most comprehensive metaphor for the medium—is characterized by *receptivity* or *openness,* in this case to incorporation of the transformative spirit that negates the everyday self by suddenly expanding its potential actualizations. This openness to assimilation of the unknown constitutes the accomplished medium's receptiveness to the spirit: a trained passivity that is an act of voluntary surrender to the beyond through which man becomes momentarily other and more.

The literature of spirit possession repeatedly emphasizes the contrast between the convulsive spasms of the disoriented novice and the controlled trances of the authoritative medium who is no longer, in the Afro-Brazilian distinction, an undisciplined child but a mother or father of the god. The initial seizure is not always a call to the medium's vocation. Unexpected encounters with the wild can lead to destruction as well as mastery, and malignant possession, whether from witchcraft or random demons of the bush, may result in wasting illness, madness, or death unless the invading spirit is exorcized or appeased. If the seizure is diagnosed as a call, moreover, the vocation to which it summons may be that of an exorcist or diviner who will not thereafter enter possession even if inducing it in others.

The early states of an incipient medium's "uncontrolled" or "unsolicited" possession, to employ Lewis's terms (55),[1] are characteristically followed by increasingly controlled states demonstrating a degree of mastery in summoning spirits to which the medium then submits. In some cultures different categories of possession represent clearly distinguished degrees of control, as among the Tonga of Zambia where the *basangu* medium plays a public role as channel to the divine largely absent in less voluntary forms of ghost possession (Colson, 70–71), or in Bali where the relatively sedate behavior of the dancing *sadeg* mediums contrasts with that of the frenzied self-stabbing maskers of Barong the Dragon. But the distinction in degrees of control pertains above all to successive phases in a given type of medium's career.

Thus the more spectacular elements of !Kung Bushman trance performances, such as fire-walking and running amok, Lee remarks (41), were not typical of experienced trancers but "were largely confined to the young novices who would plunge into trance and exhibit uncontrolled reactions." Mandari doctors "are controlled personalities, and it is the uncontrolled, the non-professional, the sick and the immature who suffer inappropriate or adventitious possession" (Buxton 1973, 42). Among the Nago-Yoruba, "the first possession fits, which come before initiation, are often wild and violent; but under the supervision of the head priest of the god, they become calm and settled after a short period in his temple" (Verger, 51). In Afro-Brazilian cults such as the Batuque of Belém, the most admired behavior is often the most apparently nor-

---

1. Lewis's "more neutral" terms *uncontrolled/controlled* and *unsolicited/solicited* or Oesterreich's comprehensive *involuntary/voluntary* (236–43) are preferable to Bourguignon's *negative/positive* or *pathological/non-pathological* (1968, 6).

mal, and in Haiti, where elaborate rites such as the kanzo or *brulé zin* ("boiling pot") mark the passage to higher stages of control, "the houngan eventually establishes a conditioned, formalized response to possession, and once this is achieved, the loa is regarded as having been tamed" (Courlander, 11).[2]

The distinction between controlled and uncontrolled spirit possession in tribal cultures is similar to that made in Oughourlian's psychology of mimetic desire between possession and hysteria. Possession, he writes (179–80), "understood in the true sense, that is, as adorcism" (in contrast to exorcism),

> is the recognition or acknowledgment [*reconnaissance*] of the interindividual relation and the mimetic character of desire. Hysteria is its misunderstanding [*méconnaissance*]. . . . Consequently, possession is *submission* to the other, the taking of the other as a *model* and as the origin of the self's desire. Hysteria, in contrast, is *revolt*, strife, insurrection against the other. . . . Possession manifests *identification*, whereas hysteria manifests an *inability to identify*. . . . Possession is accompanied by catharsis. But no cathartic process is really possible in hysteria.

The medium's true mastery thus lies in the fullness of her recognition and acceptance of the otherness to which she is willingly open and which she thereby incorporates into herself.

The novice becomes a medium to the extent that she is able, through discipline and training, to turn initially involuntary spirit possession to the *use* of others through controlled communication with the spirit world—a use requiring that her behavior be "intelligible or able to be interpreted," Firth writes (1967a, 296), and therefore that it "follow some fairly regular, predictable pattern, usually of speech." Though not a true "master of spirits" like the North Asiatic shaman, the practiced medium is far from a merely passive instrument of forces wholly external to her and thus altogether beyond the reach of her powers.

The vocation thrust upon her against her will must thenceforth be repeatedly won, for in order to convert the potentially destructive onslaught of the untamed spirit to advantageous ends, the medium must actively seek and in some measure command the transformative influx that will no longer come unbidden. To the extent that the Nuer prophet, like every medium, is "the mouthpiece of a spirit" and "speaks under its control," Evans-Pritchard remarks (1956, 304), he may seem the mere implement of another's will. But in contrast to the ordinary Nuer, the prophet is a seeker: one who "sought inspiration, entry of Spirit into

2. On the *brulé zin* and other Haitian initiation rites, see Courlander, 41–44; Métraux 1959, 192–212; and Deren, 220–24.

himself and its filling him; and in seeking it, he could not but have been aware of the influence it would bring him" (307).

The medium possessed by a spirit cannot simply be considered, then, a passive conductor of messages originating in undisciplined impulses from without or within, from the heights of the spirit or the depths of the psyche; her trained receptivity to powers beyond and within her is a hard-sought and always perilous attainment. But this necessary disciplining of initially uncontrolled seizures raises the question of the medium's susceptibility not to impulse but to the conventional expectations of her social role: the possibility, that is, of another kind of passivity. Older interpretations of possession trance (propounded for Afro-Brazilian religions by Nina Rodrigues and Ramos) as fits of hysteria or even epilepsy have rightly given way to the emphasis of Bastide (306) and others on "the discipline of the cult, the control of ecstasy," understood as a normal social phenomenon (310). But does this replacement of a psychiatric by a sociological thesis imply that the medium has exchanged one domination for another, becoming the instrument not of neurotic frenzies externalized as spirits but of pre-established behavior patterns regulated, like ritual in general, by an inflexible communal tradition to which she unconsciously conforms?

Bastide was writing in particular about possession of dancers at stylized festivals like those of Dahomey and the candomblés of Brazil, in which spirit trance shares in the putative invariability of priestly ritual. Here dance is paramount, and the dancer's movements, attributed to the possessing spirit, are regulated almost as rigorously as other aspects of ritual, leaving slender if any margin for individual expression. Up to a point, similar observations apply to almost all spirit possession, individual as well as communal, seemingly ecstatic no less than rigidly controlled. All varieties of trance behavior in Bali, Belo writes (1), "bear the imprint of cultural patterning" in children and adults, self-stabbers and *sadegs*. And among mothers of sick children possessed by *jok* in frenzied seances of the Nilotic Alur scarcely less than among performers at Dahomean tribal festivities, "dancing and trance alike are highly stylized, even at their most violent, following a pattern to which all have been mentally and physically conditioned from infancy, so that to become possessed is itself to give oneself up to a pre-ordained pattern" (Southall 243).

In this light the medium's "controlled" surrender is not to erratic psychic impulses but—with equal servility—to predictable social norms. Society masquerading as a god would appear to possess the medium, just as Society is the hidden object of worship, for Durkheim, in all ritual. So inert a conformity to collective expectations can hardly be characterized as a quest: not if the medium can discover, albeit unwittingly, only what was given to start with.

Yet involuntary and voluntary possession suggest not merely two successive phases of passivity—surrender to uncontrollable powers of the "wild" followed by compliance with socially dictated behavior patterns—but a tension between opposing demands in whose interplay lies the medium's margin of freedom and opportunity for discovery. The "remarkable general similarity" in the speech and behavior of mediums during trance among the Hill Saora of India, as elsewhere, by no means excludes an "endless diversity in detail" permitted by absence of the rigid program of priestly ritual, nor the possibility that once a medium enters trance "anything may happen" (Elwin 1955, 470). The cultural pattern, however pervasive, is not the sole determinant of the possessed medium's behavior but the matrix giving shape to forces through whose conflict the unexpected can arise. Without the cultural pattern spirit possession could not become a communicable experience, but if every impulse were defined by that pattern alone there would be no experience to communicate, and the medium's message, like that of ritual, would be a continuously repeated self-referential tautology, "communication without information."

Such would be the case if the medium's behavior were totally controlled. As Firth writes, however (1967a, 306), in most performances "there seemed to be some kind of balance between involuntary behaviour and the exercise of personal control"; trance was unpredictable, but "most of the events within it followed a fairly set pattern." Because of this tension between individual impulse and cultural pattern the medium communicates, as she professes, something beyond the socially constituted self that she shares with others—hence something transcendent.

Thus the medium's progression from largely involuntary to increasingly controlled states of possession need not be understood as passive conformity with social conventions, for these patterned states—like the seemingly self-enclosed genome, the repetitive Freudian id, the fixed grammatical component of language, and every other organic and cultural structure—are dynamic systems never wholly closed to the outside world. The behavior of both disciplined medium and the person seized by a malignant spirit "tends to be largely stereotyped, to conform to a kind of code. But what is particularly interesting here," Firth suggests (1969, xi), "is that in many societies the code of the medium is used to provide an interpretation of the code of the possessed patient. Under pressure of the social conventions, the medium in *his* spirit terms works out the stresses which the patient displays in *his*," thus turning to purposeful use, through the interplay of codes as open systems, an impetus that might otherwise remain destructively undirected.

The medium's interpretive code is pre-eminently *linguistic,* since speech during spirit possession is a hallmark of the most practiced mediums: in others the spirit may move but through these it *speaks.* And unlike the fixed movements of the dance, language, once released by the solvent of trance from the formulaic repetitiveness of ritual, can never be confined to the self-referential closure of communicating absence of newness, but by its assimilation of experience will continually create the indeterminate future to which information alone pertains.

Through the creative power of speech the medium thus introduces into spirit possession a dimension of purposeful change lacking in its involuntary manifestations; her "interpretation" typically takes the form of prognosis, revealing not only the patient's current condition and its causes but the potentiality for transforming that condition as the medium has already done. Language, quintessentially patterned by culture, is therefore truly a manifestation of spirit, conceived precisely as the potential for purposeful self-transcendence inherent in all living things: a potential apprehensible only through the symbol understood (in Peirce's sense) as *esse in futuro.* Spirit possession interpreted through the medium's never wholly stereotyped language thus opens, like myth, onto an undetermined future. To this degree the structure of ecstasy, Bastide observes (1961, 252), "is equal to the structure of myth, which serves it as a model"; both complement the invariance of ritual by extending its latent (or liminal) dynamic dimensions, and thereby reorient tribal religious activity away from exclusive concern with affirmation of the communal past toward incorporation of the variable and the new.

Even more than myth, however, whose subject matter looks back to a legendary past, verbal communication attributed to the spirit in trance pertains explicitly to present and future needs of living individuals in transition or crisis. And unlike myths, which frequently become dissociated from ritual, spirit mediumship, where it exists among tribal peoples, is an integral part of religious praxis—one which may even (as in Tikopia)[3] briefly survive more conservative forms of ritual long associated with it in the dialectic of closure and openness, stasis and change.

Inasmuch as the medium's practice finds culminating expression in speech ascribed to spirit, then, her trance can by no means be dismissed

3. Returning to Tikopia in 1952, Firth (1967a, 294–95) found only small sectors of the largely Christian community practicing such pagan rites as the Work of the Gods, yet spirit mediumship was still flourishing as in 1928–29. But during a third visit in 1966, when all pagan ritual had lapsed, everyone agreed that mediumship "had ceased completely and I could find not the slightest evidence of any private or secret practices of this order" (356).

as mere compliance with preordained social norms but must be understood as an actively pursued state of indeterminacy whose communications pertain essentially not to what is given but to what remains to be found and must therefore, with no certainty of its outcome, be continually sought. Both that uncertainty, that possibility (rigorously excluded from priestly ritual in all but its carefully confined liminal phases) that the unexpected *may* happen, and the stereotyped redundancy of most messages against which such novelty can be measured, are fundamental to the medium's capacity to convey information held to derive from a realm of the spirit surpassing the everyday self: a transcendent realm made immanent in the incarnated word. To communicate this "news of the beyond" is the never fully attainable object of the spirit medium's often arduous quest.

DANCING TOWARD THE UNKNOWN

The word "medium" carries inevitable connotations in modern western languages of dubious if not fraudulent practices ranging from table-turning to ouija boards and other forms of fortune-telling. But in contrast to the spiritism of modern Europe and America, which grew up in reaction to both institutional Christianity and positivistic science, the spirit mediumship of tribal religions is in its own context by no means reactionary. On the contrary, as the communally sanctioned complement to priestly ritual, it has generally been associated with an opening toward the unknown, a potentially transformative exploration of the new.

This does not, however, imply that the claims of mediums are universally believed by their credulous followers, or that their ecstatic performances are always free of the deceptions rampant in Western spiritism—and not unknown in Western science. Both tribesman and anthropologist may be skeptical with good reason of inspired pronouncements, knowing how easily trance can be dissembled. Yet the undoubted (and sometimes openly acknowledged) pretense noted by Nina Rodrigues in his pioneering study of Afro-Brazilian candomblés (103–04)— and by many ethnologists since—in no way contradicts the "profound conviction" of their devotees. The conclusion that for those who experience it "trance is very real" (Bastide 1961, 251), though often pretended, is reinforced positively by many instances of the possessed medium's increased physical powers and immunity to pain, and negatively by occasional failure to achieve a condition so ardently sought. "I myself saw *filhas-de-santo* desire trance, do everything, with touching good will, to be possessed by the god," Bastide writes (1973, 303–04), "without achieving anything. . . . This proves that simulation is neither general nor normal in Afro-Brazilian religion."

Not only initiates but experienced mediums may fail to enter trance: "Despite everything," Colson writes (76) of the Tonga of Zambia, "the medium may not be able to involve the spirit," which sometimes refuses to speak. Such instances, though very rare—normally the accomplished medium can enter possession almost at will—contrast sharply with the supposed infallibility of properly performed spells and rituals. However great a degree of control the medium has attained, a remote possibility exists that the unpredictable spirit, who can be summoned but not coerced by drumbeat and song, may not deign, after all, to descend.

More fundamentally, our preoccupation with distinguishing pretended from genuine states is largely alien to tribal religion. The Dinka recognize that early stages of possession may be counterfeited, Lienhardt observes (1961, 235), but "unlike us they do not think that this voluntary co-operation of the conscious person in any way invalidates his final state of possession as coming from a source other than himself." Conscious manipulation thus precedes and may even, up to a point, accompany the medium's surrender to a transcendent and therefore unknowable power, suggesting a *purposeful* quest for an indeterminate object.

"Every possession has a theatrical aspect," Métraux comments (1959, 126); in Haiti as elsewhere the medium's impersonation of a familiar spirit is a skilled performance enhanced by elaborate costumes and props. In great festivals such as the Brazilian candomblés (Bastide 1961, 249–51), dances tend toward theatrical representation in which various trances follow a mythic scenario. The fact of dramatic impersonation need not, however, any more than occasional dissimulation, suggest that spirit possession is "only" an acted and not a genuine experience. For in this primitive theater there can be no paradox of an actor self-consciously distinct from his role: person and persona are one, and to *act*—for drama is essentially praxis, or action—is to *be* the god. The theatrical aspect of possession is not a sign of deception but of involvement, by both actors and audience, in a drama of roles vastly surpassing those of everyday life, a drama of spiritual transcendence, of the human capacity for harboring the divine. The "theater" of spirit possession is not a theater of artifice only but, as Leiris (90–91) calls the Ethiopian zar, "a lived theater," *un théâtre vécu*, whose life is that of the spirit which infuses the body with its unbounded potentiality and thus immeasurably expands the momentarily nullified self.

The tribal priest, Firth writes (1970, 32), finds his role in "reaffirmation of the existing order and traditionally accepted meanings. He tends to be conservative." The medium, who responds to a personal call, generally occupies a more ambiguous social position; but as the priest's institutional counterpart does she, or the spirit possessing her, equally reaffirm, in the end, the rightness of the traditional order? Her patterned trance, as Herskovits emphasizes for Haitian voodoo (1966, 359), follows rules well understood and accepted by all. Possession, in Bastide's words (1973, 310), "is a normal phenomenon because it is a social phenomenon." Those subject to spirit possession—pre-eminently practiced mediums—appear for the most part, to both ethnographers and fellow-tribesmen, "physically and mentally normal" individuals, as Gelfand (133) writes of the Shona of Zimbabwe, well in control of their emotions. With conspicuous exceptions, African mediums, like most others, are not deviants, homosexuals, epileptics, or misfits, Beattie and Middleton observe (xxiii–xxiv); "often indeed they are chosen expressly for their moral probity and virtue," and may even (as among the Ashanti) be priests. Although attitudes toward the medium vary widely both among different cultures and within a given culture, only rarely will one be regarded, like the "nat wife" of Burma (Spiro, 209–10), with widespread contempt. As a rule, despite the extraordinary experiences she undergoes during trance, the medium is no dissenter, much less a rebel, against a social order that readily accommodates such experiences to its norms; she in no way threatens things as they traditionally are.

In contrast to priests, however, who belong to the upper classes in most socially differentiated societies, tribal mediums are often drawn from the lower orders. The priesthood is generally a closed corporation allied (when not identical) with the governing class, but communication through spirit possession is often open to all, including those (like women) normally excluded from other prestigious activities. Among the Banyoro of western Uganda, for example, women have low social status and are subservient to men, but as mediums, Beattie notes (1969, 169), they can command respect and earn a substantial income. The predominance of women is especially notable in cults like the North African zar and Brazilian candomblé, where possession is widely disseminated among the initiates. In Ethiopia, members of the lower classes, such as the Sudanese Muslim minority, find social contact across religious barriers in the zar cult, most of whose members are married women neglected in a man's world; even ex-slaves from alien tribes are admitted to full membership (Messing, 286). And in Bahia, Landes remarks in her extraordinary memoir of a visit to Brazil during 1938–39, *The City of Women* (148), "mothers" and priestesses of the candomblé did not marry, since submission to a husband was incompatible with female dominion. In this cult ruled by African American women the hierarchy of the outside world is turned decisively upside down.

Such facts led I. M. Lewis to consider "peripheral" possession cults of this kind as "thinly disguised protest movements directed against the dominant sex" (31) by women channeling, through "ritualized mutiny"

(114), the "revolutionary fervour" (116) and "pent-up resentment" (117) of "the weak and downtrodden" (72) against their social and sexual superiors—a function diametrically opposed to the conservative role of the priesthood. A "feminist sub-culture, with an ecstatic religion restricted to women and protected from male attack through its representation as a therapy for illness" (89), aspires by "an oblique strategy of attack" (117), in Lewis's view, "to achieve entirely new positions of independence and power" (97). Many forms of spirit mediumship no doubt serve as a protest, or recompense, for those whose rank or sex excludes them from a more authoritative role in societies whose immutable order priestly ritual insistently affirms, but Lewis's bellicose interpretation requires, at the very least, qualification.[4]

Indeed, although mediumship is usually open to a broader social spectrum than the priesthood (when the two are distinguished), most mediums—both male and female—in tribal societies are not downtrodden outcasts rebelling against their inferior status but highly respected members of their community admired by men and women alike. Nor is the change in condition effected by cults like the zar always liberating, since "individual adepts may become involved in new situations of dependence" even more binding than the old (Morton, 198). More fundamentally, insofar as spirit possession can be called a channel of protest at all, its main effect, as Lewis well understands (86), is to uphold "the official ideology" ("male supremacy" or whatever), since it "ventilates aggression and frustration largely within an uneasy acceptance of the established order of things" (120–21).

4. Lewis's main examples of sexual polarization, the Hausa *bori* cult and the *zar* of Ethiopia and North Africa (including Somaliland, where his field work was done), are far from typical of tribal religions. In both cases the official religion (Islam or Christianity) is an international one introduced from without and bringing major social changes. Lewis (82) quotes Onwuejeogwu's assertion (290) that "In *Bori*, women find an escape from a world dominated by men, and through *Bori* the world of females temporarily subdues and humiliates the world of men." But Onwuejeogwu also notes (281–82) that before complete Islamization of the Hausa in 1804–10, women were sometimes politically equal to men, serving as rulers and holding political office. As Muslims, they lost their pre-Islamic political, legal, and economic freedom, becoming completely dependent on husband or kin. The bori possession cult, far from arising as a protest movement, apparently occupied a central place in Hausa religious life until intensification of Islamic belief thrust it into a subsidiary position as men gravitated toward male-dominated Muslim rituals (Onwuejeogwu, 291). Only the loss of its former influence made it a peripheral cult. Sexual polarization and protest against it (insofar as a cult in which prostitution is common can be called a protest against male domination!) are thus not inherent to the bori *qua* possession cult but probably arise from its recent historical status as the remnant of a religion in which men and women once participated in mediumship together, as in many tribal societies. Even now, male experts in medical or magical practices are frequently consulted in the bori (290–91), and in the Ethiopian zar the healer in charge of the ceremony in which possessed women dance is often male.

"Homeostatic" reconciliation of social tensions by incorporating potential outsiders into communal religious life is characteristic of tribal religion in general, whether in rites of passage or rituals of stereotyped rebellion. In the end the medium too challenges social norms (if at all) only to confirm them. The Tikopia medium's wildest fantasy, Firth remarks (1967a, 314; cf. 1970, 29), uses conventional concepts and follows ordinary norms of etiquette and morality, allowing him "to express his desire for self assertion . . . harmlessly in a manner which does not conflict with existing social privileges." The medium's relative freedom of expression under the spirit's sway knows its limits within a social order indispensable to it; it is not a rebellion or protest against that order itself.

Lewis's contention that possession cults are a means of protest against dominant (mainly male) social values has been both endorsed and disputed. None of the cases adduced in support of his thesis, however, concerns the more controlled and authoritative forms of trance in which the spirit is held to *speak* through the medium. Thus Haitian voodoo, where both male houngan and female mambo speak with full authority of the god, cannot properly be classified, as Bourguignon has demurred (1976, 35; cf. 50, 53), either as an "amoral peripheral possession" cult or a "protest" religion: for only cults *un*able to challenge the pretensions of alien beliefs need confine themselves to so feeble a role. In most tribal situations, where priest and medium are allied when not identical, Firth's recognition of the interdependence of center and periphery seems a more judicious appraisal than Lewis's disproportionate emphasis on mutiny and attack.

Yet the opposite emphasis can be equally misleading. As channels for ancestral wisdom, spirit mediumship cults may indeed be "a powerful force for social conformity" (Beattie 1969, 170); by their "dramatic restatement of the ultimate values of community life" and demand for compliance with them, they can play a fundamentally conservative role in preventing changes and upholding tradition (Horton, 26–27). In this context spirit possession is little more than an appendage of institutional ritual, whose confirmation of established tradition it colorfully reinforces.

Yet even if the medium's pronouncements were "an elaboration rather than a criticism" of values upheld by priests and aristocrats in Tikopia, spirit mediums, Firth reminds us (1967a, 309), were always "a possible countervailing force" in a traditional system of checks and balances. Indeed, as Lannoy writes (201) of the ecstatic oracles of India's "Little Traditions"—the tribal religious inheritances that coexist with the "Great Tradition" of Hinduism—the potentially uncontrollable powers incarnated in the medium not only "balance" but "in some cases menace" (hence check) those of the Brahmin priest "by restoring the element of disorder which normal regulation has outlawed." The relation of spirit mediumship to priestly ritual is not simply one of protest or insurrection, then (though this may arise when "official" religion is seen as alien), but of interaction in which the less formulaic, more exploratory ecstatic cult at the institutional periphery is continually extending (above all in times of crisis) the boundaries of the more conservative priestly religion toward assimilation of the unknown.

The *creative* role of mediumship in tribal religion finds expression, Firth suggests (1970, 284–85), in expanded information about the spirit world, in creation of new spirit entities, and in initiating social action. Because the actions and words of the possessing spirit, stereotyped though they may be, are never formulaically fixed as those of ritual ideally are, they are subject to continuous individual variations endowed with the prestige of the divine. The medium's relative freedom to improvise during trance—in contrast to the priest's obligation to maintain ancient traditions to the letter—makes certain possession cults, however conservative their social function, "a promising channel," Horton observes (46), "for innovations in belief and doctrine which may eventually come to assume importance in the community at large." Spirit possession is thus a principal means by which mobility enters into tribal religions otherwise overwhelmingly oriented, by ritual, ancestor worship, and the content (if not the form) of myth, toward the timeless past.

In a religion like Haitian voodoo to which possession trance is central, religious innovation arising from states of dissociation in trance is frequent (Bourguignon 1965, 55). The Himalayan Pahari medium, too, Berreman observes (58), "has considerable leeway for choice and originality, a fact demonstrated by the diversity and the constant and surprisingly rapid turnover in gods worshiped in the Pahari village." Unlike the fixed rites performed by the Brahmin who memorizes age-old formulas, the details of each Pahari medium's performance are unique (61), thereby introducing constant novelty into the religious life of the people. Innovation alleviates the frustrations of lower-caste mediums' positions (63) not through protest against the existing religious system but by incorporation of the variations which give them, as opposed to the conservative Brahmins, their authority. The potential for adaptation and growth that characterizes any religious—indeed, any living—system, though latent in ritual and myth, thus finds full expression in the institution of mediumship which consistently ascribes it, however, not to any human effort but to the incursion of a power external to man.

The innovation characteristic of spirit-medium cults is evident not only in the expanded powers and multiple identities experienced—if not normally remembered—by the person possessed, but in the aura of newness and foreignness that often adheres to these cults as opposed to reputedly (and sometimes demonstrably) older priestly institutions. The Nuer prophet, the Mandari *jok* doctor, the Zinza *bacwezi* doctor, like other mediums, gain prestige not as upholders of age-old traditions but as innovators able to communicate with newly assimilated foreign spirits and to speak, very often, in a foreign tongue. This reaching out to embrace the alien and the new exemplifies the expansion of information, or extension of horizons, characteristic of spirit possession in its orientation toward the unknown future; and the possessing spirits, benign or malignant, may accordingly be far from traditional. The "black" *mbandwa* in Bunyoro, all of foreign origin, include spirits of tanks, airplanes, and Europeans (Beattie 1969, 161); and among the *masabe* spirits viewed by the Tonga as "something new, appearing within living memory," are an Airplane spirit and train dancers who whistle like a locomotive (Colson, 94, 86–88). By no stretch of imagination could such a possession cult be considered a form of ritual immutably inherited from ancestral times; the adaptive incorporation of change, indeed, is its essence.

As we might expect, new forms of mediumship tend to arise in response to crisis or rapid social change. In such situations, where the perennial need to explore the unknown is dramatically intensified, mediumship, Beattie and Middleton observe (xxviii–xxix), is both a means to incorporate change and a basis for legitimizing new authority. To the Nilotic Alur of northwest Uganda, *jok* possession, unlike less flexible forms of ritual, assimilates the disruptive changes that threaten the traditional, essentially closed society with disintegration. By contrast to this closure, Southall writes (265), the recently invading *jok* spirits "are as mobile as modern man." Because the new cults not only represented the problems and anxieties of a changing world but also, through controlled inducement of possession in those afflicted by these uncertain spirits, provided new techniques of treatment (266), the medium became, as in many other tribal societies, an agent of change identified not with the fixity of the old but with the mobility of the new: no mere protester against the inherited past but, in potential, a charismatically inspired prophet guiding his people in quest of an unpredictable future.

The "essentially reciprocal element in men's relations with the spirit-world" noted by Beattie and Middleton (xxii) is paramount in possession trance, with its rapidly shifting roles and its culminating exchange of questions and answers channeled through the medium from man to spirit and from spirit to man. What most characterizes the medium's relation with spirit, then, is not passivity but interaction, and in this dialogue at its fullest "man takes the initiative," like the Mandari *jok* doctor (Buxton 1973, 94–95), "in establishing a reputed communication with para-normal forces, reversing the order of traditional man-spirit communication." Instead of idly awaiting the spirit's descent, or ritually compelling its presence, he "deliberately sets out to call his Power, to question it and to discover its needs."[5] Lacking any means to coerce this protean force, or any assurance where it will lead when it seizes upon him, the medium's invocation of spirit is in essence a quest without end.

The marginal uncertainty of its outcome marks the medium's solicitation of trance as a quest, for in a domain of mobility never subject to full conscious control, no cultural pattern, however ingrained, can preclude the unexpected. In most cases Tikopia spirit mediumship, in contrast to fixed rituals, "related to situations of uncertainty," Firth observes (1967a, 293); the medium's function was "to resolve a situation of some anxiety and ambiguity." But the resolution can only be provisional, for recurrent uncertainty is itself a condition of any form of communication that (unlike the invariant repetitions of ritual) conveys information and helps create a future distinct from the determinate past. "A message conveys no information unless some prior uncertainty exists in the mind of the receiver about what the message will contain," Jeremy Campbell writes (68), summarizing the findings of twentieth-century information theory: "And the greater the uncertainty, the larger the amount of information conveyed when that uncertainty is resolved." To resolve this uncertainty once and for all would be to annul the essence of spirit possession and reduce it to ritual.

Only inasmuch as it responds to the uncertainty of a changing world, then, can the spirit mediumship of tribal religion communicate the new. The often amoral spirits with which the medium communes "stand for moral indeterminacy and an uncertain universe," and their outlook, Nadel declares (1946, 34), is "a philosophy of uncertainty"; for spirit possession "absorbs all that is unpredictable and morally indeterminate," and thus "saves the conception of an ordered universe from self-contradiction." Its practitioners explore and assimilate the seeming chaos of the undetermined without whose controlled infusion the social order insistently affirmed by ritual to be immutable could not adapt or long survive. The medium "dancing on the edge of the unknown," in Seth and Ruth Leacock's phrase (2), is dancing where she must, though she give the appearance, in doing so, of folly or madness: for on that edge, or just beyond it, the goal of every spiritual quest must continually be sought.

5. Such interdependence and human initiative characterize mediumship primarily in its more voluntarily controlled manifestations, like Mandari *jok* possession. In "orthodox" Mandari possession, Buxton notes (95), "'Above' falls upon a man arbitrarily. To attempt to summon the spirit would be unthinkable."

PART FOUR

Forms of the Shamanic Quest

CHAPTER TEN

Shamanism, Possession, and Ecstasy

Australia and the Tropics

Like myth, which looks to the undetermined future as well as the sacro-sanct past, spirit mediumship, especially in less standardized forms cul-minating in oracular speech, provides an essential counterpart to the putative closure of ritual by its continual opening toward unrealized potentialities of human existence. The practiced medium's voluntary so-licitation of a condition that surpasses her ordinary powers and leads her toward an intrinsically unpredictable goal thus exhibits the form of a spiritual quest as a purposeful exploration of the transcendent unknown.

Yet the uncertainties of this formalized quest are severely circum-scribed by its practical function within the institutional structure of tribal religion. The information imparted during trance most often pertains, as Lessa writes of Ulithi (1966b, 51), to such immediate concerns as "the feasibility of an ocean voyage, the safety of relatives away from home, the cause of an illness, the attitude of a loved one, the approach of a typhoon." The future revealed through the medium's words or the di-viner's interpretation of signs is a very constricted future holding out no prospect of fundamental change beyond restoration of health or increase of fortune; for in tribal thought the future, as we have seen, is in general an underdeveloped forward extension of the overshadow-ing past.

The medium's personal transformation by possession trance is a tem-porary change without major consequence (in most instances) for daily life. Her self-perception as the passive implement of a power beyond her control reduces, moreover, the extent to which she actively partici-pates in shaping its responses (thus in shaping the future), and increases her tendency to fall back on cultural stereotypes restricting both the uncertainty that initiates the quest and the transformative encounter with the new that is its goal. Only in exceptional cases does the recognized medium *fail* to enter trance and transmit the spirit's words—and without risk of failure the quest through spirit possession can never go far toward transcending the ancestral certainties of ritual to which it remains, in many tribal religions, firmly linked.

THE SHAMAN AS ECSTATIC MASTER OF SPIRITS

In some cultures, however, instead of awaiting descent of a spirit summoned to possess his body and speak through his mouth, the medium himself sets out, or sends helping spirits under his command, to another world in search of what cannot be found in his own. This figure, in whom the spiritual quest becomes a fully active pursuit of transcendence, we shall call the shaman, using a term which for many writers is synonymous with medium.

Thus for Nadel (25) the shaman "is a passive medium when possessed; but through his ability to induce possession, he is also a master of these supernatural powers." This criterion derives from the studies of Kroeber (1907, 327) and from those of Shirokogoroff (1935a, 271), who saw the Tungus (Evenk) shaman, from whose language the word derives, as "a *master of spirits,* at least of a group of spirits." But control over possessing spirits is characteristic of all disciplined mediums, so that any distinction based on mastery alone is one of degree. To that extent, Lewis is justified in including, like Nadel, the African medium in his understanding of the shaman (188–89) as "not the slave, but the master of anomaly and chaos," whose hard-won control of affliction he repeatedly re-enacts. The shaman, so defined, is a medium able to induce possession at will and for controlled ends by spirits whose helpless victim he, like others less in command of anomaly, once was. He cures others' afflictions by mastering his own and thus becomes a doctor by having ministered, when a patient, to himself.

This understanding of shamanism, endorsing its identification by earlier anthropologists such as Frobenius (2:561) with the "religion of possession" practiced, for example, in the *bori* cult, did not go unquestioned. Thus for Oesterreich (305) the "original Shamanism" of northern Asia consisted not in possession but in visual phenomena; to call possession states shamanism was "a misuse of words" (309). And Eliade, in his monumental study *Shamanism,* distinguished the shaman (1964, 5) not by visionary but by ecstatic trance, "during which his soul is believed to leave his body and ascend to the sky or descend to the underworld."

Ecstasy, as Eliade conceives it, is sharply differentiated from possession. The shaman's mastery is shown not in voluntarily inducing possession by spirits who control *him* during trance but in his own control over spirits through whom he communicates with the beyond without becoming their instrument. Shamans do sometimes appear to be possessed, Eliade concedes (6), but these exceptional cases often turn out to be only apparent. The shaman is always an active agent and never merely a vehicle, as is the medium, for another; his ecstasy, far from annulling the self, frees it to realize to the fullest powers normally beyond its reach.

Thus the "specific element" of shamanism, Eliade concludes (499), is not the shaman's embodiment of spirits but the ecstasy of ascent to the sky or descent to the underworld. This criterion has by no means been universally accepted. Findeisen characterizes the shaman (7) as a possession priest (*Besessenheitspriester*); and Lewis takes explicit issue (50) with Eliade's division between spirit possession and shamanism. The two regularly occur together, he remarks (51), "particularly in the Arctic *locus classicus* of shamanism"; the Tungus evidence of Shirokogoroff, for example, "makes nonsense of the assumption that shamanism and spirit possession are totally separate phenomena" (55–56). If the shaman, as Lewis affirms with Firth, is a voluntarily possessed master of spirits, all shamans are mediums who "function as a 'telephone exchange' between man and god." [1]

But if possession is sometimes part of the shaman's experience (as Eliade never denied), it is not definitive as it is for the medium. "There are certainly transitions with combinations of both phenomena, shamanism and mediumism," Paulson writes in concurrence with Eliade, "but basically there is a great difference in kind between them. Possession is more a characteristic of mediumism, the 'soul-journey' (the dispatching of the so-called free-soul, i.e., the person himself), however, a characteristic of shamanism" (Bäckman and Hultkrantz, 21). The shaman may appear to be seized by an alien spirit but he typically remains wholly himself while becoming other. In imitating the voice and gestures of his helping spirits or of the divinities he visits, he engages in a dialogue in

1. The very passage from Eliade (reaffirming his distinction between ecstasy and possession) which Lewis dismisses as "nonsense" on the basis of Tungus evidence occurs in the context of Eliade's argument (1964, 499–500) that Tungus shamanism as portrayed by Shirokogoroff is in its present form "strongly influenced by Lamaism" and "cannot be considered a 'classic' form of shamanism, precisely because of the predominant importance it accords to the incarnation of 'spirits' and the small role played by the ascent to the sky." In citing Firth's criterion of the shaman as a "master of spirits," Lewis likewise fails to note that Firth preferred to use shamanism "in the limited North Asiatic sense" (1964, 298), and found "spirit possession and spirit mediumship in Tikopia but not shamanism" (1967a, 296).

which *he* is the central actor; even if he falls into catatonic trance, his soul is thought to retain its conscious existence in the supernatural regions to which it has traveled. After waking, the shaman can precisely describe his soul journey, Paulson observes (1964, 138), whereas a possessed person has no memory of what happened during possession, since he was then a wholly different being.

Medium and shaman, then, though by no means categorically distinct, differ significantly in the beliefs most typical of them. The medium's personality or self is thought to be obliterated by the spirit that displaces it, even when seizure is voluntarily induced; the shaman's is thought to remain intact and in charge of its destiny even when it assimilates the identities of others, and its mastery of spirits extends into trance itself, where it is always an active agent, never merely the instrument of powers beyond it. Where possession plays an important role in shamanism, as among the Tungus and some other Siberian peoples, it most often does so, as Hultkrantz remarks (Bäckman and Hultkrantz, 25), during the future shaman's call, when spirits (often those who will become his helpers) may seem to drive him insane and even "kill" him in order to resurrect him as a newly empowered being. During the shamanistic seance, on the other hand, most apparent "possession" is deliberate impersonation of spirits under the shaman's command, even if the step between imitation and possession, as Hultkrantz cautions, is very slight.

Eliade's definition of the shaman as one whose soul ascends to the sky or descends to the underworld excludes, however, not only the medium but Oesterreich's visionary shaman, leaving out "the many cases in Siberia and North America where the shaman does not depart from his body, but waits for the arrival of the spirits" (Hultkrantz 1973, 29). Hultkrantz therefore suggests (Bäckman and Hultkrantz, 20) widening the concept of shamanism to include not only extra-corporeal flight but clairvoyant experience, which may accompany or precede it. Inasmuch as these remain distinct, we may differentiate a "weak" and a "strong" form of shamanism embodied respectively by the visionary and the ecstatic (Hultkrantz 1979, 87).

Visionary inspiration presupposes the widespread primitive belief in mobile spirits, including human souls capable of wandering abroad during sleep or after death; the shaman communicates with such spirits not only spontaneously in dreams, like others, but in trance under his disciplined control. Ecstatic shamanism even more particularly rests on belief in soul dualism and a detachable "free-soul" typical, Hultkrantz contends (1973, 30), of regions conspicuous for "strong shamanism," since "only the shaman's free soul can transcend the boundaries of the dead without risking his life."[2] The ultimate ecstasy of return from the dead is the fullest expression of the shaman's mastery of spirits: his ability, without losing his own identity, to assimilate the transcendent and thereby infuse the actuality of his world with the indeterminate potentiality of others beyond it.

Shamanism must be regarded, Hultkrantz writes (Bäckman and Hultkrantz, 28), as a continuous historical complex centered in northernmost Europe, northern and central Asia, and the Americas—homes of the ancient hunting and herding cultures of Arctic and sub-Arctic Eurasia and their extension, in recent millennia, into the New World. The fact of historical and geographical continuity need not imply, however, that any pure or "original form" of shamanism can be discovered or ever existed. A complex entails coexistence of many components, none of which can be isolated as uniquely essential. We can identify, in cases like the Tungus, intrusions or accretions from (for example) Lamaist Buddhism, but no pristine substratum intruded upon; for shamanism has never existed, so far as we know, without the accretions. Tungus shamanism, like any other, is "classic" in its very contamination. The widespread prevalence in the Americas of shamanistic practices clearly analogous to those of Siberia strongly suggests that forms of shamanism were brought to the New World millennia ago, but this probability need not imply that historically attested Siberian shamanisms are more nearly "original" than those of America; indeed, the relative isolation until recent centuries of most American tribes outside the Peruvian and Mexican spheres from influence by "higher" agricultural civilizations makes the opposite hypothesis equally plausible, though no doubt equally meaningless and certainly no more verifiable.

Shamanism cannot be restricted, moreover, to the "continuous historical complex" of northern Eurasia and the Americas. Paintings of human figures in bird or animal guise from such caves as Les Trois Frères in France suggest the tantalizing possibility that something resembling historical shamanism may have flourished in western Europe during the last Ice Age or even (as imagination takes flight) that it may have been common to paleolithic hunting cultures; if so, the "historical complex"

2. Hultkrantz 1953 and Paulson 1958 set forth the evidence for an ideology of soul dualism (or "dualistic pluralism") in North America and North Asia, arguing that the duality between "body soul" or "life soul" and "free soul" or "dream soul" (the individual *alter ego* which survives after death) is more primitive, especially in regions where shamanism prevails, than belief in a unitary and indivisible soul. The tendency of these two supposedly basic categories to subdivide in many different ways, however, and the existence of similar beliefs in dual or multiple souls in non-shamanistic regions, suggests that caution is in order before accepting their impressively documented hypothesis.

of shamanism might once have been coextensive with the human race. Such a possibility (like hypotheses of universal ancestor worship, mana, totemism, dying corn gods, or primal hordes devouring their fathers) can no more be entirely discounted than proved. But the questionable evidence of a few painted figures no less plausibly interpretable as gods, sorcerers, or mediums than as shamans hardly justifies so sweeping a conjecture as La Barre's (1970, 163–64) that the supernatural "is patterned simply [!] on the human master of animals," who is "simply the human shaman himself," thus the ultimate object of all human worship.

On the other hand, where no historical continuity with Eurasian-American shamanisms is probable, parallel practices may have arisen along with or after the agricultural rites and spirit possession cults too easily assumed by Eliade to be later intrusions. Even where mediumship is so prevalent as in tropical India, the Hill Saora "shaman," like his Siberian counterpart, may send his tutelary on a "spirit-hunt in the other world" to find the agent responsible for a sickness and argue with it in propria persona (Elwin 1955, 242–43). And in Africa, the only continent where ecstatic shamanism is rare, according to Eliade (1961, 153), the shamanism of the Zinza of Tanzania—distinguished from traditional mediumship by "lucid" possession in which the shaman engages in dialogue with the spirits and reports without loss of identity what they tell him—is a recent development associated with newly introduced *bacwezi* spirits (Bjerke, 139–40, 148–49).

These examples suggest not only that spirit possession and shamanism may coexist, as they often do, but that shamanism may develop from mediumship and not only, as Eliade seems to assume in speaking of shamanic "vestiges" in Polynesian mediumship, the other way round. Both the recent origin of Zinza shamanism outside any major historical complex and its rapid growth during a few decades of cultural crisis confirm the untenability of any search for a single evolutionary line uniting the various shamanisms practiced in different parts of the world since an antiquity long beyond apprehension. No doubt shamanism was once far more widespread than now, but nothing justifies the assumption that it universally preceded other forms of religion.

AUSTRALIA: IN QUEST OF THE LINGERING DREAM

If the ecstatic quest for transcendence is rare in Africa, where mediumship developed in close connection with ancestor worship and agricultural rites, it is common among the totemic hunting and gathering tribes of aboriginal Australia. Here the sparsity, over centuries and millennia, of external religious influences (except on northern coastal tribes by nonshamanic Melanesians) strongly suggests an origin inde-

pendent of any known complex elsewhere—or a connection so immemorially ancient as to be past all but hypothetical, not to say imaginary,
reconstruction.

The remarkable conservatism of Australian religion, with its "metaphysical emphasis on abidingness" (Stanner 1979, 36–38), is rooted in
the formative time widely known as the Dreaming. The tribal "ancestors" of this long gone yet hauntingly present age, whether human beings or totemic animals, were endowed with a primal creativity deriving
from ability to project their dreams in a visible landscape "considered to
be an integral part of the reality of eternity" (Strehlow 1970, 134). In
this ancestral time, the Aranda *altjiringa,* reality was as mobile as dream.
"The living Aboriginal, on the other hand," Nancy Munn writes (147),
"is faced with a *fait accompli,*" a fixed topography offering no possibility
that his dreams, too, might create or transmute reality. Through ritual,
which perpetuates that past by making it present, man maintains contact
with the ancestral beings who have never abandoned the world they
formed. Thus ritual gives purpose to men's lives (though far less to wom-
en's), but this purpose no longer embraces the possibility of changing an
inherited world that admits no variation, hence no future.

Yet the fact that creatively autonomous ancestral beings have never
abandoned the tribal lands and may be reincarnated (among the Aranda
and some other tribes) in living men through initiation shows that even
in societies so conservative as these the seeming closure of ritual does
not preclude transcendence. The purposeful quest of the First People
for a homeland is re-enacted by every living tribesman both in his physical wanderings through a countryside saturated by myth and in the spiritual journey infallibly mapped by ritual. The powers of the mythical
ancestors, including self-transformation, are latent in every man who, in
tribal initiations normally undergone by all adult males, approaches the
creative potential of the original Dreamers.

Australian, like Polynesian and African, myths tell of a time now lost
when inhabitants of earth could visit the sky and return. But whereas in
most African tales the heavens, since that primal breach, have been inaccessible to all except an occasional half-divine trickster, and in Polynesia ascent to the sky was attributed to mythical but not living beings,
in Australia a few respected elders designated by special initiation as
most advanced in knowledge of the Dreaming, the "clever men" called
by Elkin "aboriginal men of high degree," were thought in some tribes
to be still capable of journeying to the skies in spirit as the First People
had long before done in the flesh. These medicine men are not only
mediums but shamans, able after their initial possession to "fly through
space unseen, and ascertain what is happening at a distance" (Elkin
1978, 298). They are intermediaries who retain their hard-won mastery

as they venture forth in quest of fuller contact with the spirits than is given, outside participation in ritual, to their fellow tribesmen.

According to Spencer and Gillen's classic account (1899, 523–25) of the Aranda (Arunta) medicine man, in a cave south of Alice Springs a man who wishes to become the spirit-double of a Dream Time ancestor lies down to sleep. At daybreak, a spirit pierces his neck and tongue with an invisible lance, then replaces his internal organs and implants magic stones in his body. Coming to life again, the man returns to his people and after several days of odd behavior paints himself with powdered charcoal and fat: "All signs of insanity have disappeared, and it is at once recognized that a new medicine man has graduated."

Although in some respects, such as replacement of the internal organs and insertion of magic stones, the Aranda medicine man resembles others in aboriginal Australia, shamanic elements are less prominent than in many tribes. The celestial dimension, to begin with, is almost entirely absent in the accounts of Spencer and Gillen, who took pains to rebut the Rev. C. Strehlow's contention (Spencer and Gillen 1927, 2:593) that the word *Altjira* (from which *altjiringa* derives) referred not to multiple "totem-gods" but to a "good God" whose sovereignty extends over Heaven. The findings of C. Strehlow, like those of Howitt, who reported similar beliefs in a heavenly "All Father" in southeast Australia, were thus in large measure discredited by those who held, with Spencer and Gillen, Herbert Spencer, and Frazer, against the dissenting voices of Andrew Lang and later Wilhelm Schmidt, that belief in a High God was an evolutionary construct never achieved by primitive Australians (see Eliade 1971, ch. 1). Whether or not C. Strehlow's reports were contaminated, as Spencer and Gillen thought, by missionary influence, at least some Aranda shared the belief of many tribes in a sky world inhabited by spirits from which man had been cut off in a distant past. Thus T. G. H. Strehlow (1964, 2:725) reports an Aranda belief "that men had to die only because all connections had been severed between the sky and the earth." When avenging spirits chopped down a tree linking them, the bridge to unending life was destroyed forever.

Only in his initial quest for power does the Aranda medicine man remotely resemble the ecstatic shaman, for as Spencer and Gillen remark (1899, 530), he is no more favored than other members of his tribe in communicating with spirits who neither descend to possess him, nor appear in visions, nor carry him off to the heavens. Having obtained his powers, he becomes not a shaman but a magician. A very different account was given by Howitt in his roughly contemporary studies of the rapidly vanishing religions of southeast Australia, for more than a century the center of white settlement on the continent. Here, among the Kurnai, Wiradjuri, and other tribes, medicine men acquired power not only by dreaming, inheritance, or insertion of quartz crystals but by sleeping near a grave or visiting the "sky-land," to which they magically ascended by a cord or spiderweb to the heavens. Nor were these feats confined to the southeastern region; outside central Australia, according to Elkin (1954, 304), most postulant medicine men journey to the sky. Thus in the northwestern Forrest River district, a continent away from Howitt's tribes, a medicine man receives power from the rainbow snake, mediator between earth and sky, after ascending in the pouch of an older medicine man in the form of a skeleton. Unlike most mediums (and many Siberian shamans), in this and other Australian tribes one becomes a medicine man not by sudden onslaught of madness, illness, or unsolicited dreams, nor by inheritance alone, but through a deliberate quest for transcendent power.

A Bandjelang clever man of northern New South Wales told Elkin (1978, 141) that in his making he went to the mountains and fasted for two or three months. In tropical Arnhem Land, the main object of the medicine man's making is to seek a vision of bird-like spirit children while fasting alone in a solitary place (22–23); elsewhere this place is sometimes a tomb, water hole, or (as among the Aranda) sacred cave. Even when his office customarily passes from father to son, the candidate's powers are not simply given but must be won and continually renewed by perilous journeys to the world beyond. To a great extent, especially in tribes like the Aranda where personal communion with the spirits virtually ceases after his "making," the aboriginal medicine man (like the rarer medicine woman) resembles the sorcerer in other tribal societies, displaying his powers through essentially magical, therefore mechanically compulsive, techniques. But the fundamental shamanic component of interchange between the human and spirit worlds, if not always clearly dominant over the magical element (as the Aranda example reminds us), permeates Australian religion. Only because his powers are not innate and his magic not automatically effective, like those of many witches and sorcerers, does the Australian medicine man so often renew his contact with the spirits dwelling under the earth or in the sky.

The doctor, Elkin writes (32), must himself be magically cured and resurrected before he can cure others by the spirit power he now embodies. His self-transformation—in contrast to the typical spirit medium's recovery of a self theoretically unaltered by the experience of possession—is equivalent to death and rebirth, often renewing him in body as in spirit by replacement of his internal organs. Insofar as he deliberately seeks to become a medicine man, the Australian is therefore consciously pursuing the indeterminate goal of his own transformation into a being that he cannot, to begin with, fully envisage. This transformation, Elkin remarks (306), "explains why he seems so strange when he returns to his people. He now lives on a different plane from them, though in all ordinary relationships there is nothing specially noticeable about him."

He has gained spiritual power not through drugs or violent frenzies (14) but through quiet receptivity, meditation, and recollection; his powers are not a psychopathic aberration but the extension to a "high degree" of the sacred condition shared by all initiated members of his tribe. Yet because he has striven to go beyond the given in his quest for a never wholly predictable visionary knowledge that brings him into contact with the totemic ancestors of the dream time, he dwells on a different plane from those who have never been dismembered and renewed, nor left the body behind in the rapturous spirit's heavenly flight. The transmuted medicine man, Eliade remarks (1971, 157), "lives simultaneously in two worlds: in his actual tribal world and in the sacred world of the beginning, when the Primordial Beings were present and active on earth." He alone of the living is a link between them; he allows society to adjust to perpetual change while maintaining the appearance of sameness because he incarnates, in his restless quest to surpass the given, the primal creativity that has never entirely vanished from the seemingly static world to which it gave form in the Dreaming. His is the realm, in Elkin's words (1950, 282), of "the apparently contingent and unexpected, especially in the sphere of sickness and death," those inevitable accidents of human life whose issue can be foreseen with certainty by no man.

TROPICAL SHAMANS OF MALAYSIA AND INDONESIA

In parts of the Pacific islands and southeast Asia, where spirit mediumship is widely practiced, the ecstatic quest for transcendence has likewise flourished. In the isolated, unusually democratic Polynesian island of Niue, the *taula-atua* might be possessed by gods or ghosts, but could also send his own gods to recover a sick person's lost soul (Loeb 1924, 393–97)—a triumph characteristic not of the medium as instrument of the spirits but of the shaman as their master. In several Melanesian societies, a professional dreamer was thought to visit the dead in sleep and bring back the soul of a sick infant held by a deceased relative (Codrington, 208–09).[3] And in New Caledonia a Kanaka tribesman may climb up

3. On an extremely general level, the flying witches of Melanesia (and of Africa or Europe) can be compared to shamans, as Layard has done in paralleling "flying tricksters" of the New Hebrides to Siberian shamans; common traits include, in his view, initiatory death and resurrection, metamorphosis into animal form, flight through the air, epileptic

to a platform of his house where he seeks visions in a deliberate quest for transcendent knowledge (Leenhardt, 28).

But it is in the Malay peninsula and Indonesian archipelago that the prevalent spirit mediumship of these regions most strikingly intermingles with practices similar to those of northern Eurasia. The Malay *belian* actively combats his spiritual foes. If not quite a master of spirits (since the possessing tiger-spirit is thought to act through him), he is far more than a "telephone exchange" for their messages, and although his familiar spirit is inherited, he may establish communication with it through *tuntut* (Endicott 1970, 16), a vision quest involving solitary vigil beside an open grave or in the dark forest.

Possession by a tiger may not be indigenous to the Malay *belian* but borrowed from the shamanistic Negrito or Senoi (Endicott 1970, 22; cf. 81). The Negritos belong to a stock thought to have been among the first inhabitants of southeast Asia but confined in recent centuries to the Andaman Islands and pockets of peninsular Malaysia and the Philippines; like the Australians, they are mainly hunters and gatherers. The Andamanese, when first observed by E. H. Man in the late nineteenth and by Radcliffe-Brown in the early twentieth century, were among the most primitive peoples on earth, lacking not only agriculture and domestic animals (even the dog until 1858) but knowledge of making fire. The shamanism of their medicine man is visionary rather than ecstatic; through dreams he communicates with spirits of the dead and performs cures (Radcliffe-Brown 1922, 177).

Among the less isolated Negritos or Semang of the Malay peninsula, the crystal-gazing *hala* is in some respects, like his Andamanese counterpart, a visionary shaman; in others, he more nearly resembles ecstatic shamans elsewhere. The word *hala* signifies transformation into a tiger (Schebesta, 121); ability to change into so potent a spirit betokens mastery of extraordinary spiritual power. At nocturnal ceremonies he ascends on incense to the sky while singing songs in voices ascribed to celestial *chenoi* spirits (136–40); here he gains power to transform himself into spirit beings without loss of his own identity. Shamans of neighboring tribes were able to free a person's soul carried off by disease, sending familiar spirits to retrieve it from captivity (Evans, 219–20); thus they performed the supreme shamanic task of penetrating and returning from the world of the dead.

---

symptoms, and homosexuality. But shamans differ fundamentally, as Layard notes, from witches in their vocation of healing and fighting against demonic forces and death. One might speculate that witchcraft has been especially prominent in regions like Melanesia, Africa, Europe, and the Pueblo and Navajo Southwest where ecstatic transcendence, denied the communally sanctioned expression of shamanism, has taken illicit forms.

Ecstatic ascent to the heavens is especially prominent in Batek Negrito shamanism. The Batek, Endicott writes (1979, 91–96), believe that a personal shadow-soul can leave the body to make contact with the spirits in dreams. But the most effective communication with the *hala' asal* ("original superhuman beings") is trancing by a shaman, whose shadow-soul can fly anywhere in the universe (145), guided by songs to its destination. It may also make earthly journeys in its tiger-body in search of information from the spirits. At a session held several times a year (154–55), a Batek shaman sinks into trance after singing with eyes shut how his shadow-soul journeys to the sky or through deep pools to the underworld, where it visits the *hala' asal* and the dead. "It also just travels about, marvelling at the wonderful sights." Unlike the dreamer (or medium of other cultures), the shaman determines what *hala'* to visit and chooses the topic of discussion as his soul ranges in quest of transcendent knowledge.

Chinese mediums of Singapore find a shamanic counterpart in the female "soul-raiser" (Elliott, 137–39) who calls up the *shen* Kuan Yin to help her seek out the souls of the dead. Trembling violently and speaking alternately in her own voice, the sing-song chant of Kuan Yin, and the "horrible growl" of the dead, she reports the goddess's progress through the gruesome underworld and the ghosts' responses to questions from relatives, engaging in dialogue with her familiar spirit. But it is in the Indonesian archipelago above all that the juxtaposition of shamanism (both visionary and ecstatic) and spirit mediumship reveals the multiplicity of its forms. The seer of the Mentawei islands off Sumatra ascends in a boat (the communal house) to the sky, borne by eagles to the spirits who are the sole source of visionary knowledge (Loeb 1929, 78). But the most striking instances of shamanism in this great island chain are found not in prevalently Muslim Sumatra or Java,[4] but in tribal Borneo (Indonesian Kalimantan and Malaysian Sarawak and Sabah) and Sulawesi (Celebes).

In the myths of the Bare'e-speaking Toradja of Sulawesi studied by Adriani and Kruyt, people could visit the gods when heaven and earth were close together (Downs, 10), and even now the upperworld is sometimes accessible by a coconut palm or other means. Along with elaborate agricultural rituals and initiatory head hunting, ecstatic shamanism was central to Toradja religion, and was open to all women (and men who dressed and acted as women) with talent for it, even an occasional slave

---

4. In the village religions of east central Java described by Geertz (1960, 19–21), malignant spirits may answer a curer's questions through the possessed victim's mouth and agree to depart in return for food and drink, but neither spirit mediumship nor shamanism appears in highly developed forms comparable to those of other islands, including nearby Bali.

(47).[5] Shamans, whose chief function here as elsewhere was to retrieve souls of the sick captured by spirits, could journey in search of advice from celestial deities; their excursions, described in "litanies" composed in a nearly incomprehensible shamanic language (48), became common property of the tribe. The Wana of Sulawesi, also visited by Kruyt and recently studied by Atkinson, dress in rags to search for forest spirits, since power originates in the wilderness. Their shaman sees in controlled waking states what others see only in dreams; in the elaborate *mabolong* ceremony he and his spirit familiars "travel to distant realms in pursuit of lost aspects of a patient's being" (Atkinson, 123), although journeys to a celestial "Owner," Atkinson surmises, may be a recent development influenced by Christianity and Islam (159, 197).

In Borneo spirit possession and ecstatic shamanism continually intermingle. Even where the former predominates, the medium, far from passively awaiting the spirit, may boldly set out to seek it in worlds remote from her own. Especially in the northwestern state of Sarawak, shamanism is highly developed. For the Berawan (Metcalf, 58–62), illness results from loss of the soul, which the shaman must recover. To the strumming of a stringed instrument the shaman enters a trance in which her soul "makes astral journeys to locate the soul of the sick person and to wrest it away from whatever has seized it." Other shamans operate without soul flight (260–61), but their skills derive from personal inspiration, and what they teach of spirit worlds is not fixed dogma or invariant ritual but inquiry into what can never, in a world of intrinsic uncertainty, be finally known.

Among the Sea Dayaks or Iban of Sarawak, Erik Jensen writes (55), religion is almost synonymous with divinely sanctioned ritual order (*adat*). But the Iban, as Geddes describes them (3) in contrast to the Land Dayaks (or to conservative peoples like the Zuñi, Tallensi, and Aranda), are "restless innovators for gain, prestige, or sheer enjoyment of change." This restlessly searching aspect of their experience finds religious expression in a shamanism based on divine revelation communicated by a mobile soul (*semengat*) wandering to the spirit world during sleep (D. Freeman 1967, 316); for dreams, as a basis for religious belief, produce, as Freeman observes (1975, 285), "not 'ordered pattern,' but innovation and change."

Such revelations may be spontaneously communicated, but when the soul is captured by a malignant spirit, the services of a shaman (*manang*) are required. Shamans, both male and (less commonly) female, fall into three classes (Freeman 1967, 316, 320): novice, fully initiated shaman,

5. Downs notes (48n.) that Adriani and Kruyt termed those whom he calls shamans "priestesses." Cf. Wales, 63.

and transvestite shaman. The shaman's position may be passed from fa-ther to son, but no one becomes a shaman without being "summoned in a dream which is said to involve experiencing himself in a new way, com-monly the dress of the opposite sex. . . . The spirit calling the Iban," Jensen writes (144), "remains his familiar spirit, his contact, his guide, and helper in the spirit world." In the last century manangs ranked sec-ond to village chiefs, and might be chiefs themselves (Ling Roth, 1 : 265), but their recent social standing is more equivocal. Most suffer from a physical handicap such as blindness and are stigmatized as failures in terms of normal Iban values. Skepticism toward them is common, yet the most prestigious manangs are highly respected members of the community.

The manang's treatment of disease takes various forms, of which the ecstatic journey to recover a patient's departed soul is the most potent. During the *pelian* ritual, held in the longhouse at night, the manang journeys over water to the land of the dead in search of an errant soul, which he retrieves in trance and restores to the sick person's head. When all else fails, a victim of serious illness may seek a personal encounter with spirits to whom, in the vision-quest known as *nampok,* he offers food and sacrifices a cock on a solitary hillside or in a graveyard. He beats out on his drum a summons for the spirit, who rewards him, if he stands his ground, with a charm to guide him through life (Jensen, 124). In this way not only the shaman but the ordinary Iban could acquire divine power through possession of a guardian spirit or personal totem.

Nor was recovery from illness the only goal of the vision quest. "A man who was fired with ambition to shine in deeds of strength and brav-ery, or one who desired to attain the position of chief, or to be cured of an obstinate disease, would, in olden times," Ling Roth observes (1 : 185), "spend a night or nights by himself on a mountain, hoping to meet a benevolent spirit who would give him what he desired. To be alone was a primary condition of the expected apparition," for society's laws and conventions had to be left far behind in order to achieve this commu-nion with the cosmic order on which all things human depend. Here the restless need for continual innovation permeating Iban culture (if not indeed human nature) culminates in a deliberate personal quest for transcendence of the individual self through solitary encounter with a kindred if ultimately unknowable other.

CHAPTER ELEVEN

Shamanic Heartland

Central and Northern Eurasia

Australia and parts of tribal southeast Asia are one region where sha-manistic practices have survived down to the present; Arctic and sub-Arctic Eurasia from Lapland eastward through Siberia (and Alaska to Greenland), along with much of Central Asia, is another. Between these widely separated areas exist traces, in the China of Taoist-inspired folk religions, the highlands of Kachin Burma and Indian Nagaland, and above all (quite literally) the mountainous tableland of Tibet, of what may once have been a far more widely disseminated shamanism of pre-historic times.

THE ANTIQUITY OF THE SHAMAN: TIBET AND HINTS OF PREHISTORY

Beliefs derived from the largely shamanistic Bon (or Bön) religion of Tibet prior to the introduction of Tantric Buddhism in the seventh cen-tury A.D. and its development into Lamaism pervade folk religion even now, to the extent that "the so-called Buddhist population is practically Shamanist" (David-Neel, 9). Here too we find the tripartite cosmos, and a legendary time when the king, at least, could ascend to heaven until the cord linking it to earth broke (Tucci, 167, 225). A detachable "double" may leave the body involuntarily to wander abroad in dreams, and the *delog* or *'das log*[1] ("one who has returned from the beyond") can

---

1. Some Tibetan terms are given in roughly phonetic form, some in the wildly unpho-netic Tibetan orthography.

travel in trance to far-off places. These include various paradises, purgatories, and the bardo, where the dead await reincarnation, as related in the *Bar do thosgrol* or "Tibetan Book of the Dead," a Lamaist book of counsel probably influenced by Bon shamanism (Evans-Wentz, 75). The Buddhist lama who whispers this sacred text into the dead man's ear is himself, like the tribal shaman, a *psychopompos* or soul-guide (Tucci, 194) who accompanies the dead person on his difficult path during the forty-nine days of the intermediate state between death and rebirth.

Tales of *'das log* returning from the beyond, which closely recall shamanistic journeys of the soul, thus reinforce Lamaist teachings (Tucci, 198–99). Grave sickness and hallucinations usually precede the trance in which the *'das log,* believing himself dead, visits the other world, sometimes rising into the air on a horse which suddenly appears and takes him away under the guidance of invisible beings. Other Tibetan practices, whatever their source, reflect the shamanistic belief that the human soul may journey to far-off homes of the spirits in quest of superhuman powers. *Gomchen* ascetics can "kill men at a distance and fly through the air" (David-Neel, 42), and the rigorously trained *lung-gom-pa* run long distances barely touching the ground, even wearing chains to prevent them from floating in the air (210). The legend of Shambhala tells of a Pure Land, at once on earth and in the mind, tirelessly sought by those on the road to Nirvana in quest of a liberation that will eventually transform both travelers and the world (Bernbaum, 103). That Shambhala may be reached by magical flight on horseback recalls Central Asian rituals in which shamans similarly ascend to the heavens (165).

In the folk religion evidently descended from the pre-Buddhist Bon (David-Neel, 36–37), a male or female medium, dancing to drum and bell, trembles convulsively as a possessing spirit of the dead frenziedly communicates its wishes. In contrast, shamans of yore splendidly regaled themselves for bold flights on a clay deer or a drum, leaving no doubt, Tucci writes (241), of "similarities between the old Tibetan religion and shamanism; the ride through the air, the magical use of the drum, the calling back of the souls of the dead or dying." And even now, after thirteen centuries of Buddhism, the Bon sorcerer is in essence a shaman. As observed by David-Neel (38–39) among the "practically Shamanist" Tibetans of Sikkim, the sorcerer's "double" travels in trance to the dwelling of a demon holding a captive soul, then obscurely describes his fight to restore the soul to its owner.

With the gradual spread of Lamaist Buddhism northward to Mongolia and Siberia, not only those who adopted (and adapted) the new religion but others who presumably retained ancestral shamanistic practices were deeply influenced by it. Indeed, some scholars—notably Shirokogoroff—attribute not only the Tungus (Evenk) shaman's costume,

mirror, and drum but the word "shaman"[2] and Siberian shamanism itself to Buddhist influences from Tibet and Central Asia. Given the wide
diffusion of a clearly ancient shamanic complex from Lapland eastward
to Greenland (hence far beyond Buddhist influences), this conclusion is
untenable; but the undoubted impact of Lamaism on Mongolian and
Tungus shamanism suggests a complex and reciprocal relation between
them. For the Lamaist Buddhism that spread to the north had already
been profoundly influenced, as we have seen, by ancient Tibetan Bon
shamanism. Indeed, David-Neel (243) heard a learned lama maintain
that bold Tibetan mystical theories of a "Short Path" to Buddhahood by
direct ascent in this life are "faint echoes of teachings that existed from
time immemorial in Central and Northern Asia."

In most of northern Eurasia and much of Central Asia shamanism
has been practiced either as a component of tribal religion or in conjunction with Christianity, Islam, or Buddhism into recent times. These
peoples of tundra, taiga, and steppe, whether Lapp or Finno-Ugrian
to the west, Turco-Tatar, Mongolian, or Tungus-Manchu in Altaic-
speaking Siberia and Central Asia, or the "paleo-Siberian" tribes (Chukchee, Kamchadal, Koryak) and others such as the Ainu in the Far East,
have for centuries or millennia lived as nomadic hunters, fishers, or
herders of reindeer or cattle; their shamanism, in contrast to the fixed
rites of agricultural peoples, is a central expression of this mobile
existence.

The profusion of splendid animals (and a few human figures in animal garb) painted deep in nearly impenetrable caves by reindeer hunters of Ice Age France and Spain tantalizingly suggests the existence of a
paleolithic shamanism. Even evidence from Greek and Chinese writers
thousands of years later remains too scanty, however, to allow more than
speculative reconstruction of the religious practices of such ancient Central Asian nomads as the Scythians and Huns.[3] The most intriguing ac-

2. Mironov and Shirokogoroff in 1924 endorsed the derivation of Tungus *shaman*
(which entered Russian in the seventeenth and eighteenth centuries) from Sanskrit *šra-*
mana (via Pali *śamana*), a Hindu or Buddhist ascetic. Mironov, after Levi, thought the
Sanskrit-Pali term passed into China (becoming *sha-men*) through Indo-European Ku-
chean or Tokharian speakers of northwest India before the Turkish conquest of the eleventh century. Shirokogoroff uses this derivation to support his theory (127) that shamanism is "a relatively recent phenomenon" in Siberia, beginning with Lamaism. Elsewhere
(1935b, 42) he suggests that it is only about two or three centuries old among some Tungus. Eliade (1964, 498), though accepting Buddhist stimulus, argues that Tungus, and
generally Asian, shamanism "*is not a creation of Buddhism.*" Others, such as Diószegi and
Hultkrantz, derive *shaman* from an Altaic root such as Tungus-Manchu *ša* or *sa*, "to know"
(Hultkrantz 1973, 26). As far back as 1917 Laufer summarized arguments for a native
Tungusic derivation bearing witness, he thought (371), to "the great antiquity of the shamanistic form of religion."

3. Maenchen-Helfen (269) thinks it certain that the Huns had shamans, but the evi-

count is Herodotus's of the Scythians, a migratory Indo-Iranian or possibly Altaic people whose territory once stretched from near the Black Sea to the borders of China, penetrating westward into the Balkans and Prussia and southward, for a brief time, into Palestine and almost to Egypt. Some of their soothsayers, Herodotus remarks (IV.67), belong to "the class of effeminate persons called 'Enarees'," who suffer from what he elsewhere (I.105) calls the "female disease." After a burial (IV.73–75), the Scythians cleanse themselves in a vapor bath formed by stretching woolen cloth over a framework of sticks, and "inside this little tent they put a dish with red-hot stones in it. Then they take some hemp seed, creep into the tent, and throw the seed on to the hot stones. At once it begins to smoke . . . The Scythians enjoy it so much that they howl with pleasure."

Few though these details are, the androgynous prophets, purification by steam bath, intoxication by cannabis, and subsequent howling strongly suggest affinities with Central Asian, Siberian, and American shamanisms observed over two thousand years later. Transvestite shamans are found, Meuli notes (2:826), in much of Siberia and North America, especially among the "Paleo-Siberians" and Asiatic Eskimo; sweat baths such as Herodotus described are widely used by Native Americans for ritual purification, notably before vision quests; and narcotics ranging from tobacco to Siberian fly-agaric mushrooms and South American yagé induce visions throughout much of the Eurasian-American shamanic complex. And since shamans often act as "psychopomps," conducting souls of the recently dead to the underworld, Meuli plausibly conjectures (2:821–22) "that the Scythian too in his sweat-hut was striving for the same object, that his 'howling' was a singing-over of the dead man's soul—that the Scythian," in short, far from howling with pleasure in his primitive sauna, "was shamanizing."

Ancient Central Asian shamanism may have profoundly influenced religious practice in Greece, as Dodds (ch. 5) and Meuli believed, and conceivably in Persia, India, and China as well. Such heady speculations aside, we have clear accounts of shamanistic sessions from European travelers to the courts of Genghis Khan's successors in Turkestan, Mongolia, and China. "The oracle (cham) intending to invoke the spirits begins his sorcery and frenziedly beats the ground with a drum," wrote the Franciscan monk Ruysbroeck, King Louis IX of France's envoy to Mon-

---

dence he cites is the component *kam* (Turkic for "shaman") in the names of high-ranking Huns. He also notes that in Chinese writings *kan* (ancient *kam*) is equated with Chinese *wu*, usually translated "sorcerer" or "shaman." References to Hun *wu* in such Chinese annals as the *Han Shu* (*History of the Former Han*) generally emphasize their magical powers, however, and give little indication of specifically shamanistic attributes.

golia in 1253–55. "At last he begins to get wild and lets himself be bound. Then the evil spirit comes in the dark, he gives it meat to eat, and it utters the oracular answer." Such an account, Siikala writes, "proves that the séance has in the main remained almost unchanged" for at least seven hundred years.[4]

Subsequent accounts of Central Asian and Siberian shamans express intense fascination with their incomprehensible frenzies. Thus Richard Johnson (354–56) vividly describes the "devilish rites" of the northern Siberian Samoyeds whom he visited in 1556:

> first the Priest doeth beginne to playe upon a thing like to a great sieve, with a skinne on the one ende like a drumme . . . Then hee singeth as wee use heere in England to hallow, whope, or showte at houndes, and the rest of the company answere him with this Owtis, Igha, Igha, Igha, and then the Priest replieth againe with his voyces. And they answere him with the selfe same wordes so manie times, that in the ende he becommeth as it were madde, and falling downe as hee were dead . . . I asked them why hee lay so, and they answered mee, Now doeth our God tell him what wee shall doe, and whither wee shall goe.

In the remainder of his performance the "priest" thrust a heated sword "through his bodie, as I thought, in at his navill and out at his fundament," and was decapitated (behind a curtain) by a drawn cord, his head falling into a kettle of boiling water. "And I went to him that served the Priest, and asked him what their God saide to him when he lay as dead. Hee answered 'that his owne people doeth not know: neither is it for them to know: for they must doe as he commanded.' "

With expansion of the Russian empire into Turkestan and Siberia, detailed accounts of shamanistic performances proliferated; and though some observers regard shamans as mere charlatans, others openly admit the powerful impact of their wild behavior on imperfectly civilized modern man. "Every time that here or elsewhere I have seen shamans operate they have left on me a dark impression which was long in fading," von Wrangel writes (Oesterreich, 295) of his experiences in Siberia during the 1820s. "The wild glance, blood-shot eyes, raucous voice which seemed to come forth with extreme effort from a chest racked by spasmodic movements, the unnatural convulsive distortion of the face and body, the bristling hair, and even the hollow sound of the magic drum—all this gives to the scene a horrible and mysterious character which has gripped me strangely every time . . ."

Extensive observations in the eighteenth and nineteenth centuries,

4. Siikala, 77, citing Charpentier, *Vilhelms av Ruysbroeck resa genom Asien 1253–1255* (Stockholm, 1919), 258–59. Siikala (77–87) summarizes accounts of shamanism since the thirteenth century.

and ethnographical studies by Shirokogoroff, Bogoras, Jochelson, Sternberg, Anisimov, and others in the late nineteenth and early twentieth,
when shamanism was in evident decline, are central to the mass of materials in Russian, German, English, French, Finnish, Swedish, and Hun-
garian on which such twentieth-century scholars as Harva, Eliade, Paulson, and Hultkrantz have drawn for their studies of North Eurasian
shamanism. From these voluminous writings one fact that emerges (allowing us to deal with Eurasian shamanism as a whole rather than tribe
by tribe) is the extraordinary extent to which, despite countless variations, not only has shamanism remained "almost unchanged" in many
respects from the time of Ruysbroeck (if not Herodotus) until its recent
decline, but despite "the variety of races and the enormous distances that
separate them," as Mikhailovskii (158) long ago observed, many of its
practices are "repeated with marvellous regularity." Insofar as the shamanism of the hunters and herders of northern Eurasia (and beyond)
has pre-eminently expressed the restlessly mobile, transcendently questing dimension of primitive religion, nothing about it has been more
striking than its consistency and persistence in these regions throughout
immense expanses of space and time.

THE SHAMANIC COSMOS AND THE IMPERIOUS CALL

The cosmology common to many North Eurasian tribal peoples com-
prises three regions linked together by a central *axis mundi,* whether pil-
lar or tree, mountain or river (Eliade 1964, 259); though not unique to
shamanistic cultures, it is fundamental to their view of the world, high-
lighting the transitional place in the cosmos of man in general and the
shaman in particular. Similar tripartite divisions are found in Tibet and
as far away as Sulawesi, and some North Eurasian tribes, like the Chukchee, distinguish five, seven, or nine vertical worlds (Bogoras, 330). The
sacred and profane, divine and human, are not opposed in insuperable
dualism but linked by the axis that provides, for those between, the perpetual opportunity of passage between them.

In some cases the tripartite cosmos corresponds to a threefold soul;
in every case a mobile soul is believed to depart temporarily from the
body during dreams and illness and permanently at death (Harva 1927,
472–74). Because of this peripatetic capacity, those who inhabit the
middle world can voyage to the heavens or the world of the dead: a
latent potentiality continually impeded, however, by the limits of the
everyday human condition.

Thus the Koryak near the Bering Sea believe that in the mythological
age of Big Raven, "men could ascend to heaven, and get down to the
underground world, with great ease. Now only shamans are capable of

doing it" (Jochelson 1908, 121). As Eliade remarks (1964, 259), the shaman alone "knows the mystery of the break-through in plane" and can
communicate to those who have half forgotten it this transcendent potentiality of everyone who inhabits our liminal world.

Although shamans may perform priestly functions, Mikhailovskii observes (91), their chief importance derives from duties which distinguish
them sharply from priests. Moreover, nowhere (apart from shamans
who continued to practice after a tribe's conversion to Lamaism, Islam,
or Christianity) do we find a sharp dichotomy, as in many cultures where
spirit mediumship is practiced, between the shaman and a more prestigious guardian of tribal ritual. The shaman, unlike most mediums, is the
supreme and often the sole intermediary between his people and the
spirit world. On the other hand, although many shamans practice magic
(often against shamans of other clans), they characteristically *seek* communion with spirits instead of attempting to coerce it through mechanical formulas; the shaman's performance, unlike the magician's, is in
theory a venture in the unknown.

Shamanic ecstasy is no mere technique, like magic or ritual, then, but
a transcendent ("ek-static") quest to restore the harmony shattered for
the individual by illness or death, and for the people by loss of primordial unity with kindred spirits in the heavens and fellow creatures on
earth. The widespread conception of a soul inherent in natural objects
was closely connected, among the Altaic and other peoples, with belief
in an inspiriting power identified as the owner or master of phenomena
ranging from forest or sea to species of plants and animals. It was in
general this owner, not individual members of a species, that ceremonies
sought to propitiate after the killing of a kindred animal, notably, among
Boreal hunting peoples, the bear (Hallowell 1926, 154). In the Finnish
bear feast called "the wedding," Bishop Rothovius observed in 1640
(Harva 1927, 97–98), "when they capture a bear, they must hold a feast
in the dark, drinking the health of the bear from its skull, acting and
growling like the bear, procuring in this way further success"; similar
rites are common throughout the Eurasian-American complex.

The shaman can mediate between men and spirits (of animals or others) because he has been empowered by his own guardian spirit in the
shape of an animal or ancestral shaman, the two being not clearly distinct. This tutelary spirit or genius (often assisted by various helping
spirits in bird or animal form) is no doubt, as Harva suggests (1927, 284),
in essence the shaman's own mobile soul, a universally latent power to
which the shaman intermittently gives rein, at the risk of madness, while
others regard it as dangerous and strive to hold it in check. The secret
language of many shamans, moreover, is frequently thought to be an
animal language, and the shaman's costume may be adorned with bird

and animal features. Such costumes, Harva believes (1927, 519), originally represented the shaman's soul-animal, to which he remains inseparably joined long after the cleavage between human and animal has taken place for others.

Through the metamorphic capacity of the mobile soul, shamans are thought to be able, among the Koryak and elsewhere, to transform themselves into other shapes (Jochelson 1908, 117), above all into the animal forms they assume upon donning their costumes. Such transformations are a common motif of myths throughout the world; the shaman, even in a time when bodily transformation, like bodily flight, is no longer possible, perpetuates the versatility of the mobile soul shared by all animate creatures in the mythic past. "Each time a shaman succeeds in sharing in the animal mode of being," Eliade writes (1964, 94), "he in a manner re-establishes the situation that existed *in illo tempore*, in mythical times, when the divorce between man and animal had not yet occurred": the lost paradise of the dawn of time. To re-establish this condition cannot be simply to recapture a timeless past, however, for it is the capacity for inherently uncertain *change* that the restless shaman repeatedly embodies in his endless quest to actualize a unity with all creation that is now forever potential and thus forever future.

The vocation of shaman in most of North and Central Eurasia, like that of spirit mediums in much of the world, is not voluntarily chosen but "ineluctably and fatally determined" (Paulson 1964, 135). Predisposition to the call may be hereditary, but the "gift" is normally "accepted as a heavy burden, which man takes up as the inevitable, submitting to it with a weary heart as of one doomed. It is not the shaman who elects the protecting spirit, but the protecting spirit who elects the shaman" (Sternberg, 473). This call, again like the spirit medium's, is characteristically communicated by onslaught of illness, whose often bizarre symptoms led some observers to consider shamanism a pathological condition: epilepsy, neurosis, or "Arctic hysteria" resulting from long nights, malnutrition, and cold. Among the Yakut, a person destined to shamanism, Mikhailovskii writes (85–87), suddenly "gabbles, falls into unconsciousness, runs about the woods, lives on the bark of trees, throws himself into fire and water, lays hold of weapons and injures himself, so that he has to be watched by his family; by these signs they know that he will be a shaman." A future Buryat shaman, marked by solitary thoughtfulness, Mikhailovskii continues, "begins to have fits of ecstasy, dreams and swoons become more frequent; he sees spirits, leads a restless life, wanders about from village to village and tries to *kam*," that is, to be the shaman he is becoming.

In these and other instances the transformation into a shaman is more protracted than the spirit medium's call, which may be as sudden as that of the Ashanti who rushes wildly into the bush and emerges hours or days later as a medium-priest, even if weeks of disorientation and months or years of instruction follow. The shaman, too, receives training from other shamans, but it is typically by spirits themselves—above all his guardian spirit—that he claims to be instructed during his long preparation. His relationship with a guardian spirit of the opposite sex is frequently (like that of some mediums) a sexual one. Thus a shaman of the Gold tribe told Sternberg (476–77) of a spirit who approached him, on his sick bed, in the shape of a beautiful woman, saying: "I love you, I have no husband now, you will be my husband and I shall be a wife unto you." Threatening to kill him if he resisted, she has come to him ever since from her solitary mountain hut, sometimes as an old woman, sometimes as a wolf or winged tiger, "and I sleep with her as with my own wife, but we have no children."

In this story, as in many from Siberia, the spirit takes the initiative in instructing the resisting novice, who appears as passive as a typical medium. Sometimes, however, the shaman's vocation, though initially involuntary, takes on the shape, as he gradually identifies with the transcendent spirit within, of an initiation or quest for realization of hitherto unsuspected powers. In the vivid account of the Tavgi Samoyed shaman Sereptie Djaruoskin reported by Popov (137–43), the novice must find out everything for himself; hence the quest is especially prominent.

After Djaruoskin felled the shaman's tree of which he had dreamed the previous night, "a man sprang out of its roots with a loud shout," commanding the terrified woodsman to come down through the root. Like Alice following her theriomorphic guardian spirit in the ecstasy of Victorian dream, Djaruoskin noticed a hole in the earth. "My companion asked: 'What hole is this? If your destiny is to make a drum of this tree, find it out!'" Recognizing the hole through which a shaman gained his voice, he descended and saw a river with two streams flowing in opposite directions. "'Well, find out this one too!' said my companion." And so with every strange sight, Djaruoskin must divine its meaning and his destiny as a shaman. To the repeated injunction "Find it out!" he repeatedly gives the correct answer, which he had not known before. "You will be a great shaman indeed, you find out everything," the spirit says, clapping his hands, " . . . since you have seen all these things": Djaruoskin's own wish is of no account. Finally (like Virgil crowning Dante lord of himself atop Mount Purgatory), "'Now that we have arrived here, I will leave you alone,' said my companion. . . . 'Shamanizing, you will find your way, by yourself.'" Hereafter the reluctantly questing shaman will guide others on a path which he himself must continually discover, since it leads forever beyond him.

The Chukchee compare the preparatory period of a shaman's call,

Bogoras writes (421), "to a long, severe illness; and the acquirement of inspiration, to a recovery." The call may be reluctantly shouldered at first, but during his long initiation by a guardian spirit the shaman increasingly acquires the spirit's powers (which are those of his own mobile soul) and thereby control of the forces assaulting him. Seized by spirits, Krader says of the Buryat shaman (115), "he uses the power thus derived to seize the spirits . . . to his own ends." His hard-won ability to make use of his own affliction is thus the first and most crucial sign of the mastery of spirits that defines him as a shaman and enables him to minister to the afflictions of others. Therefore the shaman "is not only a sick man," Eliade rightly insists (1964, 27), but "a sick man who has been cured, who has succeeded in curing himself." By courageously enduring affliction and transforming it into spiritual grace, he becomes, to quote Lewis again (188–89), "the master of anomaly and chaos. . . . In rising to the challenge of the powers which rule his life and by valiantly overcoming them in this crucial initiatory rite which reimposes order on chaos and despair, man reasserts his mastery of the universe and affirms his control of destiny and fate."

Far more than most mediums, whose personalities are unchanged by periodic possession, the shaman's extraordinary experience sets him apart from his world. "I think it was mine," Djaruoskin says of a tent seen in his vision (Popov, 142), strange though it seemed: "I went in, not as a man but as a skeleton." This sense of no longer fully belonging to a society which he alone sees *sub specie aeternitatis* leaves the shaman a conspicuous outsider even after recovery from his initial "disease" has made him a socially honored (if widely feared) magician and healer. Despite the reverence, even posthumous worship, sometimes accorded him, the Siberian shaman often seems unhappy in a personal life "wholly isolated" and deprived of constant communication with human beings (Shirokogoroff 1935b, 89–91). His startling nonconformity is perhaps a counterweight (like the antics of the peripheral Pueblo clown) to the intense collective pressures of tribal societies: he is a "safety valve" (Shirokogoroff 1923, 247) not only for psychic maladies but for latent individualistic impulses of his tribespeople, which could never be realized by more than a few without shattering their unity. The Buryat are divided, Krader writes (132), between the aberrant shaman and the social conformity of others; the shaman thus embodies "transcendence by the individual of the social norm." As such, he remains perpetually estranged from the society whose need for vicarious transcendence he fulfills: a figure inherently in between.

One example of this transcendence of the socially given is the adoption by some Siberian shamans, especially in the Far East (as also among the Iban of Borneo and many American tribes), of the dress and manners of the opposite sex: a potent expression of the shaman's self-transformative powers. By this ultimate metamorphosis he (or less frequently she)[5] subverts the conventions even of shamanic society and endures the isolation of having restored, in a divided world, the long-lost unity not only of human and animal, heaven and earth, but of the primal androgyne in which male and female, too, are one.

ECSTATIC ASCENT AND DESCENT: IN QUEST OF A SOUL

The shaman's communication with spirits can be conceived, as we have noted, in two ways: either his soul journeys in ecstasy to the world beyond, or spirits enter and inspire him (Harva 1938, 540). These are by no means exclusive, since the guardian spirit may enter his body before departing as his alter ego: in this case possession or inspiration is preliminary to ecstasy. To the extent that the second way predominates, however, shamans may seem "entirely passive," like those of the Ainu (Ohnuki-Tierney, 113), and thus indistinguishable from mediums. Far more distinctive of North Eurasian shamanism is trance, ranging from cataleptic stupor to ecstatic frenzy, in which the shaman's own soul (often identified with his guardian spirit) in the company of his helpers, or these alone at his command, set forth to the spirit world in active quest of knowledge or to retrieve a soul whose loss has endangered another's life. In addition to hypnotic singing and beating of drums, Eurasian shamans, to induce visionary trance, frequently make use of stimulants and narcotics, including the indigenous fly-agaric mushroom, eaten dry or drunk in a potion and recirculated by drinking the urine. This hallucinogen, Bogoras writes (205–07) of the Chukchee, makes a man "unconscious of his surroundings, . . . walking or tumbling about on the ground, sometimes raving, and breaking whatever happens to come into his hands" while "the agaric spirits take him through various worlds and show him strange sights and peoples."

Despite the effects of this and other stimulants, the shaman is not typically considered (like the medium) a vehicle swept away by overwhelming powers but is distinguished precisely by retaining a crucial margin of self-control which allows him, at the height of seemingly de-

5. On transvestite Siberian shamans, see Krader, 112, on the Buryat; Sternberg, 493, on the Gold; Jochelson 1926, 194, on the Yukaghir and Yakut; and Bogoras, 450–53, on the Chukchee. In much of northern Eurasia and Central Asia shamans have in recent historical times been mainly male. Female shamans are also found, though in general, Harva observes (1927, 499), "these can in no way be compared with the male in power and importance." As a rule, only on the outer fringes of the Eurasian shamanic complex (from the Tajiks and Uzbeks of Central Asia to Korea and the Ainu of northern Japan), in mainly agricultural cultures, have female shamans predominated both in number and in prestige.

mented ecstasy, to orient his visionary experience toward a purposeful goal. Anyone can assimilate spirits, Shirokogoroff writes (1935b, 50), but only shamans "can subordinate them to themselves, doing with them as they please." The shaman can be guided by a guardian spirit that is both within and beyond him only inasmuch as he does not surrender wholly to it; its very guidance is thus the proof of his mastery.

By this guidance, the shaman's trance becomes a fully purposeful quest. In initiatory rites of Central Asia, Siberia, and (as Eliade emphasizes[6]) much of the world, his journey often takes the form of ascent to the sky. The elaborate ceremonies performed by the Turkic Altai for their celestial deity Bai-Yulgen, for example, as described by Radloff (Mikhailovskii, 74–78), include ritual ascent by the *kam* of a birch tree in which steps have been carved. Walking several times round the tree placed in his yurt, he beats his tambourine while his body quivers and he mutters unintelligible words. In ecstasy he climbs the tree, one step for each heaven, thumping his tambourine and shouting. "The more powerful the *kam* is, the higher he mounts in the celestial regions; there are some, but few, who can soar to the tenth, eleventh, twelfth, and even higher.... After his conversation with Yulgen, the ecstasy of the shaman reaches its highest point, and he falls down completely exhausted."

In most instances, however, the shaman's soul travels to the heavens while his body remains below. Often he ascends by his magical drum, painted with shamanistic animals or birds and sometimes depicting the sky above and the underworld beneath. The Tofa shaman Kokuev modestly told Diószegi (1968b, 311–12) that he flew only about four meters from the ground, "because I was a small shaman." Yet even at this far-from-celestial height he journeyed astride his drum to sacred lakes and mountains to learn from their spirit masters whatever he wanted to know.

Such ascents, in body or spirit, were among the principal means by which Eurasian shamans could gain and renew the visionary knowledge indispensable to their people's well-being. In their central task, however, diagnosis and treatment of disease, and in some others like safe conduct of the souls of the dead, their goal was usually not the upper but the lower world, to which shamans alone of the living could penetrate and hope to return. Entry to these subterranean realms (as to the heavens

6. See esp. 1964, ch. 4. Eliade's discussion is dominated by the hypothesis (1961, 154) "that ecstasy as ascension preceded ecstasy as *descensus ad inferos*" (descent to the underworld), on the grounds that dreams of ascent are "universally attested" (are not dreams of falling?) and that flight is "universally known" in archaic myths (but so is enclosure in caves). To stress the temporal or theoretical priority of one over the other is to forget what Heraclitus (and T. S. Eliot and Eliade himself) well knew, that "the way up and the way down are one and the same."

also) might be by a hole in the middle of each vertically ordered plane through which the world-axis passes from the North Star to the center of the earth. Among the Altaic peoples, Harva writes (1938, 347–48), everything in the lower world "seems to be other," its day corresponding to our night and its night to our day.

The songs and ceremonies of shamans who have returned from this realm vividly describe its geography and its perilous roads over raging rivers or streams of blood. The Reindeer Gold shaman's itinerary crosses high mountains and primeval swamps until reaching the village of the dead, where smoke rises "and reindeer feed as among the living Reindeer-Tungus" (Harva 1938, 485–87). Many northern Siberian peoples believe the realm of the dead lies to the north, at the mouths of rivers flowing into the Arctic Ocean or beyond the death-sea, and many in both North and Central Asia tell of an evil prince (Erlik-Khan for the Altai) who rules over the dead and carries off souls to his realm.

Nor is this mirror world a place of eternal stasis: it may be a beginning as much as an end of life, and thus a source of perpetual regeneration. Some peoples believe souls of the dead may be reborn in children of the same family. The Yenisei Ostiaks, or Kets, "believe that the soul can take up its dwelling, or live again in some animal, especially in bears, and also *vice versa*," in a cycle of continual renewal (Harva 1938, 481). Yukaghir shamans often go to the land of shadows to request a soul for living childless relatives, or to seize one by force and put it in a woman's womb—though such a soul will soon escape from the body and return to the world below (Jochelson 1926, 160). Because of this dual nature of the underworld, some shamans not only escort souls of the dead to their future homes but bring back to the world of the living souls of the unborn. The other world of Siberian cosmology is thus no eternally changeless realm but partakes in a dynamic interchange of living, dead, and unborn, an interchange—pertaining to the future as much as the past—in which the shaman, both psychopomp and midwife, plays the indispensable role of mediating between the two worlds.

The most common reason for a shaman's descent to the underworld was not to escort souls of the dead, however, or replenish the living, but to retrieve the soul of a sick person feared to be in danger of death, or to gain advice from the dead on how to expel disease. This hazardous quest, in which shamans might risk their own lives, occasioned their most elaborate performances as well as dramatic accompanying narratives and retrospective sagas commemorating their heroic achievement.

Many in the centuries since Richard Johnson have described ceremonies for recovering a sick person's soul. Thus the old Yukaghir Samsonov re-enacted for Jochelson (1926, 196–99) the curing rite of his clan. After beating a drum and conjuring up spirits of animals and birds, the shaman lay motionless while his soul descended through his drum to the world below; he then described his journey. Having crossed a river and entered the tent of his ancestors, he rescued the sick man's soul by force and stuffed it up his ear to prevent it from escaping. Finally, after two virgins revived him by rubbing his legs, the shaman, beating his drum and jumping, returned the soul to the patient.

The shaman frequently enacts his quest (commonly in a darkened tent) for his patient and others. Among the Tungus or Evenk, performances were especially stormy, Jochelson noted (1926, 199–200) after watching Samsonov's son-in-law "call forth his spirits with such wild onomatopoetic screams, whistling, grinding of teeth and terrible facial contortions, that the Yukaghir would be terrified." A generation later, Anisimov (1963b, 100–101) witnessed an Evenk curing session which he describes in detail. Swaying slowly to the drum, by a glimmering fire, the shaman invoked spirit helpers through song, vividly describing their responses. In the silence after the drumming ceased, "the voices of the spirits could be clearly heard: the snorting of beasts, bird-calls, the whirring of wings." Then to thunderous drumming and agitated song the shaman's animal double (*khargi*) and attendant spirits descended to the lower world by the world-tree and learned from an ancestor the cause of the clansman's illness. If the shamanic ancestor failed to provide the needed information, the shaman sent his khargi to the supreme heavenly deity, the ultimate source of knowledge to which only he of the living, by virtue of his ecstatic vocation, had access.

So vividly is the khargi's journey evoked, with "comic and dramatic dialogues, wild screams, snorts, noises, and the like," Anisimov recalls (101–03), "that it startled and amazed even this far from superstitious onlooker." At the height of his ecstasy, the shaman threw his drum to his assistant, seized the thongs connected to the tent pole, and danced a pantomime illustrating how the *khargi* rushed on his dangerous journey at the shaman's command. While the hypnotized audience "fell into a state of mystical hallucination, feeling themselves active participants in the shaman's performance," he leaped into the air with the help of the tent thongs, imitating the flight of his spirits, "reached the highest pitch of ecstasy, and fell foaming at the mouth on the rug." Gradually revived by his assistant, he began to dance a pantomime symbolizing the khargi's return to the middle world. Then, rhythmically swaying on the thongs, he told in recitative of the khargi's deeds in the other world, reported the ancestral spirits' advice on fighting the disease spirit, put the drum aside, and paused; the first part of the performance had ended.

After resting, the shaman again seized the thongs and began to whirl around the tent pole in a furious dance, attempting to expel the spirit of the disease (Anisimov, 103–05). When all else failed, a contentious dialogue ensued, in which the shaman persuaded the disease-spirit to pass into a sacrificial reindeer; his helpers then showered the spirit with jibes and threats. Once more the shaman seized the thongs and threw himself into a frantic dance, accompanied by wild screams and snorts and flying coals and ashes. As the ecstasy of shaman and onlookers reached its highest pitch, the captured disease-spirit was defecated into the abyss by one of the shaman's spirit birds. The shaman and his spirits then returned to the middle world, barricading all passages from the world below. After sacrificing the reindeer and dancing through various heavens up to the supreme god into whose safekeeping he gave an image of the patient's soul, the shaman, in a strenuous dance of ecstasy, celebrated his triumph and that of his people over the forces afflicting them—the always-provisional triumph of life over death which must continually be sought anew because it can never be final.

For both shaman and audience such a performance is no mere theatrical representation but an undertaking demanding supreme effort and entailing possible failure or even death from loss of the shaman's soul. Deep trance, in which the soul is thought to leave the inanimate body for the other world, resembles a coma; Shirokogoroff (1935b, 76–77) found that the pulse of a Tungus shamaness rapidly dropped in half, while her body turned cold and showed no vital signs. "The shaman knows that his soul is going forth, he knows too that on its way back to his body it can be robbed or detained, he knows that a life without soul is impossible, and if he has convinced himself that it has really not returned, nothing further remains for him but to suspend the action of his heart, and to die." Knowing well that transcendence of the here and now is no trifling matter, shamans try to avoid going on such dangerous journeys more than once a year.

SHAMANIC NARRATION: HEROES OF THE SPIRIT

More than most priests or mediums, the shaman is frequently venerated by those whose aspirations (however worldly) he strives to fulfill through quests to other worlds above and below. His dramatic account of his adventures, in story, song, or recitative, was no doubt "a primordial form of poetry" descending from ancient times, and very possibly also, as Meuli suggests (849), a "germinal form" for myth, folktale, and poetry in general. In the shaman's wild songs, vividly describing the strange sights and adventures, trials and dangers experienced on his difficult journeys in the spirit world (Harva 1927, 523), with their perilous battles against demonic foes, is one possible kernel of full-blown epic and dramatic poetry (see Kirby) celebrating the spiritual quest of the conquering hero.

No language of North or Central Eurasian shamanistic peoples was written until recently, but a large body of oral poetry from these regions has been recorded in which the shamanic quest is central. Unlike much early oral literature of Europe, Nora Chadwick suggests (1936, 291)—though like Homer's Nekyia (Odysseus's visit to the underworld) and some poems of the Elder Edda—oral sagas of the Turkic peoples or "Tatars" of Central Asia, as collected by Radloff in the late nineteenth century, relate, insofar as the distinction can be made, "not to the actual, but to the spiritual experiences of their heroes," and the search motif "plays perhaps a larger part than any other single theme in these poems," whose hero himself usually performs shamanistic feats (325).

The hero's career in these oral epics typically takes him over rivers and seas on a "hero horse" by whose aid, in Radloff's summation (Chadwick 1936, 292),[7] "he climbs the mountain ridges which tower to Heaven, and finally he mounts to the very sea of the gods; . . . dives down into the depths of the nether world and there does battle with fearful giants and swan women." The hero or heroine of the poems communicates with spirits through music, the heroine often transforming herself, like some shamans, into a bird, the hero riding away, like others, on his magical horse. Visits to worlds above and below are common themes (302). Several poems describe heroic underworld journeys like that of the maiden Kubai Ko who visits Erlik, king of the dead, to seek her brother's head, returns with it to earth, and with the water of life restores him to health (306). Visits to the heavens are also frequent, especially by women, on horseback or as birds, with the purpose of saving souls. The hero or heroine of these Turkic epics is engaged, for the people's good, in a perilous quest open to all in those far-off times, but in these latter (and lesser) days restricted to the shaman alone.

Apart from narrations of their spiritual travels, made by shamans themselves and recorded by others during performances, accounts like these from Central Asia of journeys to other worlds are seldom found in the cultures of aboriginal Siberia. The impact of shamanism is evident, however, in the oral epics of such widely separated peoples as the Finns to the west and the Ainu and Manchus to the east.[8] Prominent

7. Chadwick draws primarily on Wilhelm Radloff (V. V. Radlov), *Proben der Volkslitteratur der Türkischen Stämme und der Dsungarischen Steppe*, published in 10 volumes between 1866 and 1907; this citation is from 5:vii.

8. Shamanistic elements, including flights through the air and attempted ascent of the sky, also pervade the Tibetan/Mongolian epic of Gesar of Ling. "There is good reason to believe that the most ancient traditions relating to Gesar appeared among the Bonpös," David-Neel writes (David-Neel and Yongden, 19), ". . . and that subsequently a Buddhist gloss was given to these traditions" in an epic "impregnated with shamanism." In extant versions, however, this purportedly shamanistic substratum has been overgrown by lush accretions of Tibetan magic and Buddhist marvels.

among the fabulous adventures of the Finnish hero Väinämöinen handed down in the oral tales collected by Lönnrot as the *Kalevala* are descents to the dead in Poems 16 and 17 (96–112). In order to fetch the charms needed to complete the boat constructed by his magic singing, Väinämöinen visits the Abode of the Dead where "Death's stumpy daughter," washing laundry in Death's dark river, warns him that "many have come here, not many returned," and lulls him to sleep. Escaping the river of Death by transforming himself into an otter and a snake, Väinämöinen warns against voluntarily going to Death's Domain and tells of the evil wages paid to wrongdoers there. He next seeks the needed charms from the long dead Antero Vipunen, who lies outstretched with trees growing from him, and when this earthy corpse swallows him, builds a smithy in his entrails and forces Vipunen to reveal the charms. Väinämöinen then emerges from Vipunen's mouth and completes the wondrous boat of his travels.

Despite motifs common to widely disparate peoples, much in these and other adventures of the *Kalevala* suggests that its strange heroes, "smiths, singers, and magicians," may in essence, as Meuli suggests (2:693–95), be shamans. Their chief weapon is song, such as the "eternal sage" and master harpist Väinämöinen learns from the dead Vipunen through his shamanistic initiation in the bowels of the earth; and when he finally sets out in a copper boat "toward the upper reaches of the world, to the lower reaches of the heavens" at the end of Lönnrot's compilation (337), he leaves his harp behind as "the eternal source of joyous music for the people, the great songs for his children." In short, Meuli concludes, the adventure with Vipunen and other exploits of Väinämöinen "are shamans' journeys" like those known among the Siberian Samoyed tribes distantly related to the Finns.

Some five thousand miles to the east, on Japan's northernmost main island, Hokkaido, the Ainu epic tradition "is one of the richest and most interesting bodies of archaic oral folklore in existence" (Philippi, 21). Recorded mainly in the early twentieth century, when the language was fast beginning to vanish, these remarkable songs have unmistakable shamanistic affinities. Human, animal, and divine mingle inseparably in poems narrated, like shamans' accounts, in the first person singular, whether by a human being, a semi-divine culture hero, or a god or goddess associated with an animal species such as the bear.

Although the epic reciter, usually a woman (like almost all Ainu shamans), "does not go into a trance, the gods borrow the reciter's lips in the same way as those of a shaman" (Philippi, 3). Indeed, some female reciters double as shamans, and the heroines of epic literature are normally depicted as such (45), suggesting that age-old north Asiatic shamanism "is an all-pervasive influence in Ainu life" (27). In the poems, shamanistic feats are performed by divinities themselves (the active agents during shamans' trances) or by animals incarnating divinity. Thus the Owl God sends Dipper Boy to request the Gods of Game and Fish to replenish the food from whose lack human beings—until they learn to treat the slain properly—are dying (111–14). In another song a she-bear obeys the Fire Goddess's commands to cure a chieftain's daughter by licking her wounds and blowing on them, like a shaman (129–31; cf. Kitagawa, 119–21).

Clearly shamanistic though these poems are, they remain peripheral to our concerns, since the Ainu shaman's personal self is thought to be passively displaced by the god possessing her rather than journeying forth in ecstatic quest of transcendent knowledge. (The Hokkaido Ainu were not nomads but salmon fishers who in some ways more resembled sedentary agriculturalists than the restless hunters and herders of North Asia.) Turning to the *Tale of the Nišan Shamaness*—a Manchu folk epic dating, in origin, to perhaps the seventeenth century and surviving in three written redactions discovered in the early twentieth—we find a full-blown rendition, in prose interspersed with verse incantations, of the ecstatic otherworld quest most fully attested among the kindred Tungus who gave the shaman his international name.

Here there can be no doubt of shamanistic influence, since the heroine is a shamaness rescuing a soul from the land of the dead. In the longest version, a son, Sergudai Fiyanggo, is born to a wealthy village official, Baldu Bayan, and his wife in their fiftieth year, after the loss of their previous son in a hunting accident at age fifteen. When Sergudai reaches fifteen he asks to go hunting, for "none of us escapes the fate that comes bringing life and death to us all" (40). Fever suddenly fells him, and he dies. At the funeral, an old hunchback tells the stricken father a skilled shaman can bring the boy back to life: "Go quickly and seek her!" Having said this (50), he walked leisurely away, "sat on a five-colored cloud and was lifted upwards"; Baldu Bayan joyously recognizes that a god has instructed him.

A young woman hanging out clothes directs him to the other bank, where he learns that she herself was the shaman he sought. Having thus deceived him, she yields to his tearful pleas and begins her divination by throwing objects in the water and beating a tambourine while "the spirit permeated her body" (52). In rhythmic mutterings she reveals that Sergudai died when Ilmun Han, Lord of the Dead, sent an evil spirit to seize him, and divines that Baldu Bayan owns a dog born on the same day as his son. But as to bringing the boy back to life: "How will I, a small and weak shaman, be able to accomplish this? . . . What do I know?" (55).

Offered half of Baldu Bayan's property, she consents to try, and is borne to his house as quickly as if she were flying; there her old assistant,

Nari Fiyanggo, joins her. After she dons her shaman's garments, bells, and cap, "her tall, slender body waved like a trembling willow" as "the spirit entered, permeating her fully. Suddenly, gritting her teeth, she began to mumble" (57–58), calling for rooster, dog, lumps of bean paste, and bundles of paper: "I am going to pursue a soul into a dark place. . . . Truly try hard to revive me when I come back" (59). Her assistant begins to mutter, using the drumstick to conduct the spirits, as the shaman starts on her perilous quest.

Leading the rooster and dog, she sets out to seek Ilmun Han. A lame one-eyed man ferries her over a river, informing her that Monggoldai Nakcu, kinsman of the Lord of the Dead, had passed the same way with Sergudai's soul. Crossing the Red River on her drum like a whirlwind, she tells the gatekeepers, "I am going to seek Monggoldai Nakcu in the realm of the dead" (63–64). At the third pass of the underworld she shakes her skirt bells and calls on Monggoldai Nakcu to restore, for a fee, one who did not reach the full length of his life; but he scornfully refuses, saying that Ilmun Han has "made Sergudai his son and is raising him lovingly! Could it be possible to give him back to you?" (65).

The shamaness angrily says she is "finished" (66) if she fails to retrieve him. She bids her bird and animal spirits fly into Ilmun Han's city and bring the boy to her; they rise up like fog, and a great bird carries Sergudai away. Ilmun Han angrily sends Monggoldai Nakcu in pursuit, and after bargaining with the shamaness he promises, in return for rooster and dog, to add ninety years to the boy's life: "Until his hair turns white, his teeth turn yellow, his waist becomes bent, his eyes grow dim, and his feet begin to lag, let him urinate standing up and defecate squatting down" (70).

As she leads Sergudai back, a resentful spirit angrily asks why she has not revived "your dear warm husband who was married to you from youth" (71), and threatens boiling oil if she refuses. She quickly rids herself of him—"Without a husband, I shall live happily" (74)—and continues on her way, "now walking merrily as the breeze, now running quickly as a whirlwind" (75). She sees an ugly old woman, Omosi-mama, distributor of souls, "manufacturing small children" and placing them in bags (77); when the shamaness was born, Omosi-mama recalls, "I placed a shaman's cap on your head, tied bells on your skirt, put a tambourine in your hand, and causing you to act as a shaman, I playfully brought you to life." Omosi-mama shows her punishments of the underworld to instruct her in consequences of good and evil while a bodhisattva, by a bridge of souls, assigns future incarnations, from Buddhas to worms. The shamaness bows and promises to report these things to the living.

After she returns to the home of Baldu Bayan, her assistant revives her, and she fans the soul into Serguddai's body, which awakens as from a long sleep. She then lives respectably, "making a break with all strange, dissolute matters" (88–89). When her mother-in-law accuses her of killing her husband a second time by refusing to resurrect him, the Emperor, in sparing her life, decrees that her shaman's cap and bells, tambourines and implements, be bound with steel rope in a leather box and thrown into the village well. "Let us," the epic's redactor piously concludes, "overcome and abstain from evil" (90).

Profoundly influenced though this tale clearly is by popular Mahayana Buddhism in important details—its descriptions of hellish punishments, its moralistic ending, and above all its need to declare shamanism a thing of the past—its account of a shaman's underworld journey is surely an authentic reflection of the far older Tungus-Manchu culture of pre-Buddhist times. In this vivid Manchu folk epic, as in those of Turks and Finns (and more marginally of the Ainu), an unmistakably shamanic figure engages in the central undertaking of shamans everywhere, the quest in other worlds for means of restoring human life in this one.

For this world, the here and now of immediate human experience, is not autonomous but can only attain fulfillment through interaction with what lies beyond it—with the transcendent yet potentially immanent worlds of the spirit. In the traditional cultures of these vast regions the shaman alone can bring about communication between them, thereby breaching the closure of a world in which man would otherwise be less than human. In mythical times, to be sure, there were others, as the quests of the Turkic and Finnish epic heroes attest, no less spiritually adventurous than shamans themselves, but since those far-off days when men could speak the language of animals, change shape, and ascend to the heavens at will, the shaman alone, in the solitude of his (or her) demanding vocation and the hazards of spiritual journeys on others' behalf, has made of life, in Shirokogoroff's words (1935b, 96), "a kind of hero's existence," continuing at whatever personal cost the indispensable quest for ecstatic transcendence through communication with the beyond on which the life and wellbeing of others depend no less than before. It is doubtful that any imperial edict will be able to silence this telltale drumming forever or dispense for long with the visionary services of some wise one (or fool) speaking with the indefeasible authority bestowed by cap and bells.

PART FIVE

Forms of the Quest in Native America

CHAPTER TWELVE

The Arctic and Western
North America

The unmistakable affinity and probable common ancestry of Eurasian and American shamanisms is especially striking in the case of the Eskimo (or Inuit) and the tribes of the Northwest Pacific coast, the peoples closest to Siberia. The Eskimo in particular belong to an Arctic culture circling the globe from Lapland through Siberia to Alaska, Canada, and Greenland, and their once-universal shamanism was until recently central to their culture.

AURORA BOREALIS: THE ESKIMO

Given the immense extent of these sparsely populated barren lands, the uniformity of a culture unmistakably Eskimo in spite of every regional variation is astonishing. The isolation of the traditional Eskimo from all but sporadic contact with other peoples, and their constant struggle with a signally harsh environment, fostered for centuries an extraordinary conservatism not only in language but in virtually every aspect of their life.

Subsisting largely on fish and sea mammals, even tribes that winter in fixed houses of wood or sod are constantly on the move during much of the year, and always ready to adapt to unexpected circumstances. Their conservatism is therefore an expression not of habituated routines in a static world but of inventive responsiveness, in time-tested ways, to a world of continual change. Their characteristic "symbolism of fluidity, changeability of life, even of unreliability," and their "lack of symbolism indicating attachment to the land," probably reflect, as Lantis suggests (334–35), "the ancient as well as modern mobility of the Eskimos, who must be continually moving about in search of food and who most often seek that food from the sea." The religious expression of this mobility cannot, of course, be the invariant ritual of the hierarchic priest, wholly foreign to the egalitarian Eskimo, but the restless shaman's inherently unfinished quest to assure the welfare of his people in a world of constant flux.

Eskimo cosmologies are generally less developed than those of Old World shamanistic peoples, who were often in contact both with one another and with foreign civilizations from Scandinavia to Japan. Even so, a tripartite division of the universe into heaven, earth, and underworld is widely attested, with the underworld most often located beneath the sea. Within this universe, the "ability of men and animals to transform themselves into other beings, while always retaining their *inuas* [souls or spirits], results in an unpredictable world in which one cannot be sure of the true identity of any given creature" (Fitzhugh and Kaplan, 187). In earlier times, the Canadian Netsilik and other tribes believed, human beings and animals changed into one another at will and spoke the same tongue (Balikci, 210). But since then only the shaman can exercise this power and visit the underworld in the shape of a seal, or the sky in the shape of a bird.

Personal names were often identified with the souls which most Eskimo, like many Siberian peoples, thought were reborn in children named after dead relatives; belief in reincarnation, Hultkrantz asserts (in Paulson et al., 409), is more characteristic of the Eskimo than of other North American peoples. Absence of the mobile soul from the body is widely held to be the main cause of illness; after death, which its permanent departure effects, it travels to one of several worlds in the sky or beneath the earth or sea. The number of these worlds varies greatly, and Eskimo eschatology is seldom highly systematized.

The most accessible of the *inuat* (spirits or divinities) to shamanistic mediation is the Old Woman of the undersea world commonly known by the mercifully short name of Sedna given to her on Baffin Island. "The Central Eskimo say that at one time she had been a woman who escaped in her father's boat from her bird-husband, and who, on being pursued by her husband," Boas writes (1940, 504–05), summarizing this widespread myth, "was thrown overboard by her father. When she clung to the gunwale of her boat, her father chopped off her finger-joints one after another. These were transformed into seals, ground-seals, and whales. . . . After this had happened, she was taken to the lower world, of which she became the ruler." Here she has power both to provide and, when angered, withhold the sea beasts needed for food, blubber, and skins, and to raise storms, steal human souls, and cause sickness. "It is not strange therefore," Rasmussen writes (1929, 123–24), "that it is regarded as one of a shaman's greatest feats to visit her where she lives at the bottom of the sea, and so tame and conciliate her that human beings can live once more untroubled on earth."[1]

The shaman, commonly known by some variant of the word *angakoq* (plural *angakut*), was the pre-eminent Eskimo religious specialist; as in Siberia, his only human rival was another shaman. In a culture lacking the hierarchical institutions of more sedentary peoples his prestige—or, less frequently, hers; as in Siberia the female shaman was the exception—was extraordinarily great, even though he was generally an outsider. "He may be an orphan or a cripple who is unable to hunt or otherwise contribute to routine village life," Fitzhugh and Kaplan write (188) of the Bering Sea shaman. "He may be prone to fits or seizures, sure signs that spirits are at work within."

The initial call, as in Siberia, was involuntary, and its signs might be remarked from early childhood if not birth. "A man does not become an angakoq because he wishes it himself, but because certain mysterious powers in the universe convey to him the impression that he has been chosen, and this takes place as a revelation in a dream" (Rasmussen, 1927, 81). Here too the vocation of shaman tended to run in families, but a personal vision was usually essential; only rarely were the shaman's powers acquired in a mechanical fashion, as among the Kobuk of northern Alaska (Curtis, 20:211–12), where the son obtained his father's supernatural gifts by eating a piece of his flesh. The extent to which the initiative for the visionary call was beyond the individual's control is emphasized not only by shamans' accounts but by various myths, including several—from Alaska to Greenland—that tell of persons who became shamans after being carried off to the moon (Curtis, 20:235–37; Rink, 440–41).

But if the initial summons was involuntary, the preparation that followed often involved an arduous quest. It was above all the Central and Eastern Eskimo, as opposed to those of Siberia, the Bering Sea, and southern Alaska, Lantis suggests (313), who "deliberately sought power through solitude, concentration, and physical self-mortification."[2] Here the classic accounts are those of Rasmussen's Fifth Thule Expedition

1. The Iglulik call this goddess Takánapsâluk; here as elsewhere, even in quotations, I substitute the more familiar name Sedna. For other versions of this myth see, e.g., Rasmussen 1931, 225–27, and Boas 1964, 175–83.

2. Lantis's generalization concerning the Eskimo parallels Benedict's about the North American Indians (1923, 26–27): "East of the Rocky Mountains the emphasis is upon the sought vision induced by hunger, thirst, purgatives, and self-laceration. To the west of the Rockies, though we find there also the deliberate vision quest, a very widespread attitude regards the vision as unsought, involuntary, a thing of predisposition."

across the Canadian Arctic by dogsled in the early 1920s, when shamans, with whom Rasmussen could fluently converse in their own language, were still practicing even though already, perhaps, in decline.

In some cases, like that of the Iglulik woman Uvavnuk, who was struck by a ball of fire while making water outside her ice hut in the winter (Rasmussen 1929, 122–23), the shaman might be the seemingly passive recipient of a "sudden enlightenment" descending upon her unawares, much as the spirit might seize a future medium in the African bush. Generally, however, a Central or Eastern Eskimo could acquire shamanic spirits only through a determined quest involving rigorous ordeals. Thus Igjugarjuk of the Caribou Eskimo was visited as a young man by incomprehensible dreams, but his visionary election by a spirit was only the first step in the difficult process of making himself a shaman. In the depth of winter, he was carried on a small sledge to a faraway spot where his instructor built a tiny snow hut. Here he sat meditating without food or water for thirty days, he told Rasmussen (1927, 82–84; cf. 1930, 52–55), until a helping spirit in the shape of a woman crowned his potentially lethal quest with success. Even with this hardwon acquisition, his preparation was not ended; five months of strict diet and sexual abstention followed, culminating in five days of formal initiation.

This quest sets the shaman apart from the community whose needs he will serve, since "the best magic words are those which come to one in an inexplicable manner when one is alone out among the mountains. . . . The power of solitude is great and beyond understanding" (Rasmussen 1929, 114). In the midst of his deliberate isolation, the Iglulik shaman Aua recalls (118–19),

> I would sometimes fall to weeping, and feel unhappy without knowing why. Then, for no reason, all would suddenly be changed, and I felt a great, inexplicable joy, a joy so powerful that I could not restrain it, but had to break into song, a mighty song, with only room for the one word: joy, joy! And I had to use the full strength of my voice. And then in the midst of such a fit of mysterious and overwhelming delight I became a shaman, not knowing myself how it came about. But I was a shaman. I could see and hear in a totally different way. I had gained my qaumaneq, my enlightenment, the shaman-light of brain and body, and this in such a manner that it was not only I who could see through the darkness of life, but the same light also shone out from me, imperceptible to human beings, but visible to all the spirits of earth and sky and sea, and these now came to me and became my helping spirits.

Aua's enlightenment, like Igjugarjuk's, is the climax of a lonely quest entailing "inexplicable terror" and "peril of death" (121) from spirits who become helpers only when mastered by mastery of self; Aua's luminous joy arises from victorious confrontation with this mortal danger that threatens all but the few who by looking within can see through and beyond it, thereby gaining the transformative spirit they have long sought but could not attain till it suddenly descended upon them.

The Eskimo shaman's principal purpose was to remedy disease and other misfortunes, including bad weather and bad luck in the hunt. Some of his performances resembled those of diviners or mediums elsewhere. In the "head-lifting" technique, for example, a thong held by the shaman was tied to the head of a reclining person to whom questions were addressed; when the head could not be lifted the answer was affirmative (Boas 1975, 135; Balikci, 227). And the Netsilik, like so many tribal peoples, believe that the spirit takes possession of the shaman and speaks through his mouth (Rasmussen 1931, 294). But in many instances the Eskimo shaman was by no means simply a passive implement of the spirits; his active quest for shamanic powers continued as an unending search given dramatic expression in his public performances. Far from being completed with initiation, his quest for spiritual knowledge in a world of sudden change and radical uncertainty was inherently open-ended; what he gained by the ordeal of becoming a shaman was not so much knowledge itself as the repeatedly renewed impetus to seek it beyond the normal round of everyday tribal existence by which others were largely shut off.

One source of superhuman knowledge was the Land of the Sky, in particular the Moon, which shamans of both mythical and recent times frequently visited. In a legend recorded by Boas (1964, 190–91), "A mighty angakoq, who had a bear for his tornaq [helping spirit], resolved to pay a visit to the moon. . . . He had his hands tied up and a thong fastened around his knees and neck. Then he summoned his tornaq, which carried him rapidly through the air and brought him to the moon," where he gained the favor of the man of the moon by passing the difficult test of not laughing at his hollow-backed wife as she danced. "During his visit to the moon, his body had lain motionless and soulless, but now it revived. The thongs with which his hands had been fastened had fallen down," the story concludes, "though they had been tied in firm knots. The angakoq fell almost exhausted, and when the lamps were relighted he related to the eagerly listening men his adventures during his flight to the moon."

The procedure by which a shaman seeking higher knowledge was bound in a dark room by thongs from which he somehow freed himself during his performance was by no means only mythical, but was a core component of the "Spirit Lodge" or "Shaking Tent" complex throughout much of native North America (and elsewhere), associated by the Eskimo with celestial flights of the shaman's spirit (Hultkrantz 1981,

61–90; cf. Boas 1964, 186). In the Iglulik shaman Aua's vivid account (Rasmussen 1929, 129–31),

> strange sounds are heard by the listening guests; they hear a whistling that seems to come far, far up in the air, humming and whistling sounds, and then suddenly the shaman calling out at the top of his voice:
> 'Halala—halalale, halala—halalale!'
> And at the same moment, all visitors in the house must cry:
> 'Ale—ale—ale!'; then there is a sort of rushing noise in the snow hut, and all know that an opening has been formed for the soul of the shaman, an opening like the blowhole of a seal, and through it the soul flies up to heaven, aided by all those stars which were once human beings. . . . When the shaman has amused himself for a while among all the happy dead, he returns to his old village. The guests, who are awaiting him with closed eyes, hear a loud bump at the back of the sleeping place, and then they hear the thong he was tied with come rushing down. . . . Afterwards he tells of all that he has seen and heard.

Such a spirit journey may be made, Aua states, "for joy alone," but also for more practical purposes such as diagnosis of disease, or even resurrection of the dead. Theories of disease among the Eskimo included both intrusion of a foreign object (or assault by an inimical spirit) and loss of the wandering soul, theories by no means incompatible; belief in soul loss was especially prominent. Whatever the cause, disease was treated (in a region lacking the medicinal herbs of less rigorous climates) not only by sucking or extraction but by soul flights to the sky or beneath the sea, and frequently, as in much of Siberia, by direct combat between the shaman and the afflicting spirit.

Since disease and other misfortunes were commonly thought to result from infringement of one or more of the many taboos governing Eskimo life, including the much violated taboo against abortions, a shamanistic seance was often followed by communal confession of transgressions—a practice widely prevalent in non-Eskimo native North America also, especially among Eastern Indian tribes. This was preeminently the case when a shaman journeyed to the underwater realm of Sedna to refurnish the tribal food supply, either at a regular festival or a time of famine. The classic account of this uncertain spiritual quest on which the life and wellbeing of the community depended is again Rasmussen's (1929, 124–27). After sitting for a while in silence, breathing deeply, the shaman calls upon his helping spirits. "Then all know that he is on his way to the ruler of the sea beasts," on a perilous journey over the sea floor past rolling stones to Sedna's house or—for the greatest shamans—directly down "through a tube so fitted to his body that he can check his progress by pressing against the sides."

When the shaman enters the house, he at once sees Sedna, who, as a sign of anger, is sitting with her back to the lamp and with her back to all the animals in the pool. . . . And now he must grasp Sedna by one shoulder and turn her face towards the lamp and towards the animals, and stroke her hair, the hair she has been unable to comb out herself, because she has no fingers. . . . The shaman must now use all his efforts to appease her anger, and at last, when she is in a kindlier mood, she takes the animals one by one and drops them on the floor, and then it is as if a whirlpool arose in the passage, the water pours out from the pool and the animals disappear in the sea. This means rich hunting and abundance for mankind. . . . Those who have been in attendance during his dangerous journey close the session by confessing the breaches of taboo by which the communal welfare has been endangered.

Despite undoubted elements of compulsive or hortatory ritual, these ceremonies—on which there were many variations among the Central Eskimo (see Rasmussen 1932, 24–26; Boas 1975, 138–39)—were not in essence coercive. The increase in the food supply or the restoration of health at which they aimed could be achieved, most notably for the Iglulik, not by repetition of magic formulas or actions but by the shaman's hazardous descent to the sea bottom, in which failure was always at least theoretically possible, to seek out the favor which Sedna alone, goddess, human, and animal in one, could decide to grant or deny.

It was above all the knowledge won through his solitary initial quest and renewed through further wanderings or flights to the sky that now allowed the shaman, on return from the wilderness, to undertake this greater quest on behalf of the people. Their resurrection could be achieved only by one who had looked unflinchingly on his own skeleton and knew that despite his apartness from others and transcendence of everyday experience he was fundamentally one with them, so that their quest was his. By his unending search for what he knew he was lacking and might never find, the disoriented outsider became the necessary guide who infused the frozen present with a visionary if always uncertain light without which life itself would soon perish.

PRIESTLY SHAMANS: THE NORTHWEST COAST

Despite the close affinities between the peoples of the Northwest Pacific Coast and the shamanistic cultures of the Eskimo and Siberia, which led Benedict to categorize the Kwakiutl as "Dionysian" in their excess, the communal ceremonies of these settled salmon fishers reflect their stratified social structure and in this regard more nearly resemble the "Apollonian" rites of agriculturalists like the Zuñi. This striking manifestation of conflicting tendencies latent in every culture is one reason for the fascination their seemingly bizarre traditions exert.

Only rarely, as among the Nootka of Vancouver Island, do a few myths—"imports from other peoples," in Drucker's view (1951, 151)—tell of heroes who climbed to the sky or descended to the underworld; in general the cosmology of these peoples seems less developed than in shamanistic cultures of Eurasia. But nowhere were myths and rites affirming the intimate relation of human and animal more prominent than in this land of totem pole and mask. The most widely diffused rite was the First Salmon ceremony, in which this seasonal visitor was ritually propitiated before being cooked and eaten. Thus the creative power of animals was shared by all, even if it could be fully acquired by the shaman alone.

Among some tribes like the Wishram of the Columbia River, religion centered almost wholly in shamanism and there were no ceremonials unconnected with it (Spier and Sapir, 236). But even to the north, where formal rituals were highly developed, shamans were the essential intermediaries between human and natural forces. Shamanism was frequently "the surest route to prestige for one who found himself doomed to low status in a rigid social system" (Drucker 1965, 92). Women could become shamans, and in most Northwest Coast tribes there seem to have been more female than male shamans, even though the most powerful were generally men (Drucker 1951, 183). Male or female, noble or commoner, however, the shaman was the central religious figure, preeminently able (as among the Kwakiutl) to "cross what should be an absolute divide and return safely": the indispensable "marginal person who straddles the boundaries between his own kind and the universe of spirits" (Goldman 1975, 100), fostering reciprocal communication between these continually interacting realms.

The shaman's initial call was widely considered involuntary, even violent. Among the Kwakiutl, the shaman may acquire powers by killing a supernatural being or by being taken to a lonely spot where a supernatural helper injects him with shamanistic power in the form of a quartz crystal (Boas 1966b, 135), as among the Aranda and other Australian tribes half a world away. But among some peoples the shaman-to-be is the spirits' unwilling prey, vainly fleeing a summons he cannot refuse. Thus Isaac Tens, shaman of the Gitskan of northern British Columbia, told Barbeau (39–41) how he strove to escape from a large owl that tried to carry him away and tall trees that crawled after him like snakes, and how he resisted the visionary shamans who bade him join them, until finally "I began to sing. A chant was coming out of me without my being able to do anything to stop it."

A strong tendency toward automatic inheritance of shamanic powers existed among several peoples like the Haida (Swanton 1905, 38; Curtis, 11:136), especially in the north. Even here, however, at least a pro forma quest was required, and for most Northwest Coast shamans neither inheritance nor involuntary seizure was sufficient preparation unless followed by a prolonged solitary quest culminating in personal encounter with the empowering spirits. Thus among the Coast Salish of British Columbia, ritual transfer of shamanic power from father to son was preliminary to the boy's personal spirit encounter (Barnett, 149–50).

For these peoples, and many others of the Americas, the ritualized quest for supernatural powers was not limited—as it generally was, outside myth and legend, in Eurasia and the American Arctic—to potential shamans but was open to virtually all. Even among the northern Tlingit and Haida, who tended toward routine inheritance of spirit helpers by the population at large, a residual quest for a spirit belonging to one's lineage remained indispensable, and among many tribes from southern British Columbia to northern Oregon, notably the Coast Salish, the quest was the central spiritual experience of each individual's life, corresponding to tribal initiations of other peoples.

Its object was acquisition of a personal guardian spirit, usually in animal form. In some Salishan tribes, like the Twana and Upper Skagit of northwestern Washington, shamanic spirits were sharply differentiated from those of laymen, but a quest was essential to the acquisition of both. It was fundamental to this as to every quest that each person, as Collins writes of the Skagit (4), "obtained his own spirit through his own efforts," and that the vision, as Amoss (13) affirms of the Nooksack, "was his own and not given to him by anyone."

Among the Twana and other Coast Salish tribes, systematic training might begin at age five or six, to be followed in adolescence by solitary fasts in quest of a guardian spirit (Elmendorf, 491–94). After this the seeker was "expected to 'forget' the vision encounter until the occasion of his first repossession by the spirit at a winter spirit dance," which might take place as long as twenty years after the first vision (495). This dance displayed the quester's spirit power, now revealed as under his or her control; it culminated in possession by the spirit, which sang its song while the quester ritually danced. Cleanliness was essential to the guardian spirit quest, of which bathing rituals were frequently part. A Nootka went out secretly at night to a bathing place in stream, lake, or ocean, where he sang a prayer while mortifying his flesh, then "entered the water, in which he remained as long as he could stand the cold. Some men would be almost unable to walk by the time they emerged," Drucker writes (1951, 167), and others "have been found dead at their bathing places." So fundamental was the spirit quest to the Coast Salish tribes of the Puget Sound region that children who refused to go were whipped and deprived of food; many seekers went out in stormy weather and plunged into deep water, weighted down by large stones.

Thus the dangers of the quest were intensely real, and success by no means guaranteed. One Puget Sound boy was sent out thrice on solitary quests, fasting and bathing for ten, fourteen, and fifteen days before attaining a vision (Haeberlin and Gunther, 68–69), which to some never came. When it did appear, a vision might be so terrifying, as among the Quinault of the Washington coast, that "the faint-hearted usually ran away" (Olson, 136). Clearly, mastery of such powerful spirits presupposed the difficult mastery of self, a principal goal of the arduous quest which nearly everyone, among Coast Salish and some other tribes, undertook: for the guardian spirit was an alter ego resulting from purposeful self-transformation, an expanded self acquiring transcendent power through communion with a larger than human world, and therefore a self not given but created and found.

The shaman's quest resembled that of others, though directed to the acquisition of far greater powers, including power to harm (even kill) and to cure. According to Bella Coola belief, men used to be "so much more powerful than at present, and so close to the supernatural, that all were virtually shamans" (McIlwraith, 1:539), but nowadays only shamans could attain—through a quest that might require thirty years or more (548)—what was once the birthright of all. Even a hereditary shaman, as among the Yakutat Tlingit of Alaska, had to go into the woods to encounter a spirit (usually in the form of an animal or bird whose tongue he cut out), and thereafter strengthened his power by repeated quests for new spirits (F. de Laguna, part 2, 676–77).

Nootka Shamans underwent years of ritual bathing before confronting a spirit. Some fainted, Drucker reports (1951, 184–87),

> with blood still trickling from mouth, nose, and ears, and even from the temples and hollows over the collar bones, so potent was the spirit power. . . . No seeker after power dared to forget, if he wished to avoid misfortune, that the encounter with a spirit was tremendously charged with danger. . . . He might drop dead on the spot, or he might last to make his way home, to collapse in front of his house, with rigid limbs and horribly contorted face.

The newly found spirit taught the future shaman songs of curing, and instructed him night after night. Further encounters were repeatedly sought, for this, like all true quests, was unending.

Despite his involuntary initial call, the Northwest Coast shaman's profession frequently required not only a quest but an active struggle to master, even "kill," the spirit whose power the shaman sought to acquire—a struggle reminiscent of the conflicts of myth. For these North-west Coast Indians saw no essential hiatus between the heroes of myth and the living man or woman of spiritual powers, depleted though these may have become since the time when all were heroes and shamans in one.

A Kwakiutl or Tsimshian shaman might be designated against his will by spirits who made him sick or pursued him through the shadowy forest, but in myth the human being often triumphed over the spirits. Typical Kwakiutl stories, recounted by Boas (1966b, 309), tell of those who succeed, by guile or force, in wresting power from the supernaturals, even at the price of death and rebirth. And a Tsimshian myth of the Gyilodzau tribe relates the triumphant descent of the would-be shaman Only-One into a dark pit where he learns to restore the dead to life (Barbeau, 76–77). In myth as in life extraordinary powers were bestowed as the fruit of courageously pursued efforts of indeterminate outcome.

Here as elsewhere disease might be caused either by intrusion or soul loss (Drucker 1965, 87). The former was treated by extraction, especially sucking, but a shaman most fully demonstrated his powers by recovery of a lost soul, typically in a public performance. Some techniques, indeed, were more magical than ecstatic; thus among the Kwakiutl, a shaman passed his purifying ring of hemlock branches over a patient until the soul re-entered his body. Even this highly ritualized ceremony frequently involved, however, at least a rudimentary quest, as the shaman ran about looking for the patient's soul (Boas 1966, 137–39).

To travel to the spirit world was among the greatest accomplishments celebrated in the myths of Northwest Coast peoples. Thus a Bella Coola shaman descended into the ocean by a rope lowered from his canoe "until he found himself in a land where everything was much the same as on this earth"; he rescued his wife and later revived the son who had rotted away to a skeleton during his father's absence of nearly a year (McIlwraith, 1:544–46). Such feats were thought to have been performed by living shamans into recent times. Curtis (11:49) describes how a Nootka shaman's spirit apparently left his body to search for a sick man's soul, "visiting house after house in the land of the dead, until it found the object of its search" in the form of a small image which "he pretended to replace in the patient's head."

Among the Coast Salish the shaman's ritualized journey to other worlds was highly developed. In British Columbia, a Coast Salish shaman searched for a lost soul with outstretched arms and closed eyes; finally he received the soul, cold and nearly dead, blew gently on it, and restored it to its owner (Barnett, 215). The Upper Skagit shaman, too, went to the land of the dead to retrieve a lost soul, describing the events as he went (Collins, 201). But the dangers were great, and success uncertain. Among the Quinault a guardian spirit from the "twice dead" dared accompany the shaman only to where he had stayed while dead: "If he ventured farther both he and the shaman died" (Olson, 160). If a soul had gone too far, the shaman reported failure, for not even the boldest spiritual quest could now restore it.

Among the most elaborate Northwest Coast ceremonies was the *sbetetdaq* or "spirit canoe" rite performed by the Coast Salish of Puget Sound and some neighboring tribes. The ceremony, as Haeberlin describes it (252–57) from informants' memories of a ritual already defunct in the early twentieth century, took place in midwinter at night, since in the other world it would then be a bright summer day. The shamans stood in two parallel rows, facing westward as they poled their imaginary canoe toward the land of the dead, and eastward for the return journey. In the village of the dead a fight broke out (dramatized by boys shooting burning splints) between the shamans and ghosts who held a patient's spirit captive; this continued as the ghosts pursued the canoe back to the land of the living.

In crucial respects, then, including the journey to another world in search of a lost soul, the shamanistic quest of Pacific Northwest America paralleled that of Eurasia and the American Arctic. In others, however, the practices of these hierarchical salmon-fishers more nearly resembled the communal rituals characteristic of sedentary agriculturalists like the Zuñi, to whom Benedict so categorically opposed the "Dionysian" Kwakiutl.

Such rituals are prominent among both northern peoples like the Kwakiutl and peripheral California tribes to the south. The elaborate Kwakiutl organization of the people, during the winter season, into groups distinguished by degrees of spiritual power (an organization paralleled among the Nootka and others) carried collectivization to a point seemingly unknown among the migratory and egalitarian peoples of Central Asia and Siberia. Unlike the individual quest, which allowed for uncertainty and variation, the winter ceremonials performed by these groups were dramatizations of ancestral supernatural experiences transmitted, through shamanistic societies, from the legendary past.

Initiation of a shaman is "analogous in all details to that of participants in the winter ceremonial" (Boas 1966, 135); and both the Kwakiutl "Cannibal Dance" and the Nootka "Wolf Dance," like the societies that performed them, were known in their very different languages as "The Shamans," though most participants did not actually practice shamanism. "The Ceremonial shaman is the curing shaman translated," Goldman writes of the Kwakiutl (1975, 99), "to the more general and hence higher level of ritual performance." To this extent, the "shamanism" of the tribal ceremonials is a collective repetition of ancestral tradition rather than a perilous search for never fully attainable knowledge. Ceremonial shamanism in these rigidly structured cultures thus partially forfeited its questing dimension, which was nevertheless implicit in its communal endeavor to transcend nature through the sanctions of a precariously maintained social order.

Far from fomenting ecstasy, the Kwakiutl ritual transformed the "Cannibal's" hunger "from a destructive act to an affirmation of self-control" (Walens, 162), since the Kwakiutl, more Apollonian than Dionysian, "seek not excess but order" (41), which can only be won by overcoming its opposite. In consequence their shaman was almost priestly in the insistent ritual correctness of his actions, able to summon the spirits "only because he observes the correct ritual taboos and performs the correct prayers" (25).

The Northwest Coast shaman not only resembled a priest in reliance on ritual coercion, he also frequently shared his power (unlike his Siberian or Eskimo counterparts) with still more formalistic priests or ritualists. On the southern fringes of the Northwest Coast culture, among the Yurok, Karok, Hupa, and other small tribes of the Klamath River region of northern California, only vestiges remained of the quest for transcendent knowledge and power that had been among the hallmarks of Eurasian-American shamanism from Lapland to Puget Sound and beyond. In northwestern California, the almost universal American Indian association between the shaman and personal guardian spirits "is very weakly and indirectly developed," Kroeber writes (1925, 3). Shamans, almost all women, diagnosed disease not by communicating with spirits but through a clairvoyance attained by dancing and smoking, and cured a patient not by journeying forth in quest of his soul but by sucking out the intrusive "pain" within him. Magical techniques and concepts were "as abundantly developed among the Yurok and their neighbors as shamanism is narrowed" (Kroeber 1925, 4), and the formulaic character of their recitations suggest that the Yurok, unlike the intrepid nomads who once brought a primeval shamanism to American shores, "did not venture into the unknown and had no desire to" (13).

If this passive shamanism was restricted mainly to women, male priests conducted ceremonies intended (like the First Salmon Rites of more northerly tribes) "to renew or maintain the established world" (Kroeber 1925, 53), and in them the uncertain quest for knowledge of an indeterminate future gave way to ritually guaranteed prolongation of a sacrosanct past. These peoples, Kroeber concludes on the evidence of their own statements (Kroeber and Gifford, 5), "wanted their world small, compact, closed, stable, permanent, and fixed." Their quest was not to transcend the world as it is but forevermore to repeat it as it was from the first and must always (until it vanished completely) remain.

SHAMANIC CULTS: CALIFORNIA

However much the Yurok and their neighbors resembled some salmon-fishing tribes of the Northwest Coast in their sharp division between female curing shaman and male priest officiating over renewal of the world, they did not differ greatly, in the relative passivity of a shamanism remote from any quest for transcendent knowledge, from other peoples of California. Lacking priestly rivals in a region where plentiful acorns and pine-nuts provided little incentive, outside the far south, for agriculture or highly differentiated societies, Californian shamans were generally unrivaled in their authority. Sometimes chief and shaman were one, sometimes they collaborated closely; in either case, the shaman's standing was high and his prestige, though tinged with ambivalence, great. Where formalized cults had not arisen, as among the Shasta in the north, virtually all ritual centered in shamans and their ceremonials; and even where collective rites had taken over functions of individual shamans, the latter often remained, in the absence (outside the southernmost tribes) of other religious officials, key figures in their performance.

In contrast to his counterparts in Eurasia and the American Arctic, and in some Pacific Northwest tribes, however, this curing shaman did not in general enter frenzied trances or set out on flights to the heavens or descents to the dead. His shamanism was not of the ecstatic but of a visionary kind: he did not journey in quest of knowledge but solicited its coming. In most of California, shamans cured by sucking out disease objects (Kroeber 1925, 851). Apart from Yuman-speaking tribes of southeasternmost California, whose affinities were mainly with cultures of the desert Southwest, soul loss was very exceptionally a cause of disease, and conceptions of the soul remained somewhat vague.

Shamans had no need to seek what was not lost and could devote themselves, with much uniformity throughout most of the state, to singing, dancing, smoking, applying herbs, and sucking forth intruding "pains." Sometimes their functions were divided. In northern California, Kroeber writes (855), a distinction was made between shamans who diagnosed by singing, dancing, and smoking and those who cured by sucking. Some specialized shamans were concerned with the weather, rattlesnake bites, or specific diseases. Despite such partition of functions, the curing shaman remained a paramount figure whose supernatural power was respected and feared. Nowhere was the merging of shaman and sorcerer carried further than in central and southern California, where witchcraft and medicine were "indissolubly bound up together" (853; cf. 136). Killings of shamans for suspected malice were often reported; the dangers of the profession were real.

West of the Rockies, Benedict noted (1923, 26–27), visions were normally unsought. In some California tribes, such as the Patwin, Pomo, and Nisenan, hereditary transmission of the shaman's office was so strong that even involuntary visions were dispensed with, making transmission of power almost automatic. Visions seemed unknown to the Coast Central Pomo (Loeb 1926, 320), "and a man became a shaman by inheriting a place in the secret society," so that priest and shaman were one. Even where visions were necessary, as among the Shasta, a shaman's spirit or "pain" was hereditary (Dixon 1907, 477).

In most tribes one or several visions (usually involuntary) were required for acquisition of shamanic power, and deliberate quests were not unknown. Among the north-central Yana, a shaman's quest resembled that of some Pacific Northwest tribes, or of the Klamath of Oregon (Spier 1930, 94–100). A would-be shaman, Sapir and Spier relate (279–80), descended by grapevine to pools where he swam under water, then lived alone in the woods for six days to acquire a song. Like all true quests, this one was not final; the shaman periodically repeated it to renew his powers. Nor were quests confined solely to northern peoples like the Yana or Atsugewi, possibly influenced by cultures of the Northwest Coast. A prospective Tachi shaman of the San Joaquin Valley "bathed nightly for a whole winter in a pool, spring, or waterhole until the creature dwelling in it met him face-to-face and gave specific instructions" (W. Wallace, 457–58).

More typically, the California shaman was summoned in a dream or waking vision, though fasting, abstinence, and instruction by older shamans might follow. In a wild desolate place, Kroeber recounts (1907, 422–23), recapitulating many similar narrations, a person suddenly falls unconscious and receives supernatural power. "On his return to his people he is for a time demented or physically affected. After he again becomes normal he has control of his supernatural influences," and is thus a master of spirits, or shaman. Even though bodily possession— rare in aboriginal America[3]—seldom occurs, this overwhelming infu-

3. Oesterreich (286, 289–90) found "not one single account of spontaneous possession amongst the American aborigines" except on the Northwest coast. Stewart cites other instances, but says that outside the Eskimo, Northwest Coast, and Plateau, spirit possession of shamans in North America is "exceptional" or even "aberrant" (339). Malignant possession was so rare that Teicher (112) found possession by the cannibalistic windigo of the Canadian Algonquians unique in the Americas. To Hultkrantz (1979, 98), "psychologically speaking there is rarely a question of true possession"; cf. Bourguignon's statistical tables (1973, 16–18).

sion of power through unsolicited vision is similar to initial seizure of spirit mediums in many cultures, and the resultant shamanism is of a correspondingly "weak" inspirational form in which the ecstatic quest plays little or no part.

A future Shasta shaman (often female) had a series of stereotyped dreams (Dixon 1907, 471–76), culminating in swarms of yellow-jackets identified as "pains," and a visionary man threatened to shoot her if she refused to sing. She danced, holding onto a rope from the roof, like the Tungus shaman clutching his tent thongs, and repeated this ceremony for three nights, falling into a cataleptic trance followed by further dancing and fasting. But such intricate ceremonies were rare; in most cases, repeated nocturnal dreams or visions—sometimes induced by tobacco or, in the south, datura (jimsonweed or toloache)—followed by fasting, instruction, and initiation, could inaugurate a shaman's career.

In central California a shaman's guardian spirit was much like those of the central and eastern United States (Kroeber 1925, 851), and in parts of southern California, too, as among the Cahuilla (Bean 1972, 109–10), guardian spirits were the source of shamanic power. Such spirits most often took the shape of an animal or human being. Celestial inspiration by an eagle or other bird (Foster 1944b, 213) was exceptional, not only in California but among most North American Indians, for whom, Dixon notes (1908, 9), the spiritual flight of Siberian shamans "seems on the whole rare." In California, though stories of flying shamans survive, even in myth there are few accounts of heroic visits to the sun or other celestial powers. An occasional myth, like one from the Chumash near Santa Barbara (Blackburn, 198–201), may tell of a visit to the sky, here by Coyote, who hitches a downward ride on an eagle but is thrown to earth and killed when he plucks its feathers. ("But Coyote never dies," as Snyder remarks [1977, 427], "he gets killed plenty of times, but he always comes back to life again, and then he goes right on traveling.") The shamanic parallels remain implicit, since there is no more a deliberate quest for celestial powers here than in similar tales of African tricksters momentarily encroaching, like the Zande Ture, on the alien heavens.

In much of southern California, as in the Southwest, the guardian-spirit idea basic to American shamanism is lacking or undeveloped, possibly, Kroeber believes (1925, 680–81), because Pueblo collectivism "spread from this culturally most advanced group to other southwestern tribes as far as the Pacific." Be that as it may, once automatic accretions of impersonal power replaced the individual guardian spirit, neither deliberate quest nor spontaneous vision could create the reciprocal relationship between human and divine characteristic of shamanistic religions.

Some northern tribes, like the Shasta, practiced few rites apart from shamans' ceremonies, but in various parts of California highly ritualized cults overlapped with and partly displaced the shamanism with which they were no doubt closely affiliated in origin. The Kuksu and related north-central cults were characterized by male secret societies—into which females were sometimes admitted—and esoteric rites for initiates; these often involved, like Kwakiutl winter ceremonials and Pueblo masked dances, impersonation of spirits by initiated members, and the enacted death and resurrection of novices. The *hesi* cult of the River Patwin included virtually all males, who enacted spirit dances at periodic performances, often attaining, with age and through payment to elders, esoteric knowledge or "medicine" entitling them to the rank of master (Kroeber 1932, 331–32).

Many north-central tribes practicing variations of the Kuksu also observed ceremonies for the dead. Beginning with the northeastern Maidu, a great annual (or biennial) mourning ceremony was given throughout the Sierra Nevada and southern California (Kroeber 1925, 29).[4] In the south these ceremonies often coexisted with initiatory cults in which hallucinogenic jimsonweed was ingested, and in some tribes coexisted with cults of a dying god. Collective taking of datura during puberty initiations lasting for days or weeks was differentiated from individual usage to stimulate personal visions, though the two functions might overlap, since, as in shamanism, an individual supernatural relation was believed "to exist forever after between the dreamer and the dream" induced in these rituals (Kroeber 1925, 669–70).

Thus these cults, which might easily have hardened into ritualized institutions antagonistic to individual inspiration, remained closely linked with a shamanism whose practices they complemented. There was no rigid division between populace and shaman, who for all his eminence (and fearful power) was not set essentially apart from others. Here as elsewhere in North America, attainment of guardian spirits was not usually confined to shamans, and the sharp distinction between shamanistic and lay spirits frequent among some tribes to the north was generally absent. As Margolin (137) observes of Costanoan or Ohlone life in the San Francisco-Monterey Bay area, "A shaman differed from ordinary people mainly because he or she plunged deeper into the spirit world." The difference in power tended, as among the Yokuts and Western Mono, to be "of quantity rather than of quality" (Gayton 1930, 389), though the quantitative difference was often very large. Among these

4. For other accounts see Gayton 1948, 124–31; Strong, passim; and Bean 1972, 135–38. On ghost-impersonating ceremonies in northwestern California, see esp. Loeb 1926, 338–54.

territorially stable, socially homogeneous hunter-gatherers, a hierarchical priesthood found no place even when initiatory cults arose. Shamanism was too deeply rooted in tribal ecology to be readily displaced; only exceptionally, as among the Pomo, did a shamanistic religion seem to be evolving toward a priestly one like that of the Pueblos.

Further south, a ritual hierarchy partially distinct from the shaman was in charge of most jimsonweed initiations. "Rituals were strictly governed," among the Luiseño and others, "by rules and procedures administered by religious chiefs and shamans, who comprised a hierarchical power pyramid" (Bean and Shipek, 556). Along with increasing formalism we find a veneration, wholly alien to shamanistic exploration of the unknown, of an immutable past. "Tradition was authority, and the past was the referent for the present and future," Bean writes of the Cahuilla (1978, 583; cf. Bean, 1972, 170–71); thus "innovative actions were seen as potentially dangerous." With this attitude, utterly foreign to the ecstatic quest for an indeterminate future, we are closer to Zuñi or Navajo ceremonialism, in which individual variation had been largely eclipsed, than to Eurasian or Arctic shamanism.

To this extent, southern and central California religions approached the cultic ritualism of Northwest Coast salmon fishers and Pueblo agriculturalists. Yet just as Kwakiutl and Nootka winter ceremonies gave collective expression to shamanic impulses, jimsonweed and Kuksu initiations both incorporated individual shamans as participants (even when others presided) and allowed wide variation in visionary acquisition of guardian spirits by initiates who, in their hallucinatory transformation into animals, re-enacted the shaman's individual experience.

The ritualism of these cults may reflect early stages of social stratification among once nomadic peoples whose way of life had changed little for millennia.[5] Thus gradations of wealth in the Kuksu suggest an emergent hierarchy, and the use of datura in southern ceremonies, far from being a gesture of nonconformity, "was frequently correlated with leadership positions and almost always with professional orientation or social rank" (Bean and Vane, 668). Yet because of their close association with shamanism these cults could not merely celebrate the past but played— as all rites of passage do—a dynamic function as well. In the south, Bean suggests (1976a, 417), powerful hereditary elites "were in continual conflict with individuals from beneath their ranks who sought to acquire power, since power was potentially available to anyone." Such "control mechanisms" as secret societies and initiations permitted capable per-

---

5. In the San Francisco Bay region, archaeology suggests that "at a time when Troy was besieged and Solomon was building the temple, . . . the native Californian already lived in all essentials like his descendant of to-day" (Kroeber 1925, 930).

sons to move upward in society while protecting its structure from disruption. Even if the dichotomy between elites and others is too sharp for most California tribes, it places proper emphasis on reciprocal accommodation, through rituals of shamanic provenance, between closed and open, static and dynamic tendencies by which social structure is both preserved and incessantly transcended.

"In spite of their performance of communal and often public rituals," Kroeber writes (1925, 859), "American religious societies are never wholly divorced from shamanism, that is, the exercise of individual religious power." Yet the interdependence of individual shamans and collective cults found in much of California could only have occurred, perhaps, where the shaman, unlike his ecstatic Siberian or Eskimo counterpart, was of a relatively passive kind no longer given to arduous journeys in quest of celestial knowledge or lost souls, and where the organization of ritual was relatively undeveloped. With further elaboration of tribal ceremony and its hierarchy of specialists, the shaman, who in California still maintained his paramount prestige, was likely to become increasingly the representative of alternative and even marginal practices (like the spirit medium in some societies) or to be confined, like the Pueblo clown, to the protest of dissident individuality against the burdensome demands of a rigid social order.

CEREMONIALISM AND ECSTASY: THE SOUTHWEST

Shamanistic forms of religion prevailed in the sparsely populated Great Basin from northeastern California through Nevada and Utah, to which cults—possibly of recent origin—like those of the Northwest Coast and central or southern California had not spread. Other rites, Park observes (14), "play a minor rôle in the religion of the Paviotso," or Northern Paiute, "compared to shamanistic beliefs and practices." Dreams, which are central to acquisition of spiritual power, may either come unsolicited or be sought by quest, most commonly in a mountain cave.

The shaman was the natural leader of his people, and when the boundaries of the long unenclosed world of the western Indian began to shrink under the white man's rapacious impact, it was a Paviotso dreamer, Wovoka or Jack Wilson, who (following the path of his father) was taken up to the other world and given the doctrine of the Ghost Dance: a messianic faith proclaiming that "the whole Indian race, living and dead, will be reunited upon a regenerated earth, to live a life of aboriginal happiness, forever free from death, disease, and misery" (Mooney 1965, 19). By this powerful vision of a boundless future transcending a meager present the tribal shaman became a prophet to the nations who eagerly took up his word and danced till they fell from exhaustion—or bullets—in their fervent endeavor to bring on the new day.

At the opposite extreme, Navajo and especially Pueblo religion emphasize the ritual and collective to near exclusion of the shamanistic and individual. Most of the long settled Pueblos met the intrusions of the white man, beginning with Coronado, with entrenched resistance and stubborn continuation of ancient rites performed—even after formal adoption of Roman Catholicism—with newly urgent secrecy in the face of a militantly hostile outside world.

In the ideology of such a community, as Dozier (a native of Santa Clara Pueblo) writes of the Tewa pueblo of Hano (1966a, 81), "individual subordination to group effort is believed to be an essential part of maintaining balance in the universe." The personal and unpredictable are suppressed (though not, of course, entirely), and the organization of religious life into ceremonial societies is nearly all-embracing. These societies vary from pueblo to pueblo but often include an association responsible for calendrical ceremonies; a society of masked kachina dancers who impersonate rain gods sometimes conceived as ancestral; one or several medicine societies; a hunters' or warriors' society; and at least one clown society which provides a communally sanctioned outlet for otherwise repressed anti-social impulses.

Despite its formalism, much southwestern ritual shows strong shamanic affiliations. Masked kachina dances and calendrical rites are best known to outsiders, but most secret societies, especially in eastern pueblos, are devoted principally to curing, the shamanistic profession par excellence, and even their relentlessly collective procedures suggest something of the ecstatic shaman's unpredictable quest. In the curing practices of the Keresan and Tewa medicine societies the individual shaman still plays a part, when illness is not severe; he is often called first, as in Santo Domingo (White 1935, 121–22), even though he can do little more than diagnose illness by feeling the patient's body, and administer medicinal potions. Shamanic parallels are most prominent in practices of the society as a whole, which attends a patient when an individual shaman's efforts have failed. "The medicinemen do not possess power to cure disease in and of themselves," White writes (1928, 608–09) of the Keresan; "they receive it from animal spirit doctors (the bear is the chief one, others are mountain lion, badger, eagle, etc.)," elemental powers characteristic of an ancestral, pre-agricultural shamanism.

If witches have stolen a patient's heart, medicine men go out to fight them (White 1928, 609–10), armed with flint knives, wearing a bear paw, bear claw necklace, and whistle of bear bone as they speed forth, sometimes flying through the air. Cries and thuds are heard in the darkness, and medicine men found tied up on the ground; smeared with blood, they frequently fall into a trance. The patient swallows a "heart" (corn wrapped in rags), and thus his lost soul is retrieved after a perilous quest and restored to the body which cannot long survive its absence.[6]

Curing is more prominent than rain-making in rituals of the eastern pueblos (Eggan, 172; Dozier 1966b, 141), but is important also among the Zuñi and Hopi to the west. At Zuñi, twelve of thirteen secret societies "function as shamans in the curing of individuals or the public, besides participating . . . in various masked ceremonies" (Curtis, 17:146). As in eastern pueblos, cures for critical illness are performed by the society as a whole. The Beast Gods, the most dangerous in the Zuñi pantheon (Bunzel 1932, 528), are the source of both curative magic and witchcraft; most powerful is the Bear, whose paws, drawn over the hands, are as potent as masks of the gods. In the winter solstice ceremony, costumed dancers "utter the cries of animals and otherwise imitate beasts, especially the bear," and by gazing into a crystal discover hidden sickness (531–32).

On the isolated mesa-tops of the Hopi, who fiercely resisted Spanish Catholicism after the Pueblo Revolt of 1680, spectacular calendrical rites purportedly unchanged (despite evident Zuñi accretions) for millennia absorbed the attention of nineteenth and twentieth century observers.[7] Their neglect of curing practices results from the fact, E. Parsons suggests (1933a, 9), that these are more esoteric than weather control and less readily communicated to whites. Secretiveness is common to all pueblos, but lack of communal curing ceremonies or specific medicine societies seems peculiar to the Hopi. Far from being devoted exclusively to continuation of the solar cycle and inducement of rain, however, "nearly every one of the secret societies has a particular form of illness which it controls" (Titiev 1944, 106). Their curing practices, though apparently far less shamanistic than those of Zuñi and the eastern pueblos—cures are generally performed by waving ashes over a patient while the society's song is sung—may institutionalize nearly forgotten shamanistic healing traditions now openly perpetuated only by sorcerers who transform themselves into animals both to injure and to cure.

Among the sedentary Pueblo agriculturalists, then, despite near-total absence of unpredictably visionary inspiration, a vestigial shamanism survived even when relegated, at the Hopi extreme, to witchcraft. Else-

6. See White on individual Keresan pueblos (e.g., 1935, 122–28), and E. Parsons 1926a, 118–22, on Laguna pueblo.

7. Stephen, whose *Hopi Journal* was mainly written between 1891 and 1894, was an initiate in several Hopi societies; J. Walter Fewkes drew on his accounts. Waters's *Book of the Hopi* is based on reports by Oswald White Bear Fredericks, which Albert Yava, a Tewa-Hopi who praises Fewkes, calls (80) "a hodgepodge of misinformation . . . full of inaccuracies and sometimes . . . farfetched."

where in the Greater Southwest "ceremonialism swings between the two poles," Underhill writes (1948, ix), "of uncontrolled individual vision and standardized ritual," with various degrees of uneasy accommodation. Among scattered semi-nomadic Apache bands, both the visionary shamanism of their Athapascan heritage and the ritualized ceremonies of their settled Navajo cousins mingled together. The White Mountain Apache attains supernatural power "in both a mechanical and spiritual way" (Goodwin 1938, 27–29), by ceremony or individual prayer, neither of which exclusively dominates. The effectiveness of a ritual, Keith Basso writes (58) of the Cibecue Apache, depends on "precise coincidence with established pattern," so as not to "inject an unexpected and unwelcome element of disorder"; yet though most ceremonies are meticulously learned in return for payment, those "based on personal experience with supernatural power are held in greater esteem than the traditional" (Goodwin 1938, 31–32).

Ceremonies among the mobile Apache were associated, like those of the Navajo, with the individual life cycle, and were in large measure rites of passage intended not to commemorate what eternally is or promote its cyclic recurrence but to facilitate change in a world where almost nothing, apart from these rituals, is stable and sure. The shaman's acquisition of these ceremonies was not in every case simply a matter of inheritance or purchase, as among the Navajo; it might even require a solitary quest. A candidate for medicine man, Bourke writes (1892, 452–53), must "show that he is a dreamer of dreams, given to long fasts and vigils, able to . . . withdraw, at least temporarily, from the society of his fellows and devote himself to long absences, especially by night, in the 'high places' . . ." In consequence, Opler writes of the Chiricahua Apache (1941, 257), there was no religious hierarchy and no two ceremonies were exactly alike, even though all conform to a general pattern. The songs may be invariant in any given ceremony, but accompanying prayers tend to be extemporaneous. At the height of this ritualized performance, moreover, the visionary component often manifests itself when the shaman hears a voice or sees a vision. Throughout the rite, "a constant interchange between the power and the shaman takes place" (208), a questioning and questing relationship far from the "one-way communication" of standardized ritual.

Thus although the initiative may be another's, the Apache shaman must himself, through a vision quest or through arduous apprenticeship, seek to acquire the power that revealed itself to him, and thus establish a reciprocal communion between them. In some cases, Cibecue Apache say, "power finds you," in others "you find power" (K. Basso, 40); these processes differ mainly in starting point and emphasis, for the shaman must seek through mastery of ritual the power that seeks him in unsolicited vision. Ceremony remains permeated with an inveterate shamanism, and for the Apache, unlike the Navajo and the Pueblos, personal vision is central: the essence of Mescalero religion, to Opler (1969, 24), was the individual quest. The components of unpredictable vision and established ritual, openness and closure, mobility and repose, were inseparably interdependent, and the creative tension engendered by their polarity was at the heart of Apache religion.

Among the Yuman tribes along the lower Colorado and Gila rivers in the far southwestern United States and adjacent regions of Mexico, for whom agriculture was secondary to hunting and gathering, highly stereotyped dreams were the central or only source of shamanic power. Dreams "cast in mythological mold," Kroeber writes (1925, 755–56), were the foundation of Mohave life; recitations of long song cycles "strung on the thread of myth" were almost their only ceremonies. These myths related the journey of a single person or a pair of brothers from their beginning to their transformation into an animal or a landmark. No quest, and no active effort, was involved in a Mohave shaman's acquisition of power; on the contrary, Bourke noted (1889, 172), "they can talk to the spirits before they have left their mother's womb," and therefore had no need to seek what was theirs to begin with. They believed a shaman retrieved a patient's "shadow" by dreaming of the primal time when the god Mastamho regulated the world. Other Yuman tribes, such as the Yuma, Cocopa, and Maricopa, follow a similar pattern, although none have such elaborate mythic cycles as the Mohave.

In a polarity of southwestern cultures between visionary and ceremonial, the river Yumans should belong to the first, for no peoples gave greater importance to individual dreams in which a spiritual journey or quest was often central. A Yuma dream vision usually involved a journey to the scene of creation or to a mountain visited by the Yuma creator gods (Forde 1931, 201; cf. J. Harrington, 326–27), and similar ascents of a sacred mountain to attain medicinal instruction typified both the Cocopa (W. Kelly, 74) and Maricopa (Spier 1933, 247). Yet if the religion of these tribes suggests a close affinity with visionary shamanism in its emphasis on dream and the spirit journey, there was normally nothing active, nor anything unpredictable, even significantly variable, in these dream experiences: no deliberation or choice in the somnambulistic progression of the dreamer to summits of spiritual revelation. The most striking characteristic of the dreams is their uniform reflection of a traditional paradigm. What is dreamed, especially among the Mohave, is what will always be in the eternally present past, so that the truth of a dream, and the validity of the mythical cycle that gives it public expression, are determined by strict adherence to a well-known prior model. Thus if Apache ceremonialism was permeated by visionary shamanism,

Yuman dreaming was standardized to the point of becoming, among the Mohave, an all but invariant ritual eternally repeating, in the preconditioned experience of each individual, the immutable past in which everything now dreamed was reality.

Among the marginally agricultural, semi-nomadic Pima and Papago of the southern Arizona desert, vision and ritual again coexisted in fragile union. A Pima shaman generally inherited office, but might also acquire power by surviving a rattlesnake bite or receiving a summons in unsolicited dreams. To this extent, Pima religion inclined toward the passive visionary shamanism of California, the Great Basin, and the river Yumans; their shaman too cured by singing, puffing tobacco smoke, and sucking. Such a shamanism was compatible with the highly ritualized Navichu cult, in which masked impersonators performed ceremonial cures probably derived from Pueblo medicine cults (E. Parsons 1928, 461–62). Instead of being merged in a single complex, then, the shamanic and ceremonial (or proto-priestly) poles of Pima religion existed side by side and, like the shaman and the Kuksu cults of central California, combined visionary inspiration and ritual coercion.

Among the Papago, calendrical ceremonies coexisted with "the democratic concept of the guardian spirit, opening the power quest to everyone," not to priests or shamans alone (Underhill 1946, 17). No clear demarcation existed between standardized ritual and individual vision. In the salt pilgrimage, visions were all but automatic for individuals participating in the communal undertaking, and the ritual act of killing an enemy or an eagle likewise infallibly brought power if followed by a purificatory ordeal. Yet shamans, as seekers par excellence of powers potentially accessible to all, actively sought empowering dreams, often by killing an eagle and submitting to the ordeal that followed. Their songs, which recounted not fixed tribal mythology but personal visions, were meant to induce a trance in which the cause of disease would be revealed. Some trace of the shaman's ecstatic quest for knowledge transcending ordinary human powers thus survived in a tribal religion dominated by the all but wholly predictable movements of seasonal ritual.

Even in the Southwest, then, shamanism was not wholly displaced by coercive ritual, as a first impression of Pueblo and Navajo ceremonialism might suggest, but continued to embody, in weakened form, the possibility of transformation through visionary access to the extrahuman that finds fullest expression in the ecstatic shaman's quest of spiritual power. Both here and in California, shamans were mainly empowered by involuntary dreams. In consequence, this relatively passive shamanism, like divination and spirit mediumship elsewhere, proved easily compatible with communal rituals that either coexisted with it, as in much of California or among the Papago, or more or less absorbed it, as among the

Pueblos, Navajo, and (less completely) Apache. Even where the individually inspired shaman remained, like the Mohave dreamer, the predominant religious figure, his visions, far from opening toward the unexpected, were made to conform to a largely invariant communal mythology. Yet in every case, however repetitiously formalized tribal ceremonies might be, especially among the settled agriculturalists of the Pueblos, the need for visionary transcendence of ritual tradition continued to find expression, whether in the bear garb of the Tewa or Zuñi dancers, the quest of Keresan doctors to recover a captive soul, or even in the menacing transformations of the ostracized but still potent sorcerer on the fringes of Hopi society.

CHAPTER THIRTEEN

Mesoamerica and South America

In much of Middle America, from the northern borders of Mexico to the Isthmus of Panama, and especially in Mesoamerica—the large regions once dominated by ancient Mexican and Mayan civilizations—native peoples were Christianized earlier than further north, and populations more extensively mixed. Thus whatever vestiges of ancestral shamanism survive will be intertwined, in most cases, with hardly less primordial ritualisms, aboriginal and Christian. Continuation of an impulse toward personal transcendence not fully satisfied by the fixed rites of these settled agriculturalists bears witness to an unsatisfied need to expand human limits through pursuit of a spiritual goal indispensable to the degree that it remains beyond attainment.

ANCIENT MESOAMERICA AND ITS TRANSFORMATIONS

From earliest times the Mesoamerican archaeological record bespeaks highly stratified societies in sharp contrast to the generally mobile and egalitarian cultures of North America (with conspicuous exceptions like the Pacific Northwest). Corresponding to this hierarchical social structure was a tightly centralized religion whose priests sometimes wielded overt political authority. Their central function was perpetuation of cosmic and social order through performance of seasonal rituals for an elaborate pantheon of gods in a continual effort to make the universe "routine and predictable" (Wolf, 84). Intermeshed with a highly accurate solar calendar developed by the Olmec and Maya was a sacred calendar of two hundred sixty days; the priests, who alone knew its intricacies, were the indispensable interpreters of divine order.

Seasonal festivals were correlated with the solar year; only their correct performance—with increasing bloodshed—"assured the regular succession of the seasons, the coming of the rains, the springing of the plants . . . and the resurrection of the sun" (J. Soustelle, 147). The second calendar, the Aztec *tonalamatl,* was mainly used to divine the destiny of individuals born on particular days. Every human being, Soustelle writes (114–15), "was governed by predestination; neither his life nor his after-life was in his own hands, and determinism ruled every phase of his short stay on earth." There was no apparent place for personal vision when whatever would be was immutably established, nor anything that a quest could accomplish or alter.

Yet this seemingly rigid universe was extremely precarious. Even before the cataclysm of Spanish conquest, ancient Mesoamericans knew how suddenly worldly glory could pass, as city after splendid city fell to ruin. The legend of the exile and expected return of Quetzalcoatl—the ancient plumed-serpent god identified with a Toltec king who tried to abolish human sacrifices to him—suggests both a challenge to the bleak determinism of this homicidal religion and the lingering possibility of seeking an alternative to it: a possibility ironically culminating in the disastrous identification of Quetzalcoatl with Cortés.

The universe was in continual peril. Our world of the fifth sun, the Aztec believed, will be destroyed like its four predecessors; all the rituals of the calendrical round can only defer the sun's extinction, after a fifty-two year cycle, bringing the world to an end. The world's instability troubled the poet-king of Texcoco, Nezahualcoyotl: "What does your mind seek? Where is your heart?" he asked in the perplexity of an inchoate quest that could find no place to begin: "Can anything be found on earth?" (León-Portilla, 4–5). Among his Aztec allies, human sacrifice in mounting numbers was the only conceivable response to the insecurity of a continually threatened world (J. Soustelle, 99).

If ritual coercion is one response to the uncertainties of a world never fully conformable to human need, incorporation of more flexible means of transcendence through personal communication with the divine is another. In most North American tribes, even when ritualized cults arose the shaman either performed their rites or remained dominant among those who did. Only in the Pueblos and tribes influenced by them was shaman clearly subordinated to priest, though even here (with the possible exception of Hopi) he found a place as a member of a curing or clown society, providing an institutionalized alternative from within.

E. Parsons (1933b, 613) suggests important parallels between Aztec and Pueblo religious practices both in impersonation of gods and organization of curing societies. It would not be surprising, then, if curers of shamanic origin marginally eluded the despotism of priestly ritual in ancient Mesoamerica also. Very little is known of these putative figures, however, since the Spanish friars who remain our principal source of information (along with archaeological excavation and a few codices in native languages) were concerned primarily with recording—and extirpating—the priestly religion which they saw as the devil's work. To what extent shamanic practices provided alternatives to the deathly rigidity of a fatalistic ritualism therefore remains uncertain.

A few sixteenth-century sources hint at Mayan and Aztec religious specialists other than priests. The Yucatec Mayan *chilans,* "mouthpieces" of the gods whom Bishop Landa mentions, may have been, Tozzer suggests (112), diviners who read the *tonalamatls,* or horoscopes; but a visionary component is unmistakable in a manuscript telling how the prophet Chilam Balam retired to a room where he lay in a trance while the spirit perched on the ridgepole of the house spoke to him (Roys 1967, 182). Even if the *chilan* was "a kind of visionary shaman who received messages from the gods while in a state of trance" (Coe, 154), however, he had been so subordinated to priestly ritual that in times of crisis he might, Landa tells us (Tozzer, 115), order human sacrifice.

Only after the Spanish conquest did the legendary Chilam Balam, who was said to have foretold it, achieve a posthumous fame outlasting the priesthood. As for the curers, whom Landa also mentions, they may have cast lots, or kernels of maize, to make prognoses—like the divine soothsayers of the *Popol Vuh* (36), the mythological epic of the Quiche Maya, who "could tell the future by throwing beans"—sucked disease objects, applied herbal remedies, and recited magical incantations (Roys 1965), but there is little suggestion of anything resembling visionary quests. Among the Aztec, as among the Hopi, it was to sorcerers (*nahualli*), who could change themselves into animals and kill from afar (J. Soustelle, 57), rather than to doctors that the remnants of shamanism appear to have been mainly consigned. Here was no visionary alternative to the lethal exactions of ritual but only the dark underside of a shamanism placed effectively outside the pale of officially sanctioned religion.

One means of transcending an intolerable present was through hallucinogens, widely known in ancient as in modern Middle America. The "divine food" of the Aztec described by Durán (115–16) was brewed from ashes of poisonous beasts, pulverized with tobacco, live scorpions, spiders, and centipedes, and topped with ground morning-glory seed, "which the natives apply to their bodies and drink to see visions." Besides tobacco and morning-glory seed (*ololiuhqui*), which intoxicates those who imbibe it and makes them "see visions and fearful things" (Sahagún, 3:40), ancient Mexican hallucinogens included the sacred mushrooms known as *teonacatl* (3:293) or *nanacatl* (3:40). The effect of these, too, in Sahagún's meticulous descriptions, was far from uniformly emancipatory: "Some saw in a vision that they were dying, and wept, others saw that some wild beast was eating them, others that they were taking captives in war," and so forth.

Another visionary agent, the cactus *peyotl*, generated "fearful or ludicrous visions" in those who ate or drank it (3:292). We have no clear reason to believe that any of these played a role, at the time of the conquest, in shamanistic rites distinguishable from black magic. On the tenuous basis of accounts by disapproving Spanish friars, indeed, it would seem that such substances did not provide a liberating alternative communication with the beyond so much as they confirmed the nightmarish closure relentlessly affirmed by the murderous rites of the priestly religion—that grim cult which Brundage (1979, 186) calls "a staged hallucination," surely the most nightmarish of all. This fanatically ritualized Aztec culture epitomizes a self-enclosed world with no effective means of transcendence, a world so rigidly organized as to preclude any possibility of a quest for something beyond it, and thus a world doomed less from without than from within: a world that fascinates us, as it did the conquistadors and friars, by being so grotesque a reflection of our own.

In modern Middle America there is no aboriginal culture wholly uninfluenced by Catholic Christianity. From the time of the Spanish Conquest, however, observers have noted that obliteration of pre-Columbian religions by worship of Christ and the saints was far from complete. "I believe that, incited by the cursed devil," Friar Durán regretfully wrote (152–53), ". . . these wretched Indians remain confused and are neither fish nor fowl in matters of the faith." In the following century, Jacinto de la Serna more stridently lamented that the unrepentant Indians, "the better to dissemble their poisonous deception, . . . revere Christ Our Lord and His most holy Mother and the saints (some of whom they hold as gods) while worshiping their idols at the same time" (G. Soustelle, 192). Clearly, pagan beliefs and practices had not altogether vanished—how could they?—with the advent of a zealous new faith.

Yet only in isolated pockets of Mexico, mainly mountainous regions on the fringes of ancient Mesoamerican culture, did a few scattered groups openly reject the Christian sacraments after their conquest, and even these inevitably absorbed many Christian beliefs. Nor could the systematic deception feared by Serna, or the "cabalistic guild" romantically imagined by Brinton (37), with its lascivious "bands of naked Nagualists" (57), plausibly have survived for long among a large segment of the population. Instead, the new missionary faith assimilated, in different degrees, pre-Columbian practices that survived—often in strange guises—through increasing toleration by priests who preferred an imperfect Catholicism to none. Thus the deeply venerated Virgin of Guadalupe, the patron saint of Mexico, incorporated traits of the Aztec

Mother Goddess Tonantzin (see Lafaye). Rites similar to confession and baptism could continue in the new religion, and even the cross might be simultaneously Christian and "pagan."

The extent of religious fusion varied greatly even in relatively homogeneous areas, as Redfield demonstrated for the Yucatec Maya (1941). For the most part—except in cities where pagan rites survived only as "superstitions," or a few remote tribes stubbornly resistant to Christianity—elements have inseparably mingled. In Mayan areas a long tradition of coexistence prevails: the Chorti of Guatemala, Wisdom writes (1940, 18), recognize no "difference of origin of any religious or ceremonial elements in the culture." In formerly Aztec realms of central Mexico, indigenous elements were more completely suppressed, surviving mainly in curing rites. Widespread substitution of saints for gods has not meant equation between them, as in some Haitian and Brazilian cults; rather, G. Soustelle writes (191) of the Nahuatl village of Tequila, they have "*taken the place* of ancient divinities," thereby filling the void their departure left behind.

Extensive though such religious fusion has been among descendants of ancient Mayans and Mexicans, in some cases ethnography has revealed an indigenous substratum hardly affected by Christianity. The Zinacantecos of Chiapas, Vogt writes (1970, 12), "were Maya tribesmen with a Spanish Catholic veneer" of increasingly evident thinness. Especially among Mayan peoples, large elements of indigenous ritual, ecclesiastical hierarchies, and even (as La Farge and Byers discovered in Jacaltenango, Guatemala) calendrical lore have survived. Indeed, from researches in nearby Santa Eulalia, La Farge (161–62) found indications that the tonalamatl calendar of 260 days was known to the common people. And local systems of annually rotated offices, or *cargos*, combining ceremonial and secular administration, function much like the native hierarchies they replaced (see Carrasco 1961).

Native rites of priestly origin complement Catholic ceremonies by asserting the need for control of a partly predictable world. But other surviving pagan rites are mainly associated with the limitless domain beyond this imperfectly closed circle, the unpredictable domain of the wild called in Spanish *el monte*. Traces of hunting rites to appease supernatural owners of natural phenomena survive among long-agricultural Mayan peoples (La Farge and Byers, 132; Wisdom, 72), and centuries of calendrical rites have not wholly suppressed the interdependence between humans and the undomesticated beings that surround them on the open margins of a world finally beyond their control.

In barren northern Mexico and southern Arizona, the Mayo and Yaqui (known together as the Cáhita), who lay outside the ancient Mesoamerican sphere, continue to practice, despite fervent devotion to Christianity, a "Religion of the Woods," in Beals's phrase (1945a, 190), associated with hunting ritual, witches and wizards, disease and its cure. Neither Jesus as curer nor Saints attired in Yaqui garb wholly displaced the unbaptized ancestral spirits of the *Monte,* the source of mysterious music for *pascola* dances. These spirits, Spicer recounts (1954, 123), "are around and about eternally in a sort of 'other world' which surrounds and yet is an integral part of the world in which baptized Yaquis live"—a menacing other world beckoning, like goat-footed Pan or the Erl-king, beyond the given world we insistently ritualize to make it safely, if never wholly, our own.

Still more significant than survival of particular spirits is this fundamental opposition between the given world and "the other" beyond yet inseparable from it. In Yaqui belief, as Spicer analyzes it (1980, 64–66), the *huya aniya,* the "tree-world" of the *monte,* embraced the *yo aniya,* the ancient realm of nature spirits who conveyed their transformative power through unsolicited dreams. After the coming of the Jesuits and the imposition of town life, the once all-embracing huya aniya "became the other world, the wild world surrounding the towns,"[1] to whose geometrically ordered structure it was consistently opposed. In contrast to the predictable regularity of work and ritual, the uncontrollable power of the huya aniya came unexpectedly to individuals from "a world where there was much uncertainty, where there was much over which men had no control, concerning which there were no well-defined rules." The segregation between the realms was never complete: what remained was an "oppositional integration," as Spicer calls it (1980, 70), involving continual interaction between the regular and the wild, the closed and the open, the fixed communal pattern of ritual repetition and the unpredictable individual variation of shamanic vision which transcends and potentially transforms it. In this dynamic opposition, as we have seen, the spiritual quest is always latent.

---

1. The *huya aniya* may recall the vague "nonordinary reality" supposedly revealed by the Yaqui *brujo* Don Juan, according to Castaneda's increasingly dubious accounts. Yet peyote, datura, and mushrooms, by whose aid Don Juan and his pupil allegedly attained this condition, are not reported by reliable ethnographers to be used by the Yaqui for visionary purposes, as peyote is by the Huichol and Tarahumara. According to Beals (1945a, 195), peyote was unknown in any form, and toloache (datura) used externally only, as a medicine. In a caustic 1972 *New York Times* review of Castaneda's second volume, La Barre, author of *The Peyote Cult,* found Castaneda's epistemology "too noodleheaded and naive to merit comment. . . . The total effect is self-dramatizing and vague, and Castañeda curiously manages to be at once disingenuous and naive. Even as belles lettres the book is wanting, for the writing is pretentious." The *Times* substituted a reviewer who could not "even begin to point out all the delights to be found in these books" (which by then were three), and who lauded "the excellence of Castañeda's writing" (La Barre 1975, 271–73).

CURANDERO AND SHAMAN IN MODERN MESOAMERICA

Among peoples still aware of an unpredictable wild surrounding the closure of ritual we might expect to find significant traces of ancestral shamanisms. Many Mesoamerican curers are indeed often characterized as "shamans," though most learn their technical craft, especially in Mayan areas, without personal visions. Thus in Mam-speaking Santiago Chimaltenango in Guatemala the *chimán,* with his bagful of beans and rock crystals, is both soothsayer and curer; through his divinations alone "can a Chimalteco order his life to suit the unchangeable future" (Wagley 1949, 71). Most divinatory techniques in Guatemala (see Oakes, 178; Wisdom 1940, 344) and throughout Middle America produce automatic results through strict procedures rather than individually variant visions or ecstatic flights of the spirit.

The impersonal nature of the curer's call in most of this region is underscored by absence of the personal guardian spirit central to shamanism in much of Eurasia and the Americas. The guardian-spirit concept has a Mesoamerican parallel, however, in the animal companion called *nagual* or *tonal.* (The former term, from Aztec *nahualli,* is also used of a witch capable of transformation into animals.) As early as 1530, Antonio de Herrera y Tordesillas (in Foster 1944a, 89–90) noted such beliefs in the Honduran mountains: "The devil deceived these people and appeared in the form of a lion, *tigre* [jaguar], coyote, alligator, bird, or serpent; and these are called *naguals,* which is to say 'guardians' or 'companions'; and when the animal dies the Indian bound to it also dies." Acquisition of this companion, as Herrera describes it, is strikingly similar to guardian spirit quests in many North American tribes. The searcher went to a secluded place "and cried out to obtain the favors which his ancestors had had." After the animals he sought appeared in a dream, he made a pact that the first one he encountered would be his "*nagual* and companion for all time." It is a procedure which a Nootka or Twana, Crow or Sioux, would instantly have understood.

But in virtually no modern account of Middle American nagual beliefs is any personal initiative found, much less a purposeful quest nor even, in many instances, a vision. The name *tonal,* by which the animal companion is known in parts of Mexico, stems from Aztec *tonalamatl,* or calendrical book of fates; designation of this alter ego is almost always involuntary and at least implicitly predestined, from birth or before, by forces beyond individual control. The Tzeltals and other Mayan peoples of Guatemala and Chiapas believe that shamans assign naguals "according to the day of one's birth" (La Farge and Byers, 133); but even where no explicit connection with the sacred calendar is made, a sense of fatality is generally strong. Because no one, in many Mayan villages, knows the identity of his nagual (see Wagley 1949, 65), the sickness or death of any animal at any time may lead without warning to one's own.

Whether the animal companion's identity is known or not, the individual almost never takes an active part in its acquisition. Among the Chatino of Oaxaca a specialist determines which animal has left its "tracks" in ashes around the house of a newborn child and ascribes the tracks to its *tona* (Greenberg, 91–92). A Mixe *nagual* might be known from a birthmark (E. Parsons 1936, 225), and in virtually every case, as G. Soustelle stresses (124) in discussing the Nahuatl village of Tequila, the nagual (here identified with a species) is not a guardian but only a companion to whose destiny the human being's is bound[2] in a passive relation from which the individual derives no new knowledge or power.

Thus the Mesoamerican animal companion differs fundamentally (despite probable historical connection) from the guardian spirit elsewhere in the Americas. No quest and usually no vision is needed to acquire this shadowy and often unrecognized "secret sharer" allotted by forces beyond human ken. The nagual, not unlike the natal day-god of the ancient calendar, represents, as Bunzel writes (1952, 275) of the Quiche Maya villagers of Chichicastenango, "an utterly arbitrary and capricious destiny."

Affliction of the animal companion, which automatically leads to one's own, is one cause of disease; others widespread throughout Mesoamerica include invasion by evil "airs," witchcraft and the evil eye, sudden fright (*espanto*), and imbalance between hot and cold (Redfield and Villa Rojas, 160; Wisdom 1952, 129–32). Most native curers rely principally (apart from herbal medicines) on magical and thus automatically effective practices in accord with their mostly involuntary vocation. No visionary quest is involved in their cures any more than in their call, and they are thus "shamans" in only a residual sense, by distinction from the priestly officials responsible for communal ceremonies. It is hardly surprising, given their fatalistic legacy, that most curers, instead of perilously venturing into the unknown, rely on infallible techniques to dispel disease from the patient's body.

Thus the Mayan *h-men* of Yucatán, far from being a Siberian shaman of the southern jungle, recites prayers, offers food to the gods, and cures by exorcism, herbal medicine, and bleeding (Redfield and Villa Rojas, 75). Another ancient Mayan technique, practiced by the Chorti of Guatemala and the villagers of San Antonio in Belize, is to "seize" the foreign matter from the patient's body by applying an object such as a fish or tortilla, chicken or tobacco leaf, which draws the sickness into itself

---

2. But in San Pedro Chenhalhó, some animal souls "protect the souls of their compañeros" (Guiteras-Holmes, 248).

(J. Thompson, 71–73; Wisdom 1940, 347–49). Other common curing methods are blowing tobacco smoke, spitting, and sucking.

Even if Mesoamerican curers descend from primeval shamans, long centuries of settled agriculture, stratified societies, and ritualized religions (aboriginal and Catholic) have made them, in most cases, not ecstatic explorers of the unknown but diviners, herbalists, and ritualists, "shaman-priests" empowered by birth and training, not personal vision, to practice standard curing techniques. The questing dimension has not vanished but has been largely confined (as in the Pueblos) to set forms, so that curers embody less a visionary alternative to priestly hegemony than an extension of its dominant outlook from public to private sphere.

Largely confined, but not entirely: in some regions shamanistic traits remain prominent, whether surviving from preagricultural times or generated anew by historical and ecological changes. Herrera's account of nagual acquisition in sixteenth-century Honduras testifies to a pre-Columbian guardian spirit quest on the fringes of Mesoamerican civilizations, and far to the north, among the pagan Cáhita, "the source of curing power was the dream or vision, through which the individual acquired the assistance of a spirit, in animal form usually, which helped him or over which he had a certain control" (Beals 1943, 64).

Among Mayan descendants of perhaps the oldest continuous New World civilization, emphasis on hereditary office does not preclude a personal bond between curer and spirit, even without a vision. In Todos Santos, Guatemala, this bond takes the form of a metal chain thought to be "the pact between the *chimán* and the Spirit" (Oakes, 110; cf. 151); if the latter fails him, the chimán can go to its mountain home and break his chain and thus his connection with it. The bond symbolized by the chain distinguishes the shaman-curer, even in a culture so remote from ecstasy as the Maya, from the priest who derives automatic authority from his office and whose rituals depend not on relationship to a particular spirit but on their own efficacy, *ex opere operato*.

In the Valley of Mexico, the center of Aztec ritualism and Spanish missionary zeal, Madsen (1955, 49–56; cf. 1960, 181–86) reported in the 1950s an extraordinary parallel to Siberian shamanism among Nahuatl speakers in San Francisco Tecospa south of Mexico City. Here Don Soltero Perez's vocation was no mere matter of birth or training. One night in 1918 lightning struck, subjecting him to recurrent loss of consciousness. During these spells, "his spirit was kidnapped by the 'enanitos,' dwarf-size rain deities who have existed in the Valley of Mexico since Aztec times," and detained in mountain caves until he agreed to become a curer. After six months he consented and was given a spirit wife by whom he had children. He "and all other 'curanderos de aire' die twice a year; their spirits then go to a cave of the enanitos where they receive instructions for curing." In his coercive call and ability to enter the other world when summoned, this curer, Madsen suggests, resembles Siberian (and especially Gold) shamans, even though his treatment of disease remains typically Mesoamerican in its reliance on magical techniques.

Among some peoples, mainly in isolated mountain regions, disease and its cure are thought to involve loss and recovery of the mobile soul. Thus the Sierra Popoluca of Veracruz believe that in cases of *espanto* a person's soul will leave his body, captured by dwarfish "masters" of fish and game, until the curer retrieves it by pleading, sucking, or both (Foster 1945, 185). Among the Highland Totonac, a curer "goes, in spirit, beneath the earth, to negotiate ransom" for a soul held captive by evil airs (I. Kelly, 402–03); the pattern is that of the visionary shaman's journey to the world of the dead. In northern Mexico, among the Tarahumara of the Sierra Madre Occidental, soul loss is the main cause of disease, and the curer must bring it back by projecting his own soul in a dream (Kennedy, 129–31; Bennett and Zingg, 259). Though he owes his office to birth or purchase, his power issues, Lumholtz writes (1:322), "from the light of his heart, which was given him by Tata Dios (God the Father)," and this visionary enlightenment enables him not only to descend to the world below but "to see Tata Dios himself, to talk to him, to travel through space at will, for the shamans are as bright as the sun."

Contributing to Tarahumara visionary ecstasy are intoxicants, especially *tesgüino* corn beer (Bennett and Zingg, 253), widely used for inspiration by others, including some generally sober Mayan groups. Use of alcohol before sacred performances in Santa Eulalia, La Farge remarks (161), seems "a mild approach toward ecstasy, a means of achieving a state in which the limited human being can more readily consort with divinity." Some trace of the Siberian shaman's frenzied raptures appears to survive even in formalized rituals of the sedate and long civilized Maya.

More important to traditional practices of Middle American peoples are hallucinogens familiar for centuries. Tobacco, peyote, mushrooms, and morning-glory seeds were, Wasson says (1966, 329), "the four great divinatory plants of Mexico at the time of the Conquest," mediating between men and gods; all are widely used today for medicinal, narcotic, or visionary ends, both by shamans and the people at large. There is little indication in Durán and Sahagún, as we have seen, that such substances were employed at the time of the Conquest to transcend the closure of this world through visionary access to another, but their continued use by widely scattered contemporary peoples, mainly of the mountains, may reflect that shamanistic purpose.

Among the Mize of northern Oaxaca, the mushrooms called "Our

Lords" are believed to give visionary knowledge of cures. But the vision "is always the same" (Miller, 318): a dwarf who answers questions. Far more varied are visions of the nearby Mazatec. In Soyaltepec an apprentice curer goes to the wild to gather seeds of a vine called "Seed of the Virgin" (Villa Rojas, 118); he drinks a potion prepared from it and withdraws to await a vision. After repeated doses, he is transported to the sky, where he sees Our Lord and converses with curers already dead.

Beginning in 1955, when Wasson first attended a vigil by the "wise woman" Maria Sabina, the Mazatec mushroom cult gained a notoriety that may have contributed, he ruefully confessed (Estrada, 20), to undermining a possibly ancient curative practice. Ever since hearing a Wise Man sing for her sick uncle at a vigil with the "saint children" (as the mushrooms are called), María Sabina was attracted by a mysterious language "that spoke of stars, animals, and other things unknown to me" (39), and drew her beyond the limits of her impoverished existence. After eating the mushrooms she heard voices "from another world" (40) and, though illiterate, read from a Book of Wisdom which taught her to summon the Lord of the Mountains, to "see from the origin," and to "cure with Language" and the wisdom it bestows (56). In her vigils she was transformed into God and entered another world, the vision of which gives meaning to this one.

The Mazatec mushroom experience thus makes explicit the deep affinity between ecstatic vision and language: both breach the closure of the given world and open continually toward one being formed. "The Mazatecs say that the mushrooms speak," H. Munn writes (88). "The shamans who eat them . . . are the oral poets of their people, the doctors of the word." By means of "mushrooms that liberate the fountains of language" (92), the Mazatec shaman "has a conception of *poesis* in its original sense as an action": the mushrooms inspire him with language and "transform him into an oracle" (93) of the mobile spirit. The process is by nature a perpetual quest: "We are going to search and question," the doctor woman says (94), and what she seeks are tracks toward "the unexplored, the unknown and unsaid into which she adventures by language, the seeker of significance, the questioner of significance, the articulator of significance."

Far to the northwest, among the Tarahumara, peyote induces visionary transcendence, and the quest takes form as a pilgrimage for the sacred cactus. The christianized Tarahumara, Lumholtz observed (1:357) in the 1890s, regard the *híkuli* (as both they and the linguistically unrelated Huichol call the cactus known to the Aztec as *peyotl*) as a demi-god to whom sacrifices are offered as the brother of Tata Dios (360). By the 1930s, the peyote shaman was rare, but the *híkuli* pilgrimage, lasting as long as a month, continued (Bennett and Zingg, 291–92).

But it is the nearby Huichol, perhaps "the least acculturated major contemporary Indian population in Mesoamerica" (Furst, 5), who have developed the peyote pilgrimage most fully. The Huichol shaman-priest, as depicted by Myerhoff (94–100), is summoned spontaneously in a vision revealed to a solitary young boy (or rarely girl); only after he has undergone rigorous probation and led as many as five peyote pilgrimages will he assume office. Like Eurasian shamans, he can transform himself into various animals, make the magical flight to the land of the gods, and follow souls to the underworld. He divines causes of illness, which he treats by blowing smoke, spitting, and sucking, but he is also a priest who presides, in the absence of both Catholic clergy and a cargo system, over public ceremonies, "embodying and promoting traditional values, jealously guarding the Huichol cultural heritage and identity." Fixed agricultural rituals and ancestral celebrations are not antitheses of the quest but its prelude, by which the shaman inculcates his followers with the itinerary of the peyote pilgrimage, thus firmly rooting this visionary journey in the communal present and inherited past.

Its goal is Wirikuta, the sacred home of the peyote in San Luis Potosí, some three hundred miles from the Huichol homeland. After purification and confession, the pilgrims themselves become the Ancient Ones (Myerhoff, 136), re-enacting—in the liminal communitas that binds them together throughout their journey—the primeval quest of the gods for renewal of life. Henceforth everything once predictable is "upside down and backward" (149), so that words and actions take on significances hilariously reversing the normal. After traveling to a place called Vagina and following the trail sanctified by the mythical first pilgrims, these hunters of the Deer-peyote reach the oasis of Our Mothers (167) and track the life-giving cactus. The shaman shoots arrows toward a peyote cluster identified as the Deer and implores this Elder Brother not to be angry, for it will rise again. Having shared the plants they have shot, the pilgrims leave the dangerous place at a run, "as though pursued and in great peril" (158). The shaman, after eating peyote, receives messages from the gods and learns the names of things, as he does when he drums and sings at sacred ceremonies. The arduously hunted peyote thus reveals knowledge of other worlds which he shares with those to whom hallucinations induced by the cactus could otherwise communicate nothing transcendent.

The Huichol complex of maize, deer, and peyote entails continual interaction between the shamanism predominantly practiced by nomadic hunters and the priestly rites of agriculturalists: ways of life mediated through the shaman-priest who re-enacts the hunt for peyote that originated in the mythical times celebrated in agricultural ritual. The peyote hunt aims "to return to the birthplace of the gods, to Wirikuta, where all will be a unity, to gather *híkuri*, which is the maize and the deer, so that 'we may have our life' " (240), becoming the gods who first sought the peyote that each must now find for himself. But this pilgrimage, unlike rites for the corn, looks not toward a fixed ancestral past but toward a never completed future; by openness to this quintessentially shamanic dimension the Huichol "accommodate to new situations" (125) with an innovative flexibility that helps perpetuate their culture. To a Huichol shaman, unlike the once-mighty priests of aboriginal Mesoamerica, "answers were not self-evident or automatically provided" by ritual: for this reason he continues to question, and to quest, long after the ancient priests' confident answers have been forgotten.

The Mixe and Mazatec, Tarahumara and Huichol examples suggest the adaptive survival (and repeated renewal) in these mountainous regions of the shamanic quest for transcendent knowledge. These peoples were marginal, however, to the civilizations of pre-Columbian Mesoamerica, among whose Maya- and Nahuatl-speaking successors (and others in the Mexican cultural sphere) we find only scattered traces of practices more ecstatic than the traditional *curandero*'s ritualized cures. In at least one culture descended from the ancient civilizations, however—the Tzotzil Mayan *municipio* of Zinacantan—the curer's role, despite millennia of priestly ritual, shows strong affinities with the primordial quest of earlier shamans. While cargoholders of the religious hierarchy perform the annual round of mainly Catholic ceremonies in Zinacantan Center, the *h'iloletik* or shamans practice in the hamlets. These too have their hierarchy, and many of their public functions are priestly (though only superficially Catholic), presumably adapted from practices of their ancient forebears.

But in other respects the Zinacantec *h'ilol* embodies not priestly ceremonialism but the questing spirit of the shaman searching for what can never be finally found. The most common way of becoming a shaman is not through heredity or instruction alone, but through a divine call in a series of three dreams over several years. In these the future shaman's soul is summoned by the supernatural *alcalde* (corresponding to the highest officer of the cargo system) inside "Senior Large Mountain," where he agrees to be a shaman and performs his first cures (Vogt 1970, 26–27).[3] In curing rites above all, the pervasive ceremonialism of Zinacantec life reveals its continued affiliation with the spiritual quest. In addition to an animal spirit companion, each Zinacanteco possesses a *ch'ulel*, an indestructible personal soul whose identity is learned in a childhood dream voyage to Senior Large Mountain, and whoever loses

---

3. On Zinacantec dreams see Laughlin's introduction and collection of dream accounts. For variants of the shaman's call see Fabrega and Silver, 31–32.

one or more of its thirteen parts requires a special ceremony to recover them (Vogt 1969, 370).

All shamanism inherently allows for unpredictable variations on its accustomed patterns, opening a space of indeterminacy for a spiritual quest that could never take place if everything sacred were given once for all and retrievable only by repetition of an immutable past. It is highly significant, then, that public ceremonies performed by the Zinacantec *h'ilol* in his priestly role, like calendrical rituals of the cargoholders, "take place without great variation," whereas his private ceremonies, Silver writes (145–46), "are subject to no such adherence to generally held notions of proper procedure," making possible a degree of innovation that priestly ritual in theory denies and in practice retards. "The basic patterns of organization resemble a syntax," Silver suggests, and the ritual symbols a vocabulary: "The ceremonial expressions that result from the interaction of the two are similar to the sentences of a language in their combination of patterning and variability." It is an interaction fundamental, as we have seen, to the spiritual quest.

The most elaborate of the Zinacantec shaman's variable ceremonies, "the Great Vision," is a quest to recover the animal spirit companion, embodying the soul, which has gone astray from its corral. Formalized though the procedure is, with its nineteen steps, fixed prayers, set arrangements of candles, pine boughs, and flowers, ritual baths and meals, and sacrifices of black chickens, the shaman's ancient search remains its recognizable core. The quest takes the form of a pilgrimage, lasting hours or even days, as the curing party travels up and down mountain trails from the patient's hamlet to the Ceremonial Center, then to a series of shrines at each of which the shaman prays to the Ancestral Gods inside the mountain, and finally, after sacrificing a chicken, back to the patient's home. Here the shaman proceeds (if "fright" is involved) to call back the patient's personal soul, shouting "Come, come!" as he strikes the ground with a staff. The parts of the soul are gathered up, Vogt writes (1970, 96),[4] and led back into the patient's body, terminating the ceremony by the archetypal shamanic deed of retrieving life from the world of the dead.

Far as the sober Zinacantec shaman's quest may be from the visionary ecstasies of his Huichol or Mazatec (not to mention his Eskimo or Siberian) counterpart, it testifies to a continued need for transcendence even among so ritualized a people as the modern Maya. Interviews by Guiteras-Holmes with Manuel Arias, a former curer of the Tzotzil-speaking Mayan village of San Pedro Chenalhó near Zinacantan, suggest how es-

---

4. For fuller accounts see Silver, 153–205; Fabrega and Silver, 172–88; Vogt 1969, 425–46, and 1976, 61–83.

sential the hazardous quest of the mobile spirit remains despite centuries of native and Christian ritual. The settled world may be a square and the ceremonial center its navel, and rites inherited from a mythical past may perpetuate its sacred order, but Manuel knows that this world is not a self-sufficient whole. Unlike the cultivated fields, the forest is dark and dangerous: yet this half-alien world of the *monte,* too, belongs to the experience of being human. When we fall asleep our ch'ulel, or soul, escapes to faraway places where the animal companion roams. But those alluring realms are hostile to human life insofar as they, too, threaten to be sufficient; the healer, in his effort to rescue the patient's soul from exclusive allegiance to this world of the gods and the dead, cannot rely on coercive rituals alone but "struggles against powerful forces in order to recover the ch'ulel that has been lost, exposing himself to danger by sending out his own ch'ulel in search, and by combating the forces of evil" (137). In this fundamental task he proves true to the shaman's primordial calling as heroic explorer of the boundless unknown in which the open-ended quest of imperfectly sapient man to expand his intrinsically limited knowledge and power incessantly takes place.

CIVILIZATION AND SAVAGERY:
FROM THE ANDES TO TIERRA DEL FUEGO

The artistic grandeur of Andean civilizations preceding that of the Inca, who had dominated the area for less than a century when Pizarro brought a brutal end to their vast empire, wholly belies the Inca Garcilaso de la Vega's claim (30) after the Spanish Conquest that these peoples were little better than beasts. So completely did the Inca impose their culture, imperial religion, and adoptive Quechua language during their brief dominion, however, that it is only of their beliefs, recorded mainly by Spanish writers, that we can speak with any confidence.

The highly efficient Inca empire "was one of the most thoroughly regimented societies the world has ever known" (Steward and Faron, 5–6). Local populations were organized into family groups (*ayllus*), and all power and land belonged in theory to the Inca himself, who as descendant of the Sun held absolute authority by divine right. "Formal religious organization with priests, as distinct from medicine men" (Bennett, 9), prevailed in this highly stratified agricultural state. The gods were hierarchically ordered, with the heavenly Creator Viracocha or Pachacámac at the summit, and the Sun, divine ancestor of the Inca dynasty, as his regent. (The Inca appear to have fatally confused Pizarro with Viracocha, as the Mexicans confused Cortés with Quetzalcoatl, and *viracocha* continued to be a common noun for the white man.) In addition to other major deities officially worshiped throughout the empire, like Pachamama, the Earth Mother, and Mamacocha, Mother Sea, countless natural and man-made objects were venerated as sacred *huacas* (or *wakas*): anything extraordinary was *huaca*. The bones of lineal ancestors were also revered; and every family seems to have had its household gods, called *conopas* or *chancas*. [5]

An imposing priestly hierarchy formed what Mason (202) calls "the only instance in aboriginal America of an established church," with the High Priest of the Sun in Cuzco, a brother or uncle of the Inca, at the top. Inca religion "emphasized ritual and organization rather than mysticism and spirituality, and its chief interests were for food supply and curing" (Rowe, 293), which an elaborate ceremonial cycle aimed to promote. As in Mesoamerica and intervening kingdoms, human sacrifice was practiced, at least at times of crisis, and as many as two hundred children might be strangled at a coronation; other victims, as in Mexico, had palpitating hearts torn from their chests. [6]

In its emphasis on sin (understood as violation of ritual or natural order), confession (often individual and secret), and purification, Inca religion resembled the Catholic, as Spanish priests who denounced it uncomfortably recognized. The confessor belonged to the priestly hierarchy; especially heinous sins might be confessed to the High Priest. Curing too pertained in large part to the priestly order. At the summer festival of *Situa,* as Molina (20–34) described it in the sixteenth century, the people of Cuzco went to the Temple of the Sun calling on sickness to depart, and armed men ran to distant destinations where they bathed to purge evils causing disease. The people lighted torches; days of sacrifice and prayer, feasting and singing followed.

Not only communal but individual curing appears to have been largely performed by priests. But the curer-diviner, though incorporated—insofar as the imprecise terminology of Spanish sources permits us to judge—into the lower ranks of the priestly hierarchy, nevertheless retained traces of his putatively shamanic origin, to the extent that Brundage (1963, 55–56) even suggests that "a fundamental shamanism lies behind all sacred offices in ancient Peru." This curer, unlike higher priests, received a personal supernatural call to his or her office. Molina (14) speaks of a class of "wizards" called *camascas,* "who declared that their grace and virtue was derived from the thunder," and Cobo (2:227–28) specifies that most healers called *camasca* or *soncoyoc* said that someone appeared in dreams and taught them to cure. Both light-

5. See, e.g., Arriaga, 28; also Cobo, 2:163–65, on worship of the dead, and Garcilaso, 76–77, on *huacas.*

6. For early accounts of human sacrifice in Peru, which the Inca apologist Garcilaso (86–87) vigorously denies were performed by his people, see Molina, 54–59, and Cieza de León, 150–51, 180. On the Inca calendar, see Rowe, 308–11, and the sources he cites.

ning and dreams are common forms of the shaman's (or medium's) call, and an Inca curer's initial vision may have remained the guardian spirit from which his or her power derived.

Cures for diseases caused by malevolent spirits, evil winds, and soul loss through fright (Mason, 219) included—besides confession—massage and sucking, sacrifice and prayer, a rich variety of herbal medicines (many of which Europeans adopted), and sophisticated surgical methods such as trepanation. A relative absence of horrified denunciations supports Rowe's contention (291) that narcotics were unimportant in Inca culture, unlike that of Mexico. Coca, whose dried leaves were chewed with lime to release cocaine, was less widely used before than after the Spanish Conquest (von Hagen, 110–12); its main religious use was in divination and sacrifice, and far from producing frenzied visions it assuaged hunger and gave strength to those who chewed it, substituting for food (Cieza de León, 259–60). Other visionary substances, such as hallucinogenic cactuses, were probably known to ancient Andean peoples (Sharon, 40), and intoxication with chicha beer was common on festive occasions, but nothing indicates that ecstatic trance was an important element, even for curers or diviners, in the highly ritualized Inca culture.

Divination was largely mechanical, by grains of maize, beans, or colored stones, spiders' legs, masticated coca, or lungs of slaughtered birds or animals (Cobo, 2:226–27). A more solemn form of divination on critical occasions communicated with spirits answering questions out of flaming braziers around which food and drink were set (Rowe, 302–03; cf. Molina, 14). And a wide range of "oracles," from the High Priest to local practitioners, carried on the shamanic tradition, in very constricted form, of direct communication with the divine. At the annual festival of Capaccocha, at which two male and two female infants were said to be sacrificed, the High Priest and his assistants questioned the principal "idols" about the future of the Inca people; drunken priests, Cieza de León scornfully writes (19), "invented what they saw would most please those who asked the questions, assisted by the devil." At much lower levels "sorcerers" in charge of innumerable huacas talked incomprehensibly with spirits in the dark in order to find lost articles or learn what was happening at a distance (Rowe, 302; cf. Molina, 14–15; Arriaga, 32–33; Polo de Ondegardo, 26–34). In such ways, and by interpretation of dreams, an unpredictable element lingered at the outer margins of the Incas' rigidly ordered world, as if to remind them of a residual shamanic quest or to presage the dark uncertainty soon to descend inexplicably upon them from beyond the farthest borders of this four-cornered empire of the Sun.

Not surprisingly, Andean cultures since colonial times have continued, despite the shattering impact of Spanish Conquest, to reflect attitudes already ancient, no doubt, when the Inca ruled. The rigidity of indigenous (now outwardly Catholic) ritual has been maintained and intensified among the Quechua of Peru and the Aymara and other peoples of highland Bolivia in reaction to centuries of exploitation in the mines and encomiendas. The Andean village is a "closed corporate community" in which the ayllu, a group of families claiming common descent, is the basic unit of social organization as it was for the Inca and possibly their predecessors. Aboriginal social stratification has been heightened by polarization between natives and Europeans, and here as in Mesoamerica ceremonial life in many communities is directed by holders of rotating "cargos" ranked by expense and prestige (Buechler, 44–49). Closure and immobility, though never total, typify both the reality of these societies as perceived by outsiders and the ideal of many Indians: to be left to themselves.

In such societies ritual tends to be stereotyped and invariant. Besides public festivals of the Catholic calendar, personal rites are performed, but no important cults of ancient gods have openly survived. For the Aymara around Lake Titicaca, as for the Colla before them, "religion was and is," La Barre writes (1948, 165), "a worship of strongly localized, sometimes ancestral and totemic, place-deities." In the Quechua community of Qotobamba in southern Peru, too, deities of earth and mountains intimately partake of the life of the people (Nuñez del Prado, 242–49).

If Inca priests vanished, or adopted a new faith, diviners, curers, and sorcerers flourish much as before. Aymara diviners employ ancient techniques of reading coca leaves; they may claim power from lightning but learn mechanical methods by observation (Tschopik, 563–64). The most powerful of them can converse with a dead person's soul (Radin 1942, 285–94). These diviners are sometimes called shamans, but there is little of visionary trance in their procedures: their rituals, like those of their ancestors, are hardly less standardized than a priest's. Curers too "belong rather to a 'priestly' than to a 'shamanistic' tradition," Tschopik (558) notes of the Aymara; though accompanied by herbal medicines, cures are essentially magical, employing blood sacrifice, libations, and food offerings to restore the individual or communal harmony (Métraux 1967, 276–80; Bastien, 129–49).

Central Andean religion thus appears to exclude ecstatic shamanism, yet within this closed world, openness to an indeterminate beyond has sporadically made itself felt. The late sixteenth-century millenarian Taki Onqoy ("Dancing Sickness"), like other Native American revivalist cults, aimed to replace the Christian God with native huacas, which swept down and seized its followers, causing them "to shake, tremble, fall, and dance insanely" (Stern, 52) in a frenzied contact with the divine that was largely foreign to the sober religion it strove to reinstate. Such revitalization movements arise, A. Wallace notes (1966, 157), when members of a traditional community no longer practice the values they profess and must therefore seek new ones, which they equate with the old. Their nearly inevitable failure to restore a vanished past projected into the future often eventuates in embittered acceptance of a once again closed and now demonstrably immutable order.

On the north coast of Peru, where Moche civilization flourished, folk healing has preserved much of its presumably shamanistic content. At a session observed in the 1940s (Gillin, 119–22), the *brujo* summoned spirits by shaking his rattle, chanting, and whistling until he sank into trance and learned from the saint's picture on his table how to treat a patient, while his helper attacked hostile spirits with a knife. In Trujillo, northwest of Moche, the folk healer Eduardo Calderón Palomino was educated in a Catholic seminary, but his practices were overwhelmingly indigenous. Denunciations by Catholic priests in the seventeenth century (Sharon, 43) attest to ancient use of the San Pedro cactus and other hallucinogens by means of which the modern *curandero,* too, is able to transcend mortal limits, voyage to supernatural realms, divine the future—"in short, to attain 'vision,' to 'see'" (45). His soul sets forth in "ecstatic magical flight" (46) to sacred lagoons where it learns the causes of illness and sometimes battles spirits, performing somersaults with sword in hand. Such a figure, bridging ancient tribal and modern urban worlds, embodies not the closed conservatism of the ritualistic Andean healer but the "restless search for meaning" (11) and "constant innovation and growth" (22) characteristic of the age-old shamanic quest.

The vast Inca empire dominated only a fraction of South America, and beyond its confines shamans continued to flourish, often without priestly rival. Nowhere south of Alaska are parallels with Eurasian shamanism more striking than among the Araucanian peoples of the southern Andes, who for centuries resisted both Inca and Spaniard until driven over the cordillera to Argentina or herded onto reservations in Chile. The Araucanians have long practiced agriculture, and among the Mapuche, the largest Araucanian group, priestly ritual probably influenced by ancient Andean civilizations remains central. Indeed, in continuing to worship gods of Sun and Moon, Earth and Sea, the Mapuche have quite possibly perpetuated rites long vanished in the Inca's own domains. In their worship of ancestral deities, too, the Mapuche resemble the Inca and other agricultural peoples. Their most elaborate funeral ritual in recent times is the *ñillatun,* in which prayers to ancestors were probably once the central component. Far from being strictly calendrical, however, this ceremony, as Titiev (1951, 129–30) observed it in the late 1940s, was characterized by lack of standardization. Formulaic invariance was apparently foreign to this traditionally warlike people.

The ritual priest's power derives from social standing and knowledge of ritual. The *machi,* on the other hand, though she too has frequently taken a leading role in the ñillatun "largely by default" (Faron 1964, 102), is in many ways an archetypal shaman showing extraordinary affinities with counterparts in Eurasia and the American Arctic. Although now usually female, the machi was formerly more often, as in some Siberian and Eskimo tribes, a transvestite male; nineteenth-century reports suggest that unlike most of his female successors, he often resembled classic Siberian shamans in being neurotic, epileptic, or otherwise sickly or deformed (Métraux 1967, 183–84; cf. Titiev 1951, 117–18).

A vision, sometimes in conjunction with a serious illness or handicap, is a normal sign of shamanic vocation (Faron 1964, 141–43), and appears to have been standard for centuries past. This initial vision often involves ecstatic ascent to the heavens and revelation from the ancestral sky god Ñenechen or his Christian counterpart; training by an experienced elder follows election and culminates in an initiation ceremony strikingly parallel to those of some Siberian peoples. The machi induces trance not principally by the gourd rattle nearly universal in the New World but by the shallow wooden drum common in Eurasia but rare in America south of the Pacific Northwest. A still more conspicuous shamanistic appurtenance is the *rewe,* a squared tree trunk three meters high with a human head carved at the top and a stairway hewn into the back. On the culminating second day of a ceremony, having demonstrated her curative powers and entered trance, dancing to drum, rattle, and chant, a machi wildly struggles to escape those restraining her, then slowly climbs the *rewe*—much as the Altaic *kam* climbed his birch tree—stands swaying on a platform at its top, then descends to the halfway point from which, shaking her bells, she falls unconscious into a young man's arms.[7]

The Araucanian machi resembles spirit mediums and many Siberian shamans, in contrast to most American shamans outside the Northwest Coast, in being possessed by a spirit—usually a supernatural animal or bird helper or the soul of a dead shaman—and communicating through an interpreter what was revealed during trance. While possessed, she "is unaware of what she says and does and often uses a secret language" (Faron 1964, 139); she sometimes handles hot coals and passes her arms through fire. But machis not only incorporate possessing spirits but "visit

---

7. Based on Robles Rodríguez's account summarized in Métraux 1967, 193–95. See also Métraux, 195–201.

them in the lands where they stay in order to obtain from them the knowledge they need" (Métraux 1967, 208–09). The shaman, an old and blind male machi told Faron (1968, 79), "is inbetween," linking this world to another both by receptively opening herself and by setting actively forth in search of what transcends her. Possession and ecstasy are thus complementary moments in the unending quest to enlarge the given human condition through interchange with what is forever beyond yet inseparable from it.

The most dangerous illnesses are caused by soul loss (Faron 1964, 146), usually inflicted by a witch hostile to the shaman. At the climax of the *machitun* curing ceremony, in another striking parallel to Siberian practice, the machi drinks copiously of urine, then sings and beats the drum, jumps over the patient, and works herself up to a frenzy of possession. She speaks in the possessing spirit's voice without revealing its name, begins a violent dance, often rushing out to climb her *rewe*, then dances around the pole, accompanied by a young man charged with catching her when she falls (Titiev 1951, 115–16). The machi may also directly combat the witch responsible for the disease, or the demons under her command, through powers won from the heavens she is thought to revisit during trance (Métraux 1967, 216).

The impressive parallels between Araucanian and Siberian shamanism must surely be attributed, as Métraux contends (234), to "survival of a great number of traits which elsewhere have been retained in a partial or incomplete fashion and which here have persisted in a coherent complex." In contrast to highly ritualized Mesoamerican and Incan priests, the machi—whether female or transvestite male—is an outsider to dominant hierarchies, and the high esteem bestowed on her without regard to sex or birth provides "compensation for the overwhelming attention given to males in both the mundane and the spiritual segments of the Mapuche world" (Faron 1964, 152). By preserving much of the primordial shaman's mobility in an increasingly sedentary world, Araucanian machis assured that their people's religion would not be only an invariant round of repetitive ritual oriented toward a sacrosanct past but would remain open to the uncertainties of a changing present and indeterminate future. Variant procedures characterize even priestly ceremonies, and healing rites, Titiev notes (1951, 117), leave ample room for "individual whims." Like rites of other mediums or shamans who open themselves to the unknown, they are not automatically effective, as magic and formal ritual are thought to be, but depend upon unpredictable dialogue with spirits who can never be infallibly coerced or commanded.

This dialogic openness to the unexpected accounts for the machi's exhilaration in exploring new realms of the spirit, but also for the sense of peril that often attends it. "When I am possessed by a spirit, I am close to death," one of Faron's informants told him (1964, 142): "It is dangerous, and I do not like to do it," exciting though she found it when young. Both the danger and the excitement derive in large measure from the intrinsic incertitude of the authentic shaman's interaction with a world of boundless transformative potentiality that is not given and cannot be wholly foreknown.

Far to the south the Selk'nam (or Ona) and Yamana (or Yahgan) eked out a livelihood by hunting, fishing, and gathering on the frigid islands of Tierra del Fuego at the southernmost tip of the inhabited world. Among the now nearly extinct Selk'nam of the main island, society was "egalitarian and individualistic" (Chapman, 40), with no chiefs, council of elders, or governing institutions; the seafaring Yamana of the smaller islands south to Cape Horn, whom hunger kept perpetually on the move, likewise recognized no external authority. "An inner unrest moves these people," Gusinde remarks (1961, 2:363 = 1937, 612), "which they themselves cannot account for, because they were born with it."

Repelled by these "miserable, degraded savages" (1962, 208) during the visit of the *Beagle* in 1832–33, Darwin could hardly think them inhabitants of the same world (213), or attribute to them belief "in what we should call a God" (1936, 470) or practice of any religious rites except "the muttering of the old man before he distributed the putrid blubber to his famished party" (1962, 216). Later missionaries and scientists likewise found that the Fuegians "have no knowledge whatever of God" and "are completely lacking" in religious ideas.[8] Such opinions arose from misconceived identification of religion with the priestly rituals of more settled peoples, relegating the shaman, if noticed at all, to the peripheral role of "wizard or conjuring doctor" whose existence Darwin noted (1962, 216) but "whose office we could never clearly ascertain."

But the shaman, however simple his practices, was central to Fuegian religion. A Selk'nam received the shamanic spirit of a dead relative from a living shaman who rubbed his body; thereafter he could accomplish nothing when not possessed by this spirit (Gusinde 1931, 740). Every Yamana shaman maintained an intimate connection with a guardian spirit invoked with songs learned in his vision. While treating disease he sang himself into a semi-trance during which he took counsel with his spirit (1961, 5:1340–48 = 1937, 1415–21). The Selk'nam shaman like-

---

8. Quoted from G. P. Despard (1863) and C. Spegazzini (1882) by Gusinde (1961, 4:951 = 1937, 1035); cf. Lothrop, 35. For Darwin the distinction was not racial; though ranking the Fuegians "amongst the lowest barbarians" (1936, 445), he was surprised "how closely the three natives on board H. M. S. 'Beagle', who had lived some years in England, and could talk little English, resembled us in disposition and in most of our mental faculties." On Darwin's attitudes toward the Fuegians, see Gould 1993, 267–74.

wise consulted with the spirit who entered him during trance, and cured by singing, massaging, and sucking (1931, 757–62). These familiar procedures show little resemblance to ecstatic journeys by Siberian, Eskimo, or Araucanian shamans, for transcendence of the Fuegians' harsh conditions was difficult to envisage.

Yet even in this peripheral outpost of American shamanism, indications remained of a once—and, until their extinction, always a potentially—larger role for Fuegian shamans. According to a Selk'nam myth, the first man and woman descended from the sky by a rope which broke behind them (Lothrop, 98); in other myths the culture hero Kenós came down from the heavens, then near the earth, to mediate between the Highest Being and inhabitants of this world (Gusinde 1931, 573; cf. 1975, 21). Such myths suggest a lingering memory of spirit realms to which Fuegian shamans, like spirit mediums of Polynesia or Africa, no longer had access.

If access to the heavens was not in his power—had it been lost in the distant age when men slaughtered the women who once ruled over them, driving their primordial shaman, the Moon, to the skies in anger at her husband, the Sun?—the vast realm of the future might still reveal itself to the rare Selk'nam shaman who became a "father of the word," a prophet able, through knowledge of celestial lore, to foretell events (Chapman, 44–47).[9] Here mastery of the limitless heavens is again associated with the dynamism of language through which the indeterminate future can be apprehended. The restless Yamana "believe that their medicine men can see into the future and that they have infallible prescience" (Gusinde 1961, 5:130 = 1937, 1422). In this orientation, as in their access to dream and myth, both Yamana and Selk'nam shamans continued to embody, in however attenuated a form, the age-old shamanic vocation of enlarging the boundaries of the bleak and seemingly ineluctable here and now.

TROPICAL QUEST: SHAMANS OF THE AMAZON

On the high plains and western slopes of the Andean cordillera and its narrow Pacific strip, from the Colombian tropics to the frigid wastes of Tierra del Fuego, shamanistic practices either coexisted with priestly rit-

---

9. Few Selk'nam shamans were prophets, and not all prophets were shamans; some prophets were "mothers of the word." With the Selk'nam myth of men's seizure of power from women (Chapman, 66–70), cf. the Yamana myth in Gusinde 1961, 5:1237–49 = 1937, 1337–45. Similar myths of women's primordial pre-eminence (for Australian examples, see Berndt 1951, 18–19, and Strehlow 1947, 93–94) gave rise to theories of aboriginal matriarchy which Bachofen supposed, mainly on the basis of classical literary sources, to be a fundamental stage in the development of civilization.

ualisms or continued, as among the Fuegians, in depleted form. In the sparsely populated regions east of the Andes, on the other hand, above all in the rain forests and highlands watered by the vast Amazon and Orinoco systems, complex shamanisms survived into the present as the predominant, if not unrivaled, expression of tribal religion. With its small semi-migratory bands combining hunting and gathering with slash-and-burn horticulture, the Amazon Basin has been for the most part, in contrast to Mesoamerica and the Central Andes, "a region of the shaman and of minor cults rather than of priests and of the worship of important deities" (Goldman 1963, 4).

Not that communal rituals of fertility, healing, or initiation were absent; on the contrary, studies of Tukanoan peoples of the Colombian Vaupés in northwest Amazonia have demonstrated the extent to which intricate rituals of these relatively settled longhouse communities restore the equilibrium of "an ordered cosmos created in the ancestral past" (C. Hugh-Jones, 1) and allow participant males to be identified with mythical forebears. In the *He* House rites of the men's Yorupary cult among the Barasana, "Regular contact with the world of spirits and ancestors . . . ensures that the human world is attuned to a wider and more embracing cosmic order" (S. Hugh-Jones, 38).

But here, as in central and southern California, the principal officiant is normally a shaman (who is sometimes the headman), not a priest of a rival order, and the use of hallucinogens transforming celebrants into animals able to traverse cosmic layers is distinctly shamanistic. The festivals provide the opportunity for participants "partially to experience what shamans experience—to 'see' beyond everyday reality" (Jackson, 202). Mythical progenitors are venerated, but there is no lineal "ancestor worship" as in Africa, and few signs of sharp division between shaman and priest such as Lévi-Strauss (1973, 269) found among the dualistic Bororo of Brazil. Spirit possession, though attested in some tribes, is relatively infrequent.

Shamans, Métraux observes (1944, 1:197), display "remarkable uniformity in the entire tropical zone extending from the Antilles to the Gran Chaco" two-thirds of a continent to the south. Like the Tapirapé of northern Mato Grosso in central Brazil (Wagley 1977, 174), many of these peoples had no true religious rituals and therefore no priests, but shamans whose personal characteristics gave direct access to the supernatural. Differences in religious practice are great, but in so vast a region it is again, as in northern Eurasia, similarities that are most striking. The near universality of ecstatic shamanism bears witness to the urgency of the spiritual quest among these tropical peoples.

Some Amazonian peoples divide the cosmos into three layers, others into four or more, but many give the impression, as the Shavante of

eastern Mato Grosso did to Maybury-Lewis (284), "of having compara-
tively little speculative interest" in its structure or origin. Opinions concerning the soul vary greatly, and often seem contradictory to outsiders.
Belief in a guardian spirit or nagual attached to an individual for life is
fairly rare (Chagnon, 48–50; Montgomery, 124), but belief in a mobile
soul capable of traveling forth in sickness or dream—the precondition
of visionary shamanism—is very widespread.

The headhunting Jívaro of the Ecuadorian Amazon have developed
a rich doctrine of multiple souls in which the quest has a crucial role. Of
their three souls, the visionary *arutam* which protects against violent
death is not given at birth but must be acquired. A boy (rarely a girl)
begins seeking it at about age six. Accompanied most commonly by his
father (Harner 1972, 136–39), he makes a pilgrimage to a sacred water-
fall where these wandering souls meet. By day the vision seekers bathe,
by night they fast, drink tobacco water or *datura*, and await an arutam
for as long as five days, departing if unsuccessful. If the seeker is fortu-
nate, he wakens to find the earth trembling and a great wind felling trees
amid thunder and lightning; while he grasps a tree trunk the arutam
appears as a pair of creatures, a disembodied head, or a ball of fire. The
seeker boldly touches the arutam, which explodes and disappears; he
then returns home, telling no one he fulfilled his quest. After nightfall,
the arutam he touched comes as a dream in the form of an old ancestor
who promises success and enters his body. Unlike the guardian spirit of
many American peoples the Jívaro arutam departs each time a man kills
an enemy, so that new arutams must continually be sought by successful
warriors. Among most other South American tribes the visionary soul is
not acquired through a quest or dream encounter but is a potentiality
inborn in every woman and man.

Early and recent writers alike have remarked on the prominence of
belief among these peoples in the power of the mobile soul, above all the
shaman's, to transform itself into a bird or animal. In central Brazil, von
den Steinen observed a century ago (351), human beings, birds, animals,
and fish "are all only persons of different appearance and different attributes" into any of which the shaman can transform himself "and understand all languages that are spoken in the forest or in the air or in
the water"; and myths of the Gê, Bororo, and other Amazonian peoples
compiled in Lévi-Strauss's *Mythologiques* bear witness to this all-but-
universal conviction of the interchangeability of human and animal particularly characteristic of shamanistic peoples. The shaman is the self-
transformer par excellence, and the animal into which he especially
changes himself throughout the forested regions of South America is
the swift and powerful jaguar.

If transformation into animal form is one means of transcending the normal human condition, contact with the heavens is another. The sky, the ancestral land where history began for the Bakaïrí of central Brazil, "previously lay near the earth, and one could easily cross over to it" (von den Steinen, 349–50); but after men migrated to earth it rose to its present distance. Some peoples worshiped an astral pantheon based on careful observation of the skies (W. Roth, 254–70), and a star-divinity might appear in a vision, Nimuendajú reported (1942, 86) for the central Brazilian Sherente, to reveal supernatural knowledge. At their Great Feast, already a thing of the past when Nimuendajú visited in 1930 (97–98), a man carried a wad of rosinous bast to the top of a pole called "road to the sky" and raised it to be ignited by a heavenly spark. Others climbed up to learn from dead kin how long they would live; finally, an official received a message from the Sun god. In this way the primordial connection between the earthly and heavenly spheres was restored.

Spirits of the dead are widely believed to reside in the sky, in or beyond the Milky Way, which the living—especially shamans—are thought to visit in quest of knowledge or power. Among the Desana of northwest Amazonia, the Milky Way is the zone of contact, through drug-induced visions, between terrestrial and supernatural beings, including the divine Master of Animals (Reichel-Dolmatoff 1971, 43; cf. Koch-Grünberg, 173; Murphy and Quain, 75). Here animal and celestial transcendence intersect in a complex realization of the transformative spiritual quest.

Twins, sometimes identified with Sun and Moon, were prominent South American culture heroes; and although the quest is often submerged in a tangle of other motifs rather than being found in the "practically unmixed form" of Navajo and Pueblo myths (Radin 1942, 81), it finds striking expression in tales from widely dispersed Tupí-Guàraní–speaking peoples. In a myth of the long-extinct Tupinamba of coastal Brazil, recounted by Métraux (1948, 132; cf. 1928, 31–43), twins of the culture hero Maira by Opossum seek their father, who imposes a series of tasks before acknowledging them as his children. Each is killed and revived by the other during these ordeals, but in the end Maira recognizes both.[10] Such widely disseminated tales give mythical expression to the arduous quest re-enacted by the shaman and indeed by every person who combines celestial and animal powers potentially surpassing the normally human.

10. For more recent Tupí-Guaraní versions, see Wagley and Galvão, 137–40, and Bartolomé, 16–40. Myths of twins exist among many other groups; see, e.g., the Carib versions from the Guianas and Brazil recorded in W. Roth, 130–36, and E. Basso, 10–12.

Shamans acquire their powers in several ways. In the Guianas, the office was apparently hereditary (W. Roth, 333), and among the Jívaro, where warriors must seek a vision-soul, a shaman obtains power through purchase (Harner 1972, 118). But in most cases a visionary call, followed by isolated apprenticeship, is necessary. Thus among the Mehinaku of Mato Grosso a monkey demon offers to be the dreamer's "pet"; instruction in smoking and three months of seclusion and taboos follow (Gregor, 335). Among the Tapirapé, all young men who wished to be shamans gathered each evening to seek dreams, swallowing smoke and falling into trance. Those who succeeded (as not all did) later took part in a ritualized "fight against the beings of Thunder" and performed cures alongside their mentors (Wagley 1977, 197–99).

Tobacco and other hallucinogens—notably the potent concoction of the *Banisteriopsis caapi* vine widely known as *yagé* or *ayahuasca*—are frequently used to induce the shaman's visionary call. Even Jívaro candidates, whose purchase of shamanic powers is nearly routine (about one of four men is a shaman!), make contact with the "real" or supernatural world (Harner 1972, 154) only after imbibing the drink. Elsewhere the apprenticeship is normally more arduous and uncertain. Helena Valero, a Brazilian peasant girl captured by the Shamatari of northwest Amazonia, observed the rigors of a secluded young initiate (Biocca, 71–73) who became so drunk with hallucinogenic *epená*, inhaled day and night, that he could not stand while learning to repeat his teacher's chants. If he survived this ordeal of up to a month, the initiate would have mastered the spirits and become a true shaman: an experience equated with death and rebirth. Novice shamans of the Colombian Desana, secluded for a year or more, strove in a slow and difficult quest to attain "weapons" in a drug-induced visit to the celestial House of Thunder (Reichel-Dolmatoff 1975, 78–79), until finally "they will see a tree, a piece of wood, or a stone and will suddenly know: this is mine, this is what thunder sent me!" With this, the long search to transcend the given by uniting powers of earth and sky embodied in the most familiar objects attains fruition.

Disease is thought to be caused by intrusion or soul loss, evil spirits, sorcerers, or broken taboos. Métraux (1944, 2:325) finds belief in soul loss widespread in the Andes and Gran Chaco but rare in tropical America, even suggesting (1967, 133) that its prevalence in the Chaco may derive from Andean civilizations rather than native traditions. Many accounts testify, however, to persistence of this ancient belief in widely separated parts of the immense Amazonian region. Only when the soul has been robbed does the otherwise "singularly uniform" shamanistic treatment of illness change, Métraux remarks (1944, 2:325), as the widespread methods of massaging, blowing tobacco smoke or swallowing tobacco juice, and sucking out intrusive objects, along with singing, dancing, and shaking of rattles, are supplemented by spirit possession[11] and ecstatic flight. Some Amazonian shamans, moreover, directly engage hostile spirits in dialogue or battle. One dramatic instance is the cure Im Thurn (336–37) underwent in the 1880s, when suffering from fever, by a Macusi shaman of Guyana. As he lay in total darkness, roars filled the house; the shaman thundered questions and disease spirits shouted answers: "I seemed to be suspended somewhere in a ceaselessly surging din; and my only thoughts were a hardly-felt wonder as to the cause of the noise, and a gentle, fruitless effort to remember if there had once been a time before the noise was."

Many Amazonian peoples believe, like the Jívaro, that the "real" world can be seen only with the aid of hallucinogens (Harner 1972, 134; cf. Karsten 1935, 444–45). Drinking of yagé and similar substances, not only by shamans but in communal celebrations like those of the Tukanoans (C. Hugh-Jones, 209), "creates an alternative experience of time and space." The thin shell between the two worlds can be traversed only in hallucinatory trance, and "people say they have visited this other dimension and have seen its inhabitants" (Reichel-Dolmatoff 1975, 192). Whether drunk, smoked, or inhaled through a blowpipe in the form of snuff, the drug enables the soul to communicate with spirits, and sometimes frees it to rise above this world to another. Thus tobacco not only attracts spirits, Wilbert observes (34), but transports man into their realm, "where he can learn how 'to see' things that are beyond his physical field of vision."

After drinking yagé (known as ayahuasca in Peru), the nineteenth-century Ecuadorian geographer Villavicencio reported (Harner 1973a, 155–56), natives "feel vertigo and spinning in the head, then a sensation of being lifted into the air and beginning an aerial journey," though elevated visions of lakes, forests, and birds are followed by terrible horrors. For the Desana of Colombia, hallucinogenic snuff, or its supernatural master, is the intermediary through which those chosen by it "ascended to the Milky Way and turned into jaguars" allowing them to roam in the forest unrecognized (Reichel-Dolmatoff 1975, 109).

---

11. Métraux (1944, 2:322) notes, contrary to Loeb, that shamanistic possession is far from unknown in South America. Sometimes the shaman is possessed, sometimes another specialist (see Gregor, 339, on the Mehinaku). In most tropical tribes, however, as Reichel-Dolmatoff writes of the Desana and other Tukanoan peoples (1975, 104), "the concept of spirit-possession seems to be completely lacking. . . . A payé [shaman] is always himself; never is he seized or invaded by a spirit; he simply interprets and transmits what this spirit shows him or tells him."

Among some Tukanoan tribes only great shamans of the past could travel to the sky (C. Hugh-Jones, 62), but belief in celestial ascent by living shamans has persisted elsewhere. A Tapirapé shaman could travel to villages of the dead by turning himself into a bird (Wagley 1977, 185), and certain shamans traveled to the sky in their canoes or visited the Pleiades as "Jaguars of the Skies." Such celestial journeys are a quest for renewal of superhuman powers lost by the primordial schism of earth and sky, but still possessed by hawk, jaguar, and other animals.

The heavenly quest is central to cures for soul loss. In the Gran Chaco, where this diagnosis is common, the shaman sends his own soul in quest of his patient's, traveling in the sky and under the earth to discover and restore it (Métraux 1967, 133–34). When a Taulipáng shaman of northwest Amazonia wishes to communicate with the *Mauarí*, or spirits, during a curing session, Koch-Grünberg reported (211–12) in the early twentieth century, he cuts some pieces from a vine resembling a ladder and drinks the brew concocted from them: "In this way this vine . . . becomes a ladder for him to climb up to the land of the *Mauarí*."

When her baby appeared to be dying among the Namoeteri, Helena Valero recalls (Biocca, 211–13), the old *shapori* or shamans, having inhaled *epená* snuff, sought his shade, examining the various paths it might have taken. The chief shaman then announced that spirits of the Sun had stolen him, and bade the others follow him to the Sun, for when drunk with *epená* "they really believe they are rising into the air." Finally, having sung, sucked, invoked the spirits, and sprinkled invisible water, the chief went away. The child, as his mother remembers, "had truly improved."

The shamanistic quest for knowledge of a transcendent heavenly realm thus plays an important part in tropical South America. Yet the prominence of hallucinogenic drugs in inducing these visions both diminishes the heroic effort required of the spiritual quest—the shaman may be less exception than norm, so easily attained are his visions—and reduces its indeterminate exploration of the beyond. "In spite of the individual nature of the hallucinogenic experience," Kensinger notes (12) of ayahuasca among the Cashinahua of eastern Peru, "there is a high degree of similarity . . . from individual to individual during any one night of drinking," giving their visions a repetitively standardized quality. Among the Desana, the shaman "is not a mystic, and the mechanisms he employs are not sacred" (Reichel-Dolmatoff 1975, 201–02). As mechanisms they share the invariability of compulsive rites, and to that extent do not so much open toward the unknown as guarantee a repetition of the expected.

Yet like patterns of ritual or spirit possession, use of hallucinogens does not preclude the exploratory quest but guides it in restricted channels toward a finally unpredictable goal. Its initial effect is often disorienting—"It can ruin a man's mind," the Amahuaca shaman-chief Xumu warned his Peruvian captive, Córdova-Rios (Lamb, 131)—if he cannot control his visions; successful effort to gain an always imperfect control distinguishes the shaman from those who submit to stereotyped hallucinations. In Xumu's chant, as his pupil later remembers it, the emphasis is on incessant search for knowledge (Lamb, 89–90):

> We are here again to seek wisdom
> give us tranquillity and guidance
> to understand the mysteries of the forest
> the knowledge of our ancestors . . .
> to translate the past into the future . . .

To transcend past in future is to enter a realm of indeterminate danger, as myths of shamanic flight repeatedly stress. The shaman is thus far more than a channel for monotonous hallucinations; indeed his social role, as among the Sharanahua of eastern Peru, may be the only one not determined by kinship or marriage (Siskind, 52). He is therefore uniquely qualified to explore the unknown, so that new songs created from his observations and experiences may become as much a part of traditional knowledge as the old songs had been (162), expanding tribal horizons and effecting change within a framework of perceived continuity.

The ecstatic shaman is no mere technician, then, but an explorer as well: "the reformer of received traditions, the preserver and innovator alike" (Bödiger, 54). The quasi-mechanical effect of communally shared hallucinogens may indeed diminish individual endeavor and constrict the indeterminacy of the quest by channeling it, like ritual formulas, into expected patterns. But wherever unpredictable chance prevails—as among semi-nomadic forest tribes it often does—the Tapirapé and other peoples of the Amazon basin "depended markedly upon their shamans" (Wagley 1977, 195) to assimilate the new and unknown. As religious leader of his people, the shaman is often not only curer but prophet or even messiah; and it is rare, Métraux remarks (1967, 38), "that a messianic movement, even if it aims at re-creating the past, is not at the same time innovative."

The close relation between Amazonian messianic movements and native myths of a culture hero who leads his people to a paradise on earth or beyond it strongly indicates, Schaden asserts (172), that millenarian conceptions were indigenous to these cultures—above all to the wandering Tupí-Guaraní tribes dispersed in historical times from the Atlantic coast of Brazil to the Peruvian montaña, and in particular to the Apapocuva of southern Brazil and their neighbors.[12] For these peoples the questing culture heroes of myth were no mere legend of long ago but a present reality embodied by the shaman as leader of his people. Maira, father of the mythical twins, according to the Tenetehara of northeastern Brazil, came to earth in search of a "Beautiful Land," and there created man and woman, and taught them to procreate, plant, and prepare manioc before he returned to his carefree "Village of the Gods" (Wagley and Galvão, 100–01). In widely separated parts of the Amazonian forests his people have continued his quest.

The classic account of their wanderings was written by a young German, Curt Unkel, adopted by the Apapocuva as Curt Nimuendajú. At the beginning of the nineteenth century shamans from this and other Guaraní tribes prophesied imminent destruction of the world, gathered disciples, and with dances and chants set off "in search of the 'Land without Evil,' which . . . most thought was in the east, over the sea" (Nimuendajú 1914, 87). The roots of such movements, in which whole tribes migrated hundreds of miles through hostile terrain, go back at least to the sixteenth century; to Nimuendajú (335) the apocalyptic belief of the Apapocuva expressed the "disconsolate pessimism" of a dying tribe which had lost its faith in the future. Yet by his own account (357–60), it is their unshaken perseverance in this desperate quest that is most compelling. For as long as a year after the shaman's visionary summons his people strenuously danced to elicit a revelation of the way to the east, demonstrating "an utterly astonishing determination and persistence" and enduring the harshest privations with no thought of retreat: forward was the only direction they knew. Reaching the coast, they danced again in hope of being lifted through the air to the Land without Evil beyond the sea, until "the way to the beyond had been shut off forever."

A small band of Paraguayan Guaraní whom Nimuendajú met, to his amazement, near São Paulo in 1912 showed how persistent this quest could be. "They wished to go over the sea to the east, and their confidence in the success of this plan," he writes (361–63), "brought me almost to despair." Only after utter failure of chants and dances on the shore had at last brought disillusionment did they reluctantly follow him to a reservation west of the coast; but when he returned a month later he saw them packing up their belongings and setting out once more, "very probably again to the sea; I have never heard of them again." This

12. Among the Avá-Chiripá or Avá-Katú-Eté, a Guaraní tribe that returned to the Paraguayan forest after 150 years under the Jesuits, Bartolomé (70) suggests that "little or no interruption took place in the transmission of mythical narratives and of tribal cosmological concepts inside the Missions."

small band of undaunted seekers, like other Tupí-Guaraní speaking tribes over centuries of recorded history (cf. Métraux 1967, 9–41; Eliade 1969, 101–11), and perhaps long before, had taken the shaman's vision of another world in the literal sense and unstintingly committed themselves to its realization, however long it might take, and whatever price they must pay for their intransigent resolve in the face of insuperable odds. The spiritual quest had become too vital a part of their life as a people to conceive of abandoning one without surrendering the other as well.

CHAPTER FOURTEEN

Eastern North America
and the Great Plains

To the extent that hallucinatory drugs make the visions they induce predictable or even stereotyped, it is not in the Amazonian tropics that the quest for an indeterminate transcendence found fullest realization south of the Arctic, but among the mobile hunters and gatherers of eastern and central North America, where the solitary vision quest practiced in parts of the Pacific Northwest took on an importance in tribal religious life perhaps unparalleled elsewhere in the world.

RITUALISM AND VISION IN THE SOUTHEAST

The tribes of southeastern North America possessed, in economic, political, and ceremonial terms, "the richest culture of any native people north of Mexico" (Hudson, 3)—a culture strongly influenced by Mesoamerican civilizations. Most tribes combined hunting and gathering with intensive farming of maize, beans, and squash; their societies were hierarchically ranked by age or achievement (203). These linguistically diverse but culturally similar peoples were organized into highly centralized chiefdoms: "not only as King," Captain John Smith wrote of the Virginia Powhatan chief (31), "but as half a god they esteem him." The Natchez of the lower Mississippi, who venerated their hereditary leader as the "Great Sun," may have been perpetuating a tradition of "truly powerful chiefdoms or primitive states" (206) that had flourished centuries before de Soto set out in 1539 to explore these territories for the King of Spain.

Ritual specialists exercised great powers. Although often called "prophets," "doctors," and "shamans," they are properly designated priests (337) because they were valued for their training "rather than for some innate ability or power." Office was often hereditary (Adair, 81), but sometimes, as among the Chickasaw of Mississippi and Tennessee, a priest was elected for life (Speck 1907, 51). Candidates underwent long study to gain the knowledge of sacred mysteries that qualified them for office (Adair, 364), and some tribes, like the Creek (or Muskogee) of Georgia and Alabama, recognized degrees of expertise marked by distinctive insignia. The procedure was ritually formalized with much emphasis on tradition and sacred formulas excluding as far as possible the variable and unexpected.

Bartram (390) summarized a priest's functions in the 1770s, noting that he exercises great political influence, particularly in military affairs, communes with invisible spirits, can "foretel rain or drought, and pretend to bring rain at pleasure, cure diseases, and exercise witchcraft, invoke or expel evil spirits, and even assume the power of directing thunder and lightning." Captain John Smith (29) reports that priests, like chiefs, when dead, "go beyond the mountains toward the setting of the sun, and ever remain there . . . doing nothing but dance and sing, with all their predecessors. But the common people they suppose shall not live after death, but rot in their graves like dead dogs." [1]

This priestly religion was practiced in the most elaborate sanctuaries north of Mexico. At Cofitachequi in South Carolina de Soto visited (and plundered) an immense elevated temple decorated with shells and pearls and containing statues, armor, and chests with "remains of dead notables" (Hudson, 111). Sanctuaries like those depicted in Hariot's *Brief and True Report of the New Found Land of Virginia* of 1588 (Lorant, 267–69) contained "idols" or embalmed bodies of dead chiefs displayed on a high scaffold; some of these sanctuaries were so holy, both Captain Smith (27) and Bartram (360n.) report, that only chiefs or priests could enter them. Apart from grand structures such as these and the Natchez temples (Swanton 1911, 158–67), every important town appears to have had its holy place for performance of ceremonies intended to promote fertility of the crops on which tribal livelihood depended.

The Natchez celebrated each new moon with a ceremonial feast, and throughout the region major rites were associated with ripening of the corn. Among the Waxhaw of North Carolina, as early as 1701, Lawson (33) attended a feast commemorating the harvest, and Adair (99–111) later described "the grand festival of the annual expiation of sin" at the first ripening of the corn. As Bartram (399) summarized the annual "busk" (a Creek word), or green corn dance, the people cleansed their houses and the whole town of filth, which they burned, extinguishing

---

1. From *Generall Historie of Virginia* (1624); cf. the version in *A Map of Virginia* (1612), rpt. in Barbour, 2:368–69.

the fire after three days of fasting. The high priest then lighted a new fire, and women brought newly harvested grain from the fields; after a public feast the people danced, sang and rejoiced all night for days thereafter. Ceremonial lighting (as in ancient Mexico) of the new fire signified tribal renewal through "the beginning of a new year with a purified social order" (Hudson, 318; cf. Swanton 1946, 775). The near universality of the Green Corn Ceremony throughout the known history of southeastern tribes (and most others of the eastern United States) makes this "by far the most important of their seasonal ceremonies" (Hudson, 366).

Human sacrifice, rarely attested (except for captives in war) elsewhere in North America, is another parallel with Mexico. Even allowing for horrified exaggeration and possible confusion of initiatory with bodily death, accounts are too frequent to be dismissed. Thus the artist Le Moyne affirms (Lorant, 103) that Florida Indians "offer their first-born son to the chief," clubbing him to death on a stump around which "the women who have accompanied the mother dance in a circle . . . with great demonstrations of joy." And Henry Spelman, after capture by the Powhatan and Potomac Indians of Virginia, reports (Swanton 1946, 743) that "once in the yeare, ther preests which are ther coniurers with ye men, weomen, and children doe goe into the woods, wher ther preests makes a great cirkel of fier in ye which after many obseruanses in ther coniurations they make offer of 2 or 3 children to be giuen to ther god." Many Natchez submitted to be strangled to death, or strangled their children to death, at the funeral of a Great Sun or a member of his family.

So dominant was communal ritualism that even healing, the shaman's pre-eminent domain, was often a priestly activity. Most important to successful treatment, Swanton asserts (1946, 782)—along with the usual herbal medicines, sucking, and blowing—was "repetition of the proper magical formulae," such as the invocations meticulously recorded by Cherokee doctors (in the script devised by Sequoiah) and published by Mooney (1891 and 1932). The priestly Chickasaw "shaman" administered an emetic and sang a formulaic song, then blew medicine on the patient's head, a treatment "kept up with little variation for three days" (Speck 1907, 55). In the Chickasaw *Picófa*, or "fast," a communal curing ceremony mainly consisting of propitiatory songs and dances performed in unison, the formulaic ritualism of southeastern Indian life reached an apex, all but precluding any ecstatic quest to recover a wandering soul from the uncircumscribed beyond.

Traces of shamanistic beliefs survived, however, as they did in the priestly cultures of the Southwest, Mesoamerica, and the Andes. The southeastern cosmos consisted of an orderly Upper World, an Under World epitomizing disorder and change, and a world between (Hudson, 122, 125). To the extent that emphasis fell not on celestial deities widely worshiped throughout the Southeast (Swanton 1942, 210) but on man's intermediate position in this world and potential connection with the others above and below, the quest for transcendence remained a possibility not wholly foreclosed.

Origin myths of the Caddo (Swanton 1942, 25) and Choctaw (Swanton 1931, 5), like those of the Southwest, told of the people's emergence from the earth, but some tribes, including the Creeks (Swanton 1928, 480), told also of descent from the sky, a transcendent world potentially accessible to the human. Several myths of the Alabama (Swanton 1929, 138–43) recounted celestial journeys. In one, people descended from above in a canoe, singing and laughing, played ball on earth, then returned to the sky; a man who observed them seized one of the women, married her, and had children by her. When the wife and children reascended, the father attempted to follow but fell and was killed. In a Choctaw myth from Bayou Lacomb, Louisiana (Bushnell, 35), two brothers set out together at age four to follow the Sun; as men, they traversed a wide water and entered his home. Sun asked "why they had followed him, as it was not time for them to reach heaven. They replied that their only reason for following him was a desire to see where he died." Even in priestly societies of the Southeast, the ancient quest to surpass humankind's given limits thus remained a theoretical possibility, at least for heroes of myth.

Although curing remained primarily a priestly function, early writers often noted a distinction between priests and "conjurers or wonder workers" (Swanton 1946, 743), also called sorcerers, prophets, soothsayers, or medicine men. Creek "Knowers" could prophesy and diagnose diseases; their abilities were inborn, and members of certain groups, such as twins, were most likely to join their number (774). Seemingly ecstatic behavior was not unknown: in North Carolina around 1700 a doctor, after chanting and sucking, began "to cut Capers and clap his Hands on his Breech and Sides," with "Grimaces, and antick postures, which are not to be matched in Bedlam" (Lawson, 227). The "juggler" (*jongleur*), the eighteenth-century French traveler Bossu reported (Swanton 1928, 616), entered a skin-covered cabin entirely naked and spoke incomprehensible words to invoke the spirit: "after which he rises, cries, is agitated, appears beside himself, and water pours from all parts of his body. The cabin shakes, and those present think that it is the presence of the Spirit."

The contrast between two types of specialist is illustrated by two of de

Bry's engravings: in one (Lorant, 235) an elderly priest stands dignified and erect, in the other (247) a "sorcerer" or "juggler" runs making "strange gestures" as if possessed: "For they are very familiar with devils, from whom they obtain knowledge about their enemies' movements." Le Moyne described a sorcerer consulted by a Florida chief who whispered unintelligible words and made animated gestures: "his appearance became so frightful that he looked scarcely human; he twisted his limbs until the bones snapped out of place and did many other unnatural things" (Lorant, 59). Not expertise in ritual but direct access to the divine was the source of such prophets' knowledge.

Shamanistic visions were not limited to sorcerers or soothsayers, moreover, but might be required of priestly doctors also. A novice priest of the Creek was expected to have a dream (Swanton 1928, 619), and in some tribes a visionary quest may have been essential to a priest's calling. A Chickasaw candidate went into the woods for three days, naked and alone, and kept the knowledge he gained secret (Speck 1907, 56), and among the ritualistic Natchez, according to the anonymous early eighteenth-century "Luxembourg Memoir" (Swanton 1911, 178), a novice fasted alone in a cabin for nine days. Shaking his rattle,

> he invokes the Spirit, prays Him to speak to him and to receive him as a doctor and magician, and that with cries, howls, contortions, and terrible shakings of the body, until he gets himself out of breath and foams in a frightful manner. This training being completed at the end of nine days, he comes out of his cabin triumphant and boasts of having been in conversation with the Spirit and of having received from Him the gift of healing maladies, driving away storms, and changing the weather.

Southeastern ritualism had thus not altogether obliterated the ancient tradition of direct communion with the divine.

In at least one tribe, the Chitimacha of Louisiana—and fuller observation before the forced removal or extinction of southeastern peoples might surely have revealed similar practices elsewhere—not only the shaman (whether "priest" or "sorcerer") but "Each youth underwent solitary confinement in some house until he obtained a guardian spirit, and this is also affirmed of each girl" (Swanton 1946, 781). However important communal ceremonies, public sacrifices, and standardized formulas had come to be for peoples of these hierarchically structured agricultural societies, they remained hunters, gatherers, and warriors, too, and had not entirely relinquished the need for individual quests by their leaders, or even by all, for visionary experience of a never wholly predictable or communicable reality transcending the established routines of their everyday world.

COMMUNAL AND PERSONAL QUESTS
OF THE NORTHEASTERN WOODLANDS

Largely subordinated to priestly ritual in sedentary cultures of the Southeast, the shamanic quest remained central to more mobile peoples of the northeastern United States and adjacent regions of Canada. As early as 1612 the Jesuit Father Pierre Biard described the wild Montagnais and other Algonquian tribes of a newly discovered New France (Kenton, 1:23–24) as practicing a religion of "incantations, dances and sorcery" in which "medicine men . . . consult the evil Spirit regarding life and death and future events." Other Algonquian and especially Iroquoian peoples lived in settled communities and cultivated corn, beans, and squash; for the Iroquois League, Morgan recognized (199), hunting had become "a secondary, although a necessary means of subsistence." Yet even in their sturdy longhouse villages the restless mobility of a recent past lingered on, especially for more nearly nomadic males who prided themselves on dominion in war. Communal values were strong, as in all tribal societies, but many northeastern peoples, especially in the Algonquian hunting tradition, were nonetheless strongly individualistic: the traditional Ojibwa, Landes observes (1968, 14), "brooked no laws that clashed with his whims" and took joy "in sabotaging the social game."

Collective ceremonies played a major role here as elsewhere in North America. The Iroquois in particular mapped out a familiar trail amid the uncertainties of daily existence in an ancient cycle of calendrical rites renewed in the early nineteenth century by the Seneca prophet Ganeodiyo, or Handsome Lake. Among less complexly organized Algonquian tribes communal festivals were seldom so elaborate, but some, like the annual Big House of the Delaware (or Lenape), with its representation of the soul's journey along the Milky Way after death and its kindling of new fire symbolizing renewal of life, were highly developed (Speck 1931).

Both Iroquoian and Algonquian rituals prominently included public ceremonies by curing societies. The Iroquois Company of False Faces not only healed individually but "conducted a public exorcism of disease . . . and ill luck of all kinds" each spring and fall, shouting terrifying cries as they visited each house in grotesquely carved masks and frightened away disease spirits (A. Wallace 1970, 81–82). The Huron, who seem never to have practiced regular calendrical rites (which the kindred Iroquois may have adopted from southeastern tribes since the seventeenth century), devoted the winter Ononharoia, or "upsetting of the brain," to curing illness by communal enactment of dreams, and several societies performed public dances to heal disease (Trigger 1969, 96–99).

Such collective rites, bearing clear traces of ancient shamanic practices, continued to be performed by the Iroquois despite the initial opposition of Handsome Lake, into whose reformed religion they were eventually assimilated.

Among Algonquian peoples, who almost entirely lacked fixed agricultural ceremonies, communal ritual centered on the society the Ojibwa called the Midéwiwin, whose initiatory rites climaxed in shooting each candidate with the sacred shell that killed and revived him. Midé priests inscribed their myths in pictographic characters on birch bark scrolls (see Dewdney), and these, like the sacred formulas of the Cherokee, gave written sanction for ceremonies held to date back to the origin of the world.

Communal ritual, though much less developed than in the southern United States and Mesoamerica, thus played an important role in the Northeast, but both agricultural and curing rites may in fact have been recent developments. The supposedly ancient Algonquian Midéwiwin may have been a relatively late codification of ancient shamanic practices in response to European dislocations. Among many peoples, including Chippewa,[2] Ottawa, and Fox, evidence suggests that until the eighteenth century, when the Midéwiwin emerged as a solidifying tribal tradition for Ojibwa groups dispersed by the European fur trade, "medicinal and magical practices were in the hands of shamans, individual practitioners" (Hickerson, 76–79). Iroquois medicine societies, too, give ritual form to "shamanistic behavior once free and innovative," as described in seventeenth-century accounts of the Huron before such societies regulated individual shamans (Fenton 1978, 318). The communal rituals recorded during the last three centuries by white observers may therefore have been in large part a defensive response to disruptions introduced by the whites themselves.

Major central Algonquian rites unmistakably suggest shamanistic affinities. The Delaware traced their Big House ceremony to dreams revealed to ancient tribal leaders (Speck 1931, 18), and recitation of dreams was central to it (85). Its leader, as observed by M. R. Harrington in Oklahoma (1921, 92), was not a hereditary custodian of tradition but a visionary "in communication with the supernatural world." The Midéwiwin, too, not only seems to have originated later than the guardian spirit quest among the Ojibwa (whose northern tribes seldom performed it), but retained important affinities with it. Hoffman (1891, 192) noted that its songs, far from being fixed, vary with the singer's inspiration,

2. "Chippewa," a corruption of "Ojibwa" accepted by the Bureau of American Ethnology, is either a synonym for Ojibwa or more specifically designates southwestern Ojibwa tribes living in the United States.

and Densmore remarked (1910, 13) that exactness is not obligatory in a ritual whose details vary in different localities. The Midéwiwin, Landes suggests (1968, 42), was thus "an academy of shamans" whose prestige rested mainly on visions (79).

Even the relatively fixed agricultural rites of the Iroquois may have been originally dictated by dreams and could be altered by them (Tooker 1970, 33), and despite its sacrosanct "code," Handsome Lake's Gospel has no one canonical text but varies with each recitation (Deardorff, 101). But the mobility—and the impulse to transcend the socially given—of the shamanistic quest survived above all, among the Iroquois, in rites of the curing societies which Handsome Lake's reforms could not abolish. The grotesque masks of the Falseface Company were modeled on dreams, and like sacred clowns elsewhere, these performers delighted in saturnalian inversion of their culture's values. In this masquerade, Edmund Wilson remarked (238), young and old, male and female, inseparably mingle with "a certain sense of liberation."

In a ceremony observed by Wilson (290–307) on the Tonawanda Seneca reservation in June 1959, the questing impulse of shamanism manifests itself still more clearly. Members of the Little Water Company, keepers of a medicine able to revive the dying, sing together several times a year to keep up its strength. Suddenly the lights are switched off: "The room with its Corn Flakes had vanished: you were at once in a different world." A man and a woman are searching for the Little Water by which the animals have brought back to life the mythical Good Hunter known for kindness to them, and taught him a wonderful song in their language. The animals congregate, and in "the climax of the symphony" guide the questers to a mountaintop from which the marvelous song emanates: "at the top they find a great stalk of corn growing out of the barren rock, and from this stalk comes the song that has drawn them." Its bleeding root instantly heals, and the seekers learn from the animals to mix the miraculous medicine. "In each of the first two sequences, the songs all follow a pattern; but in the third, they begin on unexpected notes and follow unfamiliar courses. This is magic, a force beyond nature is tearing itself free," and with this climactic liberation "a paean is let loose: it fills the room with its volume. One finds oneself surrounded, almost stupefied."

The quest for the Little Water thus ritually enacts a people's continuing transcendence of its given condition through communal search for its deepest sources. The adepts of this ancient medicine society whose rites Wilson found flourishing in twentieth-century New York State "have mastered the principle of life, they can summon it by the ceremony itself. Through this, they surpass themselves" (310).

Wilson remarks (310) on the closeness of the Iroquois, even today, to the animal world, and many forms of hunting magic, including bear ceremonials, have been widespread, as among the Ojibwa (Hallowell 1960, 159), throughout the Northeast. Transformation between human and animal was thought to have frequently taken place, at least in mythical times, as enacted in masked dances and curative rites of secret societies such as those, among the Iroquois, of the otter, buffalo, and bear. Healing as well as hunting might derive from identification of humans, through ritual propitiation, with beneficent animal powers; this too was a common form of the quest for transcendence.

French Jesuits repeatedly marvel at the credence given to dreams in New France. Father Brébeuf, in the Jesuit Relation of 1636 (Kenton, 1:264–65), calls the dream the "oracle" and "principal God of the Hurons." Among both Huron and Iroquois, dreams were thought to express wishes of the soul, and attempts were made to carry out their commands to the letter, sometimes by curative ceremonies whose overt sexuality dismayed French visitors. In the Huron *andacwander* ceremony recorded by Father Lalemant in 1639 (Kenton, 1:388–89; cf. Trigger 1969, 118–19), a dying old man's dreams were fulfilled by public copulation of twelve girls and young men, with a thirteenth girl for himself. Dream spirits, often in animal form, were sometimes thought to transport the soul to distant lands, but even when the soul did not leave the body, dreams gave vent to its desires in accord "with the theme of freedom in the culture as a whole" (A. Wallace 1970, 74). Variation was continually introduced into communal ritual by individual dreams, introducing a "vibrant and creative" dimension into cultures such as the Huron (Trigger 1969, 118). Through the mediation of dream, ritual itself shared in the mobility of a soul forever being formed and transformed.

Father Le Jeune reports in the Jesuit Relation of 1639 (Kenton, 1:377–78) that the Indians of Canada distinguish several souls. "Some of them imagine a Paradise abounding in blueberries. . . . Others say that the souls do nothing but dance after their departure from this life; there are some who admit the transmigration of souls, as Pythagoras did"; but all believe it is immortal. Among some tribes the journey to the land of the dead became a dangerous quest across a roaring river bridged by a slender tree trunk (Blair, 1:377–78), past a giant strawberry and over a shaking log bridge (Kohl, 214–16), or through other perils. Spirit realms were potentially accessible not only to souls of the dead but, on rare occasions, to a daring few of the living, whose mythical quests bear eloquent witness to continuation among recently migratory peoples of the search for knowledge and power through personal communication with the unknowable beyond.

"Tales of the recovery of a beloved person from the land of the dead are common in North American mythology," and however much they vary in detail, "they are one and the same story," Gayton contended (1935, 263). In a Huron legend recounted by Brébeuf in 1636 (Kenton, 1:258–60), three months after her death a man seized his reluctant sister's soul in the underworld and corked it into a pumpkin, placing her brains in another. Returning home, he retrieved her body from the cemetery and had almost revived it when a curious onlooker broke the prohibition against raising his eyes: "At that moment the soul escaped, and there remained to him only the corpse in his arms." In a tale of the Micmac of the Gaspé Peninsula and New Brunswick, recorded by Father Le Clercq in 1691 (208–13), a giant gives a father his son's soul to carry home from the land of the dead in a little bag; but a curious woman opens it, "and the soul escaped immediately and returned whence it had come."

Countless such legends, many strikingly similar to the Greek myth of Orpheus and Eurydice, have been recorded in much of North America, indicating the high importance attributed to personal communication with the spirit world. Nor were such journeys possible only in a mythical past. "Many of our tribe have been there and returned," Kohl's Ojibwa informants told him (220–25), citing a living hunter who had overcome great obstacles in returning from the dead to care for his children; nearly a century later Hallowell (1955, 151–71) found that visits to the spirit world by the dead or dying still played a major part in the life of the Berens River Saulteaux, a hunting people of Ojibwa derivation living east of Lake Winnipeg in Manitoba.

These tales perpetuate ancient shamanistic beliefs and possibly even seances aimed at reviving a dead person: according to Hultkrantz (1957, 240), "the Orpheus tradition may in its core be regarded as the text to a shamanistic act." In contrast to ritualistic agrarian ideologies, "its basic tone is individualistic, not collectivistic; it is founded on a shaman's ecstatic experiences, not upon the more sober therapeutic methods of a medicine society" (263), and it has been kept alive in North America— more perhaps than anywhere else—by the widespread guardian-spirit quest whose fundamental assumptions closely resemble its own.

The land of the dead in "Orpheus" myths is generally located near the setting sun. It is "a happy land" in a tradition created, Hultkrantz suggests (1957, 92–93), by peoples with a harmonious view of life and little terror of death. At least equally prominent in North American myth and ritual is a spiritual realm connected with the sky, and this realm, like the other (which is sometimes the same), may be the goal of a quest by the living.

The Onondaga and Seneca, two of the five (or six) Iroquois nations, believe they sprang from the ground (Morgan, 6–7), but such origin myths are as rare in the Northeast as they are common in the Southwest. The Huron "have recourse to the Sky in almost all their necessities," Brébeuf wrote in 1636 (Kenton, 1:261), and among Algonquian peoples the Great Spirit and his delegates lived in the sky, and stories were told, Copway wrote in the mid-nineteenth century (152), "of some of these high born personages coming to earth to dwell among the people; also of men going up and becoming inhabitants of the skies." The Montagnais-Naskapi of Labrador believe, Speck writes (1935, 50), that souls are transformed into stars until they become reincarnated in babies.

The living, too, have access to this realm, and one main purpose of certain Algonquian rituals was to raise participants' souls to the heavens. Each day's performance of the twelve-day Delaware Big House "lifts the worship a stage higher in the series of twelve successive sky levels until on the final day it reaches the Great Spirit himself" (Speck 1931, 61). And the Ojibwa Midéwiwin incorporated "eight successive grades of curing—the first four called Earth grades and the second four called Sky grades—the 'power' rising with the grade," that is, with closeness to its source in the heavens (Landes 1968, 52).

Most Iroquoian peoples, Brébeuf wrote of the Huron (Kenton, 1:250), trace their origin to the fall of a woman from the skies. In one version (251–52), Aatensic threw herself after a heavenly tree whose felling her sick husband dreamed could cure him. Turtle then bade other aquatic animals dive down, bring up soil, and put it on her shell, so that Aatensic dropped gently on an Island; her daughter thereafter brought forth two boys, one of whom killed the other. In later Iroquois legends the twins, "Good Mind" and "Evil Mind" in Parker's version, contend for influence in the human world, but the story is basically the same.[3] Its major elements—the fall of a human progenitor from the skies, the creation of land from the waters by an "earth diver," and the exploits of heavenly twins—are widely paralleled in myths from different regions of North America.

Along the "path of souls," or Milky Way, the soul returns after death to its home, the transcendent sphere from which it has been partly cut off during life. Among the Iroquois, "a beautiful custom prevailed in ancient times, of capturing a bird, and freeing it over the grave on the

---

3. For Iroquois versions see, e.g., Hewitt 1903 and 1928; Parker, "A Seneca Cosmological Myth" (1923), in Tooker 1979, 35–47; and Fenton 1962. On the "earth-diver" myth see Dundes 1962.

evening of the burial, to bear away the spirit to its heavenly rest"; on the invisible road to the sky, Morgan reports (174–76), "the soul ascended in its heavenly flight until it reached its celestial habitation."

Like its terrestrial counterpart this heavenly home could in exceptional cases be visited by the living (at least by mythical heroes) as well as the dead. A Seneca myth told to Parker (132–35) by Edward Cornplanter, a descendant of Handsome Lake's brother, gives clearer expression to the soul's quest for its celestial home than we have found in other Native American stories outside the Southwest. In old times, the youngest of three brothers suggested that they travel to the edge of the earth, where sky touches sea. Watching the sun slip under the rim of the sky, the two younger brothers ran under in time but the oldest was crushed, "and his spirit shot past the other two" (like Homer's Elpenor), meeting them on the far side where "everything is different." The father of the Sky people purified them by skinning them and washing their organs, and his son Haweníio sent them back to their country by the path of the sun. "The brothers did not care for the earth now, but wished themselves back in the upper world"; they were later struck by lightning, and killed.

In this myth of a realm beneath the western rim of the sky, the two seemingly distinct afterworlds of North American Indian myth are found to be one; at the liminal horizon earth and sky meet. This is the celestial (or subterranean) realm to which shamans, pre-eminently of the living, have been thought to have access from time immemorial, and even religious leaders who repudiated traditional shamans claimed a heavenly source for their revelations. Thus the Delaware Prophet of 1762–63 dreamed of receiving a divine message from the heavenly "Master of Life" (A. Wallace 1970, 117). Handsome Lake in 1799 envisioned a sky journey to the afterworld where he was told the moral plan of the cosmos on which his reformed religion was based (243). And the Shawnee Prophet, transformed into Tenskwatawa, "the Open Door" for his people's salvation, was borne to a spirit world and saw past and future in a paradise of abundant game and fertile fields where spirits of virtuous Shawnees could flourish (Edmunds, 33). However much Christian doctrine may have influenced these visions, their core appears to be the indigenous quest for spiritual transcendence variously expressed in medicinal rites, initiation ceremonies, and origin myths of Algonquian and Iroquoian peoples throughout the northeastern woodlands.

Various classes of traditional shaman coexisted among northeastern peoples, some obtaining power through visions, others by purchase. Among the Minnesota Ojibwa, Hoffman (1891, 156–58) distinguished not only the Midé priest but the *wabeno,* a visionary healer and fire-handler often associated with evil spirits, and the ecstatic *jessakkid* "seer and prophet" commonly called a *jongleur;* similar distinctions have been made for various Algonquian groups.[4] All except the Midé priests practice alone and appear to embody traditions of individual shamanism older than the Midéwiwin, which by communally sanctioning personal vision guided the questing impulse into more predictable channels.

Early French accounts make it clear that individual ecstatic practices as well as collective ceremonies were a widespread means of curing disease and probing the future. When a Huron is sick, Father Sagard reports (200–01), the medicine man manipulates hot stones and chews hot coals ("the deed of an unchained devil") and rubs, blows, or spits on the patient; both medicine man and sick person "make grimaces and utter incantations and throw themselves into contortions" until "the sick man appears quite mad, with eyes flashing and frightful to see, . . . throwing about everything that comes in his way, with a din and damage and outrageous behaviour that have no equal."

A few years later, in the Jesuit Relations of 1633 and 1634 (Kenton, 1:114–15), Father Le Jeune described how a Montagnais sorcerer treated both a sick child and himself. In ministering to the child he "howled immoderately" while whirling his tambourine, then blew on the patient's body, "as I conjectured, for I could not see what he was doing" in the surrounding darkness. And in treating himself he "acted like a madman," with truly Siberian frenzies, "singing, crying, and howling, making his drum rattle with all his might; while the others howled as loudly as he." After hissing like a snake, hurling the drum to the ground, and running round the fire, "he went out of the cabin, continuing to howl and bellow" in a display, the Jesuit missionary asserted, of "foolishness, nonsense, absurdity, noise and din."

Both the Franciscan Sagard and the Jesuit Le Jeune are among those who noted the use of sweat baths to induce ecstasy by Iroquoian and Algonquian tribes. Le Jeune's description of 1634 (Kenton, 1:115; cf. Sagard, 197–98, and Raudot in Kinietz, 365) is especially reminiscent of Herodotus's account of Scythian vapor baths two thousand years before. "They plant some sticks in the ground, making a sort of low tent," and after heating it with red-hot stones, "slip entirely naked into these sweat boxes," where they sing, cry, groan, and make speeches while the "sorcerer" beats his drum and prophesies; nor could the skeptical remonstrances of the "black robes" diminish belief in their "oracle."

4. See Landes 1938, 133, and Jenness, 60. Hoffman (1896, 138–61) distinguishes three classes of Menomini shaman: "jugglers," *wábeno,* and "dreamers." Generally in the Northeast, Ritzenthaler and Ritzenthaler write (101), "there were two types of shamans, whose concerns were primarily those of healing, and a third, whose art seemed to lean toward the darker side"; the first two (who sometimes coincided) were the conjurer or "juggler" and the sucking doctor, and the third was the *wábeno.*

Such descriptions confirm that curing and prophecy in northeastern North America required supernormal powers attained through ecstatic trance. Whether this condition implies departure of the shaman to distant realms in quest of power, or of errant souls, is less clear from our sources, in which frenzies of "sorcerers" tend to be considered diabolic possession. But the frequency of quests to the underworld or the skies in "Orpheus" tales and other myths suggests that the shaman's spirit was indeed thought to journey to transcendent worlds in search of a dead or dying person's soul, and similar beliefs persisted among some Algonquian peoples into the twentieth century. "If an Indian dies and a good medicine man starts after him quickly enough he may be brought back," Hallowell's Ojibwa informant claimed (1955, 174–75); thus one shaman restored a dead girl to life by following her to the Land of the Dead and catching her soul "just in time."

The soul's journey to distant places is most evident in the "shaking tent" seance of Algonquian "jugglers" attested since the earliest European observers. "In all their encampments," Champlain (159) wrote of his Algonquian and Huron allies, describing his journey of 1609 from the Saint Lawrence to the lake that now bears his name, one of their "soothsayers" builds a cabin and

> places himself inside, so as not to be seen at all, when he seizes and shakes one of the posts of his cabin, muttering some words between his teeth, by which he says he invokes the devil, who appears to him in the form of a stone. . . . They frequently told me that the shaking of the cabin, which I saw, proceeded from the devil, who made it move, and not the man inside, although I could see the contrary. . . . These rogues counterfeit also their voice . . . and speak in a language unknown to the other savages.

To the pious Champlain, such "impostors," as he called medicine men in general (96), were defrauding benighted peoples who "do not recognize any divinity, or worship any God and believe in anything whatever, but live like brute beasts" (321).[5]

Le Jeune in 1634 (Kenton, 1 : 106–07) tells how a Montagnais juggler howled like a French puppeteer and "fell into so violent an ecstasy, that I thought he would break everything to pieces," speaking several languages while others urged the spirits to enter. Some imagined he "had been carried away, without knowing where or how. Others said that his body was lying on the ground, and that his soul was up above the tent." Finally, "the Savages believing that the Genii or *Kichikouai* had entered, the sorcerer consulted them," and to his questions the spirits, "or rather

---

5. Parkman, who also described the "magic lodge" rite (1983, 1 : 254 and 398), believed two and a half centuries after Champlain that the Indian conjurer's remedies "were to the last degree preposterous, ridiculous, or revolting" (1 : 362).

the juggler who counterfeited them," gave answer. "I could have said as much myself," the skeptical (and possibly envious) Jesuit remarks of his savage rival's oracular pronouncements.

The Algonquian "shaking tent" or "spirit lodge" has remained essentially the same in the centuries since Le Jeune. (In one common variation, the shaman is tightly bound at the beginning of his performance and frees himself, like his Eskimo counterpart, by the end.)[6] Among the Saulteaux of the Berens River, Manitoba, a shaman seeks supernatural revelation during the puberty fast (Hallowell 1971, 19), and soul abduction is the "characteristic *modus operandi*" of the conjurer (59), who occasionally engages a rival's guardian spirits in "a dramatic struggle to the death" while the audience watches the tent shaken by spirits thumping within it, sometimes with fatal results to one of the antagonists (62–63). His other main functions are prophecy and location of lost articles through his spirit companion, the turtle (66–68). The Algonquian conjurer is no mere charlatan, Hallowell stresses (73–83), but an explorer of the liminal zone between the given condition of human beings and the world of undetermined potentialities—the world of the spirit—to which they likewise belong.

Among the relatively settled Iroquoian peoples we find only traces of individual vision quests, by shamans or others. "Time was when it was necessary to fast thirty entire days, in a Cabin apart," Brébeuf wrote of the Huron in 1636 (Kenton, 1:274); but those times were vanishing when the French arrived, and a modern scholar can only infer that Huron shamans probably obtained power through visions (Tooker 1964, 97; cf. Trigger 1969, 65). Among Iroquois of the Five Nations, the vision quest seems once to have been more prominent. At puberty some boys withdrew to the woods under supervision of an elder, fasted, abstained from sexual activity, and mortified the flesh (A. Wallace 1970, 37–38); dreams at such times "were apt to be regarded as visitations from supernatural spirits who might grant *orenda,* or magical power, to the dreamer, and who would maintain a special sort of guardianship over him" through a charm or talisman associated with the dream.

Among Algonquian peoples the individual quest seems to have been nearly universal, at least for boys; we find it among the Delaware, for example (M. Harrington 1913, 214–15; cf. 1921, 61–80), and above all among the Ojibwa, who retained many of their indigenous practices after eastern Algonquian tribes had been exterminated or displaced. An

6. Densmore 1932a, 45–46; 1932b, 104–05. Hultkrantz (1981, 79) considers such seances "forms of a jugglering complex" ranging from northern Asia and the Americas to Southeast Asia.

Ojibwa father, the Jesuit Dablon reported around 1670 (Kinietz, 326–27), made his son fast until he saw a vision of "Sun, or Thunder, or something else"; more recent descriptions have richly elaborated on this early account.

Girls too, Jenness writes of the Ojibwa of Parry Island, Ontario (1935, 50), fasted under their mothers' supervision. But a girl's quest coincided with first menstruation, thought (as in many tribal societies) to bring pollution; therefore, unlike a boy's "hopeful striving for broader horizons," her puberty ceremony "is a conscientious withdrawal of her malignant self" (Landes 1938, 5). The quest was more central for boys than girls, Barnouw suggests (20), because "a man's activities—hunting and warfare, etc.—involved unpredictable elements in which magical support was essential for success." Women might be more open to spontaneous visions, but mastery of spirits through the disciplined quest was an overwhelmingly male prerogative.

An Ojibwa boy driven out to fast in a lonely spot (Landes 1968, 8–11) might lie naked on the ground or make himself a huge "nest" in a tree as he fasted for as many as ten days. "When he swooned, the Ojibwa said he was being carried to the sphere of the manitos," or spirits. A successful visionary kept his dream secret and continued fasting in later years; over time he would come to resemble his guardian spirit—moose, bear, or other—and at night "would leave his human shape on his bed to stalk the country" in its shape. A shaman might eventually identify himself with the manito, even at the price of madness or death.

As the "nest" suggests, a connection with the sky is characteristic of Ojibwa visions. Thus the Christian convert George Copway, a friend of Longfellow and Parkman, tells how his visionary spirit made a lofty pine, "reaching towards the heavens," heave as he sang, and told the youth, "I am from the rising sun" (Zolla, 238–39). A decade or two later, one of Kohl's Ojibwa informants recalled (204–07) climbing a tall tree after his mother's death and being escorted through the air above high mountain tops and out into the sunshine, where the Sun revealed earth, sky, and his own image, and gave him protecting spirits.

An old Ojibwa told Kohl (232–42) how his grandfather took him as a boy into the forest and made him a bed high up in a pine. His first attempt to fast failed, and the next spring, determined not to return "till my right dream had come to me," he again bedded himself in a pine and after days of deprivation fell into a dream in which he followed a spirit through the air to a mountaintop. There four men disclosed the earth and the "glorious sight" of the sky, and bade him choose his destination: "I will go up," he replied. Four white-haired men revealed the gifts of God; from then on he was "a perfect man." Similarly (375–76), a great chief, "the Little Pine," followed a visionary path "higher and higher into heaven," and was told he would be a mighty hero: "And the dream was really fulfilled."

Few early European accounts of vision quests survive, no doubt largely because of their individual nature (since observers largely thought of religion in terms of communal rites) and because visions were normally kept secret until old age or death (Jenness, 50). But on the basis of later evidence, quests appear to have been nearly universal; a shaman was not set apart by his unique call, as in Siberia, but by inten- sification of a visionary experience common in some degree to every member of the community, especially among the mobile and "highly in- dividualistic society" (Landes 1938, 119) of the Ojibwa and other Algon- quian hunting peoples. The first (and principal) quest normally took place in early adolescence, and others could be occasioned by any per- sonal crisis; they were individual rites of passage substituting for the collective ceremonies of more settled peoples.

Individuality and unpredictability were characteristic also of visions themselves, which despite recurrence of common motifs were by no means as standardized as the drug-induced hallucinations of tropical South America. The outcome of the quest could not be known in ad- vance, and the possibility of failure ratified its inherent uncertainty. Years of preparation were required, and though "complete failures were very rare" (Densmore 1932a, 71), repeated and increasingly rigorous fasts might be necessary before a vision came; it was far from automa- tic. Ojibwa men who never attained visions were disdained by fellow tribesmen, and on the modern reservation, where suicide is endemic to some Ojibwa communities, this once-exceptional failure may seem to characterize a whole society from which the vision quest "molding a child's sense of identity" has vanished, leaving nothing in its place (Shkilnyk, 86–88). For the guardian spirit quest is "no passive relation- ship," Landes observes (1968, 9), but requires lifelong self-discipline, and in the solitary individual's uncertain endeavor to surpass his given condition lies a heroism all the more extraordinary, Kohl remarks (228), in that "every Indian, without exception," displays it. Small wonder that in the absence of that potentially transformative hope for a future dif- fering from the present, life might cease to have meaning.

VISIONARIES OF THE GREAT PLAINS

The vision quest is most fully documented not among northeastern Al- gonquians, who were soon uprooted by invading whites, but among the migratory buffalo hunters who briefly but memorably dominated the Great Plains. These tipi-dwelling horsemen—Sioux, Crow, Cheyenne, and others—were quintessential exemplars of the visionary shamanism once practiced by hunters and nomads in much of the world.

Yet the mobility of Plains life was not an immemorial inheritance. The tribes that entered this region in the centuries after the horse was introduced from Europe appear to have been displaced agriculturalists driven westward by the Ojibwa and others under pressure from the whites. Siouan and Algonquian peoples who had previously cultivated the land now embraced a nomadic life made possible by the horse and the seemingly inexhaustible buffalo; some, such as the Mandan and Pawnee, combined agriculture with seasonal hunting. Prominence of the Plains vision quest thus reflects not simply persistence but renewal, under conditions of heightened instability, of an openness to the unknown never wholly subordinated to the invariance of ritual.

"The American Indian was an individualist in religion as in war," the mixed-blood Wahpeton Sioux Charles Eastman, or Ohiyesa, declared (Eastman, 27). On the Plains, above all, this quality deeply impressed outsiders; thus every Comanche "could be his own priest and his own prophet—the individual interpreter of the wills and ways of the spirits" (Wallace and Hoebel, 155). Such "individualism" did not, of course, imply lack of communal affiliation: a profusion of organizations with elaborate ceremonies embraced almost everyone in a network of tribal traditions (Wissler 1916; Mails 1973). Yet few cultures have more emphasized individual achievement, and to none has the vision quest been more central.

A visionary dimension is evident in many communal rites. The Hako of the Caddoan Pawnee differs from fixed calendrical ceremonies in its collective quest for Mother Corn; other tribes, such as the Omaha (Fletcher and La Flesche, 1:74) and Teton Sioux (Densmore 1918, 68–77; J. E. Brown, 101–3), may have derived a similar rite from the Caddoan Arikara. Among the Teton Sioux, this ritual, with its "song of search" for children, was associated not with Mother Corn but with the White Buffalo Woman who gave the sacred pipe (Dorsey 1906; Walker 1980, 109–12, 148–50; Brown, 3–9). Purification by sweat bath— Teton Sioux *inipi,* considered their "oldest and most revered ceremony" (Walker 1980, 104; cf. Black Elk in Brown, 31–43, and Lame Deer and Erdoes, 174–82)—was nowhere more important than on the Plains; this ritual of kinship among those in the tiny sweat lodge and their "relatives" beyond was often a prelude to the vision quest.

Among explicitly shamanistic public ceremonies on the Plains were "shaking tent" rites like those of the northeastern Algonquians, in which a "conjurer" learned of hidden matters from spirits who freed him from his thongs. In the Teton Sioux *yuwipi* ("wrapped") ritual, a holy man versed in bird and animal languages both cures and locates lost objects

(Powers 1982, 21). In a curing session (Densmore 1918, 246), a medicine man bound inside a dark tent sang amid flying objects and animal noises until he was found "wedged between the poles near the top of the tipi, with all the restraining cords cast from him"; ascent of the pole, like ventriloquism, flying objects, and animal language, is reminiscent of Eurasian shamanism. Usually the *yuwipi* shaman's soul does not set forth in search of visions; thus spirits came to Fools Crow and showed him where to find the medicine of which they told him (Mails 1979, 94). But formerly a *yuwipi* shaman like Black Thunder learned the ceremony after long fasting in the hills (Hurt and Howard, 293), and *yuwipi* spirits themselves were thought to set forth with pounding noises from the darkened room of the seance and fly to caves, clouds, woods, or water to bring power to the shaman freed from his bonds (Feraca, 34).

But by far the most elaborate Plains ceremony is the festival commonly known (from its Dakota name) as the Sun Dance and widely considered, as by Fools Crow (Mails 1979, 44), "the highest expression of our religion." Like the Ojibwa Midéwiwin or the Winnebago Medicine Rite (Radin 1945, 72), the Sun Dance may have developed as a reaffirmation of tribal solidarity in response to massive cultural disruptions since the seventeenth century. Black Elk of the Oglala Sioux ascribes its origin to a revelation from the Great Spirit, *Wakan-Tanka,* "many, many winters after our people received the sacred pipe from the White Buffalo Cow Woman" (Brown, 67). Some form of the ceremony was all but universal on the Plains; its principal features were already apparent when Catlin (1973, 1:155; cf. 1967), in the 1830s, portrayed the "appalling scenes" he witnessed among the Mandan of the Upper Missouri shortly before their decimation by smallpox.

Since Catlin, many have described the Sun Dance, especially in its Sioux versions.[7] In setting up the twenty-eight poles of the lodge around a central tree on the third day, Black Elk explained to Brown (80), "we are really making the universe in a likeness," the circle representing creation and the tree *Wakan-Tanka,* the center of everything. The number of poles is the number of days in the lunar month, of a buffalo's ribs, and of feathers in the war bonnet: "You see, there is a significance in everything." On the fourth day, participants begin their arduous dance with hands and eyes stretched toward the sun; the dancer's intense mental concentration, Curtis writes (3:95−96), "produces that state of spiritual exaltation in which visions are seen and the future is revealed." Bleeding profusely from wooden skewers fastened from his chest by

7. See, e.g., on the Sioux, Curtis, 3:87−99; Walker 1921; Alexander, 136−69; Brown, 67−100; and Mails, 118−38. (For studies of the Sun Dance of other peoples, see Wissler 1921.)

thongs to the Sun Pole, the chief dancer lunges to free himself while others dance and sing; finally he tears loose and collapses before rising again to resume the dance. A feast, sweat bath, and prayer conclude the ceremony.

Catlin (1967, 39; cf. Wied-Neuwied 1906, 23:324–34) surmised that the Mandan Sun Dance, the "O-kee-pa," was an annual ceremony to which the people owed their existence through increase of the buffalo on which life depended; in a *folium reservatum* for scholars (83–85) he described a buffalo dancer pretending to impregnate others with a colossal red wooden penis. To the extent that these rites aimed to replenish the animal food supply, they resembled Green Corn ceremonies of southern agriculturalists and bloodier rituals of the Pawnee, who as recently as 1838 sacrificed a maiden to the Morning Star to promote the fertility of the corn.[8] In contrast to this priestly ritualism, however, individual visions remained indispensable to most Plains Sun Dances, which were set in motion not by the inflexible calendar but by the pledge of the chief dancer. His ordeals were prompted, Alexander observes (162), by "a quest of understanding" culminating in a vision of an animal power that would henceforth be his personal helper. In former times, Fools Crow remarks (Mails 1979, 120), "every pledger was required to go on a vision quest before he did the Sun Dance," and so strong did the connection between individual vision and communal ritual remain, even after that practice lapsed, that Lame Deer (199) describes the ceremony as the *hanblechia,* or vision quest, "of the whole Sioux nation."

The close relation between vision and ritual is conspicuous in two more recent movements, the messianic Ghost Dance of 1890 (Mooney 1965) and the visionary "peyote cult" that became the Native American Church (La Barre 1975). Both originated to the south and west (the Ghost Dance among the Paiute of Nevada, the peyote cult ultimately in Mexico), both incorporated Christian elements, and neither was by any means limited to the Plains. But each attained particular intensity in this region, where during the crisis of the old tribal culture both the frenzies of the Ghost Dance (before its bloody suppression at Wounded Knee) and the hallucinations of peyote gatherings found a place denied or severely restricted by ritualistic ceremonialisms of the Southwest. On the Plains the Ghost Dance reached its culmination, and on the Plains peyote "facilitated obtaining visions already sought" (Shonle, 59) by allowing the Indian to "get into immediate touch with the supernatural without

8. See Weltfish, 106–18. The Caddoan Pawnee, unlike the Siouan Mandan (who also combined agriculture with buffalo hunting), had no fully developed Sun Dance, and their ceremonies—even the Hako—retained much of the priestly ritualism, culminating in human sacrifice, characteristic of agricultural religions.

the long period of fasting" demanded by the vision quest; for this reason it took strong root.

The individual quest is central to a rare celestial myth of the Blackfoot recounting the origin of the Sun Dance, or Medicine Lodge (Grinnell 1892, 93–103). (Another Blackfoot tale [113–16] on the origin of the medicine pipe relates a rare Plains "Orpheus" myth.) In earliest times, the story of "Scarface" relates, a beautiful girl told her parents the Sun had said she could marry none but him. When a poor scarfaced boy asked her to be his wife, she said he must gain the Sun's permission and ask him to remove his scar as a sign. He traveled many days, asking animals to help find his home, until he finally met a young man, Morning Star, whose mother, Moon, protected Scarface when his father Sun returned. After Scarface saved Morning Star from great birds that had killed his brothers, Sun permitted him to marry, told him how to build a medicine lodge, and removed his scar; he gave the couple long life without sickness, and at last their shadows departed together for the Sand Hills, where the dead reside.[9]

Just as Scarface returned to earth enlightened by the Sun, some tribes attributed a heavenly origin to shamans; a Canadian Dakota medicine man was said, for example, to have dwelt with Thunders before being born on earth (Wallis, 81). But most of their power, like that of fellow tribesmen, derived not from birth but from guardian spirits repeatedly sought. Shamans might fast for a vision at least once a year, and this persistent devotion to a quest shared by all was what set them apart.

If priestly inflexibility was largely foreign to the Plains, especially among wandering hunters such as the Sioux, visionary experience was lavishly developed. Many Sioux were empowered by visions, including *heyokas* or "contraries" and "berdaches" who dressed and lived as women. But the principal shaman was the "holy man" (*wicasa wakan*)— less commonly "holy woman" (*winyan wakan*)—who gained transcendent insight through repeated contact, above all by mastery of the vision quest, with the supernatural.

Vision, the Oglala George Sword told Walker (1980, 79),[10] may come at any time to anyone, unsought or by seeking. The vision quest (*hanble-*

9. For two other versions see Wissler and Duvall, 61–66; in one of these, Scarface and Morning Star "looked alike" (63) and were mistaken for each other by the Sun. (In Highwater's retelling the hero is Anpao, Dakota for dawn.) For a Winnebago analogue, see Radin 1954, 75–80; here ascent to the heavens is effortless.

10. This volume consists of documents Walker collected as agency physician of the Oglala branch of the Teton division of the Sioux between 1896 and 1914; other documents are included in Walker 1982 and 1983. *Dakota*, which properly refers to the Sioux *language*, is subdivided into three dialects, Dakota, Nakota, and Lakota, the last of which is that of the Teton Sioux (though Walker used "Lakota," as others have more commonly used "Dakota," to refer to the Sioux in general). See Powers 1977, 3–14.

ceya or *hanbleyapi,* "crying" or "lamenting" for a vision) is a means for seeking what does not come unsought, or following up the "call" of a dream. Like the *inipi* sweat lodge, with which it is closely linked, the Sioux vision quest antedated the gift of the sacred pipe, according to Black Elk (Brown, 44; cf. Walker 1980, 104), and is therefore thought to be far older than the Sun Dance and other ceremonies influenced by it; it is an ancient shamanistic heritage—possibly revived by renewal of migratory life on the Plains since the seventeenth century—that remains, for traditional Sioux, central to their religion.[11]

Native Americans of the Woodlands and Plains "democratized shamanism," Lowie conjectured (1940, 312), by making the vision quest— elsewhere often the prerogative of religious specialists or secret societies—open to all. Whatever the historical sequence may have been, among many Plains peoples such as the Crow "there was no limitation either as to age or sex," and even little boys sometimes quested in imitation of their elders (Lowie 1922, 332).

Where communal puberty rituals were generally lacking, as in much of North America, the vision quest might be a boy's rite of passage to manhood; thus among the Winnebago, on the eastern fringes of Plains culture, it "constituted the only puberty rite" for boys (Radin 1970b, 87). But this was not its sole nor always main function; both east and west of the Plains the vision quest, Benedict wrote (1922, 2; cf. Kroeber 1983, 418, on the Arapaho), is "a ritual at entrance to maturity," but on the Plains "it is *mature men* who characteristically seek the vision," not once alone on the threshold of adulthood but repeatedly throughout it, especially in times of crisis. "Every Crow, battered by fortune, writhing under humiliation, or consumed with ambition," Lowie writes (1935, 237), sought a vision which was by nature a continually varying response to the unpredictable hazards of life.

The outcome of the quest depended in part on the character of the seeker, purified in body and mind by the sweat bath that preceded it. The quester sought a vision alone—often on a solitary hilltop—but not unassisted; a shaman or relative instructed him before the quest and interpreted its meaning afterward, and no quest, of course, could succeed without help from the spirits. These might be supreme powers (*Wakan Tanka* or the Grandfathers for the Sioux),[12] but were usually per-

---

11. "The oldest and most revered ceremony," Walker's informants told him (1980, 104), "is the *Inipi* (sweat bath). The next oldest is *Hanblepi* (seeking a vision)."

12. On *wakan* (roughly, "sacred") and *Wakan Tanka* ("the Great Spirit"), see Walker 1921, 151–52, and 1980, 68–75, 98–99; Powers 1977, 45–47; and DeMallie, 80–82. Cf. Fletcher and La Flesche, 2:597–99, on Omaha *wakonda*. On the Grandfathers (*Tunkashila*), see Powers 1977, 200–201. Although both *Wakan Tanka*, often identified with the Christian God (Mails, 120), and *Tunkashila* are singular in recent Sioux accounts, it seems

sonal guardian spirits—animals or other natural forces—in their own or in human form. As early as 1847 Parkman noted (1949, 247–48) that the Indian's guardian spirit "is usually embodied in the form of some living thing: a bear, a wolf, an eagle, or a serpent." Most important of all, for Black Elk (Brown, 58–59), are the birds or "wingeds" nearest to the heavens: for like them, "we humans may also leave this world, not with wings, but in the spirit." The vision quest, he declares (Brown, 46), "helps us to realize our oneness with all things, to know that all things are our relatives"; through it, Fools Crow too believes (Mails 1979, 183), we regain the primordial human ability to communicate with birds and animals.

Power gained by the quest was not given once for all, as in quasi-automatic rites of passage; on the contrary, a Plains visionary's quest always placed him at risk. "I mistrust visions come by in the easy way—by swallowing something. The real insight, the great ecstasy," Lame Deer protests (217; cf. 64–65), comes from "the hard, ancient way" of the vision quest, with its demanding rigors and intrinsic uncertainty. Success was by no means guaranteed, and a "persistent record of failure" (Benedict 1923, 25) typifies many Plains accounts. "Sometimes men quest and don't see or experience a thing. In fact," Fools Crow says (Mails 1979, 86), "not many people do manage it successfully."

Some acknowledged lifelong failure; others pretended visions not seen; still others succeeded after several tries. Nor were success and failure, sincerity and pretense, always clearly distinct, especially once tribal traditions began to crumble. A displaced Winnebago whose autobiography Radin recorded confessed (1926, 26) he had seen "nothing unusual" during a four-day quest in which he claimed a vision; but after learning his boasts had helped a niece in labor, "I was really convinced that I possessed sacred power" and "the authority of a great medicine man" (137). The spirit moves in unpredictable ways, and who can be certain when—or whether—he was deceiving himself, or others?

The basic pattern of the Plains quest, similar (with many variations) to that of the northeastern Algonquians, is apparent in the earliest descriptions. "When they wish to choose their medicine or guardian spirit," Prince Maximilian of Wied-Neuwied remarked (23:318) of the Mandan after his journey of 1832–34,

---

probable (DeMallie, 91) that the Grandfathers were always plural until reinterpreted by Black Elk under Catholic influence, and almost certain that *Wakan Tanka* "was a collective term, embodying various *wakan* beings in many different aspects." For a brief summary of the long controversy over supposed affinity of Dakota *wakan*, Algonquian *manitou*, and Iroquois *orenda* with Oceanic *mana* as a pre-animistic force at the origin of religious experience, see Hultkrantz 1979, 10–14.

they fast for three or four days, and even longer, retire to a solitary spot, do penance, and even sacrifice joints of their fingers; howl and cry to the lord of life, or to the first man, beseeching him to point out their guardian spirit. They continue in this excited state till they dream, and the first animal or other object which appears to them is chosen for their guardian spirit or medicine.[13]

A Blackfoot boy of fourteen or fifteen, Catlin wrote a few years later (1973, 35–37), explaining acquisition of the "medicine-bag" which Catlin considered "hocus pocus, witchcraft, and animal magnetism," wanders off for several days, "lying on the ground in some remote or secluded spot, crying to the Great Spirit, and fasting the whole time." The first animal or bird of which he dreams ("or pretends to have dreamed") becomes his lifetime protector; he later sets forth to procure its skin, which he keeps to bring good fortune in battle, act as his guardian spirit in death, and "conduct him safe to the beautiful hunting grounds, which he contemplates in the world to come."[14]

The basic accuracy of these early accounts has been largely confirmed by later observers. Curtis gives a vivid description of the Teton Sioux vision cry (which he believed had "not been performed within very recent years") in the third volume (65–70) of *The North American Indian*, in 1908. Whoever pledges to pursue the quest solemnly passes a pipe to others, and a holy man raises it to the four winds, sky, and earth. Holy man and quester purify themselves and others in a sweat bath, and the quester cries aloud as the holy man sings. Taken to a distant hill, the quester stands with uplifted face, holding the pipe up to the sun and praying, as he stands until sunset and lies until dawn, to spirits of the four directions to grant him a vision. At some time during his four-day vigil a supernatural being—bird or animal, tree, rock, or ancestral spirit—appears, if his prayers are granted, reveals the future, and points out a potent medicine: "Thus every man who has seen such a vision

13. Rpt. in Wied-Neuwied 1976, 246, a volume of selections from the *Travels* and accompanying watercolors by Karl Bodmer. A still earlier mention of the Mandan vision quest occurs in Lewis and Clark's entry for December 4, 1804 (1902, 1:148), in Biddle's edition of their *History*, first published in 1814: "Each individual selects for himself the particular object of his devotion, which is termed his medicine, and is either some invisible being or more commonly some animal, which thenceforward becomes his protector or his intercessor with the great spirit, to propitiate whom every attention is lavished, and every personal consideration is sacrificed." This passage, lacking in Clark's brief entry in the *Original Journals* edited by Thwaites (1959, 1:233), was presumably added by Biddle on the basis of his supplementary sources.

14. For Grinnell (1892, 275) the Blackfoot world of the dead was a monotonous, unending, "altogether unsatisfying existence." Had Catlin romanticized their eschatology, or had they learned with the vanishing of the buffalo how bleak the future could be?

becomes, to a certain degree, a medicine man." Back in the sweat lodge, the holy man interprets his vision and the two again purify themselves.

With many variations, this underlying pattern—purification, self-denial, and solitary communion with transcendent forces culminating, if successful, in an unpredictable vision followed by return with magnified powers—has remained remarkably constant since the earliest accounts. The vision quest of the Teton Sioux and Crow was open to both sexes, moreover, whereas most girls among the Plains Cree, as among their distant Algonquian cousins, the Blackfoot, Cheyenne, and Arapaho, "never deliberately sought visions but were apt to acquire power during menstrual seclusion" or from unsolicited dreams (Mandelbaum, 159–60).[15] The Plains vision quest, above all in its Teton Sioux version, thus represents the furthest extension of "democratized shamanism" in North America, offering a possibility of deliberate visionary self-transcendence, confined in many cultures to shamans alone, to mature adults as well as adolescents and to women no less than men.

Purification by sweat bath and fasting in solitude, usually for four days and nights but sometimes for as many as ten, were virtually universal to the Plains vision quest, but important variations from the Teton Sioux pattern occurred in the self-mortifications endured. The Teton Sioux quester, like his counterpart among the northeastern Algonquians, "cried" for spirits to take pity and grant a vision; but apart from fasting in isolation, standing for hours facing the sun, and lying unsheltered through cold nights, he normally underwent no extreme afflictions. Attainment of a vision no more depended on bodily mutilation or intense pain than on mental disorientation by drugs, for in his appeal to powers beyond him he strove to bring his own full powers to bear. The southern Comanche went further still in rejecting not only physical torments but every form of self-abasement as he quietly awaited whatever might come (Wallace and Hoebel, 157).

Among some other Plains tribes, however, the quester inflicted self-torture to signal his resolve in seeking a vision. Severing the joint of a finger was a widespread practice; among the Crow, Lowie writes (1935,

15. Female shamans are prominent in many Algonquian tribes of both Northeast and Plains, but vision quests are largely confined to men. Mandelbaum found "many women doctors" among the Plains Cree (162), but their power came mainly from spontaneous visions like that of Fine-day (160–61)—whose initial dream was followed, however, by eight days of fasting as she stood facing the sun: a quest as rigorous as any man's! A medicine woman plays the leading role in the Blackfoot Medicine Lodge (Sun Dance), but her power derives not from a vision quest but from a vow to the sun in a time of family crisis (Grinnell 1892, 263–64; Ewers, 175). Andrews claims (1981; 1984) to relate the teachings of a Plains Cree medicine woman. Women are repeatedly said to have taken part in vision quests of non-Algonquian Plains tribes such as the Teton Sioux and Crow, but firsthand accounts are sparse; Linderman, e.g., contains almost nothing on the subject.

240; cf. Nabokov, 62–65), "cutting off a finger-joint was so popular a form of self-mortification that in 1907 most of the old people I met were disfigured in this way." A Crow quester might also choose to stand on a hill painted with white clay and run around a forked pole to which he was fastened by thongs piercing his chest or back. A Cheyenne quester, too, while "starving" for a vision, might be tied to a pole by thongs from skewers piercing his skin, which he attempted to tear by lunging against his bonds (Grinnell 1923, 1:84; 1920, 79–82). This self-torturing search of a vision was incorporated into the Sun Dance not only of the Crow and Cheyenne but of the Teton Sioux and others; whether it originated in communal ceremony or solitary quest, it bears witness to their close connection and to the supreme importance ascribed to visionary revelations by peoples willing to suffer such anguish to attain them.

In chiefs and holy men of the Plains the visionary experience shared with everyone in his tribe attained its greatest intensity. It is again from the Teton Sioux, especially the Oglala branch, that the most detailed accounts have survived. According to Black Elk (Neihardt, 70), the great Oglala warrior Crazy Horse, who led the Sioux and Cheyenne against Custer at the Little Big Horn, "became a chief because of the power he got in a vision when he was a boy." In traditional Plains belief, extraordinary accomplishment of any kind derived from personal vision (spontaneous or sought) vouchsafed by spirits without whose assistance no man could ever surpass himself.

Several Teton Sioux holy men, including Frank Fools Crow and John Fire Lame Deer, have told their stories to observers, but the classic testimonial remains that given by Nicholas Black Elk to the Nebraska poet John G. Neihardt and published as *Black Elk Speaks*.[16] Born in 1863, Black Elk was thirteen when Crazy Horse defeated Custer and twenty-seven when the last armed revolt of his people ended at Wounded Knee: "A people's dream died there. It was a beautiful dream" (Neihardt, 230). He was sixty-seven when Neihardt, then forty-nine, met him at Pine Ridge in 1930, and he lived another twenty years. In 1931 Neihardt transcribed and retold the story of Black Elk's life, feeling it (xii) "a sacred obligation" to be true to his meaning and manner. (Sixteen years later, in 1947, J. E. Brown [xiv] found Black Elk on a Nebraska farm still hoping "to tell of the sacred things before they all passed away.") Neihardt's book, neglected for years, is itself a "quest for understanding" (DeMallie, 99) by two Americans, Black Elk and Neihardt (or Flaming

16. DeMallie's *The Sixth Grandfather* contains transcripts of the interviews on which Neihardt based both *Black Elk Speaks* and his novel *When the Tree Flowered*. I mainly follow *Black Elk Speaks*, with occasional reference to the transcripts. (See, e.g., DeMallie, 94–99, for comparison of the two accounts of Black Elk's Great Vision.) Neihardt wisely knew that the truth of Black Elk's story did not rely on literal transcription of his words.

Rainbow), who bridged widely sundered worlds and found them essentially one.

As a child Black Elk heard a prophecy made long before the coming of the Wasichus, or white men, that "you shall live in square gray houses, in a barren land, and . . . shall starve" (Neihardt, 8). Bleak confirmation of this prophecy soon intensified, for those who fought despair, their deep-rooted need to transcend the given conditions of a world in which no abiding fulfillment could be found. The spiritual power given to the people by the white buffalo woman through the sacred pipe could be attained by anyone who courageously sought and followed his dream, but in its absence nothing was worth attaining. In old age, "as from a lonely hilltop," Black Elk considered his life "the story of a mighty vision given to a man too weak to use it; of a holy tree that should have flourished in a people's heart with flowers and singing birds, and now is withered; and of a people's dream that died in bloody snow" (1–2).

Black Elk remembered (15–16) hearing voices when he was four. A year later, a kingbird ("This was not a dream, it happened") called him, and he saw two men coming from the clouds like arrows, singing a sacred song to the drumming of thunder; they wheeled toward the sunset, turned to geese, and were gone. These voices later recurred (17–21), "but what they wanted me to do I did not know." Then at age nine a voice said, "It is time," and as he lay sick he saw the same two men descend headfirst from storm clouds and heard them say, "Your Grandfathers are calling you!" In the great vision that became the formative experience of his life, he followed these men to the skies, where a bay horse showed him "a whole skyful of horses dancing round me." The bay then led him (21–26) through a rainbow door into a tipi in which six men were sitting, old as the hills or stars; in fear, Black Elk recognized the Powers of the World: the four directions, Sky, and Earth. Each of the Grandfathers exhorted him, and before changing to a bird or animal gave a gift able to bless or cure: a bowl of water and a bow, a white wing, a pipe, a branching red stick, and a red road. The sixth Grandfather, Spirit of the Earth, slowly turned to a boy, and Black Elk recognized "that he was myself with all the years that would be mine at last." Old again, he started toward the east, not on the red road of salvation but the black road of troubles and war.

Descending to earth (27–35), the boy slew drought and planted a red stick which grew into a cottonwood tree. Then the people, changing to animals and birds, set out on the red road, led by the twelve horsemen and followed by the boy, who became a spotted eagle, riding the bay. As they ascended the third generation, they were traveling the black road and each "seemed to have his own little vision that he followed and his own rules," and everywhere the winds were at war like wild beasts fighting. Atop the third hill, "the nation's hoop was broken" and the holy tree stripped of birds. But a herb sprang up where a bison had been and the tree flowered again; amid gathering storm clouds "a song of power came to me and I sang it there in the midst of that terrible place. . . . It was so beautiful that nothing anywhere could keep from dancing."

A flaming rainbow arose and all around the earth was green (35–39). "I was standing on the highest mountain of them all, and round about beneath me was the whole hoop of the world." From this height "I saw more than I can tell and I understood more than I saw; for I was seeing in a sacred manner the shapes of all things in the spirit, and the shape of all shapes as they must live together like one being." The people's sacred hoop was one of many that made a circle, wide as daylight and starlight, in whose center grew a mighty flowering tree to shelter all children of one mother and father: "And I saw that it was holy." The Six Grandfathers cried "He has triumphed!" as he re-entered their tipi, and the oldest bade him return with power to the place from which he came. He looked below and saw his people well and happy except one—"and that one was myself."

This Great Vision shaped the life of Black Elk, pre-eminent holy man of his people during the terrible decades to follow. Its components are inevitably drawn from tribal archetypes—the Six Grandfathers, four horses, sacred pipe, red and black paths, thunderstorms and eagle, flowering tree, and sacred hoop—endlessly interpretable (as by Black Elk himself) in terms of Sioux traditions, to say nothing of recondite Wasichu theories. But the vision's force comes from fusion of these particulars into something transcending them: a revelation as vivid and universal as the biblical Apocalypse, though without the destructive frenzy of that counterpart from an earlier time of crisis and renewal. Whatever interpretations we give it, Black Elk's Great Vision is the summoning of an individual—weak and isolated like us all—to surpass himself by absorption of superpersonal powers embodied in natural forces and tribal spirits, and thus to fulfill his own aspirations through a vision of his people's potential—though possibly unattainable—unity with themselves and the world.

Black Elk's vision was the beginning of his quest: not a possession to be hoarded but a goal to be realized in his life and his people's. At first, like the Siberian shaman, he found himself alien from others: "Everything around me seemed strange and as though it were far away . . . and it seemed I did not belong to my people" (42). Several times during the years embracing Long Hair Custer's defeat, tribal dispersal, and the death of Crazy Horse, he again had a "queer feeling" presaging return to his vision, but only disorientation seemed to have come from his involuntary spiritual encounters. Finally (136–45), at seventeen, he told his vision to an elderly holy man, who instructed him to perform a dance for his people. Through dramatic enactment of his vision, in which members of his tribe played the twelve horsemen, six grandfathers, and others while Black Elk played himself, he escaped from his imprisoning isolation. "I looked about me, and could see that what we then were doing was like a shadow cast upon the earth from yonder vision in the heavens, so bright it was and clear." Thus Black Elk learned that a man gains power over his vision only after he has performed it on earth for the people to see (173). By making his private experience communal, he transformed an unsolicited incursion of spirits into a deliberate quest for mastery of their transcendent powers.

This performance was followed (152–57) by the young man's first vision quest atop a high hill. From the nation of thunder beings, heads of dogs changed into Wasichus, and Black Elk knew the Grandfathers wanted him to perform the dog vision "with heyokas, . . . doing everything wrong or backwards to make the people laugh."[17] Only after enacting this ceremony and discovering the herb of his visions did Black Elk perform his first cure and become a holy man. His life was now a dedicated quest to realize in this world the visionary oneness he had glimpsed in the other.

As in any quest the outcome was uncertain and failure always possible—all the more so in these fearful years when the buffalo vanished as relentlessly as the Wasichus advanced. At this hopeless time, "I felt like crying, for the sacred hoop was broken and scattered" (182); the people "were traveling the black road, everybody for himself and with little rules of his own, as in my vision" (183). In Europe he traveled with Buffalo Bill's Wild West show "like a man who had never had a vision," and returned to find his people near starvation, "pitiful and in despair" (196) after the Wasichus had robbed half their land.

In these years (1889–90) news of the Paiute Messiah's Ghost Dance, which would bring back both bison and Indians from the dead, reached the Sioux; Black Elk, though skeptical, determined to participate in it: "I believed my vision was coming true at last, and happiness overcame me" (201–02). Looking back, he saw he had mistakenly followed lesser visions, for "it is hard to follow one great vision in this world of darkness and of many changing shadows" (212–13). The butchery at Wounded

17. Cf. DeMallie, 227–32. Throughout his book Neihardt altered transcripts of his interviews; among omissions at this point are the words "Many are called but few are chosen," a biblical echo deleted in accord with consistent suppression of any reference to Black Elk's longstanding Catholic faith. The shorthand transcripts by Neihardt's daughter Enid (omitted from the typescript) noted that "the dog in this vision was a symbol of any enemy and all enemies should be killed without pity like dogs."

Knee seemed (as Neihardt entitled his final chapter) "the end of the dream."

Yet Black Elk lived sixty years more, and his quest had not come to an end. Perhaps no undertaking by this Native American shaman (and Roman Catholic catechist) demanded more courage than the decision to communicate his visions to the Wasichu who visited him in 1930. "It has made me very sad to do this at last, and I have lain awake at night worrying and wondering if I was doing right; for I know I have given away my power when I have given away my vision, and maybe I cannot live very long now. But I think I have done right to save the vision in this way" (174). He could redeem his vision because he now knew that the sacred hoop embraced not only the Oglala, nor only the Indian (as the Ghost Dancers thought), but the white man as well; his visionary quest, he now understood, was theirs no less than his.

In the extraordinary postscript to Neihardt's testimonial, Black Elk (231–34) stands in the flesh on Harney Peak, where the spirits had long ago shown him the sacred hoop of the world; dressed and painted as in his great vision over sixty years before, he holds the sacred pipe as clouds gather round and prays to the Great Spirit, his Grandfather, to "make my people live" (see DeMallie, plate 8). He had persisted in striving to realize for the good of his people—and now of others as well—an exalted vision that seemed (as every transcendent goal must seem) beyond attainment; in beseeching the blessing of life at the center of earth the old man is continuing the quest he began as a boy and has never relinquished. It was "next to impossible," he well knows (DeMallie, 293), "but there was nothing like trying."

PART SIX

The Theory of the Quest

Some Closing Considerations

CHAPTER FIFTEEN

A Ternary Process

Ecstatic or visionary shamanism is not a discrete phenomenon—much less a distinct religion—but the form of tribal religious experience in which the questing impulse common in some measure to all finds fullest expression. It customarily coexists with calendrical rites, sacrifice, divination, or spirit possession, and even when the shaman has been displaced by priestly officiants, he or (frequently) she may reappear on the fringes as the still-indispensable, if more and more suspect, exorcist or medium, sorcerer or witch, clown or soothsayer, storyteller or poet.

But whereas the principal emphasis of priestly ritual is on the invariant and collective, and on the past as immutable archetype for the present—on the passive "pressure" of repetitive habit in which Bergson discerned one source of morality and religion—shamanistic vision gives expression to the individually variant, actively pursued, future-directed "aspiration" of Bergson's second source: the "forward thrust" and "demand for movement" that subject the precarious entities of self and society in an uncertain world to inherently unpredictable transformation.

Divination and spirit possession, like the liminal phase of communal rites of passage, likewise serve to open the closure of ritual toward exploration of the encompassing unknown, the wildness that can never wholly be tamed. But in both (as in more passive forms of visionary or drug-induced shamanism) the practitioner, however skilled in a difficult art, may be seen as a receptive vessel rather than a participant in search of knowledge by which she too will be transformed; she remains a vehicle or at best a "technician" of the sacred rather than one who takes active part in its discovery or invention. Only in predominantly shamanistic forms of religion does the individual deliberately undertake, in moments of ecstatic mastery, to leave the familiar world behind in search of a visionary transcendence she can never know in advance or attain in completion: a power she recognizes as her own only insofar as it forever surpasses her.

The shamanistic vision quest is primarily associated, as we have seen, with relatively mobile tribal cultures of hunters, fishers, and herders rather than with agriculturalists whose settled routines and structured societies more readily suit the repetitive rounds and hierarchical organization of priestly ritual. The shaman's connection with a powerful animal like the bear or jaguar, or a bird of prey like the hawk, as his guardian spirit or helper, totem or nagual, suggests the symbiosis (at least in recent memory) of man and beast in a world where each was both hunter and hunted, and where the animal slain for food was honored with ritual propitiation.

Indeed, the hunt was a continual prototype for the shaman's ecstatic quest in societies where animals vividly embodied transcendence of human limits. "The basic program of the 'quest,' hunting as a way to 'get' food, is, when thwarted by failure," Burkert hypothesizes (91), "transformed into a symbolic 'quest,' exploring the unexplorable, hoping for the unexpectable, overcoming despair by detour" of attention from actual to visionary animals like those depicted in paleolithic caves of France and Spain.[1] Like the food quest itself, the sublimated vision quest was subject to failure; for this reason, unlike less flexible rituals, it fulfilled an imperative need in a world from which uncertainty could never be banished. Both in migratory cultures where it flourished and in sedentary successors where it survived, the shamanistic quest continually affirmed that invariance and stability were always provisional, since the sacred space fenced off by ritual could never be hermetically sealed from the menacing dangers and intoxicating possibilities of the surrounding world.

Priestly ritual and shamanistic quest, far from being exclusive opposites, are complementary aspects of tribal man and woman's unending effort to shape and control the unknown around and beyond them: the first prevailing in sedentary cultures and times of apparent security, the second among migratory peoples and in times of heightened peril. Ritual, despite its characteristic affirmation of invariance, can be not only corroborative of the inherited past but adaptive to a changing present, and the ecstatic quest, while providing an outlet for more personal and variant aspirations, remains itself a ritualized activity unmistakably

---

1. In Burkert's view, both hunting magic and cave paintings are "evidence linking the quest for animals with the Beyond" (88), so that "entering such a cave must have meant a difficult journey to another world where one could meet animals" (90).

akin—as the close connection between vision quest and Sun Dance on the Plains reminds us—to others more rigidly patterned but not essentially dissimilar.

The opposition is not of kind, between closed ritual and open quest, but of degree, between more or less closed or open forms of the quest embodied in rituals ranging from calendrical or ancestral ceremonies to communal rites of passage and from seemingly mechanical divination to spirit mediumship and the individual search for transcendence through dreams, visions, or ecstatic flight of the soul. The quest derives, we have seen from the outset, not from the second pole alone (for neither exists in isolation) but from the perpetual interaction between them by which purposeful transcendence is both engendered and channeled into apprehensible and communicable forms, so that the individual quest latent in communal ritual is always potentially transformative of it.

This dialectic, whose varied expressions we have extensively observed, is nowhere more striking than in the shifting interrelations of communal ritual and personal vision in indigenous American cultures from the Arctic to Peru and from the Amazonian jungles to the Great Plains. For the quest to transcend the given finds expression not only at polar extremes where the shaman was most nearly unrivaled, as among the migratory Eskimo or the marginal tribes of Tierra del Fuego, nor only among mobile Algonquian or Siouan hunting bands, but among the salmon-fishing Nootka and the recently agricultural Mapuche, with their elaborate religious societies and calendrical ceremonies, and even, in more vestigial form, among the highly ritualized Pueblos of the Southwest and long-settled peoples of central Mexico and highland Peru. The quest is not simply an established institution (for like everything living, it is constantly subject to change) but repeatedly rises anew from the variegated interplay of collective and individual, inertial and dynamic dimensions of religious experience. The intimate connection of ritual and vision in the kaleidoscopic panorama of Native American religious experience thus richly demonstrates the range and complexity of this continually vital interaction.

The variety of forms the quest has taken in the tribal cultures we have examined as a result of this interaction is one of its principal characteristics; nothing could be more futile, or more contrary to the open-ended nature of the quest itself, than to try to reduce this vital diversity to a constrictively single pattern. But in accord with the underlying continuity between formal ritual and personal vision as two poles of one process, the shamanistic quest corresponds closely in structure to the most inherently open form of communal ceremony, the rite of passage from one biosocial condition to another, for which the vision quest can be a functional equivalent, substituting, for example, for collective male puberty rites among many peoples of native North America. The three phases of separation, transition, and incorporation characterize not only rites of passage, as van Gennep discerned, but the shaman's vision quest (and the spirit medium's possession trance) also.

This tripartite structure is evident in Black Elk's search for spiritual power during the crisis of his people. The visionary call comes to a boy already inclined to solitary dreaminess and separates him further from those who cannot understand what he has seen, making him (like the Siberian shaman) a stranger among his own people, "homesick for the place where I had been" (Neihardt, 42). Out of this separation comes a transitional period of terrible uncertainty when the disoriented young man, struggling with the incomprehensible destiny of being betwixt and between, is unable to turn his vision to advantage either for himself or others until he shares it and makes it fully part of himself by incorporating it, through public performance, with his people's traditions. This initially involuntary process of separation, transition, and incorporation is one that he then deliberately repeats by undertaking a formal vision quest in which isolation from his tribe after ritual purification again inaugurates a liminal passage from helpless "crying" for a vision to attainment of transcendent power from thunder beings; and a public performance again incorporates his personally acquired spiritual knowledge with that of his tribe, which it thereby enlarges. Only now, after purposefully opening himself to transformation by the transcendent unknown and returning with knowledge of it to a world to which he will never again wholly belong, can he become a holy man and bestow his curative blessing on his tribe.

Just as rites of passage may be considered a communal form of the quest, the shamanistic vision quest may be understood as an individual rite of passage beginning with separation from a state of incompletion and proceeding through a liminal region of undetermined possibilities (the realm of the quest itself) to a new condition reintegrating the self-transcendent seeker with a world which she can now help, by virtue of her own transformation, to renew. But the vision quest differs crucially from rites of passage analyzed by van Gennep and Turner. Despite the uncertainties of the liminal phase, the final outcome of these rites is determinate and thus known (though not experienced) in advance; through puberty rites, for example, the boy passes all but inevitably from childhood to the established obligations and privileges of manhood. But the result of the vision quest is never fully predictable; the nature of the vision and of the power it bestows, though of course defined in large part by tribal traditions, cannot be precisely foreknown and may vary greatly from individual to individual and occasion to occasion. This intrinsic variability of outcome is a prime characteristic of the quest and the reason why it can never be wholly reduced to a single inflexible pattern.

Whereas rites of passage, moreover, like most collective rituals, are generally thought to be infallible when correctly performed, the possibility of failure is essential to the quest, whose success depends not only on transcendent powers but on the quester's own immensely fallible endeavors. And unlike rites of passage, each of which is normally single and final for the individual or group performing it (one is born, passes through puberty, and dies once only), the quest cannot be final but may be repeated, in new ways and with unanticipated results, again and again. For a pre-eminent holy man like Black Elk it is an activity that cannot be abandoned, for how could this great venture of extending the bounds of the given through openness to the undetermined come to an end while life continues?

The vision quest thus epitomizes the self-transcendence of *animal quaerens* not only in the unquiet "Faustian" West—it would be fatuous arrogance to think that the quest to surpass our given condition sets one society apart from the rest of our species—but throughout the world from the beginnings of recorded time. We are biologically programmed (like all living things), but ours above all others is an open program; our genetic and especially cultural systems are open systems, our linguistic and social structures are self-transformative structures, processes without predetermined end. In the perpetual dialectic between closure and openness, stasis and change, inertial pressure of the past and the forward thrust of aspiration for an indeterminate future—that is, the dialectic of life—the spiritual quest for transcendence of the here and now through assimilation of the beyond is the indispensable counterpart to ritual affirmation of an immutably sacred past.

This dialectic is one which some modern physicists find characteristic not only of life but even of the "inorganic" matter of which life is composed: for the two are not, after all, discontinuous. The determinism of classical physics (and mathematics)—a determinism which, in extreme Laplacean form, would reduce any quest for the unknown to ignorance or delusion—has been badly shaken since the nineteenth century by the development of probability theory, non-Euclidean geometries, Heisenberg's uncertainty principle and Gödel's incompleteness theorem, relativity theory, and above all quantum mechanics. Among recent scientists none has argued more forcibly for a creatively indeterminate universe, and for essential continuity of the organic and inorganic realms, than Ilya Prigogine, winner of the Nobel Prize in chemistry for his work in nonequilibrium thermodynamics and his theory of dissipative structures, in his provocative book, co-authored with Isabelle Stengers, *Order Out of Chaos.*

"We find ourselves in a world," Prigogine and Stengers declare (8), "in which reversibility and determinism," cardinal postulates of Newtonian physics, "apply only to limiting, simple cases, while irreversibility and randomness are the rules," and in such a world the total predictability assumed by Laplace and others to be theoretically attainable in the Newtonian tradition has no place. In particular, "When we move away from equilibrium to far-from-equilibrium conditions, we move away from the repetitive and the universal to the specific and the unique" (13). If matter near equilibrium behaves in a predictably regular way, farther from equilibrium various types of dissipative structures may occur whose behavior is intrinsically unpredictable.

In these far-from-equilibrium conditions studied by thermodynamics, "new self-organizational processes arise" (84) that anticipate, in the "inorganic" realm, the processes of life; here, where instability is possible, fluctuations may lead to new behavior radically different from any observed in conditions at or near equilibrium. In such cases, not only the ideal determinism of Newtonian dynamics but any statistical predictions based on thermodynamic probability are no longer valid. The interaction of a system with the outside world (for such a system, in conditions of nonequilibrium, is inherently open and can no longer be treated as self-sufficient) may become "the starting point for the formation of new dynamic states of matter—dissipative structures. . . . There is no longer any universally valid law from which the overall behavior of the system can be deduced. Each system is a separate case" (143–45). The outcome of such physical or chemical processes cannot be known, even theoretically, in advance; it is Laplace's dream of a wholly predictable universe that turns out to have been the delusion.

The instability of far-from-equilibrium conditions is the source of a directional self-organization of matter essentially involved with time. Our world, in contrast to that of Newtonian (or indeed Einsteinian) physics, is one in which time and change have primacy, from the elementary particles of quantum mechanics to evolution of the cosmos from the Big Bang. "Both at the macroscopic and microscopic levels, the natural sciences have thus rid themselves of a conception of objective reality that implied that novelty and diversity had to be denied in the name of immutable universal laws" (306). The "arrow of time," the irreversibility that emerges through self-organization from the instability of far-from-equilibrium states, presupposes an indeterminate, though not a directionless, universe; for "what could an arrow of time mean in a deterministic world in which both future and past are contained in the present?" (277). It is because the future is not contained in the present but evolves from it that the irreversible process of time, through interaction of an open system with its environment, repeatedly transforms a mobile present to an unpredictable future.

If such directional processes are the norm (no longer marginal exceptions) in physics and "inorganic" chemistry, they are above all characteristic of life, which emerges from them and extends them to new dimensions. "In this context life," Prigogine and Stengers remark (175), "far from being outside the natural order, appears as the supreme expression of the self-organizing processes" occurring throughout nature, from the atomic nucleus to the cosmos at large. Biological systems, as products of evolution, "*have a past*" (153), and are therefore inseparably involved with the transitional passage of irreversible time: for only what has a past can have a future. In the processes of life, as at every level from microscopic to macrocosmic, "Irreversibility is the mechanism that brings order out of chaos" (292). Time moves not only toward increasing entropy or disorder (as it inexorably does, in accord with the second law of thermodynamics, for closed systems at equilibrium) but toward those critical moments of disequilibrium when the spontaneously adaptive self-organization of the open system—above all the living system—comes into play and future structure is generated from the flux of a liminal present.

Such a concept was anticipated, as so much in the modern philosophy of science has been, by Charles Sanders Peirce, for whom (6:197) "the idea that chance begets order" was "one of the corner-stones of modern physics" as well as biology. In evolutionary biology, Darwin's great insight was to recognize the directional organization, through time, of mutations arising by chance: "The solution of Darwin's paradox," as Mayr observes (1976, 43), "is that natural selection itself turns accident into design." The "new alliance" achieved by post-Newtonian science, as Prigogine and Stengers conceive it (286–87), has extended this concept of formative time to every dimension of the universe: "At all levels, be it the level of macroscopic physics, the level of fluctuations, or the microscopic level, *nonequilibrium is the source of order. Nonequilibrium brings 'order out of chaos.'*" Perhaps, as ancient wisdom declared, Chaos was indeed—and continues to be—the matrix of all that comes into being through the generative power of time.

In this time-oriented physics of becoming, the structure of change is inherently tripartite, anticipating the pattern of the human quest for transcendence to which only an indeterminate universe in the process of continual self-formation could ultimately have given rise. The disruption of a steady state at or near equilibrium (where statistical predictability reigns) brings matter increasingly far from equilibrium to a "bifurcation point" (Prigogine and Stengers, 160–61) at which a "choice" between alternative possibilities randomly presented by its environment takes place, a "choice" resulting in its unforeseeable reorganization, its emergence in novel form; and this process of separation, transition, and reintegration (in van Gennep's terms) is repeated whenever the provisional stability of a new equilibrium is interrupted. "The 'historical' path along which the system evolves . . . is characterized by a succession of stable regions, where deterministic laws dominate, and of unstable ones, near the bifurcation points, where the system can 'choose' between or among more than one possible future. . . . This mixture of necessity and chance constitutes the history of the system" (169–70), which apart from this history can never be understood. "In a sense," Prigogine remarks (1980, 106), "the bifurcation introduces *history* into physics and chemistry, an element that formerly seemed to be reserved for sciences dealing with biological, social, and cultural phenomena."

A similar but accelerated process occurs in the evolution of biological systems, notably as conceived by Eldredge and Gould in their theory of "punctuated equilibria," according to which "the history of evolution is not one of stately unfolding," as in the classic Darwinian version, "but a story of homeostatic equilibria, disturbed only 'rarely' . . . by rapid and episodic events of speciation."[2] Evolutionary development, on this account, is not a steady process of gradual change by slow accretions over millions of years (for the fossil record reveals that most species remain stable throughout most of their history) but one in which geographic separation, hence reproductive isolation, of a community may be followed by relatively rapid change, through natural selection in response to altered ecological conditions, culminating after a few thousand years in formation of a new species distinct from the parent group, which it may displace if its adaptation to its environment, or its reproductive capacities, give it a sufficient advantage. Here too random chance offers a "choice" at a recurrent threshold or "bifurcation point" between stable states, and time, through the slow winnowing of natural selection, brings about a reordering whose direction becomes apparent, as the process is repeated with countless unpredictable variations, only after the event.

This dynamic of chemical and biological equilibria disrupted and reestablished in new form through intensified interchange with the external world during a liminal period of heightened uncertainty is characteristic also, as we have seen, of human consciousness and language, and of social and cultural institutions. Among the latter, religious practices

2. "Punctuated Equilibria: An Alternative to Phyletic Gradualism" (1972), in Eldredge, 193. In his book, Eldredge describes development of this theory through study of two Middle Devonian trilobites.

(in particular, movements of revitalization) give expression to a "dialectic of disorganization and organization," according to A. Wallace (1966, 38), for whom the "struggle" between entropy and organization is "what religion is all about." This dialectic presupposes disruption of a prior equilibrium, transition toward an unknown outcome, and reintegration into a renewed and transformed equilibrium—a process made possible by a directional but indeterminate universe continually engendering new order from chaos. The tripartite structure of the rite of passage and vision quest is deeply rooted, therefore, in a reality shaped and reshaped by time—the reality of structured process, of self-transcendence through repeated transformation of an intrinsically mobile equilibrium in a direction that can never be known.

This ternary structure of the quest is by no means arbitrary, for though the number of its phases could easily be multiplied (three being the root of an endless plurality), it could not be less. Absolute duality precludes transition between polarized opposites just as absolute unity, the eternally static One of Parmenides, precludes beginning or end; three is the infinitely expandable number between one and two, the number of movement, relation, and change, and for this reason, perhaps, it has been the mystic number par excellence throughout much of the world. Only inasmuch as systems are viewed as closed, static, and determined can the "binary oppositions" of Saussurean structuralism[3] have their restricted validity; the open system, under the aspect not of eternity but of time, must be understood in terms not of binary oppositions but of ternary relations. Here the emphasis is not on fixed antitheses but on the process that connects (and transforms) them; not on the raw and the cooked, but on the cooking, on the present *active* participle that converts one structure to another, the given to the made, and thereby creates a future transcending the past.

The binary model has been applied not only to language and other cultural forms presumed by structuralists to be linguistically patterned but to the brain and communication itself. Attempts to equate the brain with a digital computer (in which binary oppositions reign supreme), on the grounds that the neuron can only fire or not fire, signaling either excitation or inhibition, fail to take account of the multiple synapses con-

---

3. The term *binary opposition* stems from Jakobson's analysis of the paired "distinctive features" structuring the phoneme; but as we have seen, Jakobson recognized an "ascending scale of freedom" in the combination of linguistic units, to none of which beyond the phoneme the determinism of binary oppositions applied. It was Saussure, with his rigid antitheses of *langue* and *parole*, signifier and signified, diachronic and synchronic, to whom the French structuralists harked back when they adopted Jakobson's term as a shibboleth for disciplines far removed from phonology.

necting these cells: the transition points whose function cannot be reduced to merely transmitting a predetermined "on" or "off" message.
The axon leading from the cell body to the synapses "has no choice but
to fire. At the synapses between cells," however, Rose writes (79), "lies
the choice point which converts the nervous system from a certain, predictable and dull one into an uncertain, probabilistic and hence interesting system." The intricate specificity of the human brain is counterbal-
anced by its no less essential plasticity, which differentiates its operations
from the closed programs of ants or bees (to say nothing of computers);
it follows, therefore, in Rose's view (179), that human consciousness is
not a static condition but "a *process* involving interaction between individual and environment." The synaptic structure of the nervous system,
Rose remarks (93–94), makes it "only partially predictable," since the
mode of its computation "appears to have a measure of indeterminacy
built into it." For this and other reasons, Edelman concludes (227), "little
or nothing of value can be gained from the application of this failed
analogy between the computer and the brain."

The binary model was fundamental to development of the mathematical information theory that underlies the operation of the digital
computer, with its assumption that any message expressible in language
can be communicated by means of binary digits, or bits. Far from being
deterministic in its implications, however, information theory is concerned with discrimination of meaningful information from uninfor-
mative "noise," not with specification of individual messages. The transmission of all information crucially presupposes *un*certainty, since, as
Cherry writes (170), "information can be received only where there is
doubt; and doubt implies the existence of alternatives—where choice,
selection, or discrimination is called for." And although this selection
process may be logically reducible (like all choices) to a series of binary
oppositions, on the level of actual human communication and individual
choices—the "real-life" level where uncertainty can never be eliminated,
and the meaning and truth of information are "meaning *to* somebody,
on a certain occasion" and "truth *about* some reality or experience"
(226)—choice entails no simple switching between binary alternatives
but continual sorting out of multiple possibilities by the human brain to
which the "determinate and absolutely error-free calculations" (301) of
the digital computer's closed program are intrinsically foreign.

This process suggests, Jeremy Campbell writes (265), that an open
system (whether organism, language, or society) follows "the arrow
not of entropy but of history," which "distinguishes past from future,
by moving away from the simple, the uniform, and the random, and
toward the genuinely new, the endlessly complex products of nature and

mind."[4] Communication, like life (the product of repeatedly transmitted genetic information), consciousness, and the spiritual quest that strives to transcend their given limits, is thus a self-transformative process that progresses, by unpredictable actualizations of multiple possibilities, through liminal indeterminacy toward an evolving goal.

Even in the operation of the brain and the transmission of information, then, to which the binary model has been widely applied, a connecting third term—the formative liminal phase—is essential; duality is an explanatory principle of the closed and static that can never be adequate to a system embedded in time (as all ultimately are) and open to change. Only an ideal "synchrony" cut off from both past and future can lend plausibility to the binary model of Saussurian semiology; the assumption that such an idealization is requisite to a rigorous science is a retrogression to an earlier scientific mythology.

In contrast to this deterministic tendency in twentieth-century thought, the semiotic of Saussure's older contemporary Peirce—whom Jakobson (1971, 346) and Popper (1979, 212) respectively recognized as "the most inventive and versatile among American thinkers" and "one of the greatest philosophers of all time"—fully acknowledges the critical role in human communication (as in cosmic evolution) of time and chance, and finds an explanatory principle not in binary opposition but in the ternary relation by which closure is continually transcended and signification becomes meaning.

Fundamental to Peirce's logic was the triadic relation between a sign, its object, and its interpretant, the latter—the sign created in the mind of the person whom the sign addresses—being the essential third term mediating between first and second. "To give a good and complete account of the dyadic relations of concepts would be impossible," Peirce concludes (3:387), "without taking into account the triadic relations which, for the most part, underlie them." Hence representation by a sign or "representamen" cannot be reduced (like Saussurian signification) to a static binary structure but is by nature a process. The triadic relation of Sign, Object, and Interpretant (or First, Second, and Third) "does not consist in any complexus of dyadic relations" (2:156).[5] It is not com-

---

4. See Campbell's summary (88–90) of David Layzer's argument that "even for a Laplacean superintelligence, total information about the whole universe on the scale of its individual molecules is impossible," since "the present moment always contains an element of genuine novelty and the future is never wholly predictable." See also Campbell's Afterword, "Aristotle and DNA," in which he suggests (269) that "Information is in essence a theory," like Aristotle's, "of making the possible actual."

5. On the importance of Peirce's triadic theory of the sign, in contrast to the dyadic sign which eliminates the human user, and thus the possibility of determinate meaning, in

posed of binary operations, like a computer program, but is irreducibly triadic.

So basic was this relation to Peirce's philosophy that it pervades not only logic but psychology and metaphysics. The ideas of first, second, and third "are due to congenital tendencies of the mind" (1:198), categories inherent in the structure of consciousness. Quality and Reaction, Peirce's first two categories, are connected by Category the Third, or Thirdness, which "embodies Betweenness or Mediation in its simplest and most rudimentary form" (5:68). In sum, "First is the conception of being or existing independent of anything else. Second is the conception of being relative to, the conception of reaction with, something else. Third is the conception of mediation, whereby a first and a second are brought into relation" (6:25). Any further multiplication of categories is always reducible to these three, but these three are not further reducible. "I see a great many thinkers," he lamented late in life (Peirce and Welby 1977, 28), "who are trying to construct a system without putting any thirdness into it," and who thus never go beyond the binary opposition.

Only by this mediatory third term can the static polarity of quality and reaction be overcome in the transformative potentiality of an unrealized future; only "through the medium of thirds" (1:163) does the future act upon the past and influence the present. Thirdness finds preeminent embodiment in the symbol, which differs from icon and index in being "a law, or regularity of the indefinite future"; for Peirce (2:46), "To say that the future does not influence the present is untenable doctrine." The mediating symbol engenders the indeterminate but determinative future through which the given duality of past and present designated by icon and index is continually transcended and given meaning; for meaning is "obviously a triadic relation" (1:175). The search for truth by which scientist and philosopher are motivated is thus an endeavor to overcome the constrictive closure of binary opposition, the doubt whose very derivation from Latin *duo habeo* ("hold as two") "exhibits its binarity. If we did not struggle against doubt," and thus against duality, Peirce concludes (2:45), "we should not seek the truth." As in every quest, every rite of passage, and ultimately every biological and physical change, the process is ternary: once division has occurred, the only passage from duality toward a new and always provisional unity

---

the structuralisms and post-structuralisms descending from Saussure to Derrida, see Sheriff. Hegel's logic is also triadic but his Idealism is more abstract than Peirce's pragmaticism, quirky though Peirce's multiplication of terms often seems. Peirce, who admired Hegel, remarked that "he has committed the trifling oversight of forgetting that there is a real world with real actions and reactions" (see Feibleman, 27–28 and 153–56; and cf. Peirce and Welby, 25).

is the uncertain but indispensable way of the Third, that is, not of the dual but of the *trial*.

"The irritation of doubt causes a struggle to attain a state of belief. I shall term this struggle," this crucial transitional phase between division and integration, "*Inquiry*," Peirce writes (5:231). Scientific inquiry as a quest for truth was a constant concern which distinguished him (a *summa cum laude* in Chemistry) from many contemporary thinkers. Unlike most scientists in his positivistic age, however, Peirce (1:58) firmly rejected the possibility of attaining "absolute certainty, absolute exactitude, absolute universality. We cannot be absolutely certain that our conclusions are even approximately true." Hence science, properly understood, designates not an ultimately chimerical attainment of knowledge but "the pursuit of those who are devoured by a desire to find things out" (1:x).

Consistent with this conviction, Peirce held firm to *fallibilism*, "the doctrine that our knowledge is never absolute but always swims, as it were, in a continuum of uncertainty and of indeterminacy" (1:70); he once noted his "beatific" pleasure when "a critic said of me that I did not seem to be *absolutely sure of my own conclusions*" (1:xi). This doctrine is suited to a universe where chance reigns no less than law, and the forces of nature (here again Peirce anticipates a later physics), far from being unchangeable, may have "naturally grown up" (1:72) in a cosmic evolution whose outcome must forever be unknown. But the final unattainability of knowledge does not diminish our desire to attain it; through inquiry we repeatedly transcend present uncertainty in a larger uncertainty forever beyond it. This desire—we might call it the questing impulse—is innate; for "all human knowledge, up to the highest flights of science, is but the development of our inborn animal instincts" (2:477).

The characteristic method of scientific inquiry is the formulation and testing of hypotheses that Peirce called abduction or retroduction, which forms a link (again the crucial third term) between inductive experimentation and deductive reasoning. "Peirce differed from the positivists," Feibleman writes (290), "in his regard for the reality of hypothesis; he did not seek the least hypothetical of propositions but the most." In his view (6:147), every scientific proposition is a provisional hypothesis subject to refutation, "adopted in accordance with a method which must lead to the truth in the long run." Because one hypothesis leads to another and none can ever be final, scientific inquiry is a self-transcendent quest for a goal as elusive as it is necessary: the unreachable goal of an indeterminate truth that gives direction to our instinctive pursuit of knowledge. "Inquiry properly carried on," Peirce believed (1:258), "will reach some definite and fixed result or," since the result can never be absolute certainty, will "approximate indefinitely toward that limit." Belief in a goal to be pursued is no less fundamental in the quest for truth than awareness that no goal can be finally attained: "Indeed, out of a contrite fallibilism, combined with a high faith in the reality of knowledge, and an intense desire to find things out," Peirce eloquently writes (1:11), "all my philosophy has always seemed to me to grow." Small wonder, in an age dominated by self-confident scientific positivism and dogmatic affirmations of an *in*fallible "scientific method" leading ineluctably toward attainment of incontrovertible truth, that Peirce, whose understanding of science was generations ahead of his time, never received an academic appointment and was ignored so widely and with such complacent ease.

The conception of scientific inquiry as an endless quest was not entirely new. Francis Bacon, as we have already remarked, was very much a man of the Renaissance when he affirmed (37; *Novum Organum* 48), in words reminiscent of Giordano Bruno or Marlowe's Tamburlaine, that the unquiet human understanding "cannot stop or rest, and still presses onward, but in vain." But for Bacon this urge for "something beyond" threatened to lead the mind astray from general principles that "ought to be held merely positive." During subsequent centuries most scientific thinkers held that inquiry progresses by meticulous application of an essentially mechanical inductive method. Thus Darwin, in an age when John Stuart Mill had codified experimental induction, professed with retrospective orthodoxy that he had "worked on true Baconian principles, and without any theory collected facts on a wholesale scale," reaching his conclusions by painstaking adherence to inductive procedures. Yet as Peter Medawar, who quotes this passage (80), observes, elsewhere in his writings and everywhere in his practice Darwin reveals the "self-deception" of this assertion and the irresistible attraction he found in forming hypotheses.

Despite such occasional (and mainly private) confessions, formation of hypotheses—the "abduction" central, for Peirce, to the search for truth—was widely dismissed as unscientific, with the sanction of Newton's haughty (if dubious) *hypotheses non fingo*. Few scientists, whatever their practice, openly endorsed, with the physiologist Claude Bernard, the importance of hypotheses as the starting point of experimental reasoning. In an age of triumphant positivism when science, like the Pope, was decreed infallible so long as its rituals were properly performed, Bernard was as rare among scientists as Peirce would be among philosophers in seeing theories formulated from fallible hypotheses as "only partial and provisional truths which are necessary . . . to carry the investigation forward" toward a goal continually being transformed by science itself. (See Medawar, 124, 130, 134, with quotations from Mill, Whewell, and Bernard.)

Among twentieth-century thinkers who have developed Peirce's con-

ception of scientific inquiry as a fallible search for truth through repeated testing of hypotheses, and therefore as a tireless quest for an
object forever beyond attainment, the foremost has been Karl Popper,
in a series of writings beginning with the *Logik der Forschung* of 1934.
Rejecting the so-called inductive method as a means of discovering
truth, Popper proposes instead a process of continual conjecture followed by rigorous testing culminating either in provisional confirmation
(for no final confirmation can exist) or in "falsification" leading to formulation of alternative hypotheses: a process without end. In his view
(1968, 40), "not the *verifiability* but the *falsifiability* of a system," its susceptibility to refutation, demarcates a theory as scientific, for no theory
can ever, in the nature of things, be conclusively verified.

Popper's propositions have been disputed on many grounds, including supposed inconsistency with the pursuit of what Kuhn has called
"normal" as opposed to "revolutionary" science.[6] But Popper is concerned not with the day-to-day practice but with the underlying *logic* of
scientific research. Refutation is not an end in itself, but one phase in a
process of conjecture *and* refutation that leads not to universal skepticism but to genuine, if always provisional, scientific *discovery*. Moreover,
though empirical science may be demarcated by the criterion of testable
falsifiability, it is not, Popper repeatedly emphasizes, different in kind
from other human (and animal) pursuits characterized by a similar if
less systematic process of trial and error. Both animals and human beings are born with a powerful need to seek regularities even where
none can be found, and in "the well-known method of trial and error-
elimination" common to human and animal psychology alike, "the various trials correspond to the formation of competing hypotheses" in
scientific inquiry, "and the elimination of error corresponds to the elimination or refutation of theories by way of tests" (1979, 25).

Yet although both the amoeba and Einstein "make use of the method
of trial and error elimination, the amoeba dislikes erring while Einstein
is intrigued by it: he consciously searches for his errors in the hope of
learning by their discovery and elimination" (1979, 70).[7] The critical

6. See Kuhn 1970, 146–47. In a later paper (1977, 272), Kuhn says Popper "characterized the entire scientific enterprise in terms that apply only to its occasional revolutionary parts," as opposed to normal science. But Eldredge (47) remarks that despite their
idealization Popper's views coincide with day-to-day science "in the collective effort. . . . It
is the rivals who can be counted on to falsify an hypothesis." It is in this context of the
scientific enterprise as a whole, not of the isolated theory or individual researcher, that the
logic of conjecture and refutation pertains to "normal" science, which is not perhaps so
radically different from "revolutionary" science as Kuhn proposes.

7. Cf. Lorenz 1977, 24: "The method of the genome, perpetually making experiments,
matching their results against reality, and retaining what is fittest, differs from that

method of science is not qualitatively different from the method of search and discovery through experience common to all living things; for animals and even plants, in Popper's view (145), "are problem-solvers. And they solve their problems by the method of competitive tentative solutions and the elimination of error." Even Pavlov's dog, far from acting on a "conditioned reflex" whose existence Popper denies (Popper and Eccles, 136–37), "*invents a theory* either consciously or unconsciously, and then tries it out," thus exhibiting an exploratory instinct akin to the scientist's conscious investigation of the universe. By their very nature, then, "organisms are problem solvers and explorers of their world" (138): man is but the problem solver and explorer par excellence.

For Popper (1979, 37), then, as for Peirce, "the quest for certainty, for a secure basis of knowledge, has to be abandoned" in a universe ruled not only (if at all) by strict Newtonian laws or regular movements of "clocks" (213) but by laws of chance or statistical probability, the random movements of "clouds" (Popper writes in anticipation of recent "chaos" theory) whose configurations in any individual instance cannot even theoretically be predicted. Strict determinism pertains only to an ideally self-contained and static system, but in the open system of the evolving universe (and of the evolving organism and human consciousness) it has no place; for us, exploring these worlds, "the growth of knowledge must be unpredictable in principle" (298).

Hence the pursuit of knowledge, in science as in the trial and error of ordinary experience, is essentially (as Popper entitled his intellectual autobiography) an "unended quest." For "we are searchers at best," he writes (1979, 41), "and at any rate fallible." In the words of the pre-Socratic philosopher Xenophanes, as Popper quotes them (1965, 26):

> The gods did not reveal, from the beginning,
> All things to us; but in the course of time,
> Through seeking, men find that which is the better.
>
> But as for certain truth, no man has known it,
> Nor will he know it . . .

Yet though certain truth cannot be known, truth—or at least verisimilitude, the provisional approximation to an ideal of truth forever beyond our reach—remains the continually evolving goal without which the quest could never begin and never continue. Such a goal is indispensable to scientific research (since all research is search, and every search has a goal), "For without this idea, there can be no objective standards of in-

---

adopted by man in his scientific quest for knowledge in only one respect, and that not a vital one, namely that the genome learns only from its successes, whereas man learns also from his failures." Peirce and Popper would consider the difference somewhat more vital.

quiry; no criticism of our conjectures; no groping for the unknown; no quest for knowledge" (30). Through such a quest, as much in the human as in the natural sciences, and indeed in every activity of our lives— inasmuch as "we live more for the future . . . than in the past" (Popper and Eccles, 104)—we pursue the continual self-transcendence which, in Popper's vision (1979, 147), "is the most striking and important fact of all life and all evolution, and especially of human evolution." It is this quest that has made us, and continues to make us, what we are by holding purposefully before us the elusive, indeterminate, indispensable goal of what we are in the process of becoming.

CHAPTER SIXTEEN

The Reality of Transcendence

But what is the object of this quest, the goal incessantly pursued but never fully attained? Is the pursuit no more, perhaps, than a psychological need, a sustaining illusion, and the goal a mirage that is different for every observer and that mockingly vanishes, like the Cheshire cat, as we approach it, revealing the emptiness of the hopes we have fondly attached to this evanescent will-o'-the-wisp? Much twentieth-century thought has tended toward such conclusions, viewing "reality" as a subjective construct or a fabric of rhetorical illusions: a subject for psychoanalysis or deconstruction. Even in the philosophy of science, that former bastion of confident positivism, disintegration of the once-omnipotent Newtonian synthesis has undermined faith in an objective reality capable of being discovered through disinterested search for truth. Yet both Peirce and Popper, in contrast to the relativistic tendency differently embodied by Kuhn and Feyerabend, see indeterminism as fully compatible with belief in an objective reality without which the quest for knowledge and self-transcendence could have no meaning.[1]

1. Kuhn suggested (1970, 170–71) abandoning the idea that paradigm changes bring scientists closer to truth: "Need there be any such goal?" He later sought (cf. 1977, 293–319) to modify the relativistic implications of his claim (1970, 150–51) that proponents of incommensurable paradigms "practice their trades in different worlds," changing paradigms not because one fits reality better but because of a "gestalt switch" or "conversion experience"; but he continues (206) to find the notion of a match between theory and a "real" counterpart in nature "illusive in principle." Among many critiques of Kuhn's and Feyerabend's "thesis of incommensurability" see esp. Putnam, 191–97. Kuhn and the more unabashedly relativistic Feyerabend have found a wide following among literary humanists, whereas Popper's thought has appealed both to humanists like Gombrich and to leading scientists such as Eccles in neurology, Lorenz in ethology, Medawar in medicine, and Prigogine in chemistry.

"I am myself," Peirce wrote (5:323), "a scholastic realist of a some-what extreme stripe," an admirer of Duns Scotus who condemned con-temporary nominalism and affirmed "the correspondence of a represen-tation with its object" (5:390), the belief that names refer to reality and propositions to truth (cf. Feibleman, 54–62; Hookway, 37–79). Scien-tific research could not take place without this assumption of an objective (though never finally certain) truth: "The opinion which is fated to be ultimately agreed to by all who investigate, is what we mean by the truth, and the object represented in this opinion is the real" (5:268). But for Peirce, as for the scholastic realists and Plato before them, "reality" did not consist in immediate particulars or material objects. Above all, "re-ality consists in the future" (8:199), the never fully realized potentiality to which only the "general," or universal, can refer, through the medium of thirdness embodied in the symbol. It is the quest of philosophy, as of all thought and language (for all language is symbolic and refers beyond itself), and most especially of our repeatedly formulated hypotheses or abductions, to approximate ever more closely to this objective reality.

In contrast to the Platonists, however, Peirce emphatically does not conceive of ideas or generals as immutable and eternal—his concept of thirdness, as we have seen, is relational and dynamic, and he views even natural laws as a product of evolution—nor as existing in a separate realm from the concrete realities of immediate experience: the prag-maticist, he writes (5:289), "does not make Forms to be the *only* realities in the world." In this respect he is closer to Aristotle's conception of reality as actualization or activation (*energeia*), through form, of the po-tentiality of matter than to Plato's theory of "ideas," at least in its more uncompromising versions. Far from being a changeless object of philo-sophical contemplation, truth is the objective correspondence with re-ality that must be continually (though it can never be fully) actualized by the never-ending inquiry, or quest for knowledge, of fallible human beings working alone and together toward an end that will always sur-pass them.

For Peirce the quest for knowledge is a quest, as Feibleman writes (213), "to advance from the subjective to the independently real," from the particularity of individual experience to the general that embraces it in a more comprehensive future reality. "In this way, the existence of thought now depends on what is to be hereafter; so that it has only a potential existence, dependent on the future thought of the community" (5:189). Pursuit of this transcendent goal is an ethical obligation funda-mental to being human, and it follows with inexorable logic (2:398) that "our interests shall *not* be limited. They must not stop at our own fate, but must embrace the whole community," an unlimited community ex-tending to all races and even "beyond all bounds." The heroic quest to discover and actualize an objective reality surpassing the limitations of our particular existence is therefore the proper goal of every human being in this life, the categorical imperative of Peirce's religion.

For Popper, too, science presupposes realism, and truth defined as correspondence with reality is the ultimate aim (though verisimilitude is the only attainable goal) of scientific inquiry, as of every human quest for knowledge. "Metaphysical realism . . . forms a kind of background that gives point to our search for truth" (1983, 80). The very concept of truth was one the younger Popper, like others of the Vienna Circle, viewed as vague if not meaningless. All this changed, however, when Tarski "re-established a correspondence theory of absolute or objective truth which showed that we are free to use the intuitive idea of truth as correspondence with the facts" (1965, 223). Only such a concept "allows us to say—with Xenophanes—that we search for truth, but may not know when we have found it; that we have no criterion of truth, but are nevertheless guided by the idea of truth as a *regulative principle* (as Kant or Peirce might have said); and that, though there are no general criteria by which we can recognize truth—except perhaps tautological truth— there are something like criteria of progress towards the truth" (226).

In consequence of this philosophical rehabilitation of a concept indispensable to the realist position, "we too," Popper affirms (1965, 229), "see science as the search for truth, and . . . are no longer afraid to say so. Indeed, it is only with respect to this aim, the discovery of truth, that we can say that though we are fallible, we hope to learn from our mistakes. . . . Thus the very idea of error—and of fallibility—involves the idea of an objective truth as the standard of which we may fall short." Since certainty concerning truth is intrinsically unattainable, however, the practical goal of scientific inquiry is rather approximation to truth, or verisimilitude, through rigorous falsification and progressive refinement of our hypotheses.

But if our quest for knowledge presupposes the goal, to which we can only approximate through trial and error, of a finally unattainable truth corresponding to objective reality, what is the nature, the ontological and epistemological status, of this reality? So fundamental was the triadic relation to Peirce that he speaks (Peirce and Welby 1977, 81) of his three categories as "three Universes, which are distinguished by three Modalities of Being"; of these it is the mediating universe of Thirdness that is oriented (27) not toward the past, "which is absolutely determinate, fixed, *fait accompli*, and dead," but the future, "which is living, plastic, and determinable," and provides the quest for knowledge with its goal. Popper, in his later philosophy (1979, 154; cf. 1979, 74; 1976, 180–83; Popper and Eccles, 36–38), proposes a not dissimilar triad of interacting worlds, the first of physical objects, the second of subjective mental experience, the third of objective products of the human mind; it is in this nonmaterial and relational third modality, the world of "possible objects of thought" that remain to be actualized, and are thus potential and future, that the search for truth, or approximation to truth, finds its continually evolving object.

A world of "ideas in the objective sense" (1979, 109) toward which the quest for knowledge is directed, an autonomous world of theory, of "knowledge without a knowing subject," inevitably recalls the world of Forms postulated by Plato, a thinker to whom Popper has not always been well disposed. The similarity is real, since Popper like Plato rejects the solipsistic conception of forms or ideas as having only psychological existence, hence no objective reality; but the differences are crucial. "Plato's third world was divine; it was unchanging and, of course, true," Popper writes (122), whereas "my third world is man-made and changing. It contains not only true theories but also false ones, and especially open problems, conjectures, and refutations." It is thus a world not of ultimate Truth or absolute Being, like Plato's *to ontôs on,* but of verisimilitude and becoming, a world that provides not only the goal of the individual quest (the objective and thus transcendent knowledge we seek) but its medium and the pattern on which it is modeled: a perpetually developing world—like Peirce's thirdness—of interaction and change; a product of human activity that objectifies *process* directed toward an indeterminate goal. The objective reality of world three is thus the reality of the quest itself.

This evolving world of objective ideas, which continually interacts with the worlds both of physical objects and of psychological states, engenders and gives shape to the quest (rather than merely serving, like Plato's immutable Forms, as its object) because it is both the product of the human mind and transcends it: both the activity and the goal toward which the activity is directed. "I suggest *that it is possible to accept the reality or (as it may be called) the autonomy of the third world,*" Popper writes (1979, 159), "*and at the same time to admit that the third world originates as a product of human activity.* One can even admit that the third world is man-made and, in a very clear sense, superhuman at the same time. It transcends its makers," and in doing so continually leads them to unexpected discoveries.

For Popper no less than Peirce the quest to transcend subjective experience through objective knowledge of a larger reality is the purpose and obligation of fallible man. In a universe where "no claim can be made for absolute certainty, *we are seekers for truth but we are not its possessors*" (46–47). The quester who relinquishes the chimerical hope of finality finds in determined pursuit of the quest the fullest expression of a human freedom that is no less essential because, like all things human, it can never be absolute. We fulfill our humanity not by returning to the putative harmony of a lost state of nature in which we were beasts among beasts, nor by building utopias designed to write finis to our troubles at last, but by going "into the unknown, the uncertain and insecure" (1971, 201), where the goal of our unended quest will always lie.

The scientific quest through repeated trial and error for knowledge of an objective, and thus a transcendent, reality that can never be fully apprehended finds a counterpart (however different in appearance and method) in tribal exploration of the unknown, the uncertain, and the insecure through spirit mediumship or the ecstatic shamanic quest. But what kind of truth or verisimilitude, objectivity or indeed reality, if any, can we ascribe to the visions in which this quest culminates?

Simple explanations have often been proposed, and the simplest—as for many religious phenomena—is deception. Like mediums, prophets, and other practitioners, shamans have been widely known for trickery and illusion, ranging from exhibition of foreign bodies supposedly extracted from patients' wounds to elaborate theatrical productions complete with ventriloquism, shaking tents, and escape from bondage à la Houdini. On occasion shamans have openly confided their rivals' tricks to outsiders, and on rare occasion even their own. But to see the shamanic profession itself, and the quest for spiritual knowledge central to it, as no more than an artful fraud intended to hoodwink a credulous audience would be to misconstrue it entirely. Many witnesses of traditional shamanic performances have echoed the judgment of von Wrangel, who remarked after visiting northern Siberia in the early nineteenth century that the true shaman, far from practicing deception, acts under "the involuntary and irresistible influence of his intensely stimulated imagination" (Oesterreich, 295; cf. Mikhailovskii, 136–38). Nor is use of tricks of the trade incompatible with genuine belief; indeed, shamans and other tribal doctors almost invariably call upon their colleagues, whose arts they well know, in their own time of sickness or need.

But if a shaman is something more than a sham, what reality, if any, do his visions possess? Early observers such as the Jesuits generally concurred with the "savages" in attributing to their visions an objective reality deriving from a power, albeit diabolic, beyond them: the visions were real, but delusions. More recently, when faith in both guardian spirits and devils has appreciably waned, such visions have been widely viewed as merely subjective, the hallucinatory product either of mental derangement by drugs or physical torments, or of sexual repressions. The "Arctic hysteria" of Siberian shamans is an example of the first explanation, as the sexual "perversion" of transvestite shamans is of the second.

But visionary shamanism is too varied to be explained by climate or drugs alone, and the temperament of tribal visionaries too diverse (and often too close to the cultural norm) to be categorized as psychologically deviant. More generally, subjective explanations give insufficient weight to the compelling authority these visions have not only for the visionary but for others no less inclined to ascribe objective existence—and supreme importance—to them. Both Durkheim's "collective representations," which reduce religious forms to passive reflections of a static social order, and Jung's archetypes of a vague "collective unconscious,"[2] on the other hand, locate the reality of visions in an autonomous world of cultural or psychic forms rather than in a continually changing *relation* between the vision and the envisioning subject. The latter conception, in contrast, not only accords with the "native" interpretation of visionary experience as a lifelong interaction between the visionary and a spirit both outside and intimately part of herself (a tenaciously ancient interpretation surely entitled to respect in our age of transitory isms); it concurs far more closely than purely sociological or psychological conceptions with Peirce's or Popper's view of inquiry itself as the quest for knowledge of a relational or potential third modality of being engendered by yet transcending the individual.

The spiritual quest, as a continual interrelation between the individual and a larger reality in which she transcends her personal existence—"transcends" not by leaving it behind for some separate realm of existence but by realization of its enlarging and transformative potentiality—is no less characteristic of tribal visionary experience than of scientific inquiry, or any creative endeavor. The shamanistic quest for knowledge differs, of course, from scientific research in fundamental respects: most fundamentally, perhaps, in the unquestioning credence it generally grants to visionary injunctions whose authority lies beyond question, though not beyond repeated probing through renewal of the never completed quest. "Hope and belief are as important in science as they are elsewhere; the difference," Edelman observes (208), "is that in science they must yield to experiment," and both experiment and the theory it tests are subject not only, like the vision quest, to initial failure but to repeated testing and potential disconfirmation by further experi-

2. For an attempt to redefine Jungian archetypes in a framework of Durkheimian social psychology, see Needham, 45–49. Both the "primary factors" of a complex image like the witch and the "process of synthesis that combines the components into the characteristic image" can be interpreted as "spontaneous manifestations of properties of the brain"; thus "complex images are the products of genetically inherited predispositions." Hypothetical though this notion is, it suggests an interpretation of widely disseminated archetypal images that escapes (because they *are* complex and synthetic, thus subject to renewed syntheses) both the narrow determinism of Durkheim's collective representations and the vague absolutism of Jung's archetypes of a collective unconscious that is everywhere and nowhere if it exists at all.

ments, and by the experiments (and alternative theories) of others. Yet striking as their differences are, the affinities between them are no less important, for each is a strenuous search for an *objective* knowledge—knowledge of a reality beyond yet inseparable from the perceiving self—that enlarges both the individual seeker and those with whom she shares the results of her exploration.

The reality of the vision quest is thus the reality of transcendence itself: transcendence of the envisioning subject not in a categorically distinct Other but in a larger object consubstantial with herself. This reality is located neither in physical things nor in subjective experience alone but in a "third world" of continually expanding though inherently provisional objective knowledge that relates these other two aspects of existence and, by relating, transforms them. It is this distinctively human, intrinsically potential, and always future reality—transitory by nature inasmuch as its manifestation at any one moment will always be replaced, at the next, by another—that every quest to surpass the limitations of self postulates and affirms, no less in our own time and place than in that of the aboriginal Australian, Siberian, or Brazilian medicine man. The particular shape of the vision or theory that is the goal of the quest (for every theory, the Greek origin of the word reminds us, is inherently a vision), like the path the quest follows, will change from culture to culture and moment to moment, but the need for visionary transcendence of the given which the quest embodies, and in which its truth lies, remains undiminished.

William James, toward the end of *The Varieties of Religious Experience* (497–98), boldly poses questions evaded by lesser thinkers: "First, is there, under all the discrepancies of the creeds, a common nucleus to which they bear their testimony unanimously? And second, ought we to consider the testimony true?" All religious experience, bewildering though its varieties be, gives expression, James concludes, to an *uneasiness* arising from "a sense that there is *something wrong about us* as we naturally stand," and all suggest a possible salvation through "making proper connection with the higher powers." This fundamental uneasiness leads to a need, and thence to a search, for transcendence linking subject and object when the individual (498–99) "*becomes conscious that this higher part* [of himself] *is conterminous and continuous with a* MORE *of the same quality, which is operative in the universe outside of him.*" In this "*fact that the conscious person is continuous with a wider self through which saving experiences come*" (505) is "a positive content of religious experience which, it seems to me, *is literally and objectively true as far as it goes.*" The "objective" truth of religious experience thus lies not in a changeless entity outside or beyond the human but in the continuity or interrelation between the individual and a kindred other—call it futurity, potentiality, or spirit—through which the individual self is expanded; this very transcendence is the object of a spiritual quest continually engendered by uneasiness or dissatisfaction with the given.

Nor is this impulse to transcend the given through approximation to a less narrowly personal reality characteristic of religion alone; it takes equally urgent form, Peirce and Popper remind us, in scientific inquiry, and in every search for an enlarging truth. To aspire toward a broader and more fully objective knowledge than we now possess, and to know that our aspiration can have no definitive end, nor produce any certain or final result, is as much a spiritual quest for the scientist, artist, or scholar who pursues it today, without heed for the risk of failure that every true quest must run or the indifference of those who remain content with the given, as Black Elk's lonely vigil on Harney Peak was in a place and time not so far from our own. "It is necessary to combine the recognition of our contingency, our finitude, and our containment in the world with an ambition of transcendence," a contemporary philosopher, Thomas Nagel, writes (9), "however limited may be our success in achieving it," for only by tirelessly seeking to know a transcendent reality that can never be wholly external because it is always continuous, as James recognized, with our innermost selves, can we truly become what we potentially are.

This objective reality of transcendence toward which the quest aims is a product of human consciousness at its furthest extension in language, for through language the modality of the potential arises and the transcendent dimension of the future is born. The vision, like scientific or mathematical intuition, poetic or artistic inspiration, or mystical revelation, whether it appears spontaneously or after laborious quest, may initially seem incommunicable; only through the mediating objectification of a symbolic language, however, can it become a shared reality transcending the evanescence of the subjective. It is therefore not a reality simply opposed to "fiction," for fictions too are objective and hence communicable products of language. The difference between a scientific theory and a work of fiction, Popper writes (1979, 289), "is not . . . that the theory is possibly true while the descriptions in the story are not true, although truth and falsity have something to do with it," but "that the theory and the story are embedded in different critical traditions."

As Aristotle perceived when he characterized poetry (*Poetics* 1451a–b) as more philosophical than history, fictional mimesis entails an actualization of the potential (of "what may be" in accord with probability or necessity), and is thus not a deception, as Plato thought, but a manifestation, like philosophical inquiry itself, of a truth that transcends the immediately given. Poetic fictions, like philosophical speculations, allow us to investigate the dimensions of "possible worlds" resembling our own; they are exploratory hypotheses that cannot, however, be falsified, like those of science, by contradiction with the conditions of our given reality.[3] Fiction, Ricoeur writes (1979, 152–53), "addresses itself to deeply rooted potentialities of reality to the extent that they are absent from the actualities with which we deal in everyday life under the mode of empirical control and manipulation." Like the symbolically expressed vision (which differs from it in being ascribed, as poetry long was, to a privileged external source), fiction complements but can never, because its reality *is* potential, contradict the world explored by the kindred quest of scientific investigation.

Metaphor

Of the many tropes or figures of speech that fiction, like all language, employs, metaphor most directly pertains to the quest for transcendence. For metaphor (the Greek word means a transfer or carrying over) is inherently relational and liminal, so that every metaphor is a quest to go beyond the ordinary limits of language. To the extent that all language speaks of what is absent and points beyond itself (since all language is symbolic, in Peirce's sense, and "refers to the indefinite future"), metaphor is a further extension that "gestures toward what transcends language" (Harries, 82). It is a strategy of discourse, Ricoeur writes (1977, 6), that "preserves and develops the *heuristic* power wielded by *fiction*"; it is no mere adornment, but an instrument for the discovery and exploration of otherwise unactualized (and to that degree, transcendent) potentialities of our world. For "metaphor typically involves a change," in Goodman's words (1976, 72–73), "not merely of range but also of realm," amounting to "an expedition abroad. . . . What occurs is a transfer of a schema, a migration of concepts, an alienation of categories" by which our complacent assumption of a familiar *given* reality—a reality that is ours without seeking—is called into question as our latent knowledge of the never fully realized possibilities of the world and ourselves is enriched and transformed.

But for Ricoeur in particular the function of metaphor as heuristic fiction goes far beyond disrupting expectations or making the old appear

---

3. The concept of "possible worlds" goes back to Leibniz, for whom (115) "the *possibility* of things, even of those that have no actual existence, has itself a reality founded in the divine existence." This idea (burlesqued by Voltaire after Leibniz found that the best possible world was our own) was revived by Kripke as a means of testing philosophical notions in counterfactual but possible situations; in Kripke's conception (18), possible worlds "are total 'ways the world might have been', or states or histories of the *entire* world"; they "are *stipulated*, not *discovered* by powerful telescopes" (44). Putnam (67) defends the concept so long as its language-relative character is clearly recognized. And Pavel notes the resemblance of this notion to that of fictional worlds in literary theory but remarks (49) that "the presence of contradictions effectively prevents us from considering fictional worlds as genuine possible worlds and from reducing the theory of fiction to a Kripkean theory of modality."

new: the "calculated category-mistake" with which Goodman (adapting a term from Ryle) identified metaphor complements, for Ricoeur (1977, 22), a logic of discovery at work in the metaphorical process itself. In Ricoeur's view (74), the self-referential *langue* of Saussurean semiotics, whose domain is that of the sign, "passes outside itself" in the sentence, where reference to extra-linguistic reality (Frege's *Bedeutung*) marks the self-transcendence of *langue;* semantics, as opposed to semiotics, concerns itself with the relation between language and the world (145). Metaphor, too, operates by predication and reference, but through *living* metaphor, "everyday reference to the real must be abolished in order that another sort of reference to other dimensions of reality might be liberated" (230).

Transcendence and innovation, therefore, are the essence of metaphor, whose ostensible category mistake "clears the way to a new vision" (236), an "other reference," which is "the object of our search"—clears the way to objectively existent relational potentialities, that is to say, beyond the deadening stasis of the already given. In consequence (244–45), poetry "has a referential function just as much as does descriptive discourse," and poetic mimesis (in a sense approximating Aristotle's) is not a "copy" but a "redescription" of reality through the metaphorical logic of invention and discovery. Living metaphor has *cognitive* value; it is a quest for new objective knowledge—the objective knowledge of fiction—by which the subject who brings the metaphor into being, or who imaginatively re-creates it, is herself transformed, just as a shaman is transformed by the vision of a guardian spirit with which she becomes metaphorically (but no less "really") identified precisely to the degree that it transcends and will always transcend her.

The visionary reality sought through the quest is that of living metaphor, then, the mediating "thirdness" by which self becomes more and thus other. And if this metaphorical truth, this objective reality of self-transcendence actualized by language, is its goal, the quest, as it unfolds in time, takes form as a narrative or plot (Aristotle's *mythos*),[4] in which metaphor finds a temporal analogue. Leading theorists such as Lukács have noted the close association between the novel, the dominant form

---

4. The narrative, mythos, or plot—here used synonymously—is not the underlying sequence of events (or "story") in itself, but the *recounting* of these events, as shaped by the narrator; it is thus an *objective* reality at one remove from the "real" or fictional events to which it refers: an artistic mimesis. This distinction is one of the foundations of twentieth-century narrative theory. The Russian formalists differentiated story (*fabula*) from plot (*syuzhet*) (Shklovsky, 57; Tomashevsky, 66–70), and Genette added to story (*histoire*) and narrative (*récit*) a third term, narrating (*narration*), the action that produces the narrative. In Genette's scheme narrative discourse is the objective intermediary connecting story and narrating.

of narrative in the modern age, and the quest, by both hero and novelist, for a goal intrinsically beyond realization. For Bakhtin (39), the novel is "a genre that is ever questing, ever examining itself and subjecting its established forms to review"; for Lukács (60), "the fundamental form-determining potential of the novel is objectivised as the psychology of the novel's heroes: they are seekers." Not only the novel, however, but every narrative, including such conventional forms as oral myth, folktale, and epic, is in some measure a quest.

For narrative, like metaphor, is a vehicle, as Ricoeur observes (1984, ix), for semantic *innovation,* and by its placement in time narrative reveals the temporal *process* from which this innovation results. Every quest, because it unfolds in time, takes shape as a narrative, and every narrative, insofar as it does have shape, is implicitly a quest for the metaphorical truth in which it finds, for the moment (since no truth can be more than provisional), its fulfillment. Every quest, Todorov suggests (141), may ultimately, like that of the Grail, be the quest for a narrative, since narrative is the *form* of the quest, the form through which it becomes a communicable experience. But without a Grail—or a guardian spirit, or some other living metaphor of transcendence, some other fiction made objective as vision—to give it direction, there could be no quest, and thus no narrative, to begin with. Narrative and metaphor, quest and vision are as inseparably interdependent as process and structure, movement and stasis, becoming and being.

As Alasdair MacIntyre, discussing the fundamental importance in human lives of narratives combining "both an unpredictable and a partially teleological character" (216), has observed (219): "The unity of a human life is the unity of a narrative quest. Quests sometimes fail, are frustrated, abandoned or dissipated into distractions; and human lives may in all these ways also fail. But the only criteria for success or failure in a human life as a whole are the criteria of success or failure in a narrated or to-be-narrated quest." For such a quest, MacIntyre adds, "is always an education both as to the character of that which is sought and in self-knowledge."

But what shape can we ascribe to narrative in general and the quest narrative in particular? In his *Morphology of the Folktale,* published in Russian in 1928 and translated into English thirty years later, Propp proposed (1968, 23) that all Russian fairy tales (or "wondertales")[5] "are of

---

5. Propp's intended title for his book was "Morphology of the 'Fairy Tale' or 'Wonder-tale'" (*volshebnaya skazka*), changed by his publisher to "Morphology of the Folktale" (*skazka*) (1984, 70). The terminology is further confused in English not only by alternative translations ("fairy tale" or "wonder tale") of his term for a specifically Russian type of

one type in regard to their structure," when classified not by themes but by *functions*. He distinguished thirty-one of these, and observed that although not all occur in every tale, those that do so always occur in the same order: "The sequence of elements . . . is strictly *uniform*" (22). In Propp's analysis (34–36), the tale is set in motion when the villain harms a family member, or when a family member lacks or desires something; the latter "situation of insufficiency or lack . . . leads to quests analogous to those in the case of villainy." Both functions, which are variations of one another, result in a quest to repair the initial damage or lack, the first by a "victimized hero" striving to undo an injury, the second (the explicit quest narrative) by a "seeker" aspiring to appease his unsatisfied yearnings.

Because the folktale is a nearly universal form of oral narrative (if something so ill-defined can be designated a "form"), providing, along with sacred myths, a paradigm for the epics and tales of literate cultures, Propp's analysis has often been treated as an anatomy of narrative structures in general. Such an attempt soon reveals, however, the abstractness and formulaic rigidity of reducing every narrative to a uniform sequence of thirty-one (give or take a few) functions. This was one objection Lévi-Strauss (1976, 132–33) brought against Propp in his critique of 1960: "*Formalism destroys its object*. With Propp, it results in the discovery that there exists in reality but one tale. . . . Before formalism, we were certainly unaware of what these tales had in common. Since formalism, we have been deprived of any means of understanding how they differ."

But Propp's intention, as he writes in response (1984, 70), "was not to study all the various and complex types of the folktale; I examined only one strikingly distinctive type, viz., the folk wondertale" of Russian oral tradition, which evinces the standardization characteristic of many formulaic genres of storytelling. Only when his carefully delimited functional typology is unjustifiably extended to other types of folk narrative, or when still more sweeping claims are made, as by Campbell in *The Hero with a Thousand Faces* or Frye in *Anatomy of Criticism*, to comprehend all myth in a single archetype or "monomyth," a composite quest narrative in multiple stages found throughout a bewildering spectrum of literary genres,[6] do the charges of abstraction and rigidity, to say nothing of

folktale—and by Propp's frequent use of the more general term *skazka*—but by the fact that, except in the title, the translator of the *Morphology* (as revised in 1968) renders *skazka* as "tale" and *narodnaya skazka* as "folktale." These inconsistencies have seriously affected interpretations of Propp by Lévi-Strauss and others, especially since the English translation of 1958 was the first in any language.

6. Campbell asserts (388), with the extreme generality characteristic of his book, that

vagueness and arbitrary citation of evidence, appear valid; Propp makes no such claims.

It is not Propp's linear or "syntagmatic" analysis of the sequence of functions composing the Russian wondertale but Lévi-Strauss's "paradigmatic" analysis of oral myths, with its claim, based on a shaky linguistic analogy, to discover underlying binary oppositions between raw and cooked, nature and culture, and so on, that students of folklore such as Dundes (1964, 42–47, and 1968, xii–xiii; cf. Liberman, xix–xliv) have found arbitrary, subjective, and impossible to verify. By contrast, Propp's contribution, for Dundes, is a major theoretical breakthrough in the twentieth-century study of folklore, and one not exclusively limited to the Russian wondertale. Its broader relevance is evident, however, only when Propp's thirty-one functions are whittled down to the two principal "motifemes" that Dundes (1964, 62–63), in a binary distinction of his own, finds essential: Lack (L) and Lack Liquidated (LL), in a movement "from disequilibrium to equilibrium." Here is a schema, abstracted from Propp's, broad enough to describe, on a very high level of generality, the structure characteristic not only of North American Indian folktales but of the quest narrative—if not of narrative itself—in general: a structure involving transcendence of initial insufficiency through attainment of a new, though always provisional, equilibrium, in which that insufficiency is momentarily overcome.

Yet what is slighted in Dundes's simplified binary schema is precisely the indispensable mediation, or thirdness, of the quest itself: the *movement* by means of which the hero either overcomes lack or fails (as in many North American "Orpheus" tales) to reach a goal that lies, despite his best efforts, beyond him. The model minimally adequate to the quest narrative must therefore be not a binary but a ternary model. It must have a middle (as Aristotle understood) as well as a beginning and an end; and if the beginning is typically a disequilibrium, insufficiency, or lack, and the end its resolution in a new equilibrium, or the realization that such a condition is unattainable (the alternative comic

---

"the modern hero-deed must be that of questing to bring to light again the lost Atlantis of the co-ordinated soul." His association of the quest with a parade of Jungian archetypes and cosmogonic myths tends to be more hortatory than analytic. For Frye (187), the quest is initially "the element that gives literary form to the romance," one of his four archetypes, or *mythoi* (the others are comedy, tragedy, and irony/ satire). But since each stage of romance is later associated (192) with one of the archetypes, which all become aspects of a "central unifying myth," it appears that the quest, which extends through all four stages (each subdivided into six phases), gives form not only to romance but to a unifying monomyth (to adopt Campbell's term) in twenty-four phases. The reduction of all myths to one entails, for both Campbell and Frye, a kaleidoscopic multiplication of categories which does little to confirm or elucidate the myth's putative unity.

and tragic outcomes of narrative), the middle is the transitional state of the still-undetermined quest, the necessary liminal passage, in van Gennep's terms, from separation, or disrupted equilibrium, to reintegration through purposeful transcendence of the initially given condition of things.

Narrative may begin in lack and end in lack liquidated (or reaffirmed), but its crucial middle term is the uncertain quest to transcend that initial deficiency: the eternal deficiency, perhaps, of things as they are. The structure of this mediating quest, to which the narrative owes its movement in time and thus its existence, can no more be prescribed in advance or reduced to a single model or an inflexible sequence of functions or stages than the outcome of the quest can be predicted; the liminality in which the quest takes place is an "anti-structural" in-betweenness, and patterned variability, as we have repeatedly seen, is essential to it. Narrative, like metaphor, gives rise to semantic *innovation*, a process, Ricoeur suggests (1984, 9), that no predetermined structure can ever wholly delimit; for the only structures adequate to a genuine quest are the new ones it brings into being.

The quest is narrative movement; its reality a heuristic fiction; its goal a living metaphor of transcendence. And the space of this perennial narrative embraces its audience no less than its hero: in this, too, the quest is a mediating thirdness. The reader of a story, like the hearer of a myth or spectator of a shamanistic performance, "will only begin to search for (and so actualize) the meaning," Iser writes (43), "if he does not *know* it, and so it is the unknown factors in the text that set him off on his quest," a quest for meaning that unites him (through the narrative to which he too is essential) with the quest of his magnified alter ego, the mythic shaman or hero, who likewise cannot fully know in advance the goal for which he is searching. The hero's quest parallels and patterns that of the reader or listener, who becomes an active (and indispensable) participant in a narrative that would have no existence without her; in the hero's quest she finds a paradigm for her own, which only now becomes (intel)legible to her.

For fiction, Iser too understands (53), "is a means of telling us something about reality": a reality that each reader must construct by the creative interaction that constitutes the search for meaning, not of the text alone, but (through the text that links them) of self and world. The act of reading, like the speech act, transcends the self-referential closure of grammatical or textual sense (Frege's *Sinn*) in the meaning (*Bedeutung*) opened for each speaker or reader by reference to the world. "The ceaseless and inevitable quest for the meaning shows that in assembling the sense we ourselves become aware that something has happened to us, and so we try to find out its meaning. . . . Meaning is the reader's absorption of the sense into his own existence" (150–51);[7] and in this transformative assimilation—corresponding to van Gennep's third stage of the rite of passage—the reader's or listener's quest, like that of the hero or shaman who shows the way, finds fulfillment.

To say that the quest is a narrative and its truth a fiction, its reality a metaphor of transcendence, is not to reduce it to a mere rhetorical figure, then, with reference only to itself; for through this mediating narrative the participant reader or listener, to whom it is always addressed and without whom it would remain an unactualized potentiality, becomes herself the questing hero who goes beyond her given reality to seek the never fully determined meaning of her own existence. No narrative can fulfill its function without response by a listener or reader; no quest can attain its object without giving rise to further quests without ending. This incessant response is the ultimate (because never final) act of transcendence by which the quest as narrative goes on achieving its transformative goal, thus escaping the closure that would end and, by ending, annul it.

To contemporary deconstructionist rhetoricians, the last sad heirs of a Saussurean structuralism whose signs could signify only themselves, narrative movement, like production of meaning, is a self-defeating illusion that invariably runs aground on the impasse or "aporia" of language trapped by its own inescapably figurative nature. Rhetoric, by allowing for two mutually self-destructive points of view, "puts an insurmountable obstacle," de Man writes (131), "in the way of any reading or understanding." The deconstructionist paradoxes, like those of "cruel Zeno" of Elea in ancient times, reduce the appearance of movement to the wearisome recurrence of stasis and reveal the insuperable futility of any attempted transcendence, hence of any quest for the unpredictable or the new. Unmasking of the linguistic or rhetorical aporias by which we are eternally obstructed in our vain search for a meaningless "meaning" becomes in itself the one legitimate goal of our bleak intellectual endeavors: the end beyond which is nothing but more of the same.

Yet the aporia which our modern sophists see as the uniform end point of meanings unmasked as verbal illusions is only the starting point, the indispensable impetus, for the spiritual quest, by which the new and unpredictable is brought into being. Only after recognizing that we have come to an apparent impasse (perhaps through our own acedia or inertia) that impedes us from moving further or from moving at all, a laby-

---

7. I have changed Iser's "significance" to "meaning" and his "meaning" to "sense," to correspond to the translations of *Bedeutung* and *Sinn*, respectively, used in citing Frege elsewhere.

rinth or dark wood in which the right way is lost—for in finding metaphors for our plight we have already begun to move beyond it—can we
effect the difficult separation that initiates the ternary passage from our
accustomed state to another that can never be known till we have crossed
the uncertain threshold that links and divides them.

The supreme master of aporia, the unchallenged spinner of seemingly inescapable verbal perplexities, in our western philosophical tradition is Plato's ironical Socrates, whose reputation (as Meno says and
Socrates acknowledges) was to bring others to the seemingly inescapable
paralysis in which he continually found himself.[8] But the perplexity of a
mind confronted by its own resourceless impasse was never, for Socrates, an end to intellectual endeavor but a necessary first step toward the
awareness of ignorance that separates the truly wise from others and
instigates the transformative search for truth—as it does (*Meno* 84c) for
the puzzled slave boy who can only begin to correct the fallacies of common sense after "he has fallen into aporia by realizing he does not
know," and, in consequence of this crucial realization, has only now, for
the first time, *wanted* to know.

The quest is the active mind's response to recognition of impasse, yet
its object (Socrates says in expounding Meno's dilemma) can be neither
the known nor the wholly unknown (*Meno* 80e): "You would not seek
what you know, for if you know it you have no need to seek it; nor what
you are ignorant of, for then you do not know what to seek." Socrates's
immensely fruitful postulate that the immortal soul strives to remember
what it had previously known but has largely forgotten was one resolution to this aporia of aporias; *anamnêsis,* or remembrance of an all but
immemorial phylogenetic past, made it possible for the philosophically
trained mind to seek an otherwise inapprehensible knowledge of being.
Our alternative suggestion that the spiritual quest gives shape to a self-
transcendent impulse inherent in life, or in matter itself—to their potential, that is, for directional development toward an evolving and always
unpredictable goal—is perhaps an updated variation on Plato's: a variation firmly oriented, however, in its fully purposeful human form, toward individually variant exploration of the indeterminate future rather
than dim recollection of a changeless superpersonal past.

In either case, every hindrance is potentially a point of departure,
every aporia an opportunity to renew the quest for an object that cannot
be known (to add to Socrates's paradox) even when found, since it is
continually being transformed, and only thus can satisfy the human
need for a transcendence that has no terminus this side of death. Con-

---

8. *Meno* 80a ("autos te aporeis kai tous allous poieis aporein") and 80c ("autos aporôn
houtôs kai tous allous poiô aporein"); cf. *Theaetetus* 149a ("poiô tous anthrôpous aporein").

tradictions and perplexities there will always be once the soul has separated itself from the imprisoning ignorance of the cave which must be
left behind if the quest is ever to begin. "To reach an impasse and to
seek," *aporein kai zêtein,* are for Socrates one and the same, for the soul
that knows its own aporia "stirs up thought in itself" (*Republic* VII,
524e), thereby beginning the process that will lead beyond initial paralysis and isolation through creative liminal inquiry toward a new, if always
provisional, reintegration with the uncertain beyond. "To recognize a
potential limit," Gould writes (1993, 270), "is to think about tools of possible transcendence." This is the process of the spiritual quest for shaman and scientist, slave boy and philosopher alike: the process through
which our evolving humanity, resolutely transgressing the continual impasse of the given, steps repeatedly forth in quest of the transformative
and always future unknown.

"Nothing to be done," Estragon tells Vladimir at the beginning of Samuel
Beckett's tragicomedy *Waiting for Godot,* which ends with the stage direction: "*They
do not move.*"

"Knowing that nothing need be done," Gary Snyder observes (1974, 102), "is
where we begin to move from."

BIBLIOGRAPHY

ABBREVIATIONS

AAA Memoirs	Memoirs of the American Anthropological Association
AMNH Bulletin	Bulletin of the American Museum of Natural History
AMNH Papers	Anthropological Papers of the American Museum of Natural History
BAE Bulletin	Bulletin of the Smithsonian Institution Bureau of American Ethnology
BAE Report	Annual Report of the Smithsonian Institution Bureau of American Ethnology
JAF	*Journal of American Folk-Lore*
JRAI	*Journal of the Royal Anthropological Institute of Great Britain and Ireland*
SJA	*Southwestern Journal of Anthropology*
UCPAAE	University of California Publications in American Archaeology and Ethnology

WORKS CONSULTED

Aarsleff, Hans. 1982. *From Locke to Saussure: Essays on the Study of Language and Intellectual History*. Minneapolis: University of Minnesota Press.

Adair, James. 1968. *The History of the American Indians: Particularly those Nations adjoining to the Mississippi, East and West Florida, Georgia, South and North Carolina, and Virginia*. New York: Johnson Reprint. (1st ed. London, 1775.)

Adriani, N. See Downs, Richard Erskine.

Alekseenko, E. A. 1968. "The Cult of the Bear among the Ket (Yenisei Ostyaks)." In Diószegi 1968a, 175–91.

Alexander, Hartley Burr. 1953. *The World's Rim: Great Mysteries of the North American Indians.* Lincoln: University of Nebraska Press.

Amoss, Pamela. 1978. *Coast Salish Spirit Dancing: The Survival of an Ancestral Religion.* Seattle: University of Washington Press.

Andrews, Lynn V. 1981. *Medicine Woman.* San Francisco: Harper & Row.

———. 1984. *Flight of the Seventh Moon: The Teaching of the Shields.* San Francisco: Harper & Row.

Anisimov, A. F. 1963a. "Cosmological Concepts of the Peoples of the North." In Michael, 157–229. (Translation of *Kosmologicheskiye predstavleniya narodov-Severa.* Moscow and Leningrad, 1959.)

———. 1963b. "The Shaman's Tent of the Evenks and the Origin of the Shamanistic Rite." Trans. from *Trudy Instituta etnografii Akademii nauk SSSR* 18 (1952): 199–238. In Michael, 84–123.

Arriaga, Father Pablo Joseph de. 1968. *The Extirpation of Idolatry in Peru.* Trans. L. Clark Keating. Lexington: University of Kentucky Press. (Translation of *La extirpación de la idolatría en el Perú.* Lima, 1621.)

Atkinson, Jane Monnig. 1989. *The Art and Politics of Wana Shamanship.* Berkeley and Los Angeles: University of California Press.

Auden, W. H. 1961. "The Quest Hero." *Texas Quarterly* 4, no. 4: 81–93.

Austin, J. L. 1962. *Sense and Sensibilia.* Reconstructed from manuscript notes by G. J. Warnock. Oxford: Clarendon; rpt. Oxford University Press, 1964.

Awolalu, J. Omosade. 1979. *Yoruba Beliefs and Sacrificial Rites.* London: Longman.

Ayala, Francisco J. 1970. "Teleological Explanations in Evolutionary Biology." *Philosophy of Science* 37: 1–15.

Bachofen, J. J. 1967. *Myth, Religion, and Mother Right: Selected Writings of J. J. Bachofen.* Trans. Ralph Manheim. Princeton: Princeton University Press. (Translation of *Mutterrecht und Urreligion,* ed. Rudolf Marx. Stuttgart, 1926.)

Bäckman, Louise, and Åke Hultkrantz. 1978. *Studies in Lapp Shamanism.* Acta Universitatis Stockholmiensis: Stockholm Studies in Comparative Religion 16. Stockholm: Almqvist & Wicksell International, 1978.

Bacon, Francis. 1939. *Novum Organum.* In Edwin A. Burtt, ed., *English Philosophers from Bacon to Mill.* New York: Modern Library, 24–123. (First published 1620.)

Bakhtin, M. M. 1981. *The Dialogic Imagination: Four Essays.* Ed. Michael Holquist. Trans. Caryl Emerson and Michael Holquist. Austin: University of Texas Press. (Translation of *Voprosy literatury i estetiki.* Moscow, 1975.)

Balikci, Asen. 1970. *The Netsilik Eskimo.* Garden City, N.Y.: Natural History Press.

Barbeau, Marius. 1958. *Medicine-Men on the North Pacific Coast.* National Museum of Canada Bulletin no. 152, Anthropological Series no. 42. Ottawa: Department of Northern Affairs and National Resources.

Barber, Karin. 1981. "How Man Makes God in West Africa: Yoruba Attitudes Towards the Orisa." *Africa* 51: 724–45.

Barbour, Philip L., ed. 1969. *The Jamestown Voyages Under the First Charter, 1606–1609.* 2 vols. Works Issued by the Hakluyt Society, 2d ser., no. 137. Cambridge: Cambridge University Press.

Barnett, Homer. 1955. *The Coast Salish of British Columbia.* University of Oregon

Monographs, Studies in Anthropology, no. 4. Eugene: University of Oregon Press.

Barnouw, Victor. 1950. *Acculturation and Personality among the Wisconsin Chippewa.* AAA Memoirs, no. 72.

Barth, Fredrik. 1975. *Ritual and Knowledge among the Baktaman of New Guinea.* New Haven: Yale University Press.

Bartolomé, Miguel Alberto. 1977. *Orekuera Royhendu (lo que escuchamos en sueños): shamanismo y religión entre los Avá Katú Eté del Paraguay.* Serie Antropológica Social 17. Mexico: Instituto Indigenista Interamericano.

Bartram, William. 1928. *Travels of William Bartram.* Ed. Mark Van Doren. New York: Dover; rpt. 1955. (1st ed., *Travels through North and South Carolina, Georgia, East & West Florida. . . .* Philadelphia, 1791.)

Basso, Ellen B. 1973. *The Kalapalo Indians of Central Brazil.* New York: Holt, Rinehart and Winston.

Basso, Keith H. 1973. *The Cibecue Apache.* New York: Holt, Rinehart and Winston.

Bastide, Roger. 1961. *O Candomblé da Bahia (Rito Nagô).* Trans. Maria Isaura Pereira de Queiroz. São Paulo: Companhia Editora Nacional. (Translation of *Le Candomblé de Bahia.* Paris, 1951.)

———. 1973. *Estudos Afro-Brasileiros.* São Paulo: Editora Perspectiva.

———. 1978. *The African Religions of Brazil: Toward a Sociology of the Interpenetration of Civilizations.* Trans. Helen Sebba. Baltimore: Johns Hopkins University Press. (Translation of *Les Religions Afro-Brésiliennes.* Paris, 1960.)

Bastien, Joseph W. 1978. *Mountain of the Condor: Metaphor and Ritual in an Andean Ayllu.* St. Paul: West.

Bates, Elizabeth. 1976. *Language and Context: The Acquisition of Pragmatics.* New York: Academic Press.

Bateson, Gregory. 1958. *Naven: A Survey of the Problems Suggested by a Composite Picture of a New Guinea Tribe Drawn from Three Points of View.* 2d ed. Stanford, Calif.: Stanford University Press. (1st ed. London, 1936.)

Beals, Ralph L. 1943. *The Aboriginal Culture of the Cáhita Indians. Ibero-Americana* 19.

———. 1945a. *The Contemporary Culture of the Cáhita Indians.* BAE Bulletin 142.

———. 1945b. "Ethnology of the Western Mixe." UCPAAE 42, no. 1, 1–139.

Bean, Lowell J. 1972. *Mukat's People: The Cahuilla Indians of Southern California.* Berkeley and Los Angeles: University of California Press.

———. 1976a. "Power and Its Applications in Native California." In Bean and Blackburn, 407–20.

———. 1976b. "Social Organization in Native California." In Bean and Blackburn, 99–123.

———. 1978. "Cahuilla." In Heizer, 575–87.

———, and Thomas C. Blackburn, eds. 1976. *Native Californians: A Theoretical Retrospective.* Ramona, Calif.: Ballena Press.

———, and Florence C. Shipek. 1978. "Luiseño." In Heizer, 550–63.

———, and Sylvia Brakke Vane. 1978. "Cults and Their Transformations." In Heizer, 662–72.

————. See also Blackburn, Thomas C.

Beattie, John. 1964. "The Ghost Dance Cult in Bunyoro." *Ethnology* 3: 127–51.

————. 1969. "Spirit Mediumship in Bunyoro." In Beattie and Middleton, 159–70.

————, and John Middleton, eds. 1969. *Spirit Mediumship and Society in Africa*. New York: Africana.

Beckett, Samuel. 1954. *Waiting for Godot: Tragicomedy in Two Acts*. New York: Grove.

Beidelman, T. O. 1963. "Witchcraft in Ukaguru." In Middleton and Winter, 57–98.

Bellah, Robert N. 1959. "Durkheim and History." *American Sociological Review* 24: 447–61.

————. 1970. *Beyond Belief: Essays on Religion in a Post-Traditional World*. New York: Harper & Row.

Belo, Jane. 1960. *Trance in Bali*. New York: Columbia University Press.

Benedict, Ruth Fulton. 1922. "The Vision in Plains Culture." *American Anthropologist*, n.s., 24: 1–23.

————. 1923. "The Concept of the Guardian Spirit in North America." AAA Memoirs, no. 29, 3–97.

————. 1934. *Patterns of Culture*. Boston: Houghton Mifflin.

Bennett, Wendell C. 1947. "The Andean Highlands: An Introduction." In Steward 2: 1–60.

————, and Robert M. Zingg. 1935. *The Tarahumara: An Indian Tribe of Northern Mexico*. Chicago: University of Chicago Press.

Berger, Peter L. 1967. *The Sacred Canopy: Elements of a Sociological Theory of Religion*. Garden City, N.Y.: Doubleday.

————, and Thomas Luckmann. 1966. *The Social Construction of Reality: A Treatise in the Sociology of Knowledge*. Garden City, N.Y.: Doubleday.

Bergson, Henri. 1935. *The Two Sources of Morality and Religion*. Trans. R. Ashley Audra and Cloudesley Brereton, with the assistance of W. Horsfall Carter. New York: Holt; rpt. Garden City, N.Y.: Doubleday, 1954. (Translation of *Les deux sources de la morale et de la religion*. Paris, 1932.)

Bernbaum, Edwin. 1980. *The Way to Shambhala*. Garden City, N.Y.: Doubleday.

Berndt, Catherine H. See Berndt, Ronald M.

Berndt, Ronald M. 1951. *Kunapipi: A Study of an Australian Aboriginal Religious Cult*. New York: International Universities Press.

————, ed. 1970. *Australian Aboriginal Anthropology: Modern Studies in the Social Anthropology of the Australian Aborigines*. Nedlands, Western Australia: University of Western Australia Press, for the Australian Institute of Aboriginal Studies.

————. 1974. *Australian Aboriginal Religion*. 4 fascicles. Leiden: E. J. Brill.

————, and Catherine H. Berndt. 1970. *Man, Land and Myth in North Australia: The Guwinggu People*. East Lansing: Michigan State University Press.

Berreman, Gerald D. 1964. "Brahmins and Shamans in Pahari Religion." In Edward B. Hopper, ed., *Religion in South Asia*. Seattle: University of Washington Press, 53–69.

Bertalanffy, Ludwig von. 1952. *Problems of Life: An Evaluation of Modern Biological*

Thought. New York: John Wiley & Sons. (Translation of *Das biologische Weltbild.* Bern, 1949.)

————. 1968. *Organismic Psychology and Systems Theory.* Barre, Mass.: Clark University Press.

Best, Elsdon. 1924. *The Maori As He Was: A Brief Account of Maori Life As It Was in Pre-European Days.* Wellington, New Zealand: R. E. Owen.

————. 1954. *Some Aspects of Maori Myth and Religion.* Dominion Museum Monograph no. 1. Wellington, New Zealand: R. E. Owen.

————. 1959. *The Maori School of Learning: Its Objects, Methods, and Ceremonial.* Dominion Museum Monograph no. 6. Wellington, New Zealand: R. E. Owen.

————. 1972. *Tuhoe: The Children of the Mist. A Sketch of the Origin, History, Myths, and Beliefs of the Tuhoe Tribe of the Maori of New Zealand.* . . . 2d ed. 2 vols. Wellington, New Zealand: A. H. and A. W. Reed, for the Polynesian Society. (1st published 1925 as vol. 6 of the *Memoirs of the Polynesian Society.*)

Bharati, Agehananda, ed. 1976. *The Realm of the Extra-Human: Agents and Audiences.* The Hague: Mouton.

Biocca, Ettore. 1969. *Yanoáma: The Story of a Woman Abducted by Brazilian Indians.* Trans. Dennis Thodes. London: George Allen & Unwin.

Bjerke, Svein. 1981. *Religion and Misfortune: The Bacwezi Complex and Other Spirit Cults of the Zinza of Northwestern Tanzania.* Oslo: Universitetsforlaget.

Blackburn, Thomas C., ed. 1975. *December's Child: A Book of Chumash Oral Narratives.* Collected by J. P. Harrington. Berkeley and Los Angeles: University of California Press.

————, and Lowell John Bean. 1978. "Kitanemuk." In Heizer, 564–69.

Black Elk. See Brown, Joseph Epes; DeMallie, Raymond J.; Neihardt, John G.

Blacker, Carmen. 1975. *The Catalpa Bow: A Study of Shamanistic Practices in Japan.* London: Allen & Unwin.

Blair, Emma Helen, ed. 1911. *The Indian Tribes of the Upper Mississippi Valley and Region of the Great Lakes.* 2 vols. Cleveland: Arthur H. Clark.

Boas, Franz. 1964. *The Central Eskimo.* Lincoln: University of Nebraska Press. Originally published in 1888 as Sixth BAE Report for 1884–85, 399–669.

————. 1916. *Tsimshian Mythology.* Based on texts recorded by Henry W. Tate. Washington: BAE Report, vol. 31. Rpt. New York: Johnson Reprint, 1970.

————. 1940. *Race, Language and Culture.* New York: Free Press.

————. 1966a. Introduction to *Handbook of American Indian Languages.* Ed. Preston Holder. Lincoln: University of Nebraska Press. (1st ed. published 1911.)

————. 1966b. *Kwakiutl Ethnography.* Ed. Helen Codere. Chicago and London: University of Chicago Press.

————. 1975. *The Eskimos of Baffin Land and Hudson Bay.* From Notes Collected by Capt. George Comer, Capt. James S. Mutch, and Rev. E. J. Peck. AMNH Bulletin 15, part 1 (1901), part 2 (1907); rpt. New York: AMS Press.

Bödiger, Ute. 1965. *Die Religion der Tukano im nordwestlichen Amazonas.* Kölner Ethnologischen Mitteilungen 3. Cologne: Kölner Universitäts-Verlag.

Bogoras, W. 1909. *The Chukchee.* Memoirs of the American Museum of Natural History 11. Ed. Franz Boas. (Rpt. of the Jesup North Pacific Expedition 7, 1904–1909.) Leiden: E. J. Brill; rpt. New York: Johnson Reprint, n.d.

Bourguignon, Erika. 1965. "The Self, the Behavioral Environment, and the

Theory of Spirit Possession." In Melford E. Spiro, ed., *Context and Meaning in Cultural Anthropology*. New York: Free Press, 39–60.

———. 1968. "World Distribution and Pattern of Possession States." In Prince, 3–34.

———, ed. 1973. *Religion, Altered States of Consciousness, and Social Change*. Columbus: Ohio State University Press.

———. 1976. *Possession*. San Francisco: Chandler and Sharp.

Bourke, John G. 1889. "Notes on the Cosmogony and Theogony of the Mojave Indians of the Rio Colorado, Arizona." JAF 2: 169–89.

———. 1892. "The Medicine-Men of the Apache." Ninth BAE Report for 1887–88. Washington, 443–603.

———. 1920. *The Urine Dance of the Zuni Indians of New Mexico*. Not for General Perusal. From the Ethnological Notes Collected by Him under the Direction of Lieutenant General P. H. Sheridan, U.S. Army, in 1881. Privately printed. Rpt. Topeka, Kansas, 1959.

Boyd, Maurice. 1981. *Kiowa Voices: Ceremonial Dance, Ritual and Song*. 2 vols. Fort Worth: The Texas Christian University Press.

Brain, James L. 1981. "Ancestors as Elders in Africa: Further Thoughts." *Africa* 51: 724–45.

Bramly, Serge. 1977. *Macumba: The Teachings of Maria-José, Mother of the Gods*. Trans. Meg Bogin. New York: St. Martin's. (Translation of *Macumba, forces noires du Brésil*. Paris, 1975.)

Brandon, S. G. F. 1958. "The Myth and Ritual Position Critically Considered." In S. H. Hooke, ed., *Myth, Ritual, and Kingship: Essays on the Theory and Practice of Kingship in the Ancient Near East and in Israel*. Oxford: Clarendon, 251–91.

Brinton, Daniel G. 1894. "Nagualism: A Study in Native American Folk-Lore and History." *Proceedings of the American Philosophical Society* 33: 11–73.

Browman, David, and Ronald A. Schwarz, eds. 1979. *Spirits, Shamans, and Stars: Perspectives from South America*. The Hague: Mouton.

Brown, Jason W. 1972. *Aphasia, Apraxia and Agnosia: Clinical and Theoretical Aspects*. Springfield, Ill.: Charles C. Thomas.

———. 1977. *Mind, Brain, and Consciousness: The Neuro-psychology of Cognition*. New York: Academic Press.

Brown, Joseph Epes, ed. 1953. *The Sacred Pipe: Black Elk's Account of the Sacred Rites of the Oglala Sioux*. Norman: University of Oklahoma Press; rpt. Harmondsworth: Penguin, 1971.

Brundage, Burr Cartwright. 1963. *Empire of the Inca*. Norman: University of Oklahoma Press.

———. 1979. *The Fifth Sun: Aztec Gods, Aztec World*. Austin: University of Texas Press.

Bruner, Jerome S. 1972. "Nature and Uses of Immaturity." *American Psychologist* 27: 1–22. Rpt. in Bruner, Jolly, and Sylva, 28–64.

———. 1973. *Beyond the Information Given: Studies in the Psychology of Knowing*. Ed. Jeremy M. Anglin. New York: Norton.

———. 1974–75. "From Communication to Language—A Psychological Perspective." *Cognition* 3: 255–87.

———. 1978a. "On Prelinguistic Prerequisites of Speech." In Campbell and Smith, 199–214.

———. 1978b. "The Role of Dialogue in Language Acquisition." In Sinclair, et al., 241–56.

———, Eileen Caudill, and Anat Ninio. 1977. "Language and Experience." In R. S. Peters, ed., *John Dewey Reconsidered*. London: Routledge & Kegan Paul, 18–34.

———, Alison Jolly, and Kathy Sylva, eds. 1976. *Play—Its Role in Development and Evolution*. New York: Basic Books.

———. See also Sylva, Kathy.

Buechler, Hans C. 1980. *The Masked Media: Aymara Fiestas and Social Interaction in the Bolivian Highlands*. The Hague: Mouton.

Bulmer, R. N. H. 1965. "The Kyaka of the Western Highlands." In Lawrence and Meggitt, 132–61.

Bunzel, Ruth. 1932. "Introduction to Zuñi Ceremonialism"; "Zuñi Origin Myths"; "Zuñi Ritual Poetry"; "Zuñi Katcinas." In Forty-Seventh BAE Report for 1929–30, 467–544; 545–609; 611–835; 837–1086.

———. 1952. *Chichicastenango: A Guatemalan Village*. Publications of the American Ethnological Society 22. Locust Valley, N.Y.: J. J. Augustin.

Burkert, Walter. 1979. *Structure and History in Greek Mythology and Ritual*. Berkeley and Los Angeles: University of California Press.

Bushnell, David I., Jr. 1909. *The Choctaw of Bayou Lacomb, St. Tammany Parish, Louisiana*. BAE Bulletin 48.

Busia, K. A. 1954. "The Ashanti." In Forde 1954, 190–209.

Butt, Audrey. 1962. "Réalité et Idéal dans la pratique chamanique." *L'Homme: Revue française de l'anthropologie* 2, no. 3 (Sept.–Dec. 1962): 5–52.

Buxton, Jean. 1963. "Mandari Witchcraft." In Middleton and Winter, 99–121.

———. 1973. *Religion and Healing in Mandari*. Oxford: Clarendon.

Cabrera, Lydia. 1975. *El Monte: Igbo-Finda. Ewe Orisha. Vititi Nfinda*. (Notas sobre las religiones, la magia, las supersticiones y el folklore de los negros, criollos y el pueblo de Cuba.) 4th ed. Miami: Ediciones Universal.

Campbell, Jeremy. 1982. *Grammatical Man: Information, Entropy, Language, and Life*. New York: Simon and Schuster.

Campbell, Joseph. 1959. *The Masks of God: Primitive Mythology*. New York: Viking.

———. 1968. *The Hero with a Thousand Faces*. 2d ed. Princeton: Princeton University Press. (1st ed. Princeton, 1949.)

Campbell, Robin N., and Philip T. Smith, eds. 1978. *Recent Advances in the Psychology of Language: Language Development and Mother Child Interaction*. Proceedings of the first half of the Stirling Psychology of Language Conference . . . , 1976. New York and London: Plenum Press.

Carneiro, Edison. 1961. *Candomblés da Bahia*. 3d ed. Rio de Janeiro: Conquista.

Carrasco, Pedro. 1961. "The Civil-Religious Hierarchy in Mesoamerican Communities: Pre-Spanish Background and Colonial Development." *American Anthropologist*, n.s., 63: 483–97.

———. 1970. "Tarascan Folk Religion, Christian or Pagan?" In Walter Goldschmidt and Harry Hoijer, eds., *The Social Anthropology of Latin America: Essays in Honor of Ralph Leon Beals.* Latin American Studies 14. Los Angeles, 3–15.

Cassirer, Ernst. 1955. *The Philosophy of Symbolic Forms.* 1: *Language.* 2: *Mythical Thought.* Trans. Ralph Manheim. New Haven: Yale University Press. (Translation of *Philosophie der symbolischen Formen: Die Sprache; Das mythische Denken.* Berlin, 1923, 1925.)

Castaneda, Carlos. 1968. *The Teachings of Don Juan: A Yaqui Way of Knowledge.* Berkeley and Los Angeles: University of California Press; rpt. New York: Pocket Books, 1974.

Catlin, George. 1967. *O-kee-pa: A Religious Ceremony, and Other Customs of the Mandans.* New Haven: Yale University Press; rpt. Lincoln: University of Nebraska Press, 1976. (1st ed. London and Philadelphia, 1867.)

———. 1973. *Letters and Notes on the Manners, Customs, and Conditions of the North American Indians. Written during Eight Years' Travel (1832–1839) amongst the Wildest Tribes of Indians in North America.* 2 vols. New York: Dover. (1st ed. London, 1844.)

Caudill, Eileen. See Bruner, Jerome S.

Chadwick, Nora K. 1936. "The Spiritual Ideas and Experiences of the Tatars of Central Asia." *JRAI* 66: 291–329.

———. 1969. "The Epic Poetry of the Turkic Peoples of Central Asia." In H. Munro Chadwick and Nora K. Chadwick, *The Growth of Literature,* vol. 3 (Cambridge: Cambridge University Press, 1940), 1–226; rev. in Nora K. Chadwick and Victor Zhirmunsky, *Oral Epics of Central Asia.* London: Cambridge University Press, 1–267. (Original title: "The Oral Literature of the Tatars.")

Chagnon, Napoleon A. 1977. *Yanomamö: The Fierce People.* 2d ed. New York: Holt, Rinehart and Winston. (1st ed. 1968.)

Champlain, Samuel de. 1907. *Voyages of Samuel de Champlain.* Ed. W. L. Grant. New York: Scribner's. (First published 1613–1632.)

Chapman, Anne. 1982. *Drama and Power in a Hunting Society: The Selk'nam of Tierra del Fuego.* Cambridge: Cambridge University Press.

Cherry, Colin. 1966. *On Human Communication: A Review, A Survey, and a Criticism.* 2d ed. Cambridge, Mass.: MIT Press. (1st ed. 1957.)

Chomsky, Noam. 1957. *Syntactic Structures.* The Hague: Mouton.

———. 1964. *Current Issues in Linguistic Theory.* The Hague: Mouton.

———. 1965. *Aspects of the Theory of Syntax.* Cambridge, Mass.: MIT Press.

———. 1966. *Cartesian Linguistics: A Chapter in the History of Rationalist Thought.* New York: Harper & Row.

———. 1971. *Problems of Knowledge and Freedom.* The Russell Lectures. New York: Pantheon.

———. 1972a. *Language and Mind.* Enlarged edition. New York: Harcourt Brace Jovanovich.

———. 1972b. *Studies on Semantics in Generative Grammar.* The Hague: Mouton.

———. 1973. *For Reasons of State.* New York: Pantheon.

———. 1975. *Reflections on Language.* New York: Random House.

———. 1977. *Essays on Form and Interpretation.* New York: North Holland.

———. 1979. *Language and Responsibility.* Based on conversations with Mitsou

Ronat. Trans. John Viertel. New York: Pantheon. (Translation of *Dialogues avec Mitsou Ronat*. Paris, 1977.)

———. 1980. *Rules and Representations*. New York: Columbia University Press.

———. See also Piattelli-Palmarini, Massimo.

Chukovsky, Kornei. 1963. *From Two to Five*. Trans. and ed. Miriam Morton. Berkeley and Los Angeles: University of California Press. (Translation of *Malen'kie deti* [*Little Children*]. Leningrad, 1928.)

Cieza de León, Pedro de. 1959. *The Incas*. Trans. Harriet de Onis. Ed. Victor Wolfgang von Hagen. Norman: University of Oklahoma Press. (Translation of *La Crónica del Perú*. Part 1, Seville, 1553; part 2, Madrid, 1880.)

Clarke, Kenneth Wendell. 1958. *A Motif-Index of the Folktales of Culture Area V, West Africa*. Ph.D. diss., Department of Folklore, Indiana University. Ann Arbor, Mich.: University Microfilms, 1964.

Cobo, P. Bernabé. 1956. *Obras*. 2 vols. Biblioteca de Autores Españoles 91–92. Madrid: Atlas.

Codrington, R. H. 1891. *The Melanesians: Studies in Their Anthropology and Folk Lore*. Oxford: Clarendon; rpt. New York: Dover, 1972.

Coe, Michael D. 1966. *The Maya*. New York and Washington: Praeger.

Collins, June McCormick. 1974. *Valley of the Spirits: The Upper Skagit Indians of Western Washington*. Seattle: University of Washington Press.

Colson, Elizabeth. 1969. "Spirit Possession among the Tonga of Zambia." In Beattie and Middleton, 69–103.

Cooper, John M. 1944. "The Shaking Tent Rite among Plains and Forest Algonquians." *Primitive Man* 17: 60–84.

Copway, G. 1850. *The Traditional History and Characteristic Sketches of the Ojibway Nation*. London: Charles Gilpin; rpt. Toronto: Coles Publishing Co., 1972.

Courlander, Harold. 1960. *The Drum and the Hoe: Life and Lore of the Haitian People*. Berkeley and Los Angeles: University of California Press.

Crapanzano, Vincent, and Vivian Garrison, eds. 1977. *Case Studies in Spirit Possession*. New York: John Wiley & Sons.

Curtis, Edward S. 1907–1930. *The North American Indian: Being a Series of Volumes Picturing and Describing the Indians of the United States, the Dominion of Canada, and Alaska*. Ed. Frederick Webb Hodge. 20 vols. Rpt. New York and London: Johnson Reprint, 1970.

Cushing, Frank Hamilton. 1979. *Zuñi: Selected Writings of Frank Hamilton Cushing*. Ed. Jesse Green. Lincoln: University of Nebraska Press.

Czaplicka, M. A. 1914. *Aboriginal Siberia: A Study in Social Anthropology*. Oxford: Clarendon.

Darwin, Charles. 1859; rpt. 1968. *The Origin of Species by Means of Natural Selection; or, The Preservation of Favoured Races in the Struggle for Life*. Ed. J. W. Burrow. Harmondsworth: Penguin.

———. 1936. *The Descent of Man and Selection in Relation to Sex*. (Printed with *The Origin of Species*.) New York: Modern Library. (1st ed. London, 1871.)

———. 1962. *The Voyage of the Beagle*. Ed. Leonard Engel. Garden City, N.Y.: Doubleday Anchor. (1st ed. London, 1839; rev. 1845, 1860.)

David-Neel, Alexandra. 1931. *Magic and Mystery in Tibet*. London: The Bodley

Head; rpt. New York: Penguin, 1971. (Original title: *With Mystics and Magicians in Tibet*. Translation of *Parmi les mystiques et les magiciens du Tibet*. Paris, 1929.)

————, and the Lama Yongden. 1933; rev. ed. 1959. *The Superhuman Life of Gesar of Ling*. Trans. with the collaboration of Violet Sydney. London: Rider and Co.

Deardorff, Merle H. 1951. "The Religion of Handsome Lake: Its Origin and Development." In William N. Fenton, ed., *Symposium on Local Diversity in Iroquois Culture*. BAE Bulletin 149.

de Laguna, Frederica. 1972. *Under Mount Saint Elias: The History and Culture of the Yakutat Tlingit*. 3 parts. Smithsonian Contributions to Anthropology, vol. 7. Washington, D.C.: Smithsonian Institution Press.

de Laguna, Grace Andrus. 1927. *Speech: Its Function and Development*. New Haven: Yale University Press; rpt. Bloomington: Indiana University Press, 1963.

DeMallie, Raymond J., ed. 1984. *The Sixth Grandfather: Black Elk's Teachings Given to John G. Neihardt*. Lincoln: University of Nebraska Press.

de Man, Paul. 1979. *Allegories of Reading*. New Haven: Yale University Press.

Densmore, Frances. 1910. *Chippewa Music*. BAE Bulletin 45.

————. 1918. *Teton Sioux Music*. BAE Bulletin 61.

————. 1932a. *Chippewa Customs*. BAE Bulletin 86.

————. 1932b. *Menominee Music*. BAE Bulletin 102.

Deren, Maya. 1953. *Divine Horsemen: Voodoo Gods of Haiti*. London: Thames & Hudson; rpt. New York: Dell, 1972. (Original subtitle: *The Living Gods of Haiti*.)

Dewdney, Selwyn. 1975. *The Sacred Scrolls of the Southern Ojibway*. Toronto: University of Toronto Press, for the Glenbow-Alberta Institute, Calgary, Alberta.

Diószegi, V., ed. 1968a. *Popular Beliefs and Folklore Tradition in Siberia*. Bloomington: Indiana University.

————. 1968b. "The Problem of the Ethnic Homogeneity of Tofa (Karagas) Shamanism." In Diószegi 1968a, 239–329.

Dixon, Roland B. 1907. "The Shasta." AMNH Bulletin 17, part 5, 381–498.

————. 1908. "Some Aspects of the American Shaman." JAF 21: 1–12.

Dobzhansky, Theodosius. 1970. *Genetics of the Evolutionary Process*. New York and London: Columbia University Press.

————. 1974. "Chance and Creativity in Evolution." In Francisco José Ayala and Dobzhansky, eds., *Studies in the Philosophy of Biology: Reduction and Related Problems*. London: Macmillan, 307–38.

Dodds, E. R. 1951. *The Greeks and the Irrational*. Sather Classical Lectures, vol. 25. Berkeley and Los Angeles: University of California Press.

Donner, Florinda. 1982. *Shabono*. New York: Delacorte Press; rpt. New York: Dell, 1983.

Dorsey, George A. 1904. *Traditions of the Skidi Pawnee*. Boston: Houghton Mifflin, for the American Folk-Lore Society.

————. 1906. "Legend of the Teton Sioux Medicine Pipe." JAF 19: 326–29.

Douglas, Mary. 1966. *Purity and Danger: An Analysis of Concepts of Pollution and Taboo*. London: Routledge.

Downs, Richard Erskine. 1956. *The Religion of the Bare'e-Speaking Toradja of Cen-

tral Celebes. The Hague: Excelsior. (Summary and analysis of N. Adriani and A. C. Kruijt, *De Bare'e-Sprekende Toradjas van Midden-Celebes.* Batavia, 1912; 2d ed. Amsterdam, 1951–52.)

Dozier, Edward P. 1966a. *Hano: A Tewa Indian Community in Arizona.* New York: Holt, Rinehart and Winston.

———. 1966b. *The Pueblo Indians of North America.* New York: Holt, Rinehart and Winston.

Dreyfus, Hubert L. 1979. *What Computers Can't Do: The Limits of Artificial Intelligence.* Rev. ed. New York: Harper & Row. (1st ed. 1972.)

Drucker, Philip. 1951. *The Northern and Central Nootka Tribes.* BAE Bulletin 144.

———. 1955. *Indians of the Northwest Coast.* New York: McGraw-Hill; rpt. Garden City, N.Y.: Natural History Press, 1963.

———. 1965. *Cultures of the North Pacific Coast.* San Francisco: Chandler.

DuBois, Constance Goddard. 1908. "The Religion of the Luiseño Indians of Southern California." UCPAAE 8, no. 3, 69–186.

DuBois, Cora. 1935. "Wintu Ethnography." UCPAAE 36, no. 1: 1–147.

Dummett, Michael. 1973. *Frege: Philosophy of Language.* London: Duckworth.

Dundes, Alan. 1962. "Earth-Diver: Creation of the Mythopoeic Male." *American Anthropologist,* 64: 1032–51. Rpt. in Lessa and Vogt, 278–89.

———. 1964. *The Morphology of North American Indian Folktales.* Helsinki: Suomalainen Tiedeakatemia, Academia Scientiarum Fennica.

———. 1968. "Introduction to the Second Edition" of Propp 1968, xi–xvii.

Durán, Fray Diego. 1971. *Book of the Gods and Rites and the Ancient Calendar.* Trans. Hernando Horcasitas and Doris Hayden. Norman: University of Oklahoma Press. (Translation of *Ritos y fiestas de los antiguos mexicanos.* Written 1576–78; pub. Madrid, 1854.)

Durkheim, Emile. 1915. *The Elementary Forms of the Religious Life.* Trans. Joseph Ward Swain. London: Allen & Unwin; rpt. New York: Free Press, 1965. (Translation of *Les Formes élémentaires de la vie religieuse.* Paris, 1912.)

Eastman, Charles Alexander (Ohiyesa). 1911. *The Soul of the Indian: An Interpretation.* Boston: Houghton Mifflin; rpt. Lincoln: University of Nebraska Press, 1980.

Edelman, Gerald M. 1992. *Bright Air, Brilliant Fire: On the Matter of Mind.* New York: Basic Books.

Edmunds, R. David. 1983. *The Shawnee Prophet.* Lincoln: University of Nebraska Press.

Eggan, Fred. 1950. *Social Organization of the Western Pueblos.* Chicago: University of Chicago Press.

Eldredge, Niles. 1985. *Time Frames: The Rethinking of Darwinian Evolution and the Theory of Punctuated Equilibria.* New York: Simon and Schuster.

Eliade, Mircea. 1954. *Cosmos and History: The Myth of the Eternal Return.* Trans. Willard R. Trask. New York: Pantheon; rpt. New York: Harper & Row, 1959. (Originally titled *The Myth of the Eternal Return.* Translation of *Le Mythe de l'éternel retour.* Paris, 1949.)

———. 1958. *Rites and Symbols of Initiation: The Mysteries of Birth and Rebirth.* Trans. Willard R. Trask. New York: Harper; rpt. New York: Harper & Row, 1975. (Originally titled *Birth and Rebirth.*)

———. 1959. *The Sacred and the Profane: The Nature of Religion*. Trans. Willard R. Trask. New York: Harcourt, Brace; rpt. New York: Harper & Row, 1961. (Translation of *Das Heilige und das Profane*. Hamburg, 1957.)

———. 1961. "Recent Works on Shamanism: A Review Article." *History of Religions* 1: 152–86.

———. 1964. *Shamanism: Archaic Techniques of Ecstasy*. Trans. Willard R. Trask. Princeton: Princeton University Press. (Translation of *Le Chamanisme et les techniques archaïques de l'extase*. Paris, 1951.)

———. 1969. *The Quest: History and Meaning in Religion*. Chicago: University of Chicago Press.

———. 1971. *Australian Religions: An Introduction*. Ithaca: Cornell University Press.

Elkin, A. P. 1950. "The Religion of the Australian Aborigines." In Ferm, 273–85.

———. 1954. *The Australian Aborigines*. 3d ed. Sydney: Angus and Robertson; rpt. Garden City, N.Y.: Doubleday Anchor, 1964. (1st ed. 1938.)

———. 1978. *Aboriginal Men of High Degree*. 2d ed. New York: St. Martin's. (1st ed. 1945.)

Elliott, Alan J. A. 1955. *Chinese Spirit-Medium Cults in Singapore*. Monographs on Social Anthropology, n.s., no. 14. London: Department of Anthropology, London School of Economics and Political Science.

Elmendorf, William W. 1960. "The Structure of Twana Culture." Monographic supplement no. 2, *Research Studies: A Quarterly Publication of Washington State University* 28, no. 3; rpt. in *Coast Salish and Western Washington Indians IV*. New York: Garland, 1974.

Elwin, Verrier. 1939. *The Baiga*. London: John Murray.

———. 1950. *Bondo Highlander*. Bombay: Geoffrey Cumberlege, Oxford University Press.

———. 1955. *The Religion of an Indian Tribe*. Bombay: Geoffrey Cumberlege, Oxford University Press.

Endicott, Kirk Michael. 1970. *An Analysis of Malay Magic*. Oxford: Clarendon.

———. 1979. *Batek Negrito Religion: The World-View and Rituals of a Hunting and Gathering People of Peninsular Malaysia*. Oxford: Clarendon.

Endle, Sidney. 1911. *The Kacháris*. London: Macmillan.

Estrada, Alvaro. 1981. *María Sabina: Her Life and Chants*. Trans. Henry Munn. Santa Barbara: Ross-Erikson. (Translation of *Vida de María Sabina: la sabia de los hongos*. Mexico, 1977.)

Evans, Ivor H. N. 1923. *Studies in Religion, Folk-Lore, and Custom in British North Borneo and the Malay Peninsula*. Cambridge: Cambridge University Press; rpt. London: Frank Cass, 1970.

Evans-Pritchard, E. E. 1929. "The Morphology and Function of Magic: A Comparative Study of Trobriand and Zande Ritual and Spells." *American Anthropologist*, n.s., 31: 619–41.

———. 1937. *Witchcraft, Oracles and Magic among the Azande*. Oxford: Clarendon.

———. 1956. *Nuer Religion*. New York: Oxford University Press.

———. 1967. *The Zande Trickster*. Oxford: Clarendon.

Evans-Wentz, W. Y., ed. 1960. *The Tibetan Book of the Dead; or, The After-Death*

Experiences on the Bardo Plane, according to Lama Kazi Dawa-Sandup's English Rendering. London: Oxford University Press.

Ewers, John C. 1958. *The Blackfeet: Raiders on the Northwestern Plains.* Norman: University of Oklahoma Press.

Fabrega, Horacio, Jr., and Daniel B. Silver. 1973. *Illness and Shamanistic Curing in Zinacantan: An Ethnomedical Analysis.* Stanford, Calif.: Stanford University Press.

Fakhouri, Hani. 1968. "The Zar Cult in an Egyptian Village." *Anthropological Quarterly* 41: 49–65.

Faron, Louis C. 1964. *Hawks of the Sun: Mapuche Morality and Its Ritual Attributes.* Pittsburgh: University of Pittsburgh Press.

———. 1968. *The Mapuche Indians of Chile.* New York: Holt, Rinehart and Winston.

———. See also Steward, Julian H.

Feibleman, James K. 1946. *An Introduction to the Philosophy of Charles S. Peirce: Interpreted as a System.* New Orleans: Hauser; rpt. Cambridge, Mass.: MIT Press, 1970. (Originally titled *An Introduction to Peirce's Philosophy.*)

Fenton, William N. 1962. "This Island, the World on the Turtle's Back." JAF 75: 283–300.

———. 1978. "Northern Iroquoian Culture Patterns." In Trigger 1978, 296–321.

———. See also Parker, Arthur C.

Feraca, Stephen E. 1963. *Wakinyan: Contemporary Teton Dakota Religion.* Museum of the Plains Indian Studies in Plains Anthropology and History, no. 2. Browning, Mont.: Bureau of Indian Affairs, Department of the Interior, Blackfeet Agency.

Ferm, Vergilius, ed. 1950. *Forgotten Religions (Including Some Living Primitive Religions).* New York: The Philosophical Library.

Fiawoo, D. K. 1976. "Characteristic Features of Ewe Ancestor Worship." In Newell, 263–81.

Field, M. J. 1937. *Religion and Medicine of the Gā People.* London: Oxford University Press.

———. 1960. *Search for Security: An Ethno-Psychiatric Study of Rural Ghana.* Evanston, Ill.: Northwestern University Press.

———. 1969. "Spirit Possession in Ghana." In Beattie and Middleton, 3–13.

Fienup-Riordan, Ann. 1983. *The Nelson Island Eskimo: Social Structure and Ritual Distribution.* Anchorage: Alaska Pacific University Press.

Findeisen, Hans. *Schamanentum: dargestellt am Beispiel der Besessenheitspriester nordeurasiatischer Völker.* Stuttgart: Kohlhammer, 1957.

Finnegan, Ruth. 1970. "The Divination Poetry of Ifa." From *Oral Literature in Africa.* London: Oxford University Press, 191–203. Excerpted in Rothenberg and Rothenberg, 147–54.

Firth, Raymond. 1964. *Essays on Social Organization and Values.* London: University of London, Athlone Press.

———. 1967a. *Tikopia Ritual and Belief.* London: Allen & Unwin.

———. 1967b. *The Work of the Gods in Tikopia.* 2d ed. London: University of London, Athlone Press.

———. 1969. Foreword to Beattie and Middleton, ix–xiv.

———. 1970. *Rank and Religion in Tikopia: A Study in Polynesian Paganism and Conversion to Christianity*. Boston: Beacon.

Fitzhugh, William W., and Susan A. Kaplan. 1982. *Inua: Spirit World of the Bering Sea Eskimo*. Washington, D.C.: The Smithsonian Institution Press, for the National Museum of Natural History.

Fletcher, Alice C. 1904. Assisted by James R. Murie. *The Hako: A Pawnee Ceremony*. Twenty-seventh BAE Report for 1900–1901.

———, and Francis La Flesche. 1911. *The Omaha Tribe*. 2 vols. From Twenty-seventh BAE Report for 1905–1906; rpt. Lincoln: University of Nebraska Press, 1972.

Fock, Niels. 1963. *Waiwai: Religion and Society of an Amazonian Tribe*. Copenhagen: The National Museum.

Fontenrose, Joseph. 1966. *The Ritual Theory of Myth*. University of California Folklore Studies 18. Berkeley and Los Angeles: University of California Press.

Fools Crow. See Mails, Thomas E.

Forde, C. Daryll. 1931. "Ethnography of the Yuma Indians." UCPAAE 28, no. 4: 83–278.

———, ed. 1954. *African Worlds: Studies in the Cosmological Ideas and Social Values of African Peoples*. London: Oxford University Press, 1954.

Fortes, Meyer. 1949. *The Web of Kinship among the Tallensi: The Second Part of an Analysis of the Social Structure of a Trans-Volta Tribe*. London: Oxford University Press, for the International African Institute.

———. 1959. "Oedipus and Job in West African Religion." Cambridge: Cambridge University Press; rpt. in Charles Leslie, ed., *Anthropology of Folk Religion*. New York: Vintage, 1960, 5–52.

———. 1969. *Kinship and the Social Order: The Legacy of Lewis Henry Morgan*. Chicago: Aldine.

———. 1970. *Time and Social Structure and Other Essays*. London School of Economics Monographs on Social Anthropology, no. 40. London: The Athlone Press, University of London.

———. 1975. "Tallensi Prayer." In J. H. M. Beattie and R. G. Lienhardt, eds., *Studies in Social Anthropology: Essays in Memory of E. E. Evans-Pritchard by His Former Oxford Colleagues*. Oxford: Clarendon, 132–48.

———. 1976. "An Introductory Commentary." In Newell, 1–16.

———, and Dorothy Y. Mayer. 1966. "Psychosis and Social Change among the Tallensi of Northern Ghana." *Cahiers d'Etudes africaines* 6: 5–40.

Fortune, R. F. 1935. *Manus Religion: An Ethnological Study of the Manus Natives of the Admiralty Islands*. Philadelphia: The American Philosophical Society; rpt. Lincoln: University of Nebraska Press, n.d.

Foster, George M. 1944a. "Nagualism in Mexico and Guatemala." *Acta Americana* 2: 85–103.

———. 1944b. "A Summary of Yuki Culture." *University of California Publications in Anthropological Records* 5, no. 3: 155–244.

———. 1945. "Sierra Popoluca Folklore and Beliefs." UCPAAE 42, no. 2: 177–249.

Fox, J. Robin. 1964. "Witchcraft and Clanship in Cochiti Therapy." In Kiev, 174–200; rpt. in Middleton 1967b, 255–84.

Freeman, Derek. 1967. "Shaman and Incubus." In *The Psychoanalytic Study of Society*, vol. 4. Ed. Warner Muensterberger and Sidney Axelrad. New York: International Universities Press.

———. 1975. "The Iban of Sarawak and Their Religion: A Review Article." *Sarawak Museum Journal*, n.s., 23, no. 44 (July–Dec. 1975): 275–88.

Frege, Gottlob. 1980. *Translations from the Philosophical Writings*. Ed. Peter Geach and Max Black. 3d ed. Totowa, N.J.: Rowman and Littlefield.

Freud, Sigmund. 1928. *Beyond the Pleasure Principle*. Trans. James Strachey. New York: Liveright; rpt. New York: Bantam, 1959. (Translation of *Jenseits des Lustprinzips*. Leipzig, 1920.)

———. 1939. *Moses and Monotheism*. Trans. Katherine Jones. New York: Knopf; rpt. New York: Vintage 1955. (Translation of *Der Mann Moses und die monotheistische Religion*. Parts 1 and 2 first published in *Imago*, 1937.)

———. 1949. *An Outline of Psycho-Analysis*. Trans. James Strachey. New York: Norton; rpt. 1969. (Translation of *Abriss der Psychoanalyse*. First published in *Imago*, 1940.)

———. 1950. *Totem and Taboo: Some Points of Agreement between the Mental Lives of Savages and Neurotics*. Trans. James Strachey. New York: Norton. (Translation of *Totem und Tabu*. Vienna, 1913.)

———. 1959a. *Collected Papers*. Ed. Joan Riviere. Vols. 2 and 4. New York: Basic Books.

———. 1959b. *Inhibitions, Symptoms and Anxiety*. Trans. Alix Strachey. Rev. James Strachey. New York: Norton. (Translation of *Hemmung, Symptom und Angst*. Leipzig, 1926.)

———. 1959c. *The Question of Lay Analysis: Conversations with an Impartial Person*. Trans. James Strachey. New York: Norton; rpt. Garden City, N.Y.: Doubleday Anchor, 1964. (Translation of *Die Frage der Laienanalyse*. Leipzig, 1926.)

———. 1960. *The Ego and the Id*. Trans. Joan Riviere. Rev. James Strachey. New York: Norton. (Translation of *Das Ich und das Es*. Leipzig, 1923.)

———. 1961a. *Civilization and Its Discontents*. Trans. James Strachey. New York: Norton. (Translation of *Das Unbehagen in der Kultur*. Vienna, 1930.)

———. 1961b. *The Future of an Illusion*. Trans. James Strachey. New York: Norton. (Translation of *Die Zukunft einer Illusion*. Leipzig, 1927.)

———. 1965. *New Introductory Lectures on Psychoanalysis*. Trans. James Strachey. New York: Norton. (Translation of *Neue Folge der Vorlesungen zur Einführung in die Psychoanalyse*. Vienna, 1933.)

Frobenius, Leo. 1913. *The Voice of Africa: Being an Account of the German Inner African Exploration Expedition in the Years 1910–1912*. 2 vols. Trans. Rudolf Blind. London: Hutchinson. (Translation of *Und Afrika Sprach. . . .* Berlin, 1912.)

Frye, Northrop. 1957. *Anatomy of Criticism: Four Essays*. Princeton: Princeton University Press.

Fürer-Haimendorf, Christoph von. 1969. *The Konyak Nagas: An Indian Frontier Tribe*. New York: Holt, Rinehart and Winston.

Furst, Peter T. 1968. *The Parching of the Maize: An Essay on the Survival of Huichol Ritual. Acta Ethnologica et Linguistica*, no. 14.

Gadamer, Hans-Georg. 1975. *Truth and Method.* Translation ed. Garrett Barden and John Cumming. New York: Continuum. (Translation of *Wahrheit und Methode.* Tübingen, 1960; 2d ed. 1965.)

Garcilaso de la Vega, El Inca. 1966. *Royal Commentaries of the Incas and General History of Peru.* Trans. Harold V. Livermore. Two Parts. Austin: University of Texas Press. (Translation of *Comentarios reales.* Lisbon, 1609; Córdova, 1617.)

Gardner, Howard. 1985. *The Mind's New Science: A History of the Cognitive Revolution.* New York: Basic Books.

Gayton, A. H. 1930. "Yokuts-Mono Chiefs and Shamans." UCPAAE 24, no. 8: 361–420.

———. 1935. "The Orpheus Myth in North America." JAF 48: 263–93.

———. 1948. *Yokuts and Western Mono Ethnography* 1 and 2. *University of California Publications in Anthropological Records* 10, nos. 1 and 2.

Geddes, W. R. 1957. *Nine Dayak Nights.* London: Oxford University Press.

Geertz, Clifford. 1957. "Ritual and Social Change: A Javanese Example." *American Anthropologist*, n.s., 59: 32–54; abridged in Lessa and Vogt, 531–43.

———. 1960. *The Religion of Java.* New York: Free Press.

———. 1973. *The Interpretation of Cultures.* New York: Basic Books.

Gelfand, Michael. 1964. *Witch Doctor: Traditional Medicine Man of Rhodesia.* London: Harvill.

Genette, Gérard. 1980. *Narrative Discourse: An Essay in Method.* Trans. Jane E. Lewin. Ithaca: Cornell University Press. (Translation of "Discours du récit," from *Figures III.* Paris, 1972.)

Genova, Paul. See Sylva, Kathy.

Gillin, John. 1945. *Moche: A Peruvian Coastal Community.* Smithsonian Institution Institute of Social Anthropology, publication no. 3. Washington, D.C.: Government Printing Office.

Gluckman, Max, ed. 1962. *Essays on the Ritual of Social Relations.* Manchester: Manchester University Press.

———. 1963. *Order and Rebellion in Tribal Africa: Collected Essays with an Autobiographical Introduction.* New York: Free Press of Glencoe.

———. 1966. *Custom and Conflict in Africa.* Oxford: Basil Blackwell.

Goldman, Irving. 1963. *The Cubeo: Indians of the Northwest Amazon.* Illinois Studies in Anthropology, no. 2. Urbana: University of Illinois Press.

———. 1975. *The Mouth of Heaven: An Introduction to Kwakiutl Religious Thought.* New York: John Wiley & Sons.

González-Wipple, Migene. 1982. *The Santería Experience.* Englewood Cliffs, N.J.: Prentice-Hall.

Goodman, Nelson. 1971. "The Epistemological Argument." In J. R. Searle, ed., *The Philosophy of Language.* Oxford: Oxford University Press, 140–44.

———. 1976. *Languages of Art: An Approach to a Theory of Symbols.* Indianapolis: Hackett.

Goodwin, Grenville. 1938. "White Mountain Apache Religion." *American Anthropologist*, n.s., 40: 24–37.

————. 1939. *Myths and Tales of the White Mountain Apache.* Memoirs of the American Folk-Lore Society 33.

Gorer, Geoffrey. 1967. *Himalayan Village: An Account of the Lepchas of Sikkim.* 2d ed. New York: Basic Books. (1st ed. 1938.)

Gould, Stephen Jay. 1980. *The Panda's Thumb: More Reflections in Natural History.* New York: Norton.

————. 1987a. *Time's Arrow, Time's Cycle: Myth and Metaphor in the Discovery of Geological Time.* Cambridge, Mass.: Harvard University Press.

————. 1987b. *An Urchin in the Storm: Essays about Books and Ideas.* New York: Norton.

————. 1989. *Wonderful Life: The Burgess Shale and the Nature of History.* New York: Norton.

————. 1993. *Eight Little Piggies: Reflections in Natural History.* New York: Norton.

Greenberg, James B. 1981. *Santiago's Sword: Chatino Peasant Religion and Economics.* Berkeley and Los Angeles: University of California Press.

Gregor, Thomas. 1977. *Mehinaku: The Drama of Daily Life in a Brazilian Indian Village.* Chicago: University of Chicago Press.

Grey, Sir George. 1956. *Polynesian Mythology and Ancient Traditional History of the Maori as Told by Their Priests and Chiefs.* Ed. W. W. Bird. Christchurch, New Zealand: Whitcombe and Tombs. (1st Maori ed. 1854; 1st ed. in English 1855.)

Griffiths, Walter G. 1946. *The Kol Tribe of Central India.* Calcutta: Royal Asiatic Society of Bengal.

Grinnell, George Bird. 1889. *Pawnee Hero Stories and Folk-Tales, with Notes on the Origin, Customs and Character of the Pawnee People.* New York: Forest and Stream; rpt. Lincoln: University of Nebraska Press, 1961.

————. 1892. *Blackfoot Lodge Tales: The Story of a Prairie People.* New York: Scribner's; rpt. Lincoln: University of Nebraska Press, 1962.

————. 1920. *When Buffalo Ran.* New Haven: Yale University Press; rpt. Norman: University of Oklahoma Press, 1966.

————. 1923. *The Cheyenne Indians: Their History and Ways of Life.* 2 vols. New Haven: Yale University Press; rpt. Lincoln: University of Nebraska Press, 1972.

Groos, Karl. 1976. "The Play of Man: Teasing and Love-Play." From *The Play of Man.* Trans. Elizabeth L. Baldwin. London: Heinemann, 1901. In Bruner, Jolly, and Sylva, 68–83.

Guiteras-Holmes, C. 1961. *Perils of the Soul: The World View of a Tzotzil Indian.* New York: Free Press of Glencoe.

Gusinde, Martin. 1931. *Die Feuerland Indianer: Ergebnisse meiner vier Forschungsreisen in den Jahren 1918 bis 1924, unternommen in Auftrage des Ministerio de Instrucción pública de Chile.* Vol. 1: *Die Selk'nam: Vom Leben und Denken eines Jägervolkes auf der grossen Feuerlandinsel.* Mödling bei Wien: Verlag der internationalen Zeitschrift "Anthropos."

————. 1937. *Die Feuerland Indianer.* Vol. 2: *Die Yamana: Vom Leben und Denken der Wassernomaden am Kap Hoorn.* Mödling bei Wien: Verlag der internationalen Zeitschrift "Anthropos."

———. 1975. *Folk Literature of the Selknam Indians: Martin Gusinde's Collection of Selknam Narratives*. Ed. Johannes Wilbert. Los Angeles: UCLA Latin American Center Publications. (Trans. from *Die Feuerland Indianer*, vol. 1.)

———. 1961. *The Yamana: The Life and Thought of the Water Nomads of Cape Horn.* 5 vols. Trans. Frieda Schütze. New Haven: Human Relations Area Files. (Translation of *Die Feuerland Indianer*, vol. 2.)

Haberland, Eike, Meinhardt Schuster, and Helmut Straube, eds. 1974. *Festschrift für Ad. E. Jensen.* 2 vols. Munich: Klaus Renner.

Haeberlin, Herman K. 1918. "SBETETDAQ, A Shamanistic Performance of the Coast Salish." *American Anthropologist*, n.s., 20: 249–57.

Haeberlin, Hermann, and Erna Gunther. 1930. "The Indians of Puget Sound." *University of Washington Publications in Anthropology* 4, no. 1: 1–83.

Haile, Father Berard, O.F.M. 1981. *The Upward Moving and Emergence Way.* Ed. Karl W. Luckert. Lincoln: University of Nebraska Press.

Halliday, M. A. K. 1973. *Explorations in the Functions of Language.* London: Edward Arnold; rpt. New York: Elsevier North-Holland, 1977.

———. 1975. *Learning How to Mean: Explorations in the Development of Language.* London: Edward Arnold; rpt. New York: Elsevier, 1977.

Hallowell, A. Irving. 1926. "Bear Ceremonialism in the Northern Hemisphere." *American Anthropologist*, n.s., 28: 1–175.

———. 1942. *The Role of Conjuring in Saulteaux Society.* Publications of the Philadelphia Anthropological Society, vol. 2. Philadelphia: University of Pennsylvania Press; rpt. New York: Octagon, 1971.

———. 1955. *Culture and Experience.* Philadelphia: University of Pennsylvania Press.

———. 1960. "Ojibwa Ontology, Behavior, and World View." In Stanley Diamond, ed. *Culture in History: Essays in Honor of Paul Radin.* New York: Columbia University Press, 1952. Rpt. in Dennis Tedlock and Barbara Tedlock, eds., *Teachings from the American Earth: Indian Religion and Philosophy.* New York: Liveright, 1975, 141–78.

———. 1976. *Contributions to Anthropology: Selected Papers of A. Irving Hallowell.* Chicago: University of Chicago Press.

Hallpike, C.R. 1972. *The Konso of Ethiopia: A Study of the Values of a Cushitic People.* Oxford: Clarendon.

———. 1977. *Bloodshed and Vengeance in the Papuan Mountains: The Generation of Conflict in Tauade Society.* Oxford: Clarendon.

———. 1979. *The Foundations of Primitive Thought.* Oxford: Clarendon.

———. 1988. *The Principles of Social Evolution.* Oxford: Clarendon.

Handy, E. S. Craighill. 1927. *Polynesian Religion.* Bernice P. Bishop Museum Bulletin 34. Honolulu: The Museum.

Harner, Michael J. 1972. *The Jívaro: People of the Sacred Waterfalls.* Garden City, N.Y.: Natural History Press; rpt. Garden City, N.Y.: Doubleday Anchor, 1973.

———. 1973a. "Common Themes in South American Indian Yagé Experiences." In Harner 1973b, 155–75.

———, ed. 1973b. *Hallucinogens and Shamanism.* London: Oxford University Press.

Harries, Karsten. 1979. "Metaphor and Transcendence." In Sacks, 71–88.

Harrington, John P. 1908. "A Yuma Account of Origins." JAF 21: 324–48.

———. See also Blackburn, Thomas C.

Harrington, M. R. 1913. "A Preliminary Sketch of Lenápe Culture." *American Anthropologist*, n.s., 15: 208–35.

———. 1921. *Religion and Ceremonies of the Lenape*. Indian Notes and Monographs, New York: Museum of the American Indian, Heye Foundation.

Harris, Marvin. 1974. *Cows, Pigs, Wars, and Witches: The Riddles of Culture*. New York: Random House.

Harva (Holmberg), Uno. 1927. *Finno-Ugric [and] Siberian Mythology*. Vol. 4 of Canon John Arnott MacCullock, ed., *The Mythology of All Races*. Boston: Archaeological Institute of America, Marshall Jones Co.

———. 1938. *Die religiösen Vorstellungen der altaischen Völker*. FF Communications 52, no. 125. Helsinki: Suomalainen Tiedeakatemia. (First published in Finnish, 1933.)

Heidegger, Martin. 1953. *Sein und Zeit*. 7th ed. Tübingen: Max Niemeyer Verlag. (1st ed. 1927.)

———. 1959. *An Introduction to Metaphysics*. Trans. Ralph Manheim. New Haven: Yale University Press. (Translation of *Einführung in die Metaphysik*. Tübingen, 1953.)

———. 1962a. *Being and Time*. Trans. John Macquarrie and Edward Robinson. New York: Harper & Row. (Translation of Heidegger 1953.)

———. 1962b. *Kant and the Problem of Metaphysics*. Trans. James S. Churchill. Bloomington: Indiana University Press. (Translation of *Kant und das Problem der Metaphysik*. Frankfurt, 1929.)

———. 1968. *What Is Called Thinking?* Trans. Fred D. Wieck and J. Glenn Gray. New York: Harper & Row. (Translation of *Was Heisst Denken?* Tübingen, 1954.)

———. 1971. *Poetry, Language, Thought*. Trans. Albert Hofstadter. New York: Harper & Row.

Heizer, Robert, ed. 1978. *Handbook of North American Indians*, ed. William C. Sturtevant. Vol. 8: *California*. Washington, D.C.: Smithsonian Institution.

Herdt, Gilbert H. 1981. *Guardians of the Flute: Idioms of Masculinity*. New York: McGraw Hill.

———, ed. 1982. *Rituals of Manhood: Male Initiation in Papua New Guinea*. Berkeley and Los Angeles: University of California Press.

Herodotus. 1972. *The Histories*. Trans. Aubrey de Sélincourt. Revised by A. R. Burn. Harmondsworth: Penguin, 1972. (Translation first published 1954.)

Herskovits, Melville J. 1937. *Life in a Haitian Valley*. New York: Knopf; rpt. New York: Octagon, 1964.

———. 1938. *Dahomey: An Ancient West African Kingdom*. 2 vols. New York: J. J. Augustin.

———. 1966. *The New World Negro: Selected Papers in Afroamerican Studies*. Ed. Frances S. Herskovits. Bloomington: Indiana University Press.

———, and Frances S. Herskovits. 1958. *Dahomean Narrative: A Cross-Cultural Analysis*. Evanston, Ill.: Northwestern University Press.

Hewitt, J. N. B. 1903. "Iroquoian Cosmology, First Part." Twenty-first BAE Report for 1899–1900, 127–339.

———. 1928. "Iroquoian Cosmology, Second Part." Forty-third BAE Report for 1925–1926, 449–819.

Hickerson, Harold. 1963. "The Sociohistorical Significance of Two Chippewa Ceremonials." *American Anthropologist* 65: 67–85.

Highwater, Jamake. 1977. *Anpao: An American Indian Odyssey*. New York: Lippincott; rpt. New York: Harper & Row, 1980.

Hocart, A. M. 1970. *Kings and Councillors: An Essay in the Comparative Anatomy of Human Society*. Ed. Rodney Needham. Chicago: University of Chicago Press. (First published Cairo, 1936.)

Hoffman, Walter James. 1891. "The Midewiwin or 'Grand Medicine Society' of the Ojibwa." Seventh BAE Report for 1885–1886, 143–300.

———. 1896. *The Menomini Indians*. Fourteenth BAE Report for 1892–1893; rpt. New York and London: Johnson Reprint, 1970.

Hoffmann, Helmut. 1961. *The Religions of Tibet*. Trans. Edward Fitzgerald. New York: Macmillan. (Translation of *Die Religionen Tibets*. Freiburg, 1956.)

Hogbin, H. Ian. 1939. *Experiments in Civilization: The Effects of European Culture on a Native Community of the Solomon Islands*. London: Routledge; rpt. New York: Schocken, 1970.

———. 1947–48. "Pagan Religion in a New Guinea Village." *Oceania* 18: 120–45; rpt. in Middleton 1967a, 41–75.

Holmberg, Uno. See Harva.

Hookway, Christopher. 1985. *Peirce*. London: Routledge & Kegan Paul.

Horton, Robin. 1969. "Types of Spirit Possession in Kalabari Religion." In Beattie and Middleton, 14–49.

Hose, Charles, and William McDougall. 1912. *The Pagan Tribes of Borneo: A Description of Their Physical, Moral and Intellectual Condition with Some Discussion of Their Ethnic Relations*. 2 vols. London: Macmillan.

Howitt, A. W. 1887. "On Australian Medicine Men; or, Doctors and Wizards of Some Australian Tribes." *Journal of the Anthropological Institute of Great Britain and Ireland* 16: 23–59.

———. 1904. *The Native Tribes of South-East Australia*. London: Macmillan.

Hudson, Charles. 1976. *The Southeastern Indians*. Knoxville: University of Tennessee Press.

Hugh-Jones, Christine. 1979. *From the Milk River: Spatial and Temporal Processes in Northwest Amazonia*. Cambridge Studies in Social Anthropology 26. Cambridge: Cambridge University Press.

Hugh-Jones, Stephen. 1979. *The Palm and the Pleiades: Initiation and Cosmology in Northwest Amazonia*. Cambridge Studies in Social Anthropology 24. Cambridge: Cambridge University Press.

Hultkrantz, Åke. 1953. *Conceptions of the Soul among North American Indians: A Study in Religious Ethnology*. Stockholm: The Ethnographical Museum of Sweden.

———. 1957. *The North American Indian Orpheus Tradition: A Contribution to Comparative Religion*. Stockholm: The Ethnographical Museum of Sweden Monograph Series, no. 2.

———. 1973. "A Definition of Shamanism." *Temenos* 9: 25–37.

————. 1979. *The Religions of the American Indians*. Trans. Monica Setterwall. Berkeley and Los Angeles: University of California Press. (Translation of *De Amerikanska Indianernas Religioner*. Stockholm, 1967.)

————. 1981. *Belief and Worship in Native North America*. Ed. Christopher Vecsey. Syracuse, N.Y.: Syracuse University Press.

————. See also Bäckman, Louise; Paulson, Ivar.

Humboldt, Wilhelm von. 1827. *Ueber den Dualis*. In *Werke in fünf Bänden* 3: *Schriften zur Sprachphilosophie*. Stuttgart: Cotta, 1963, 113–43.

————. 1972. *Linguistic Variability and Intellectual Development*. Trans. George C. Buck and Frithjof A. Raven. Philadelphia: University of Pennsylvania Press. (Translation of *Ueber die Verschiedenheit des menschlichen Sprachbaues und ihren Einfluss auf die geistige Entwickelung des Menschengeschlechts*. Berlin, 1836.)

Hurt, Wesley R., Jr., and James H. Howard. 1952. "A Dakota Conjuring Ceremony." *SJA* 8: 286–96.

Idowu, E. Bolaji. 1963. *Olódùmarè: God in Yoruba Belief*. New York: Praeger.

Im Thurn, Everard F. 1883. *Among the Indians of Guiana: Being Sketches Chiefly Anthropologic from the Interior of British Guiana*. London: Kegan Paul, Trench, & Co.

Iser, Wolfgang. 1978. *The Act of Reading: A Theory of Aesthetic Response*. Baltimore: Johns Hopkins University Press. (Translation of *Der Akt des Lesens: Theorie ästhetischer Wirkung*. Munich, 1976.)

Jackson, Jean E. 1983. *The Fish People: Linguistic Exogamy and Tukanoan Identity in Northwest Amazonia*. Cambridge Studies in Social Anthropology 39. Cambridge: Cambridge University Press.

Jacob, François. 1982. *The Possible and the Actual*. New York: Pantheon.

Jakobson, Roman. 1962. *Selected Writings* 1: *Phonological Studies*. The Hague: Mouton.

————. 1971. *Selected Writings* 2: *Word and Language*. The Hague: Mouton.

————. 1973. *Main Trends in the Science of Language*. London: Allen & Unwin; rpt. New York: Harper & Row, 1974. Incorporates the papers "Retrospect" (1972) and "Linguistics in Relation to Other Sciences" (1967) printed in *Selected Writings* 2: 711–22 and 655–96.

————. 1978. *Six Lectures on Sound and Meaning*. Trans. John Mepham. Cambridge, Mass.: MIT Press. (Translation of *Six leçons sur le son et le sens*. Paris, 1976, reprinting lectures delivered in New York, 1942–43.)

————. 1980. *Brain and Language: Cerebral Hemispheres and Linguistic Structure in Mutual Light*. With the assistance of Kathy Santilli. Columbus, Ohio: Slavica Publishers.

————, and Linda Waugh. 1979. *The Sound Shape of Language*. Assisted by Martha Taylor. Bloomington: Indiana University Press.

James, William. 1902. *The Varieties of Religious Experience: A Study in Human Nature*. The Gifford Lectures on Natural Religion delivered at Edinburgh in 1901–1902. New York: Longmans, Green; rpt. New York: Modern Library, n.d.

Jenness, Diamond. 1935. *The Ojibwa Indians of Parry Island, Their Social and Reli-*

gious Life. National Museum of Canada Bulletin no. 78. Ottawa: J. O. Patenaude.

Jensen, Adolf. 1963. *Myth and Cult among Primitive Peoples*. Trans. Marianna Tax Choldin and Wolfgang Weissleder. Chicago: University of Chicago Press. (Translation of *Mythos und Kult bei Naturvölkern*. Wiesbaden, 1951.)

Jensen, Erik. 1974. *The Iban and Their Religion*. Oxford: Clarendon.

Jettmar, Karl. See Paulson, Ivar.

Jochelson, Waldemar. 1908. *The Koryak*. The Jesup North Pacific Expedition, vol. 6. Leiden: E. J. Brill; rpt. New York: AMS Press, 1975.

———. 1926. *The Yukaghir and the Yukaghirized Tungus*. The Jesup North Pacific Expedition, vol. 9. Leiden: E. J. Brill.

Johansen, J. Prytz. 1954. *The Maori and His Religion in Its Non-Ritual Aspects*. Copenhagen: Munksgaard.

———. 1958. *Studies in Maori Rites and Myths*. Copenhagen: Munksgaard.

Johnson, Richard. 1907. "Certaine notes unperfectly written by Richard Johnson servant to Master Richard Chancelour, which was in the discoverie of Vaigatz and Nova Zembla, with Steven Burrowe in the Serchthrift 1556. and afterwarde among the Samoedes, whose devilish rites hee describeth." In Richard Hakluyt, ed., *The Principal Navigations*. . . . London: Dent, 1907, 1: 352–56. (1st ed. 1589.)

Jung, C. G. 1956. *Symbols of Transformation: An Analysis of the Prelude to a Case of Schizophrenia*. 2 vols. Trans. R. F. C. Hull. New York: Pantheon; rpt. New York: Harper, 1962. (Translation of *Symbole der Wandlung*. Zurich, 1952. 4th ed., rewritten, of *Wandlungen und Symbole der Libido*. Leipzig, 1912.)

———. 1962. "Commentary." In Richard Wilhelm, trans. *The Secret of the Golden Flower: A Chinese Book of Life*. Rev. ed. New York: Harcourt Brace Jovanovich. (English translation by Cary F. Baynes of Richard Wilhelm's German translation, *Das Geheimnis der goldenen Blüte: Ein chinesisches Lebensbuch*, of the Chinese *T'ai I Chin Hua Tsung Chih*. Munich, 1929.)

———. 1971. *The Portable Jung*. Ed. Joseph Campbell. Trans. R. F. C. Hull. New York: Viking; rpt. Harmondsworth: Penguin, 1976.

———, and C. Kerényi. 1963. *Essays on a Science of Mythology: The Myths of the Divine Child and the Divine Maiden*. Rev. ed. Trans. R. F. C. Hull. New York: Harper & Row, 1963. (Translation of *Einführung in das Wesen der Mythologie*. Amsterdam, 1941.)

Kant, Immanuel. 1951. *Critique of Judgment*. Trans. J. H. Bernard. New York and London: Hafner. (Translation of *Kritik der Urteilskraft*. Berlin, 1790.)

Kaplan, Susan A. See Fitzhugh, William W.

Karmiloff-Smith, Annette. 1978. "The Interplay between Syntax, Semantics and Phonology in Language Acquisition Processes." In Campbell and Smith, 1–23.

———. 1979. *A Functional Approach to Child Language: A Study of Determiners and Reference*. Cambridge: Cambridge University Press.

Karsten, Rafael. 1935. *The Head-Hunters of Western Amazonas: The Life and Culture of the Jibaro Indians of Eastern Ecuador and Peru*. Helsingfors: Societas Scientiarum Fennica.

————. 1955. *The Religion of the Samek: Ancient Beliefs and Cults of the Scandinavian and Finnish Lapps.* Leiden: E. J. Brill.

Keesing, Roger M. 1970. "Shrines, Ancestors, and Cognatic Descent: The Kwaio and Tallensi." *American Anthropologist*, n.s., 72: 755–75.

————. 1982a. "Introduction" to Herdt 1982, 1–43.

————. 1982b. *Kwaio Religion: The Living and the Dead in a Solomon Island Society.* New York: Columbia University Press.

Kelly, Isabel T. 1966. "World View of a Highland-Totonac Pueblo." In Pompa y Pompa, 395–411.

Kelly, William H. 1977. *Cocopa Ethnography.* Anthropological Papers of the University of Arizona, no. 29. Tucson: University of Arizona Press.

Kennedy, John G. 1978. *Tarahumara of the Sierra Madre: Beer, Ecology, and Social Organization.* Arlington Heights, Ill.: AHM.

Kensinger, Kenneth M. 1973. "*Banisteriopsis* Usage among the Peruvian Cashinahua." In Harner 1973b, 9–14.

Kenton, Edna, ed. 1927. *The Indians of North America.* 2 vols. New York: Harcourt, Brace. (Selections from Reuben Gold Thwaites, ed. *The Jesuit Relations and Allied Documents.* 73 vols. Cleveland, 1896–1901.)

Kessler, Clive S. 1977. "Conflict and Sovereignty in Kelantanese Malay Spirit Seances." In Crapanzano and Garrison, 295–331.

Kierkegaard, Soren. 1941. *Concluding Unscientific Postscript to the Philosophical Fragments: A Mimic-Pathetic-Dialectic Composition, An Existential Contribution, by Johannes Climacus.* Trans. David F. Swenson and Walter Lowrie. Princeton: Princeton University Press. (Translation of *Afsluttende uvidenskabelig efterskrift.* Copenhagen, 1846.)

Kiev, Ari, ed. 1964. *Magic, Faith, and Healing: Studies in Primitive Psychology Today.* New York: Free Press of Glencoe.

King, Jeff. 1967. *Where the Two Came to Their Father: A Navaho War Ceremonial.* Text and Paintings Recorded by Maud Oakes. Commentary by Joseph Campbell. 2d ed. Princeton: Princeton University Press. (1st ed. 1943.)

Kinietz, W. Vernon. 1940. *The Indians of the Western Great Lakes, 1615–1760.* Ann Arbor: University of Michigan Press.

Kirby, Ernest Theodore. 1975. "Shamanistic Theatre: Origins and Evolution." From *Ur-Drama: The Origins of Theatre.* New York: New York University Press, 1–31. Excerpted in Rothenberg and Rothenberg, 257–70.

Kirk, G. S. 1970. *Myth: Its Meaning and Function in Ancient and Other Cultures.* Sather Classical Lectures, vol. 40. Berkeley and Los Angeles: University of California Press.

Kitagawa, Joseph M. 1961–62. "Ainu Bear Festival (Iyomante)." *History of Religions* 1: 95–151.

Klah, Hasteen. 1942. *Navajo Creation Myth: The Story of the Emergence.* Recorded by Mary C. Wheelwright. Navajo Religion Series, vol. 1. Santa Fe, N.M.: Museum of Navajo Ceremonial Art; rpt. New York: AMS Press, 1980.

Kluckhohn, Clyde. 1942. "Myths and Rituals: A General Theory." *Harvard Theological Review* 35: 45–79. Rpt. in Lessa and Vogt, 93–105.

————. 1944. *Navaho Witchcraft.* Cambridge, Mass.: Harvard University Press; rpt. Boston: Beacon, 1967.

————, and Dorothea Leighton. 1962. *The Navaho.* Rev. ed. Garden City, N.Y.: Doubleday Anchor. (1st ed. Cambridge, Mass., 1946.)

Koch-Grünberg, Theodor. 1923. *Vom Roroima zum Orinoco: Ergebnisse einer Reise in Nordbrasilien und Venezuela in den Jahren 1911–1913,* vol. 3: *Ethnographie.* Stuttgart: Strecker und Schröder.

Kohl, J. G. 1860. *Kitchi-Gami: Wanderings Round Lake Superior.* London: Chapman and Hall; rpt. Minneapolis: Ross and Haines, 1956. (Translation of *Kitchi-Gami.* Bremen, 1859.)

Kopytoff, Igor. 1971. "Ancestors as Elders in Africa." *Africa* 41: 129–42.

Krader, Lawrence. 1954. "Buryat Religion and Society." *SJA* 10: 322–51. Rpt. in Middleton 1967a, 103–32.

Kripke, Saul A. 1980. *Naming and Necessity.* Cambridge, Mass.: Harvard University Press, 1980. (Lectures given at Princeton University; first published in D. Davidson and G. Harman, eds., *The Semantics of Natural Language,* 254–355. Dordrecht, 1972.)

Kroeber, Alfred L. 1907. "The Religion of the Indians of California." UCPAAE 4, no. 6: 310–56.

————. 1925. *Handbook of the Indians of California.* BAE Bulletin 78; rpt. New York: Dover, 1976.

————. 1932. "The Patwin and Their Neighbors." UCPAAE 29, no. 4, 253–423.

————. *The Arapaho.* 1983. Lincoln: University of Nebraska Press. (First published in 3 parts in the AMNH Bulletin. New York, 1902, 1904, 1907.)

————, and E. W. Gifford. 1949. "World Renewal: A Cult System of Native Northwest California." *University of California Publications in Anthropological Records* 13, no. 1: 1–155.

Kruijt (Kruyt), Alb. C. See Downs, Richard Erskine.

Kuhn, Thomas S. 1970. *The Structure of Scientific Revolutions.* 2d ed. International Encyclopedia of Unified Science 2, no. 2. Chicago: University of Chicago Press. (1st ed. 1962.)

————. 1977. *The Essential Tension: Selected Studies in Scientific Tradition and Change.* Chicago: University of Chicago Press.

La Barre, Weston. 1948. *The Aymara Indians of the Lake Titicaca Plateau, Bolivia.* AAA Memoirs, no. 68.

————. 1970. *The Ghost Dance: Origins of Religion.* New York: Doubleday; rpt. New York: Dell, 1972.

————. 1975. *The Peyote Cult.* 4th ed., enlarged. New York: Schocken. (First published as Yale University Publications in Anthropology, no. 19 [1938], with new materials appended in 1960, 1969, and 1975.)

La Farge, Oliver. 1947. *Santa Eulalia: The Religion of a Cuchumatán Indian Town.* Chicago: University of Chicago Press.

————, and Douglas Byers. 1931. *The Year Bearer's People.* The Tulane University of Louisiana Middle American Research Series Publication no. 3. New Orleans: The Department of Middle American Research, The Tulane University of Louisiana.

Lafaye, Jacques. 1976. *Quetzalcóatl and Guadalupe: The Formation of Mexican National Consciousness 1531–1813*. Trans. Benjamin Keene. Chicago: University of Chicago Press. (Translation of *Quetzalcóatl et Guadalupe*. Paris, 1974.)

La Flesche, Francis. See Fletcher, Alice C.

Lamb, F. Bruce. 1974. *Wizard of the Upper Amazon: The Story of Manuel Córdova-Rios*. 2d ed. Boston: Houghton Mifflin.

Lame Deer (John Fire), and Richard Erdoes. 1972. *Lame Deer, Seeker of Visions*. New York: Simon and Schuster.

Laming, Annette. 1959. *Lascaux: Paintings and Engravings*. Trans. Eleanore Frances Armstrong. Harmondsworth: Penguin.

Landa, Bishop Diego de. See Tozzer, Alfred M.

Landes, Ruth. 1938. *The Ojibwa Woman*. New York: Columbia University Press.

———. 1947. *The City of Women*. New York: Macmillan.

———. 1968. *Ojibwa Religion and the Midéwiwin*. Madison: University of Wisconsin Press.

Lannoy, Richard. 1971. *The Speaking Tree: A Study of Indian Culture and Society*. London: Oxford University Press.

Lantis, Margaret. 1950. "The Religion of the Eskimos." In Ferm, 309–39.

Laufer, Berthold. 1917. "Origin of the Word Shaman." *American Anthropologist*, n.s., 19: 361–71.

Laughlin, Robert M. 1976. *Of Wonders Wild and New: Dreams from Zinacantán*. Smithsonian Contributions to Anthropology, no. 22. Washington, D.C.: Smithsonian Institution Press.

Lawrence, Peter, and M. J. Meggitt, eds. 1965. *Gods, Ghosts, and Men in Melanesia: Some Religions of Australian New Guinea and the New Hebrides*. Melbourne: Oxford University Press.

Lawson, John. 1951. *Lawson's History of North Carolina*. Richmond: Garrett and Massey. (1st ed. London, 1709.)

Layard, J. W. 1930. "Malekula: Flying Tricksters, Ghosts, Gods, and Epileptics" and "Shamanism: An Analysis Based on Comparison with the Flying Tricksters of Malekula." *JRAI* 60: 501–24, 525–50.

Leach, E. R. 1954. *Political Systems of Highland Burma: A Study of Kachin Social Structure*. London: G. Bell and Sons, for the London School of Economics and Political Science, University of London.

Leacock, Seth, and Ruth Leacock. 1972. *Spirits of the Deep: A Study of an Afro-Brazilian Cult*. Garden City, N.Y.: Doubleday Natural History Press.

Le Clercq, Father Chrestien. 1910. *New Relation of Gaspesia, with the Customs and Religion of the Gaspesian Indians*. Trans. William F. Ganong. Champlain Society Publications 5. Toronto: The Champlain Society; rpt. New York, Greenwood Press, 1968. (Translation of *Nouvelle relation de la Gaspésie*. Paris, 1691.)

Lee, Richard B. 1968. "The Sociology of !Kung Bushman Trance Performances." In Prince, 35–54.

Leenhardt, Maurice. 1979. *Do Kamo: Person and Myth in the Melanesian World*. Trans. Basia Miller Gulati. Chicago and London: University of Chicago Press. (Translation of *Do Kamo: La personne et le mythe dans le monde mélanésien*. Paris, 1947.)

Leibniz, Gottfried Wilhelm von. 1965. *Monadology and Other Philosophical Essays.* Trans. Paul Schrecker and Anne Martin Schrecker. Indianapolis: Bobbs-Merrill.

Leiris, Michel. 1958. *La Possession et ses aspects théâtraux chez les Ethiopiens de Gondar.* Paris: Plon.

Lemon, Lee T., and Marion J. Reis, ed. and trans. 1965. *Russian Formalist Criticism: Four Essays.* Lincoln: University of Nebraska Press.

Lenneberg, Eric H. 1967. *Biological Foundations of Language.* New York: John Wiley & Sons.

León-Portilla, Miguel. 1963. *Aztec Thought and Culture: A Study of the Ancient Nahuatl Mind.* Trans. Jack Emory Davis. Norman: University of Oklahoma Press. (Adaptation of *La Filosofía Náhuatl.* Mexico City, 1956; 2d ed. 1959.)

Leonard, Anne P. 1973. "Spirit Mediums in Palau: Transformations in a Traditional System." In Bourguignon 1973, 129–77.

Lessa, William A. 1961. *Tales from Ulithi Atoll: A Comparative Study in Oceanic Folklore.* Folklore Studies 13. Berkeley and Los Angeles: University of California Press.

———. 1966a. "'Discoverer-of-the-Sun': Mythology as a Reflection of Culture." JAF 79: 3–51.

———. 1966b. *Ulithi: A Micronesian Design for Living.* New York: Holt, Rinehart and Winston.

———, and Evon Z. Vogt, eds. 1972. *Reader in Comparative Religion: An Anthropological Approach.* 3d ed. New York: Harper & Row.

Lévi-Strauss, Claude. 1963. *Structural Anthropology.* Trans. Claire Jacobson and Brooke Grundfest Schoepf. New York: Basic Books; rpt. Garden City, N.Y.: Doubleday Anchor, 1967. (Translation of *Anthropologie structurale.* Paris, 1958.)

———. 1969. *The Raw and the Cooked.* Vol. 1 of Introduction to a Science of Mythology. Trans. John and Doreen Weightman. New York: Harper & Row. (Translation of *Le Cru et le cuit.* Vol. 1 of Mythologiques. Paris, 1964.)

———. 1973. *Tristes Tropiques.* Trans. John and Doreen Weightman. London: Jonathan Cape; rpt. New York: Pocket Books. 1977. (Translation of *Tristes Tropiques.* Paris, 1955.)

———. 1976. *Structural Anthropology*, vol. 2. Trans. Monique Layton. New York: Basic Books.

———. 1979. *Myth and Meaning.* The Massey Lectures, broadcast December 1977. New York: Schocken.

Lévy-Bruhl, Lucien. 1925. *How Natives Think.* Trans. Lilian A. Clare. New York: Knopf. Rpt. New York: Washington Square Press, 1966. (Translation of *Les Fonctions mentales dans les sociétés inférieures.* Paris, 1910.)

———. 1975. *The Notebooks on Primitive Mentality.* Trans. Peter Rivière. New York: Harper & Row. (Translation of *Carnets.* Paris, 1949.)

Lewis, I. M. 1971. *Ecstatic Religion: An Anthropological Study of Spirit Possession and Shamanism.* Harmondsworth: Penguin.

Lewis, Meriwether, and William Clark. 1902. *History of the Expedition of Captains Lewis and Clark, 1804–5–6.* 2 vols. Chicago: A. C. McClurg. (Rpt. of 1st ed. of 1814, ed. Nicholas Biddle.)

————. 1904–05. *Original Journals of the Lewis and Clark Expedition, 1804–1806.* Ed. Reuben Gold Thwaites. 8 vols. New York: Dodd, Mead; rpt. New York: Antiquarian Press, 1959.

Liberman, Anatoly. 1984. Introduction to Propp 1984, ix–lxxxi.

Lienhardt, Godfrey. 1961. *Divinity and Experience: The Religion of the Dinka.* Oxford: Clarendon.

Linderman, Frank B. 1932. *Pretty-Shield, Medicine Woman of the Crows.* New York: John Day; rpt. Lincoln: University of Nebraska Press, 1972. (Original title: *Red Mother.*)

Ling Roth, Henry. 1896. *The Natives of Sarawak and British North Borneo.* Based chiefly on the manuscripts of the late Hugh Brooke Low, Sarawak Government Service. 2 vols. London: Truslove & Hanson.

Link, Margaret Schevill. 1956. *The Pollen Path: A Collection of Navajo Myths Retold by Margaret Schevill Link.* Stanford, Calif.: Stanford University Press.

Locke, John. 1964. *An Essay Concerning Human Understanding.* Ed. John W. Yolton. 2 vols. London: Dent. (Rpt. of 5th ed. of 1706; 1st ed. published 1690.)

Loeb, Edwin M. 1924. "The Shaman of Niue." *American Anthropologist,* n.s., 26: 393–402.

————. 1926. "Pomo Folkways." UCPAAE 19, no. 2: 147–406.

————. 1929. "Shaman and Seer." *American Anthropologist,* n.s., 31: 60–84.

Lönnrot, Elias, ed. 1963. *The Kalevala; or Poems of the Kaleva District.* A Prose Translation with Foreword and Appendices by Francis Peabody Magoun, Jr. Cambridge, Mass.: Harvard University Press. (1st published in Finnish 1835; enlarged 1849.)

Lorant, Stefan, ed. 1965. *The New World: The First Pictures of America.* Rev. ed. New York: Duell, Sloan and Pearce. (1st ed. 1946.)

Lorenz, Konrad. 1966. *On Aggression.* Trans. Marjorie Kerr Wilson. New York: Harcourt. (Translation of *Das sogenannte Böse: Zur Naturgeschichte der Aggression.* Vienna, 1963.)

————. 1977. *Behind the Mirror: A Search for a Natural History of Human Knowledge.* Trans. Ronald Taylor. London: Methuen; rpt. New York: Harcourt Brace Jovanovich, 1978. (Translation of *Die Rückseite des Spiegels.* Munich: Piper, 1973.)

Lothrop, Samuel Kirkland. 1928. *The Indians of Tierra del Fuego.* Contributions from the Museum of the American Indian, Heye Foundation, vol. 10. New York: Museum of the American Indian, Heye Foundation.

Low, Hugh Brooke. See Ling Roth, Henry.

Lowie, Robert H. 1922. "The Religion of the Crow Indians." In *AMNH Papers* 25. New York: American Museum Press.

————. 1935. *The Crow Indians.* New York: Holt, Rinehart and Winston.

————. 1940. *An Introduction to Cultural Anthropology.* Enlarged ed. New York: Farrar & Rinehart.

Luckmann, Thomas. See Berger, Peter L.

Lukács, Georg. 1971. *The Theory of the Novel: A Historico-Philosophical Essay on the Forms of Great Epic Literature.* Cambridge, Mass.: MIT Press. (Translation of *Die Theorie des Romans.* Berlin, 1920.)

Lumholtz, Carl. 1902. *Unknown Mexico: A Record of Five Years' Exploration among the Tribes of the Western Sierra Madre; in the Tierra Caliente of Tepic and Jalisco; and among the Tarascos of Michoacan.* 2 vols. New York: Scribner's; rpt. Glorieta, N.M.: The Rio Grande Press, 1973.

Lyon, Patricia J., ed. 1974. *Native South Americans: Ethnology of the Least Known Continent.* Boston: Little, Brown.

McDougall, William. See Hose, Charles.

McGovern, William Montgomery. 1927. *Jungle Paths and Inca Ruins.* New York: Century.

McGregor, Pedro. 1966. In association with T. Stratton Smith. *The Moon and Two Mountains.* London: Souvenir Press. (Published in the United States as *Jesus of the Spirits.*)

McIlwraith, R. F. 1948. *The Bella Coola Indians.* 2 vols. Toronto: University of Toronto Press.

MacIntyre, Alasdair. 1984. *After Virtue: A Study in Moral Theory.* 2d ed. Notre Dame, Ind.: University of Notre Dame Press. (1st ed. London, 1981).

McNeley, James Kale. 1981. *Holy Wind in Navajo Philosophy.* Tucson: University of Arizona Press.

Maddock, Kenneth. 1974. *The Australian Aborigines: A Portrait of Their Society.* Harmondsworth: Penguin.

Madsen, William. 1955. "Shamanism in Mexico." *SJA* 11: 48–57.

———. 1960. *The Virgin's Children: Life in an Aztec Village Today.* Austin: University of Texas Press.

Maenchen-Helfen, J. Otto. 1973. *The World of the Huns: Studies in Their History and Culture.* Ed. Max Knight. Berkeley and Los Angeles: University of California Press.

Mails, Thomas E. 1973. *Dog Soldiers, Bear Men and Buffalo Women: A Study of the Societies and Cults of the Plains Indians.* Englewood Cliffs, N.J.: Prentice-Hall.

———. 1979. Assisted by Dallas Chief Eagle. *Fools Crow.* Garden City, N.Y.: Doubleday; rpt. New York: Avon, 1980.

Malinowski, Bronislaw. 1948. *Magic, Science and Religion and Other Essays.* New York: Free Press; rpt. Garden City, N.Y.: Doubleday Anchor, n.d.

Mandelbaum, David G. 1979. *The Plains Cree: An Ethnographic, Historical, and Comparative Study.* Canadian Plains Studies 9. Regina, Saskatchewan: Canadian Plains Research Center, University of Regina. (Part 1 published as "The Plains Cree," in *AMNH Papers* 37. New York: American Museum of Natural History, 1941, 155–316.)

Mannheim, Karl. 1936. *Ideology and Utopia: An Introduction to the Sociology of Knowledge.* Trans. Louis Wirth and Edward Shils. New York: Harcourt, Brace and World. (Expanded translation of *Ideologie und Utopie.* Bonn, 1929.)

Marcus, George E., and Michael M. J. Fischer. 1986. *Anthropology as Cultural Critique: An Experimental Moment in the Human Sciences.* Chicago: University of Chicago Press.

Margolin, Malcolm. 1978. *The Ohlone Way: Indian Life in the San Francisco-Monterey Bay Area.* Berkeley: Heyday Books.

Marx, Karl, and Friedrich Engels. 1957. *On Religion.* Moscow: Foreign Languages Publishing House; rpt. New York: Schocken, 1964.

Mason, J. Alden. 1957. *The Ancient Civilizations of Peru*. Harmondsworth: Penguin.

Matthews, Washington. 1897. *Navaho Legends*. Collected and translated by Washington Matthews. New York: G. E. Stechert, for the American Folk-Lore Society.

Maximilian, Prince of Wied-Neuwied. See Wied-Neuwied, Maximilian.

Maybury-Lewis, David. 1967. *Akwê-Shavante Society*. Oxford: Clarendon; rpt. New York: Oxford University Press, 1974.

Mayr, Ernst. 1976. *Evolution and the Diversity of Life: Selected Essays*. Cambridge, Mass.: Harvard University Press.

———. 1988. *Toward a New Philosophy of Biology: Observations of an Evolutionist*. Cambridge, Mass.: Harvard University Press.

Mbiti, John S. 1969. *African Religions and Philosophy*. New York: Praeger; rpt. Garden City, N.Y.: Doubleday Anchor, 1970.

Mead, George Herbert. 1934. *Mind, Self and Society from the Standpoint of a Social Behaviorist*. Ed. Charles W. Morris. Chicago: University of Chicago Press.

———. 1938. *The Philosophy of the Act*. Ed. Charles W. Morris. Chicago: University of Chicago Press.

Medawar, Peter [Brian]. 1982. *Pluto's Republic*. Incorporating *The Art of the Soluble* (1967) and "Induction and Intuition in Scientific Thought" (1969). Oxford: Oxford University Press.

———, and J. S. Medawar. 1977. *The Life Science: Current Ideas of Biology*. London: Wildwood House.

Melatti, Julio Cezar. 1978. *Ritos de uma tribo Timbira*. São Paulo: Editora Atica.

Messenger, John C. 1982. "Ancestor Worship among the Anang: Belief System and Cult Institution." In Simon Ottenberg, ed., *African Religious Groups and Beliefs: Papers in Honor of William R. Bascom*. Meerut, India: Archana Publications for Folklore Institute, 63–78.

Messing, Simon D. 1967. "Group Therapy and Social Status in the Zar Cult of Ethiopia." In Middleton 1967b, 285–93.

Metcalf, Peter. 1982. *A Borneo Journey into Death: Berawan Eschatology from Its Rituals*. Philadelphia: University of Pennsylvania Press.

Métraux, Alfred. 1928. *La Religion des Tupinamba et ses rapports avec celle des autres tribus Tupi-Guarani*. Bibliothèque de l'Ecole des Hautes Etudes: Sciences religieuses, vol. 45. Paris: Ernest Leroux.

———. 1944. "Le Shamanisme chez les Indiens de l'Amérique du Sud tropicale," 1 and 2. *Acta Americana* 2: 197–219, 320–41.

———. 1946. "Ethnography of the Chaco." In Steward 1: 197–370.

———. 1948. "The Tupinamba." In Steward 3: 95–133.

———. 1959. *Voodoo in Haiti*. Trans. Hugo Charteris. New York: Oxford University Press. (Translation of *Le Vaudou haitien*. Paris, 1958.)

———. 1967. *Religions et magies indiennes d'Amérique du Sud*. Ed. Simone Dreyfus. Paris: Gallimard.

Meuli, Karl. 1975. *Gesammelte Schriften*. Ed. Thomas Gelzer. 2 vols. Basel: Schwabe.

Michael, Henry N., ed. 1963. *Studies in Siberian Shamanism*. Arctic Institute of

North America Anthropology of the North: Translations from Russian Sources, no. 4. Toronto: University of Toronto Press.

Middleton, John. 1960. *Lugbara Religion: Ritual and Authority among an East African People*. London: Oxford University Press.

————, ed. 1967a. *Gods and Rituals: Readings in Religious Beliefs and Practices*. Garden City, N.Y.: Natural History Press.

————, ed. 1967b. *Magic, Witchcraft, and Curing*. Garden City, N.Y.: Natural History Press.

————. 1969. "Spirit Possession among the Lugbara." In Beattie and Middleton, 220–31.

————, and E. H. Winter, eds. 1963. *Witchcraft and Sorcery in East Africa*. New York: Praeger.

Mikhailovskii, V. M. 1895. "Shamanism in Siberia and European Russia," being the second part of "*Shamanstvo*." Trans. Oliver Wardrop. *JRAI* 24: 62–100, 126–58.

Miller, Walter S. 1966. "El Tonalamatl Mixe y los hongos sagrados." In Pompa y Pompa, 317–28.

Mills, J. P. 1926. *The Ao Nagas*. London: Macmillan.

Mironov, N. D., and S. M. Shirokogoroff. 1924. "Sramana: Shaman: Etymology of the Word 'Shaman.'" *Journal of the Royal Asiatic Society of Great Britain and Ireland, North China Branch* 55: 105–30.

Molina, Christoval de. 1873. "An Account of the Fables and Rites of the Yncas." In Clements R. Markham, ed., *Narratives of the Rites and Laws of the Yncas*. Works Issued by the Hakluyt Society, 1st ser., no. 48; rpt. New York: Burt Franklin, n.d.

Monod, Jacques. 1971. *Chance and Necessity: An Essay on the Natural Philosophy of Modern Biology*. Trans. Austryn Wainhouse. New York: Knopf. (Translation of *Le Hasard et la nécessité*. Paris, 1970.)

Montgomery, Evelyn Ina. 1970. *With the Shiriana in Brazil*. Dubuque, Iowa: Kendall/Hunt.

Mooney, James. 1891. "The Sacred Formulas of the Cherokees." Seventh BAE Report for 1885–1886, 301–97.

————. 1932. *The Swimmer Manuscript: Cherokee Sacred Formulas and Medicinal Descriptions*. Rev., completed, and ed. by Frans M. Olbrechts. BAE Bulletin 99.

————. 1965. *The Ghost-Dance Religion and the Sioux Outbreak of 1890*. Abridged, with Introduction by Anthony F. C. Wallace. Chicago: University of Chicago Press. (Complete version originally published in 1896 as Part 2 of the Fourteenth BAE Report for 1892–1893.)

Morgan, Lewis Henry. 1962. *League of the Iroquois*. Secaucus, N.J.: Citadel Press. (1st ed., *League of the Ho-dé-no-sau-nee, Iroquois*. Rochester, New York, 1851.)

Morton, Alice. 1977. "*Dawit*: Competition and Integration in an Ethiopian Wuqabi Cult Group." In Crapanzano and Garrison, 193–233.

Munn, Henry. 1973. "The Mushrooms of Language." In Harner 1973b, 86–122.

Munn, Nancy D. 1970. "The Transformation of Subjects into Objects in Walbiri and Pitjantjatjara Myth." In Berndt 1970, 141–63.

Murphy, Robert F., and Buell Quain. 1955. *The Trumaí Indians of Central Brazil*.

Monographs of the American Ethnological Society 24. Locust Valley, N.Y.: J. J. Augustin.

Myerhoff, Barbara G. 1974. *Peyote Hunt: The Sacred Journey of the Huichol Indians.* Ithaca: Cornell University Press.

Nabokov, Peter. 1967. *Two Leggings: The Making of a Crow Warrior.* Based on a field manuscript prepared by William Wildschut for the Museum of the American Indian, Heye Foundation. New York: Crowell.

Nadel, S. F. 1946. "Shamanism in the Nuba Mountains." *JRAI* 76: 25–38.

———. 1954. *Nupe Religion: Traditional Beliefs and the Influence of Islam in a West African Chiefdom.* London: Routledge & Paul; rpt. New York: Schocken, 1970.

Nagel, Ernest. 1979. *Teleology Revisited and Other Essays in the Philosophy and History of Science.* New York: Columbia University Press.

Nagel, Thomas. 1986. *The View from Nowhere.* New York: Oxford University Press.

Needham, Rodney. 1978. *Primordial Characters.* Charlottesville: University Press of Virginia.

Neihardt, John G. (Flaming Rainbow). 1932. *Black Elk Speaks: Being the Life Story of a Holy Man of the Ogalala Sioux.* New York: William Morrow; rpt. New York: Pocket Books, 1972.

Nelson, Keith E., ed. 1978. *Children's Language.* Vol. 1. New York: Gardner Press.

———, and Katherine Nelson. 1978. "Cognitive Pendulums and Their Linguistic Realization." In Nelson 1978, 223–85.

Newcomb, Franc Johnson. 1964. *Hosteen Klah: Navaho Medicine Man and Sand Painter.* Norman: University of Oklahoma Press.

Newell, William H., ed. 1976. *Ancestors.* The Hague: Mouton.

Newson, John, and Elizabeth Newson. 1976. "On the Social Origins of Symbolic Functioning." In Ved P. Varma and Phillip Williams, eds., *Piaget, Psychology and Education: Papers in Honour of Jean Piaget.* London: Hodder and Stoughton, 84–96.

Nimuendajú, Curt. 1914. "Die Sagen von der Erschaffung und Vernichtung der Welt als Grundlagen der Religion der Apapocúva-Guaraní." *Zeitschrift für Ethnologie* 46: 284–403.

———. 1942. *The Serente.* Trans. Robert H. Lowie. Publications of the Frederick Webb Hodge Anniversary Publication Fund, vol. 4. Los Angeles: Southwest Museum Administrator of the Fund.

———. 1952. *The Tukuna.* Ed. Robert H. Lowie. Trans. William D. Hohenthal. UCPAAE 46.

Ninio, Anat. See Bruner, Jerome S.

Nuñez del Prado B., Juan Víctor. 1974. "The Supernatural World of the Quechua of Southern Peru As Seen from the Community of Qotobamba." Trans. Patricia J. Lyon. In Lyon, 238–50.

Oakes, Maud. 1951. *The Two Crosses of Todos Santos: Survivals of Mayan Religious Ritual.* Princeton: Princeton University Press.

Oesterreich, T. K. 1930. *Possession, Demoniacal and Other, among Primitive Races, in Antiquity, the Middle Ages, and Modern Times.* Trans. D. Ibberson. London: Kegan Paul. (Translation of *Die Besessenheit.* Halle, 1921.)

Ohiyesa. See Eastman, Charles Alexander.

Ohnuki-Tierney, Emiko. 1974. *The Ainu of the Northwest Coast of Southern Sakhalin.* New York: Holt, Rinehart and Winston.

Oliver, Douglas L. 1974. *Ancient Tahitian Society.* Vol. 1: *Ethnography.* Honolulu: University Press of Hawaii.

Olson, Ronald L. 1936. "The Quinault Indians." *University of Washington Publications in Anthropology* 6, no. 1: 1–194.

Onwuejeogwu, Michael. 1969. "The Cult of *Bori* Spirits among the Hausa." In Mary Douglas and Phyllis M. Kaberry, eds., *Man in Africa.* London: Tavistock, 279–305.

Opler, Morris E. 1938. *Myths and Tales of the Jicarilla Apache Indians.* Memoirs of the American Folk-Lore Society 31. New York: G. E. Stechert, for the American Folk-Lore Society.

———. 1941. *An Apache Life-Way: The Economic, Social, and Religious Institutions of the Chiricahua Indians.* Chicago: University of Chicago Press.

———. 1969. *Apache Odyssey: A Journey between Two Worlds.* New York: Holt, Rinehart and Winston.

Ortega y Gasset, José. 1957. *Man and People.* Trans. Willard R. Trask. New York: Norton. (Translation of *El Hombre y la gente.* Madrid, 1954.)

Ortiz, Alfonso, ed. 1979. *Handbook of North American Indians,* ed. William C. Sturtevant. Vol. 9: *Southwest.* Washington, D.C.: Smithsonian Institution.

Oughourlian, Jean-Michel. 1991. *The Puppet of Desire: The Psychology of Hysteria, Possession, and Hypnosis.* Trans. Eugene Webb. Stanford, Calif.: Stanford University Press. (Translation of *Un Mime nommé désir: Hystérie, transe, possession, adorcisme.* Paris, 1982.)

Pankow, Walter. 1976. "Openness as Self-Transcendence." In Erich Jantsch and Conrad H. Waddington, eds., *Evolution and Consciousness: Human Systems in Transition.* Reading, Mass.: Addison-Wesley, 16–36.

Park, Willard Z. 1938. *Shamanism in Western North America: A Study in Cultural Relationships.* Evanston, Ill.: Northwestern University; rpt. New York: Cooper Square Publishers, 1975.

Parker, Arthur C. 1968. *Parker on the Iroquois.* Ed. William N. Fenton. Syracuse, N.Y.: Syracuse University Press.

Parkman, Francis. 1949. *The Oregon Trail: Sketches of Prairie and Rocky-Mountain Life.* New York: Modern Library. (1st ed. Boston, 1847.)

———. 1983. *France and England in North America.* 2 vols. New York: Library of America. (Originally 9 vols., Boston, 1851–92.)

Parmentier, Richard J. 1979. "The Mythological Triangle: Poseyemu, Montezuma, and Jesus in the Pueblos." In Ortiz, 609–22.

Parret, Herman. 1974. *Discussing Language: Dialogues with Wallace L. Chafe, Noam Chomsky, Algirdas J. Greimas,* et al. The Hague: Mouton.

Parsons, Elsie Clews. 1926a. "Notes on Ceremonialism at Laguna." *AMNH Papers* 19: 85–131.

———. 1926b. *Tewa Tales.* Memoirs of the American Folk-Lore Society 19.

———. 1928. "Notes on the Pima, 1926." *American Anthropologist,* n.s., 30: 445–64.

———. 1933a. *Hopi and Zuñi Ceremonialism.* AAA Memoirs, no. 39.

————. 1933b. "Some Aztec and Pueblo Parallels," *American Anthropologist*, n.s., 35: 611–31.

————. 1936. *Mitla, Town of the Souls, and Other Zapoteco-Speaking Pueblos of Oaxaca, Mexico*. Chicago: University of Chicago Press.

————. 1939. *Pueblo Indian Religion*. 2 vols. Chicago: University of Chicago Press.

Parsons, Talcott. 1937. *The Structure of Social Action: A Study in Social Theory with Special Reference to a Group of Recent European Writers*. 2 vols. New York: McGraw Hill; rpt. New York: Free Press, 1968.

————. 1963. Introduction to Max Weber, *The Sociology of Religion*. Boston: Beacon Press.

Paulson, Ivar. 1958. *Die primitiven Seelenvorstellungen der nordeurasischen Völker: eine religionsethnographische und religionsphänomenologische Untersuchung*. Stockholm: The Ethnographical Museum of Sweden.

————. 1964. "Zur Phänomenologie des Schamanismus." *Zeitschrift für Religions und Geistesgeschichte* 16: 121–41.

————, Åke Hultkrantz, and Karl Jettmar. 1962. *Die Religionen Nordeurasiens und der amerikanischen Arktis*. In Christel Matthias Schröder, ed., *Die Religionen der Menschheit* 3. Stuttgart: Kohlhammer.

Pavel, Thomas G. 1986. *Fictional Worlds*. Cambridge, Mass.: Harvard University Press.

Peirce, Charles Sanders. 1933–63. *Collected Papers of Charles Sanders Peirce*. Ed. Charles Hartshorne and Paul Weiss. Cambridge, Mass.: Harvard University Press. Vols. 1 (*Principles of Philosophy*) and 2 (*Elements of Logic*), 1960. Vols. 3 (*Exact Logic*) and 4 (*The Simplest Mathematics*), 1933. Vols. 5 (*Pragmatism and Pragmaticism*) and 6 (*Scientific Metaphysics*), 1963. Vol. 8 (*Reviews, Correspondence, and Bibliography*, ed. Arthur W. Burks), 1958.

————, and Victoria Lady Welby. 1977. *Semiotic and Significs: The Correspondence between Charles S. Peirce and Victoria Lady Welby*. Ed. Charles S. Hardwick. Bloomington: Indiana University Press.

Philippi, Donald L. 1979. *Songs of Gods, Songs of Humans: The Epic Tradition of the Ainu*. Princeton and Tokyo: Princeton University Press and University of Tokyo Press.

Piaget, Jean. 1929. *The Child's Conception of the World*. Trans. Joan Tomlinson and Andrew Tomlinson. London: Routledge; rpt. Totowa, N.J.: Littlefield, Adams, 1960. (Translation of *La Représentation du monde chez l'enfant*. Paris, 1926.)

————. 1932a. *The Language and Thought of the Child*. 2d ed. Trans. Margorie Gabain. New York: Humanities Press; rpt. New York: Meridian, 1955. (Translation of *Le Langage et la pensée chez l'enfant*. Neuchâtel, 1923.)

————. 1932b. *The Moral Judgment of the Child*. With the assistance of seven collaborators. Trans. Marjorie Gabin. London: K. Paul, Trench, Trubner; rpt. New York: Free Press, 1965. (Translation of *Le Jugement moral chez l'enfant*. Paris, 1932.)

————. 1954. *The Construction of Reality in the Child*. Trans. Margaret Cook. New York: Basic Books; rpt. New York: Ballantine, 1971. (Translation of *La Construction du réel chez l'enfant*. Neuchâtel, 1937.)

————. 1967. *Six Psychological Studies*. Ed. David Elkind. Trans. Anita Tenzer.

New York: Random House. (Translation of *Six Etudes de Psychologie*. Geneva, 1964.)

———. 1970. *Structuralism*. Trans. and ed. Chaninah Maschler. New York: Basic Books; rpt. New York: Harper & Row, 1971. (Translation of *Le Structuralisme*. Paris, 1968.)

———. 1971. *Biology and Knowledge: An Essay on the Relations between Organic Regulations and Cognitive Processes*. Chicago: University of Chicago Press. (Translation of *Biologie et connaissance*. Paris, 1967.)

———. 1973. *The Child and Reality: Problems of Genetic Psychology*. Trans. Arnold Rosin. New York: Grossman; rpt. Harmondsworth: Penguin, 1976. (Translation of *Problèmes de psychologie génétique*. Paris, 1972.)

———. 1980. *Adaptation and Intelligence: Organic Selection and Phenocopy*. Trans. Stewart Eames. Chicago: University of Chicago Press. (Translation of *Adaptation vitale et psychologie de l'intelligence: Sélection organique et phénocopie*. Paris, 1974.)

Piattelli-Palmarini, Massimo, ed. 1980. *Language and Learning: The Debate between Jean Piaget and Noam Chomsky*. Cambridge, Mass.: Harvard University Press. (Originally titled *Théories du langage, théories de l'apprentissage*. Paris, 1979.)

Pittendrigh, C. S. 1958. "Adaptation, Natural Selection, and Behavior." In Anne Roe and George Gaylord Simpson, eds., *Behavior and Evolution*. New Haven: Yale University Press, 390–416.

Polo de Ondegardo, (el Licenciado) Juan. 1916. *Informaciones acerca de la religión y gobierno de los Incas*. Colección de Libros y Documentos referentes a la Historia del Perú 3. Lima: Sanmartí.

Pompa y Pompa, Antonio, ed. 1966. *Summa Anthropologica en homenaje a Roberto J. Weitlaner*. Mexico City: Instituto Nacional de Antropología e Historia.

Popol Vuh: The Great Mythological Book of the Ancient Maya. 1976. Trans. Ralph Nelson. Boston: Houghton Mifflin.

Popov, A. A. 1968. "How Sereptie Djaruoskin of the Nganasans (Tavgi Samoyeds) Became a Shaman." In Diószegi 1968a, 137–45.

Popper, Karl R. 1965. *Conjectures and Refutations: The Growth of Scientific Knowledge*. 2d ed. New York: Basic Books; rpt. New York: Harper & Row, 1968.

———. 1966. *The Open Society and Its Enemies*, vol. 1: *The Spell of Plato*. 5th ed. Princeton: Princeton University Press.

———. 1968. *The Logic of Scientific Discovery*. Rev. ed. New York: Basic Books; rpt. New York: Harper & Row, 1968. (Translation of *Logik der Forschung*. Vienna, 1934 [dated 1935].)

———. 1976. *Unended Quest: An Intellectual Autobiography*. Rev. ed. La Salle, Ill.: Open Court. (Originally published as "Autobiography of Karl Popper," in *The Philosophy of Karl Popper*. La Salle, Ill., 1974.)

———. 1979. *Objective Knowledge: An Evolutionary Approach*. Rev. ed. Oxford: Clarendon. (1st ed. 1972.)

———. 1983. *Realism and the Aim of Science*. Ed. W. W. Bartley III. Vol. 1 of the *Postscript to the Logic of Scientific Discovery*. Totowa, N.J.: Rowman and Littlefield.

———, and John C. Eccles. 1977. *The Self and Its Brain: An Argument for Inter-*

actionism. Berlin: Springer-Verlag; rpt. London: Routledge & Kegan Paul, 1983.

Powers, William K. 1977. *Oglala Religion*. Lincoln: University of Nebraska Press.

———. 1982. *Yuwipi: Vision and Experience in Oglala Ritual*. Lincoln: University of Nebraska Press.

Pressel, Esther. 1977. "Negative Spirit Possession in Experienced Brazilian Umbanda Spirit Mediums." In Crapanzano and Garrison, 333–64.

Prigogine, Ilya. 1980. *From Being to Becoming: Time and Complexity in the Physical Sciences*. New York: W. H. Freeman.

———, and Isabelle Stengers. 1984. *Order Out of Chaos: Man's New Dialogue with Nature*. New York: Bantam, 1984. (Based on *La nouvelle alliance*. Paris, 1977.)

Prince, Raymond, ed. 1968. *Trance and Possession States*. Montreal: R. M. Bucke Society.

Propp, Vladimir. 1968. *Morphology of the Folktale*. 2d ed. Ed. Louis A. Wagner, trans. Laurence Scott. Austin: University of Texas Press. (1st ed. Bloomington, Ind., 1958. Translation of *Morfologija skazki*. Leningrad, 1928.)

———. 1984. *Theory and History of Folklore*. Trans. Ariadna Y. Martin, Richard P. Martin, et al., ed. Anatoly Liberman. Minneapolis: University of Minnesota Press.

Putnam, Hilary. 1983. *Realism and Reason*. Philosophical Papers 3. Cambridge: Cambridge University Press.

Quine, Willard Van Orman. 1961. *From a Logical Point of View: Nine Logico-Philosophical Essays*. 2d ed. Cambridge, Mass.: Harvard University Press; rpt. New York: Harper, 1963. (1st ed. Cambridge, Mass., 1953.)

Radcliffe-Brown, A. R. 1922. *The Andaman Islanders*. Cambridge: Cambridge University Press; rpt. New York: Free Press, 1964.

———. 1952. *Structure and Function in Primitive Society: Essays and Addresses*. London: Macmillan; rpt. New York: Free Press, 1965.

Radin, Paul, ed. 1926. *Crashing Thunder: The Autobiography of an American Indian*. New York: Appleton.

———. 1942. *Indians of South America*. Garden City, N.Y.: Doubleday, Doran.

———. 1945. *The Road of Life and Death: A Ritual Drama of the American Indians*. New York: Pantheon.

———. 1954. *The Evolution of an American Indian Prose Epic: A Study in Comparative Literature*. Basel: Ethnographical Museum.

———, ed. 1970a. *African Folktales*. Princeton: Princeton University Press. (Extracted from *African Folktales and Sculpture*. Princeton, 1952.)

———. 1970b. *The Winnebago Tribe*. Lincoln: University of Nebraska Press. (Originally published in *Thirty-Seventh Annual Report of the Bureau of American Ethnology*. Washington, D.C., 1923.)

Raglan, Lord. 1936. *The Hero: A Study in Tradition, Myth, and Drama*. London: Methuen; rpt. New York: Vintage, 1956.

Ramos, Arthur. 1951. *O Negro Brasileiro*. 3d ed. 2 vols. São Paulo: Companhia Editora Nacional. (1st ed. Rio de Janeiro, 1934.)

Rappaport, Roy A. 1968. *Pigs for the Ancestors: Ritual in the Ecology of a New Guinea People*. New Haven: Yale University Press.

———. 1971. "The Sacred in Human Evolution," in Richard F. Johnston, Peter W. Frank, and Charles D. Michener, eds., *Annual Review of Ecology and Systematics* 2. Palo Alto: Annual Reviews, Inc., 23–44.

———. 1979. *Ecology, Meaning, and Religion*. Richmond, Calif.: North Atlantic Books.

Rasmussen, Knud. 1927. *Across Arctic America: Narrative of the Fifth Thule Expedition*. New York: Putnam's.

———. 1929. *Intellectual Culture of the Iglulik Eskimos*. Report of the Fifth Thule Expedition, 1921–24, vol. 7, no. 1. Trans. W. Worster. Copenhagen: Gyldendalske Boghandel, Nordisk Forlag.

———. 1930. *Observations on the Intellectual Culture of the Caribou Eskimos*. Report of the Fifth Thule Expedition, 1921–24, vol. 7, no. 2. Trans. W. E. Calvert. Copenhagen: Gyldendalske Boghandel, Nordisk Forlag.

———. 1931. *The Netsilik Eskimos: Social Life and Spiritual Culture*. Report of the Fifth Thule Expedition, 1921–24, vol. 8, nos. 1–2. Trans. W. E. Calvert. Copenhagen: Gyldendalske Boghandel, Nordisk Forlag.

———. 1932. *Intellectual Culture of the Copper Eskimos*. Report of the Fifth Thule Expedition, 1921–24, vol. 9. Trans. W. E. Calvert. Copenhagen: Gyldendalske Boghandel, Nordisk Forlag.

Read, Kenneth E. 1965. *The High Valley*. New York: Scribner's.

Redfield, Robert. 1941. *The Folk Culture of Yucatan*. Chicago: University of Chicago Press.

———, and Alfonso Villa Rojas. 1934. *Chan Kom: A Maya Village*. Washington, D.C.: Carnegie Institution; rpt. Chicago: University of Chicago Press, 1962.

Reichard, Gladys A. 1939. *Navajo Medicine Man Sandpaintings*. New York: J. J. Augustin; rpt. New York: Dover, 1977. (Originally titled *Navajo Medicine Man*.)

———. 1944. *Prayer: The Compulsive Word*. Monographs of the American Ethnological Society 7. Seattle: University of Washington Press.

Reichel-Dolmatoff, Gerardo. 1971. *Amazonian Cosmos: The Sexual and Religious Symbolism of the Tukano Indians*. Chicago: University of Chicago Press. (Translation of *Desana: Simbolismo de los Indios Tukano del Vaupés*. Bogotá, 1968.)

———. 1975. *The Shaman and the Jaguar: A Study of Narcotic Drugs among the Indians of Colombia*. Philadelphia: Temple University Press.

Ricoeur, Paul. 1974. *The Conflict of Interpretations: Essays in Hermeneutics*. Ed. Don Ihde. Evanston, Ill.: Northwestern University Press. (Translation of *Le Conflit des interprétations*. Paris, 1969.)

———. 1977. *The Rule of Metaphor: Multi-disciplinary Studies of the Creation of Meaning in Language*. Trans. Robert Czerny, with Kathleen McLaughlin and John Costello, S.J. Toronto: University of Toronto Press. (Translation of *La Métaphore vive*. Paris, 1975.)

———. 1978. *The Philosophy of Paul Ricoeur: An Anthology of His Work*. Ed. Charles E. Reagan and David Stewart. Boston: Beacon, 1978.

———. 1979. "The Metaphorical Process as Cognition, Imagination, and Feeling." In Sacks, 141–57.

————. 1984. *Time and Narrative* 1. Trans. Kathleen McLaughlin and David Pellauer. Chicago: University of Chicago Press. (Translation of *Temps et récit* 1. Paris, 1983.)

————. 1985. *Time and Narrative* 2. Trans. Kathleen McLaughlin and David Pellauer. Chicago: University of Chicago Press. (Translation of *Temps et récit* 2. Paris, 1984.)

Rink, Henrik. 1875. *Tales and Traditions of the Eskimo, with a Sketch of Their Habits, Religion, Language and Other Peculiarities.* Ed. Robert Brown. Edinburgh: William Blackwood and Sons; rpt. Montreal: McGill-Queens University Press, 1974.

Ritzenthaler, Robert E., and Pat Ritzenthaler. 1970. *The Woodland Indians of the Western Great Lakes.* Garden City, N.Y.: Natural History Press.

Rodrigues, Nina. 1896. *O Animismo Fetichista dos Negros Bahianos. Revista Brasileira,* 6 and 7; rpt. (with preface and notes by Arthur Ramos) Rio de Janeiro: Civilização Brasileira, 1935.

Roe, Peter G. 1982. *The Cosmic Zygote: Cosmology in the Amazon Basin.* New Brunswick, N.J.: Rutgers University Press.

Rose, Steven. 1976. *The Conscious Brain.* Rev. ed. New York: Vintage Books. (1st ed. New York, 1973.)

Rosenfield, Israel. 1992. *The Strange, Familiar, and Forgotten: An Anatomy of Consciousness.* New York: Knopf.

Roth, Henry Ling. See Ling Roth, Henry.

Roth, Walter E. 1915. "An Inquiry into the Animism and Folk-Lore of the Guiana Indians." Thirtieth BAE Report for 1908–1909.

Rothenberg, Jerome, and Diane Rothenberg, eds. 1983. *Symposium of the Whole: A Range of Discourse Toward an Ethnopoetics.* Berkeley and Los Angeles: University of California Press.

Rowe, John Howland. 1947. "Inca Culture at the Time of the Spanish Conquest." In Steward 2: 183–330.

Roys, Ralph L., trans. 1965. *Ritual of the Bacabs.* Norman: University of Oklahoma Press.

————. 1967. *The Book of Chilam Balam of Chumayel.* Rev. ed. Norman: University of Oklahoma Press. (1st ed. Washington, D.C.: Carnegie Institution, 1933.)

Russell, Frank. 1908. "The Pima Indians." Twenty-Sixth BAE Report for 1904–1905, 3–389.

Sacks, Sheldon, ed. 1979. *On Metaphor.* Chicago: University of Chicago Press.

Sagard, Father Gabriel. 1939. *The Long Journey to the Country of the Hurons.* Ed. George M. Wrong, trans. H. H. Langton. Champlain Society Publications 25. Toronto: Champlain Society; rpt. New York: Greenwood Press, 1968. (Translation of *Le grand voyage du pays des Hurons.* Paris, 1632.)

Sahagún, Fray Bernardino de. 1956. *Historia general de las cosas de Nueva España.* 4 vols. Ed. Angel María Garibay K. Mexico City: Editorial Porrua. (Written ca. 1570–1580.)

Sapir, Edward. 1951. *Selected Writings of Edward Sapir in Language, Culture and Personality.* Ed. David G. Mandelbaum. Berkeley and Los Angeles: University of California Press.

——, and Leslie Spier. 1943. "Notes on the Culture of the Yana." *University of California Publications in Anthropological Records* 3, no. 3: 239–97.

Saussure, Ferdinand de. 1959. *Course in General Linguistics*. Ed. Charles Bally and Albert Sechehaye. With the collaboration of Albert Riedlinger. Trans. Wade Baskin. New York: Philosophical Library; rpt. New York: McGraw Hill, 1966. (Translation of Saussure 1962.)

——. 1962. *Cours de linguistique générale*. Ed. Charles Bally and Albert Sechehaye. With the collaboration of Albert Riedlinger. 5th ed. Paris: Payot. (1st ed. Lausanne, 1916.)

Schaden, Egon. 1959. *A Mitologia heróica de tribos indígenas do Brasil: Ensaio etnosociológico*. Rio de Janeiro: Ministério da Educação e Cultura, Serviço da Documentação.

Schebesta, Paul. 1957. *Die Negrito Asiens*. Studia Instituti Anthropos 13, 2: *Ethnographie der Negrito: Religion und Mythologie*. Vienna-Mödling: St.-Gabriel.

Schieffelin, Edward L. 1976. *The Sorrow of the Lonely and the Burning of the Dancers*. New York: St. Martin's.

——. 1982. "The *Bau A* Ceremonial Hunting Lodge: An Alternative to Initiation." In Herdt 1982, 155–200.

Schleiermacher, Friedrich. 1977. *Hermeneutics: The Handwritten Manuscripts*. Ed. Heinz Kimmerle, trans. James Duke and Jack Forstman. Missoula, Mont.: Scholars Press, for the American Academy of Religion. (Translation of *Hermeneutik*. Heidelberg, 1959.)

Séjourné, Laurette. 1956. *Burning Water: Thought and Religion in Ancient Mexico*. Trans. Irene Nicholson. New York: Vanguard Press; rpt. New York: Grove Press, 1960. (Translation of *Pensamiento y religión en el México antiguo*. Mexico, 1957.)

Sharon, Douglas. 1978. *Wizard of the Four Winds: A Shaman's Story*. New York: Free Press.

Shelton, Austin J. 1971. *The Igbo-Igala Borderland: Religion and Social Control in Indigenous African Colonialism*. Albany: State University of New York Press.

Sheriff, John K. 1989. *The Fate of Meaning: Charles Peirce, Structuralism, and Literature*. Princeton: Princeton University Press.

Shipek, Florence C. See Bean, Lowell J.

Shirokogoroff (Širokogorov), S. M. 1923. "General Theory of Shamanism among the Tungus." *Journal of the Royal Asiatic Society of Great Britain and Ireland, North China Branch* 54: 246–49.

——. 1935a. *Psychomental Complex of the Tungus*. London: Kegan Paul, Trench, Trubner.

——. 1935b. "Versuch einer Erforschung der Grundlagen des Schamanentums bei den Tungusen." Trans. W. A. Unkrig. *Baessler Archiv: Beiträge zur Völkerkunde* 18, no. 2: 41–96.

——. See also Mironov, N. D.

Shkilnyk, Anastasia M. 1985. *A Poison Stronger Than Love: The Destruction of an Ojibwa Community*. New Haven: Yale University Press.

Shklovsky, Victor. 1965. "Art as Technique." In Lemon and Reis, 3–24. (Translation of "Iskusstvo, kak priyom," 1917.)

Shonle, Ruth. 1925. "Peyote, the Giver of Visions." *American Anthropologist*, n.s., 27: 53–75.

Siikala, Anna-Leena. 1978. *The Rite Technique of the Siberian Shaman*. FF Communications no. 220. Helsinki: Suomalainen Tiedeakatemia.

Silver, Daniel Ben. 1966. *Zinacanteco Shamanism*. Ph.D. thesis, Department of Social Relations, Harvard University.

———. See also Fabrega, Horacio, Jr.

Simpson, George Gaylord. 1963. "Biology and the Nature of Science." *Science* 139: 81–88.

Sinclair, A., R. J. Janella, and W. J. M. Levelt, eds. 1978. *The Child's Conception of Language*. Berlin: Springer.

Siskind, Janet. 1973. *To Hunt in the Morning*. New York: Oxford University Press.

Smith, John. 1967. *Captain John Smith's America: Selections from His Writings*. Ed. John Lankford. New York: Harper & Row.

Smith, W. Robertson. 1894. *The Religion of the Semites: The Fundamental Institutions*. Rev. ed. London: A. & C. Black; rpt. New York: Schocken, 1972. (1st ed. 1889.)

Snyder, Gary. 1974. *Turtle Island*. New York: New Directions.

———. 1977. "The Incredible Survival of Coyote." From *The Old Ways*. San Fransisco: City Light Books, 67–85. Excerpted in Rothenberg and Rothenberg, 425–33.

Soustelle, Georgette. 1958. *Tequila: un village nahuatl du Mexique oriental*. Travaux et mémoires de l'Institut d'Ethnologie, Université de Paris. Paris: Institut d'Ethnologie.

Soustelle, Jacques. 1961. *Daily Life of the Aztecs on the Eve of the Spanish Conquest*. Trans. Patrick O'Brien. London: Weidenfeld and Nicolson; rpt. Stanford, Calif.: Stanford University Press, 1970. (Translation of *La Vie quotidienne des aztèques à la veille de la conquête espagnole*. Paris, 1955.)

Southall, Aidan. 1969. "Spirit Possession and Mediumship among the Alur." In Beattie and Middleton, 232–72.

Speck, Frank G. 1907. "Notes on Chickasaw Ethnology and Folk-Lore." JAF 20: 50–58.

———. 1931. *A Study of the Delaware Indian Big House Ceremony*. In Native Text Dictated by Witapanokhwe. Vol. 2. Harrisburg: Publications of the Pennsylvania Historical Commission.

———. 1935. *Naskapi: The Savage Hunters of the Labrador Peninsula*. Norman: University of Oklahoma Press.

Spencer, Baldwin, and F. J. Gillen. 1899. *The Native Tribes of Central Australia*. London: Macmillan.

———. 1927. *The Arunta: A Study of a Stone Age People*. 2 vols. London: Macmillan.

Spencer, Herbert. 1904. *The Principles of Sociology*. 3d ed. 3 vols. New York: Appleton. (1st ed. London, 1876.)

Spencer, Katherine. 1957. *Mythology and Values: An Analysis of Navaho Chantway Myths*. Philadelphia: American Folklore Society.

Spicer, Edward H. 1954. *Potam: A Yaqui Village in Sonora*. AAA Memoirs, no. 77.

———. 1980. *The Yaquis: A Cultural History*. Tucson: University of Arizona Press.

Spier, Leslie. 1930. *Klamath Ethnography*. UCPAAE 30.

———. 1933. *Yuman Tribes of the Gila River*. Chicago: University of Chicago Press; rpt. New York: Dover, 1978.

———, and Edward Sapir. 1930. "Wishram Ethnography." University of Washington Publications in Anthropology 3, no. 3, 151–299.

Spiro, Melford E. 1978. *Burmese Supernaturalism*. Expanded ed. Philadelphia: Institute for the Study of Human Issues. (1st ed. New York: Prentice-Hall, 1967.)

Stanner, W. E. H. N.d. *On Aboriginal Religion*. The Oceania Monograph, no. 11. Sydney: The University of Sydney.

———. 1979. "The Dreaming" (1953). In *White Man Got No Dreaming: Essays 1938–1973*. Canberra: Australian National University Press.

Stengers, Isabelle. See Prigogine, Ilya.

Stephen, Alexander M. 1936. *Hopi Journal*. Ed. Elsie Clews Parsons. Columbia University Contributions to Anthropology 23. 2 parts. New York: Columbia University Press.

Stern, Steve J. 1982. *Peru's Indian Peoples and the Challenge of Spanish Conquest: Huamanga to 1640*. Madison: University of Wisconsin Press.

Sternberg, Leo. 1924. "Divine Election in Primitive Religion (including material on different tribes of N.E. Asia and America)." *Proceedings of the International Congress of Americanists* 21, part 2: 472–512.

Stevenson, Matilda Coxe. 1904. *The Zuñi Indians: Their Mythology, Esoteric Fraternities, and Ceremonies*. Twenty-Third BAE Report for 1901–1902.

Steward, Julian H., ed. 1946–49. *Handbook of South American Indians*. Vols. 1–5. BAE Bulletin 143.

———, and Louis C. Faron. 1959. *Native Peoples of South America*. New York: McGraw-Hill.

Stewart, Kenneth M. 1946. "Spirit Possession in Native America." *SJA* 2: 323–39.

Strehlow, T. G. H. 1947. *Aranda Traditions*. Melbourne: Melbourne University Press.

———. 1964. "Personal Monototemism in a Polytotemic Community." In Haberland et al. 2: 723–54.

———. 1965. "Culture, Social Structure, and Environment in Aboriginal Central Australia." In Ronald M. Berndt and Catherine H. Berndt, eds., *Aboriginal Man in Australia: Essays in Honour of Emeritus Professor A. P. Elkin*. Sydney: Angus and Robertson, 121–45.

———. 1970. "Geography and the Totemic Landscape in Central Australia: A Functional Study." In Berndt 1970, 92–140.

Strong, William Duncan. 1929. *Aboriginal Society in Southern California*. UCPAAE 26.

Swanton, John R. 1905. *Contributions to the Ethnology of the Haida*. The Jesup North Pacific Expedition 5. Leiden: E. J. Brill.

———. 1911. *Indian Tribes of the Lower Mississippi Valley and Adjacent Coast of the Gulf of Mexico*. BAE Bulletin 43; rpt. New York: Johnson Reprint, 1970.

———. 1928. "Religious Beliefs and Medical Practices of the Creek Indians." Forty-Second BAE Report for 1924–1925, 473–672.

———. 1929. *Myths and Tales of the Southeastern Indians*. BAE Bulletin 88.

———. 1931. *Source Material for the Social and Ceremonial Life of the Choctaw Indians*. BAE Bulletin 103.

———. 1942. *Source Material on the History and Ethnology of the Caddo Indians*. BAE Bulletin 132.

———. 1946. *The Indians of the Southeastern United States*. BAE Bulletin 137; rpt. Washington, D.C.: Smithsonian Institution Press, 1979.

Sylva, Kathy, Jerome S. Bruner, and Paul Genova. 1974. "The Role of Play in the Problem-Solving of Children 3–5 Years Old." In Bruner, Jolly, and Sylva, 244–57.

Taine, Hippolyte. 1877. "M. Taine on the Acquisition of Language by Children." *Mind* 2: 252–59. (Translated from *Revue philosophique*, no. 1 [1876].)

Tale of the Nišan Shamaness, The: A Manchu Folk Epic. 1977. Introduction by Margaret Nowak. Trans. Stephen Durrant. Seattle: University of Washington Press.

Tambiah, Stanley Jeraraja. 1970. *Buddhism and the Spirit Cults in North-East Thailand*. Cambridge Studies in Social Anthropology, no. 2. Cambridge: Cambridge University Press.

———. 1990. *Magic, Science, Religion, and the Scope of Rationality*. Cambridge: Cambridge University Press.

Tarski, Alfred. 1983. *Logic, Semantics, Metamathematics: Papers from 1923 to 1938*. 2d ed. Ed. John Corcoran. Indianapolis: Hackett. (1st ed. Oxford, 1956.)

Teicher, Morton I. 1960. *Windigo Psychosis: A Study of a Relationship between Belief and Behavior among the Indians of Northeastern Canada*. Proceedings of the 1960 Annual Spring Meeting of the American Ethnological Society, ed. Verne F. Ray. Seattle: American Ethnological Society.

Thompson, J. Eric. 1930. "Ethnology of the Mayas of Southern and Central British Honduras." *Field Museum of Natural History, Anthropological Series* 17, no. 2: 23–213.

Thompson, Stith, ed. 1955. *Motif-Index of Folk-Literature: A Classification of Narrative Elements in Folktales, Ballads, Myths, Fables, Mediaeval Romances, Exempla, Fabliaux, Jest-Books and Local Legends*. Rev. edition. 6 vols. Bloomington: Indiana University Press.

Thwaites, Reuben Gold. See Kenton, Edna; Lewis, Meriwether, and William Clark; Wied-Neuwied, Maximilian.

Titiev, Mischa. 1944. *Old Oraibi: A Study of the Hopi Indians of Third Mesa*. Papers of the Peabody Museum of American Archaeology and Ethnology 22.

———. 1951. *Araucanian Culture in Transition*. Occasional Contributions from the Museum of Anthropology of the University of Michigan, no. 15. Ann Arbor: University of Michigan Press.

Todorov, Tzvetan. 1977. *The Poetics of Prose*. Trans. Richard Howard. Ithaca: Cornell University Press. (Translation of *La Poétique de la prose*. Paris, 1971.)

Tomashevsky, Boris. 1965. "Thematics." In Lemon and Reis, 61–95. (Translation of "Tematika." Leningrad, 1925.)

Tooker, Elisabeth. 1964. *An Ethnography of the Huron Indians, 1615–1649*. BAE Bulletin 190.

———. 1970. *The Iroquois Ceremonial of Midwinter*. Syracuse, N.Y.: Syracuse University Press.

———, ed. 1979. *Native North American Spirituality of the Eastern Woodlands: Sacred Myths, Dreams, Visions, Speeches, Healing Formulas, Rituals and Ceremonials*. New York: Paulist Press.

Tozzer, Alfred M., ed. 1941. *Landa's Relación de las Cosas de Yucatan: A Translation*. Papers of the Peabody Museum of American Archaeology and Ethnology, Harvard University. Cambridge, Mass.: The Museum.

Trigger, Bruce G., ed. 1969. *The Huron: Farmers of the North*. New York: Holt, Rinehart and Winston.

———. 1978. *Handbook of North American Indians* 15: *Northeast*. Washington, D.C.: Smithsonian Institution.

Tschopik, Harry. 1947. "The Aymara." In Steward 2: 501–73.

Tucci, Giuseppe. 1980. *The Religions of Tibet*. Trans. Geoffrey Samuel. Berkeley and Los Angeles: University of California Press. (Translation from Giuseppe Tucci and Walter Heissig, *Die Religionen Tibets und der Mongolei*. Stuttgart, 1970.)

Turnbull, Colin. 1962. *The Forest People*. New York: Simon and Schuster.

———. 1976. *Man in Africa*. Garden City, N.Y.: Doubleday Anchor.

Turner, Edith. See Turner, Victor.

Turner, Victor. 1957. *Schism and Continuity in an African Society: A Study of Ndembu Village Life*. Manchester: Manchester University Press.

———. 1967. *The Forest of Symbols: Aspects of Ndembu Ritual*. Ithaca: Cornell University Press.

———. 1968. *The Drums of Affliction: A Study of Religious Processes among the Ndembu of Zambia*. Oxford: Clarendon; rpt. Ithaca: Cornell University Press, 1981.

———. 1969. *The Ritual Process: Structure and Anti-Structure*. The Lewis Henry Morgan Lectures, 1966. Chicago: Aldine; rpt. Ithaca: Cornell University Press, 1977.

———. 1974. *Dramas, Fields, and Metaphors: Symbolic Action in Human Society*. Ithaca: Cornell University Press.

———. 1975. *Revelation and Divination in Ndembu Ritual*. Ithaca: Cornell University Press.

———, and Edith Turner. 1978. *Image and Pilgrimage in Christian Culture: Anthropological Perspectives*. Oxford: Blackwell.

Tuzin, Donald. 1980. *The Voice of the Tambaran: Truth and Illusion in Ilahita Arapesh Religion*. Berkeley and Los Angeles: University of California Press.

Tylor, Edward. 1958. *Religion in Primitive Culture*. Chapters 11–19 of *Primitive Culture*. New York: Harper & Row; rpt. Gloucester, Mass.: Peter Smith, 1970. (1st ed. London, 1871.)

Underhill, Ruth M. 1946. *Papago Indian Religion*. Columbia University Contributions to Anthropology, no. 33. New York: Columbia University Press; rpt. New York: AMS Press, 1969.

———. 1948. *Ceremonial Patterns in the Greater Southwest.* Monographs of the American Ethnological Society 13. New York: J. J. Augustin.

Vane, Sylvia Brakke. See Bean, Lowell J.

van Gennep, Arnold. 1960. *The Rites of Passage.* Trans. Monika B. Vizedom and Gabrielle L. Caffee. Chicago: University of Chicago Press. (Translation of *Les Rites de passage.* Paris, 1908.)

Verger, Pierre. 1969. "Trance and Convention in Nago-Yoruba Spirit Mediumship." In Beattie and Middleton, 50–66.

Villa Rojas, Alfonso. 1955. *Los Mazatecos y el problema de la cuenca del Papaloapan. Memorias del Instituto Nacional Indigenista* 7.

Vogt, Evon Z. 1969. *Zinacantan: A Maya Community in the Highlands of Chiapas.* Cambridge, Mass.: Harvard University Press.

———. 1970. *The Zinacantecos of Mexico: A Modern Maya Way of Life.* New York: Holt, Rinehart and Winston.

———. 1976. *Tortillas for the Gods: A Symbolic Analysis of Zinacanteco Rituals.* Cambridge, Mass.: Harvard University Press.

von den Steinen, Karl. 1894. *Unter den Naturvölkern Zentral-Brasiliens.* Berlin: Dietrich Reimer; rpt. New York: Johnson Reprint, 1968.

von Hagen, Victor W. 1957. *Realm of the Incas.* New York: New American Library.

Vygotsky, L. S. 1976. "Play and Its Role in the Mental Development of the Child." *Soviet Psychology* 12: 62–76; rpt. in Bruner, Jolly, and Sylva, 537–54. (From a lecture of 1933.)

———. 1962. *Thought and Language.* Ed. and trans. Eugenia Hanfmann and Gertrude Vakar. Cambridge, Mass.: MIT Press.

Wadley, Susan S. 1976. "The Spirit 'Rides' or the Spirit 'Comes': Possession in a North Indian Village." In Bharati, 233–51.

Wagley, Charles. 1949. *The Social and Religious Life of a Guatemalan Village.* AAA Memoirs, no. 71.

———. 1977. *Welcome of Tears: The Tapirapé Indians of Central Brazil.* New York: Oxford University Press.

———, and Eduardo Galvão. 1949. *The Tenetehara Indians of Brazil: A Culture in Transition.* Columbia University Contributions to Anthropology, no. 35. New York: Columbia University Press.

Walens, Stanley. 1981. *Feasting with Cannibals: An Essay on Kwakiutl Cosmology.* Princeton: Princeton University Press.

Wales, H. G. Quaritch. 1957. *Prehistory and Religion in South-East Asia.* London: Bernard Quaritch.

Walker, James R. 1921. "The Sun Dance and Other Ceremonies of the Oglala Division of the Teton Dakota." In Wissler 1921, 51–221.

———. 1980. *Lakota Belief and Ritual.* Ed. Raymond J. DeMallie and Elaine A. Jahner. Lincoln: University of Nebraska Press.

———. 1982. *Lakota Society.* Ed. Raymond J. DeMallie. Lincoln: University of Nebraska Press.

———. 1983. *Lakota Myth.* Ed. Elaine A. Jahner. Lincoln: University of Nebraska Press.

Wallace, Anthony F. C. 1966. *Religion: An Anthropological View*. New York: Random House.

———. 1970. *The Death and Rebirth of the Seneca*. With the assistance of Sheila C. Steen. New York: Knopf; rpt. New York: Vintage, 1972.

Wallace, Ernest, and E. Adamson Hoebel. 1952. *The Comanches: Lords of the South Plains*. Norman: University of Oklahoma Press.

Wallace, William J. 1978. "Southern Valley Yokuts." In Heizer, 448–61.

Wallis, Wilson D. 1952. "The Canadian Dakota." *AMNH Papers* 41: 3–225.

Wasson, R. Gordon. 1966. "Ololiuhqui and the Other Hallucinogens of Mexico." In Pompa y Pompa, 329–48.

———. N.d. (ca. 1968). *Soma: Divine Mushroom of Immortality*. Ethno-Mycological Studies, no. 1. [New York]: Harcourt Brace Jovanovich.

Waters, Frank. 1963. *Book of the Hopi*. New York: Viking; rpt. Harmondsworth: Penguin, 1977.

Weber, Max. 1946. *From Max Weber: Essays in Sociology*. Trans. and ed. H. H. Gerth and C. Wright Mills. New York: Oxford University Press.

Welby, Victoria. See Peirce, Charles Sanders.

Weltfish, Gene. 1965. *The Lost Universe: Pawnee Life and Culture*. New York: Basic Books; rpt. Lincoln: University of Nebraska Press, 1977.

Werner, Alice. 1933. *Myths and Legends of the Bantu*. London: Harrap.

White, Leslie A. 1928. "A Comparative Study of Keresan Medicine Societies." *Proceedings of the International Congress of Americanists* 23: 604–19.

———. 1935. *The Pueblo of Santo Domingo, New Mexico*. AAA Memoirs, no. 43.

Whitehead, Alfred North. 1926. *Religion in the Making*. New York: Macmillan; rpt. New York: World, 1960.

———. 1929. *Process and Reality: An Essay in Cosmology*. New York: Macmillan; rpt. New York: Harper & Row, 1960.

Whitney, William Dwight. 1875. *The Life and Growth of Language: An Outline of Linguistic Science*. New York: Appleton; rpt. New York: Dover, 1979.

Whorf, Benjamin Lee. 1956. *Language, Thought, and Reality: Selected Writings of Benjamin Lee Whorf*. Ed. John B. Carroll. Cambridge, Mass.: MIT Press.

Wied-Neuwied, Maximilian Alexander Philipp, Prince of. 1839–41. *Reise in das Innere Nord-America in den Jahren 1832 bis 1834*. 2 vols. Coblenz: J. Hoelscher; rpt. Frankfurt: Bender, 1970.

———. 1906. *Travels in the Interior of North America, 1832–1834*. Trans. Hannibal Evans Lloyd. In Reuben Gold Thwaites, ed., *Early Western Travels, 1748–1846*. Cleveland: Arthur H. Clark, 1906, vols. 22–24. (1st ed. London, 1843. Translation of Wied-Neuwied 1839–41.)

———. 1976. *People of the First Man: Life Among the Plains Indians in Their Final Days of Glory. The Firsthand Account of Prince Maximilian's Expedition up the Missouri River, 1833–34*. Watercolors by Karl Bodmer. Ed. Davis Thomas and Karin Ronnefeldt. New York: Dutton. (Contains selections from Wied-Neuwied 1906.)

Wilbert, Johannes. 1979. "Magico-Religious Use of Tobacco among South American Indians." In Browman and Schwarz, 13–38.

Wildschut, William. See Nabokov, Peter.

Wilson, Edmund. 1960. *Apologies to the Iroquois*, New York: Farrar, Straus, and Giroux; rpt. New York: Vintage, 1966.

Wilson, Monica. 1951. *Good Company: A Study of Nyakyusa Age-Villages*. London: Oxford University Press, for the International African Institute.

Winter, Edward H. N.d. *Bwamba: A Structural-Functional Analysis of a Patrilineal Society*. Cambridge: W. Heffer, for the East African Institute of Social Research.

———. 1963. "The Enemy Within: Amba Witchcraft and Sociological Theory." In Middleton and Winter, 277–99.

Wisdom, Charles. 1940. *The Chorti Indians of Guatemala*. Chicago: University of Chicago Press.

———. 1952. "The Supernatural World and Curing." In Sol Tax, et al., *Heritage of Conquest: The Ethnology of Middle America*. Glencoe, Ill.: Free Press, 119–34.

Wissler, Clark, ed. 1916. *Societies of the Plains Indians. AMNH Papers* 11.

———, ed. 1921. *Sun Dance of the Plains Indians. AMNH Papers* 16.

———, and D. C. Duvall. 1909. "Mythology of the Blackfoot Indians." In *AMNH Papers* 2, part 1: 1–163.

Wolf, Eric R. 1959. *Sons of the Shaking Earth*. Chicago: University of Chicago Press.

Wyman, Leland C. 1970. *Blessingway*. Tucson: University of Arizona Press.

Yava, Albert. 1978. *Big Falling Snow: A Tewa-Hopi Indian's Life and Times and the History and Traditions of His People*. Ed. Harold Courlander. New York: Crown.

Yongden, Lama. See David-Neel, Alexandra.

Zaretsky, Irving I., and Cynthia Shambaugh. 1978. *Spirit Possession and Spirit Mediumship in Africa and Afro-America: An Annotated Bibliography*. New York: Garland.

Zingg, Robert M. See Bennett, Wendell C.

Zolla, Elémire. 1973. *The Writer and the Shaman: A Morphology of the American Indian*. Trans. Raymond Rosenthal. New York: Harcourt Brace Jovanovich. (Translation of *I Letterati e lo sciamano*. Milan, 1969.)

INDEX

Aarsleff, Hans, 36n
Acedia (spiritual apathy, sloth), 56, 292
Adair, James, 229
Adaptation: biological, 23, 24, 45, 52, 53;
  linguistic, 47, 49; physical, 267; reli-
  gious, 129–30; social, 94–95, 99, 131.
  See also Innovation, creativity
Adriani, N., 146, 147n
Africa, cultures and religions of. *See*
  Akamba; Alur; Amba; Ancestor wor-
  ship and worship of the dead; Ashanti;
  Azande; Banyoro; *Bori* cult; *Cwezi*
  complex; Dahomey; Dinka; Dogon;
  Ehanzu; Gã; Hausa; *Jok*; Kaguru;
  Konso; !Kung; Lugbara; Mandari;
  Ndembu; Nsukka Igbo; Nuer; Pyg-
  mies; Sacrifice; Spirit possession;
  Shona; Swazi; Tallensi; Tonga; Yoruba;
  Zar cult; Zinza; Zulu
Afterworld, conceptions of, 146 (Singa-
  pore), 161 (Siberia), 165 (Finns), 167
  (Manchu), 181–82 (Northwest Coast),
  236–39 and 241 (northeastern North
  America), 251 and 251 n.14 (Blackfoot). *See also* Milky Way; Myths, of ascent to heavens; Myths, of descent to
  and return from world of dead; Shaman, ascent of, to heavens; Shaman,
  descent of, to underworld; Shaman,
  recovery of souls of sick or dead by
Agriculturalists: connected with hunters
  through shaman-priest (Huichol), 207;

portrayed as aggressive, 71; sacrifice
  and slaying of deity by, 71–72; settled
  routines of, suited to priestly ritual,
  196, 204 (Mesoamerica), 207 (Huichol),
  210 (Inca), 214 (Mapuche), 229–30
  (southeastern North America), 262. *See
  also* Hunters; Ritual, agricultural
Ainu (of Hokkaido, Japan), 159, 159n,
  165–66
Akamba (of Kenya, East Africa), 79
Alabama (of southeastern North America),
  231
Alexander, Hartley Burr, 87, 246n, 247
Algonquian peoples of North America,
  185n, 233, 234, 238–42, 244, 245, 250,
  202n, 252, 252n, 263. *See also* Arap-
  aho; Blackfoot; Cheyenne; Chippewa;
  Delaware; Fox; Menomini; Micmac;
  Montagnais; Ojibwa; Ottawa; Potomac;
  Powhatan; Saulteaux; Shawnee
Altai (Turkic people of Central Asia), 160,
  161, 215
Alur (of Nilotic Sudan, Africa), 121, 130
Amahuaca (of Amazonian Peru and Bra-
  zil), 225
Amazonian and other tropical cultures and
  religions of South America, 219–27,
  263. *See also* Amahuaca; Apapocuva;
  Bakaïrí; Barasana; Bororo; Carib;
  Cashinahua; Desana; Gê; Gran Chaco;
  Guaraní; Jívaro; Macusi; Mehinaku;
  Namoeteri; Shamatari; Sharanahua;

(Zinacanteco), 211–12 (Inca), 215
(Mapuche), 222 (Amazon); combat of,
with spirits or witches, 176 (Eskimo),
180–82 (Northwest Coast), 190–91
(Pueblo), 210 (Tzotzil Maya), 214
(coastal Peru), 216 (Mapuche), 222 and
223 (Amazon), 242 (Saulteaux); costume of, 150; dangers faced by, 163
(Tungus), 180 (Nootka), 182 (Coast
Salish), 210 (Tzotzil Maya), 217 (Mapuche), 225 (Amahuaca), 243 (Ojibwa);
death and rebirth of, 143–44 (Australia), 181 (Kwakiutl), 222 (Shamatari);
derivation of word, 151, 151n; descent
of, to underworld, 137, 138, 154 (Koryak), 160–63 (Siberia), 160n, 164 (Tatars), 165 (Finns), 166–68 (Manchus),
176–77 (Eskimo), 181–82 (Coast Salish), 205 (Mesoamerica), 224 (Gran
Chaco), 241 (northeastern North
America); dialogue of, with spirits, 146
(Singapore), 162–63 (Tungus), 192
(Apache), 216 (Mapuche), 223 (Macusi); distinguished from or associated
with chief, 184 (California), 219 (Amazon), 225 (Amahuaca); distinguished
from or associated with priest, 155
(Eurasia), 183–84 (Northwest Coast
and northwestern California), 208–9
(Huichol, Zinacanteco), 219 (Amazon),
231–32 (southeastern North America);
distinguished from or associated with
sorcerer or magician, 142 (Aranda),
158 (Siberia), 184 (California); ecstatic
trance of, 136–37, 155, 159, 241; isolation or apartness of, 144 (Australia),
158–59 (Siberia), 173–74 and 177
(Eskimo), 255 and 263 (Black Elk); as
"master of animals," 140; as "master of
spirits," 136–38, 137n, 158, 160, 185
(California); physical handicap of, 148
(Iban), 173 (Eskimo); as psychopomp
or "soul guide," 150, 152, 161; quest of,
for knowledge or power, 143 (Australia), 146 (Batek), 150 (Tibet), 155,
157 (Tavgi Samoyed), 159, 160, 175
(Eskimo), 194 (southwestern North
America), 206–8 (Mesoamerica), 221
and 224–25 (Amazon), 261–62; recovery of souls of sick or dead by, 145,
146 (Singapore), 147 (Indonesia), 148

(Iban), 150 (Tibet), 159 (Eurasia),
161–63 (Siberia), 166–68 (Manchus),
181–82 (Coast Salish), 205 (Mesoamerica), 209–10 (Tzotzil Maya), 224 (Gran
Chaco), 241 (northeastern North
America); seances and ceremonies of,
138, 146 (Singapore), 147 (Toradja,
Wana), 148 (Iban), 153 (Mongol, Samoyed), 160 (Altai), 161–62 (Yukaghir),
162–63 (Tungus), 175–77 (Eskimo),
182 (Coast Salish), 182–83 (Kwakiutl
and Nootka), 207–8 (Huichol), 209
(Zinacanteco), 215 (Mapuche), 223
(Macusi), 224 (Taulipáng), 234–35
(Delaware, Ojibwa, Seneca), 237 (reflected in North American "Orpheus"
myths), 240 (Huron and Montagnais),
256 (Black Elk); spirit possession of,
136–38, 137n (Tungus), 159, 185–86
and 185n (Americas), 215–17 (Mapuche), 219 (Amazon), 223n (South
America); visionary variety of, 136,
138, 145 (Andamanese), 184 and 186
(California), 193–95 (Mohave, Pima,
Papago), 205 (Mesoamerica), 261. *See
also* Animals, transformative interchange of, with shamans and others;
Curing methods; Deception or illusion,
in shamanism; Drum or tambourine;
Failure in quest; Guardian Spirit; Marriage of medium or shaman with spirit;
Narcotics and hallucinogens, use of by
shamans and others; Narratives, of shamans' heroic exploits; Shaking Tent;
Shamanism; Soul flight; Spirit medium;
Sweat baths; Transvestism; Vision
quest; Women, as shamans
Shamanism: of Amazon and South American tropics, 218–28; of Andean peoples
of South America, 211–18; in Australia, 140–44; in California, 184–89;
in China, 151–52, 152n; in Central
Asia and Siberia, 149–68; of Eskimo,
172–77; in Greece, 152; historical complex and putative origins of, 139–40;
of Huns, 151, 151–52 n.3; in Indonesian archipelago, 146–48; in (peninsular) Malaysia, 144–45; in Melanesia,
144–45; in Mesoamerica, 196–210; of
Mongols, 152–53; of North American
Great Plains, 244–57; in northeastern

Compositor:	G&S Typesetters, Inc.
Printer:	Edwards Brothers, Inc.
Binder:	Edwards Brothers, Inc.
Text:	10/12 Baskerville
Display:	Baskerville